All information contained within the "Narrative" sections of Queen City Gothic is a matter of public record, including book research, newspaper archives, magazine articles, personal interviews, and police case files. Any rumor or conjecture is identified as such within these sections.

The "I Witness" segments at the end of each chapter are the subjective opinions of the author based on the evidence as stated in the "Narrative", and do not represent an accusation against any person living or dead.

Queen City Gothic

Cincinnati's Most Infamous Murder Mysteries

J. T. Townsend

authorHOUSE®

AuthorHouse™
1663 Liberty Drive
Bloomington, IN 47403
www.authorhouse.com
Phone: 1-800-839-8640

First published by AuthorHouse 11/07/2011
Rev. 8/24/2012

ISBN: 978-1-4490-1890-0 (sc)
ISBN: 978-1-4490-1891-7 (hc)
ISBN: 978-1-4670-5712-7 (e)

THIS BOOK IS DEDICATED TO THE VICTIMS. MAY YOUR RESTLESS GHOSTS FIND PEACE...

"Murder has a magic of its own . . . touched by that crimson wand, things base and sordid, things ugly and of ill report, are transformed into matters wondrous, weird and tragical. Dull streets become fraught with mystery, commonplace dwellings assume sinister aspects, everyone concerned, howsoever plain and ordinary, is invested with a new value and importance as the red light falls upon each."

William Roughhead

"Violent physical passions do not in themselves differentiate men from each other, but rather tend to reduce them to the same state."

T. S. Eliot

"Every murderer is probably somebody's old friend."

Agatha Christie

"The urge to kill, like the urge to beget, is blind and sinister"

Andrei Voznesenski

"Murder starts in the heart. And its first weapon is a vicious tongue."

Jewel Mayhew in *Hush, Hush, Sweet Charlotte*

Contents

PRELUDE: QUEEN CITY GOTHIC

CINCINNATI'S MOST INFAMOUS MURDER MYSTERIES

"Behold, I show you mystery; we shall not all sleep, but we shall be changed."

Corinthians

Murder is forever.

Of the countless cruelties humans inflict on one another, most don't matter in the long run. Wounded hearts heal. Discarded workers find new jobs. Careless insults are forgotten.

But murder is a binding contract, an irreversible action that is still unusual even in these violent times. Although Americans suffer the highest murder rate in the world, the act itself is still rare.

I, like many, am fascinated by true crime stories. They reveal the depth of our own malevolent power, and raise important questions about what people are capable of and how they reach the point of violence.

Exhibit A is the proliferation of TV shows and books involving cold cases laden with twisting plots that probe the undersides of our psyches. Viewers and readers eventually must ask themselves: Am I cunning and cool enough to contemplate murder—and what's more, to get away with it?

The allure lingers after the program is over or the book is closed. A primal hard drive of violence is buried inside each of us—no other creature so wantonly kills more members of its own species than the human.

Yet what happens when the killer is never caught? Since an unsolved murder has no statute of limitations, the notes, reports, photos, and evidence are exiled into the case jacket. To those with an emotional connection, those files remain open, exhausted and yellowing through the years.

When no one is ever brought to justice, the enigma only deepens with time. Unsolved murders suggest everything and prove nothing, and true mysteries offer the ultimate puzzle-solving quest. As Mark Twain wrote: "Why shouldn't truth be stranger than fiction? Fiction has to stick to possibilities."

Twain also said that if the world were ending, he would move to Cincinnati—because in the Queen City, the apocalypse would take ten years to arrive.

Once referred to by the media as "The Town Without Pity," Cincinnati is perceived as a repressive Midwestern province constantly hoisted on the petard of nationwide ridicule. As a haven for Germans, Catholics, and Republicans, the Queen City is a cloistered, spinster city, a city mired in an eternal conflict between the demand for decency and the desire for expression.

Cincinnati is an unsoiled, innocent town, and resolved to keep it that way. Opponents are never convinced, just outlived. It is a reticent place—with a collective memory that runs long and deep.

As a lifelong resident and true crime connoisseur, I remain obsessed with my city's restless spirits. In *Queen City Gothic,* I submit 13 of Cincinnati's classic unsolved homicides—murders that could play in any metropolis, yet they happened here.

How were these unlucky 13 selected? Gothic murders are appalling and impenetrable, ripening as the years unravel until they are coated with the patina of age. Each of these crimes possessed a mixture of scandal and mystery that shrieked from front page headlines and shocked the citizenry. Murder, always unfathomable to the general public, now became horrendously real.

I will be your guide and excavator on this sinister journey. We will dig out the human side of violent death, searching for the unusual, separating fascinating bones from ordinary ones. We will roust corpses to unearth secrets kept buried for decades.

In this volume, you will see marital bliss shattered when a bride-to-be is gunned down at her front door. Watch as a teenage cheerleader's vicious bludgeoning divides a close-knit community. Observe a society matron's strangulation launching the largest law enforcement mobilization in city history. And witness the slaughter of a west side family consuming detectives who identify the killer, only to leave them shaking their heads as he evades justice.

These aging mysteries could be ripped from today's headlines. Themes of racism, pedophilia, greed, vengeance, adultery, and betrayal permeate these stories just as they dominate our talk shows and mass media today.

Along with newspaper and contemporary sources to recreate the narrative, previously unpublished details of each investigation are revealed from the case jackets—this author was allowed unlimited access to these primeval files! So I won't apologize for the onslaught of facts.

For within these long forgotten details the truth is lurking.

After laying out the specifics of each case, I deliver a subjective montage of the most plausible murder scenario based on the evidence. This section is called "I Witness". I welcome the reader to challenge my verdict and delve deeper into the maze.

But while some armchair sleuths might wish these classics remain unsolved, like presents forever unopened, a true detective turns each mystery into a puzzle. Because a puzzle can be solved—it has answers.

Be forewarned! Many of these crimes are so barren of clues that even the most seasoned detectives were thwarted. Veteran cops admit that it gets to you in the long run, when endless leads consume your time and energy, until all you're left with is a tangle of loose ends.

They would be the first to tell you that unsolved murder haunts, and every tiny detail corrodes their spirit. As their investigation runs into the ground, they wonder what they missed that was just below the surface.

There is always hope. An attic may yield lost evidence. A man on his deathbed could speak. Neighbors grow weary of being discreet. Someone's conscience gets the better of him. Walls of secrecy finally crack.

Cold case detectives never forget their creed: "Let no victim's ghost say we didn't try."

Let the exhumation begin . . .

2009

Along this lonely stretch of tracks in 1909, Anna Lloyd became the 4th victim of the "Cumminsville Railroad Killer."

EMBRACE THE BEAST

THE CUMMINSVILLE "MURDER ZONE" KILLER TERRIFIES THE QUEEN CITY: 1904-1910

"I pray that love will never come to me with murderous intent, in rhythms measureless and wild."

Euripides

PROLOGUE:

Cincinnati harbored a few serial killers during the 20th century—black widow Anna Marie Hahn, "Angel of Death" Donald Harvey, and the "Cincinnati Strangler" being the most notoriously remembered.

Yet long before the term "serial killer" was coined, an unknown assassin held the Queen City in his thrall from 1904 to 1910. Five women were savagely slain within a mile of the Spring Grove and Winton Road corner in Cumminsville, thus earning the district the grisly sobriquet of "the murder zone."

Like Jack the Ripper in London, the killer was an elusive phantom, prowling dim alleys and dank railroad yards in the dead of night, searching for women walking alone who were down on their luck.

Now only ancient newspaper stories are left to recount the six-year reign of terror.

NARRATIVE:

In the spring of 1904, Teddy Roosevelt was swashbuckling toward re-election, proving that his presidency was not just a political accident sparked by the assassination of William McKinley. Japan and Russia were waging war—one of the largest armed conflicts the world had ever known. New Yorkers were marveling over their newborn subway system while being enchanted by a Broadway fantasy of eternal youth called *Peter Pan.*

Cumminsville was a mesh of narrow roads wrinkled with warehouses and taverns in northern Cincinnati, heaving with working-class residents of German descent whose stunted houses crowded the blocks and plunged into the streets. They had no reason to hurry home before nightfall, given the wide array of vice available in any back alley.

Cumminsville sheltered a wild medley of eccentric characters, some of whom may have been connected to the murders. From a one-legged peddler, to a man who pinched women's bottoms, to the letter writer known as S.D.M., the denizens of the murky streets became a bewildering aspect of this case.

By day the air was blackened with soot from belching foundries. By night the vapors of the Mill Creek mingled with smoldering waste to immerse Cumminsville in obscurity. Gloomy smoke sailed the air, allowing the moon to bleach the buildings dead white.

It was the ideal hunting ground for a sadistic killer.

It began on Saturday morning, May 4, 1904, when 31-year-old Mary McDonald was found unconscious with her skull smashed in and one leg severed near the Dane Street railroad tracks. She died hours later as her tragic past began to surface.

Also known as "Mamie," an ill-fated affair with her sister's husband had driven her to drink. After her sister died Mary became her brother-in-law's "housekeeper." He promised to marry her, but instead left town with a minister's daughter, and Mary had even made a fruitless trip to California after hearing he was living there.

FOOTPRINTS OF WOMAN

Found by Trainman on Tracks Where Mayme McDonald Was Killed—Coroner Thinks It Accidental.

In the inquest Wednesday into the death of Mayme McDonald, of 25 East Seventh-st., James Flavin, a freight conductor, of 4171 Dane-st., one of the trainmen who found her on the B. & O. S.-W. tracks, in East Cumminsville, testified that after the body was discovered he examined the ground and found footprints of a woman. He said they were between the tracks and Mill Creek, just outside of the ties. They were scattered, as though the woman had been staggering. "A mark in the earth indicated that she had slipped and fallen," he said. "There were no other footprints."

Flavin believes the woman walked from Ludlow-av. toward Winton-rd. and that while crossing the tracks stumbled and was run over by the train. The Coroner believes the woman wandered from in front of Schueler's saloon, Hoffner-st. and Hamilton-av.

Detectives Houillion and Sweeney have talked with conductors and motormen on late cars from Cumminsville, but all of them declare they did not have a woman passenger on any of their late trips Saturday night. Stagman at first claimed to have put the woman on a College Hill-Main-st. car about 11 p. m. Saturday.

Mary McDonald Who Was First of Women Victims

Mary McDonald, 31, was found unconscious and terribly beaten near the railroad track at Dane-st., May 1, 1904. She died at Cincinnati Hospital the next day. Her assailant was never caught.

The *Cincinnati Enquirer* depiction of "pathetic moth" Mary McDonald.

Returning to Cincinnati, she drank to ease her melancholy. Roving from tavern to bar with disreputable men, Mary became, in the eyes of Cumminsville, a fallen woman—one newspaper called the victim "a pathetic moth on society's fringes." Yet amazingly, she had recently become engaged to a government surveyor working in Alabama.

Despite the betrothal, she spent her final hours on one last round, drinking shots with another man in various saloons. Charles Stagman, her drinking companion, told police they had "left the last joint" and he'd put her on a trolley car at 1:30AM. His alibi appeared air tight.

But Stagman had been "tight" himself that night, and his drifting memory was a black hole. When no conductors remembered seeing a woman on their car after midnight Saturday, Stagman claimed he had put her on the College Hill car about at 11PM, and then blacked out. After giving four different stories about what time he escorted Mary to the trolley, he finally admitted he couldn't remember a thing.

Mary's landlady, a Mrs. Pritchard, told detectives that Mary used morphine, and she had smelled drugs on the dying girl's breath after being called to the hospital. Had Mary been drugged?

The coroner's inquest added to the confusion: Was Mary murdered, or was she struck by a train while in a drunken stupor? Gouges in the earth near her body showed she was staggering, and since there were no other footprints police speculated that she had tumbled into the path of an oncoming train.

They wanted to write it off as an accident, yet every engineer who made a run that night insisted she could not have been hit without their knowledge. And given Mary's capacity for alcohol, some detectives considered it a "physical impossibility" for her to have reached the scene of her death without help.

The coroner eventually returned a verdict of murder, reasoning that crew members of the slow-moving Cumminsville trains would have been aware of a collision. However, none of Mary's other "associates" could be linked to her murder, and within days the investigation was mired in the muddy spring rains.

But the terror was just beginning.

A week after Mary McDonald was found, a woman was run down by a train just north of Cumminsville. Mary Rice was struck while crossing the tracks after church services. Being somewhat deaf, she failed to hear both the approaching train and the warning of a nearby friend.

A week later, 22-year-old Kate Sanders was arrested for throwing a 3-week-old infant into a watering trough at the Cincinnati Zoo. The Kentucky woman had agonized over the birth of her illegitimate child, and claimed to have been seized by a sudden impulse. Nevertheless, she was charged with first-degree murder.

As summer faded to fall in Cumminsville, residents were soon shocked by news of another murder.

Louise "Lulu" Mueller was last seen on Friday night, October 1, near the corner of Spring Grove and Fergas Street. The comely 21-year-old was found in a clump of weeds the next morning—murdered in a "lover's lane" by the railroad tracks.

She had tried to cross through the field to a friend's house, only to be waylaid in a little thicket just moments from safety. A police constable heard a woman's screams coming from the secluded grove around 10PM, but strangely did not stop to investigate.

Her head had been battered to a pulp. There were deep wounds on either side of her face, which appeared to be inflicted by a club or an ax. The killer had added a ghoulish touch to his handiwork—a fresh grave nearby suggested he had been disturbed during a hasty burial attempt.

Among the gathering spectators at the scene that morning was a squat, swarthy man with a heavy beard. Despite the fact that he cried repeatedly in a loud voice, "It was an accident . . . it was an accident," he was allowed to slip away.

He would resurface later.

On Sunday thousands flocked to the murder scene. Streetcars were packed, and they jockeyed with carriages, buggies, and newfangled automobiles that were cruising the site.

Detectives delving into the victim's background soon found that like Mary McDonald, pretty Lulu Mueller had "been around" and was known to consort with some questionable men. Over her parents' objections, she had continued several clandestine relationships, including a serious one with 30-year-old Frank Eastman, a large, handsome man with a roguish quality. He and Lulu had kept company for more than two years, but police learned it was not an exclusive rapport. There had been recent fighting words between Lulu and another object of Frank's affection, a young singer who had gone on a carriage ride with him.

Frank was a stable hand, and his wobbly alibi depended on a group of drunken horse traders. He was supposed to meet Lulu that night, yet blew her off to carouse with his fellow hostlers. She was seen passing his house twice that evening, sometime before she was observed drinking at a Knowlton's Corner bar.

Lulu's body had been found a few hundred feet from his house, a crumpled letter from Frank in her pocket.

Lulu's paramour became the prime suspect as circumstantial evidence mounted. Her father claimed that Frank had tried to insure her life in his own favor—John Mueller had quickly put a stop to it. He admitted, "I did not like Frank, and concluded to keep him away from the house. He quit coming, but I heard my daughter used to meet him down the street."

Detectives brought Frank in for questioning on Monday. As he was escorted from his house, Eastman broke into tears and said, "I hope I am not charged with this. I know nothing of this awful thing."

He insisted that he and Lulu "were engaged to be married, and I was ready any time to marry, but the date was not set." He implored police to leave him alone: "I am as anxious to find the guilty man as anyone is. I loved that girl, but the statement that I was jealous of her is absurd . . . the sooner you get off my trail, the sooner you'll take one up that may lead to something."

Frank Eastman had a decent reputation, and expressed genuine grief over the death of his beloved. When his alibi was confirmed he was sent home with thanks for his cooperation and assurance that he was "no longer suspected of this."

On Tuesday The Cincinnati Enquirer declared, "No murder has occurred in years in Cincinnati with so few clues as that of Lulu Mueller . . . there seems to be nothing that would lift the veil of mystery . . . clue after clue is run down with tireless energy by detectives, only to be exploded."

Detective Chief Crawford favored an "accident" theory, and pointed out why a train could have dealt Lulu her fatal injuries. Her hatpin, hat, and pocketbook were scattered between the first blood pool and the tracks. The position of her body and

2009

The thicket where Lulu Mueller was murdered is gone today, as are the railroad tracks where she was found.

blood on her clothing indicated she may have walked to the spot she was found after being struck.

But Coroner Cameron strongly disagreed: "Her skull was crushed like an eggshell and her life was extinct in an instant." His verdict of homicide was upheld. The distance between the tracks and her body was too great, and she had no bruises consistent with being thrown—all injuries were to her head. And imprints on her neck hinted at a strangulation attempt.

Louise Mueller's funeral was attended by hundreds and highlighted by "intensely dramatic scenes," according to the Enquirer. Frank Eastman, looking haggard and struggling to remain upright, was the star attraction. "His face was white—even ghostly. His eyes were bloodshot. His lips were drawn as though by the pain of a thousand tortures . . . plainly he was deeply affected." When he emerged from the church doorway, "a hundred voices at once whispered, 'There's Eastman!' Their eyes glued to him, the throng shuddered at the spectacle."

Not to be upstaged, Lulu's parents both broke down at the cemetery. Her mother tried to climb onto the casket as it was being lowered into the ground, crying, "My Lulu! I want my Lulu!" Her unnerved husband promptly keeled over in a dead faint and had to be carried to their buggy.

Frank Eastman sent a bouquet of white roses to the Mueller home that night.

Public pressure on police was increasing, and they hungered to make an arrest. Detectives were taking a hard look at two men seen with Lulu a half hour before her death—a witness had observed them in an altercation near the murder scene. Taken into custody and held for questioning were a peddler named Salmon and his companion named Wilson.

Theodore Salmon operated a livery stable on Spring Grove Avenue not far from the lover's lane where Lulu was killed. The one-legged man was considered "eccentric" because he employed a wooden crutch on weekdays, but spruced up with a flamboyant red one for Sundays and "extraordinary occasions."

William Wilson was a painter, though his primary trade seemed to be loafing at Salmon's stable. He was known to make idle threats of violence that were never carried out.

A patrolman swore he saw them with two women Friday night on Fergus Street, yet Salmon and Wilson claimed these were the two girls from Chicago they had picked up earlier that evening. And they insisted that they saw Lulu Mueller for the last time near Salmon's stable around 8PM that night.

Police thought it odd that Salmon did not breakfast with his mother that Saturday morning, as was his regular habit. The mother defended her son: "My boy could not have killed her . . . no boy as good to his mother as Theodore was could do so black a deed."

Both men claimed they were home in bed at the time witnesses reported seeing them near the murder scene, and relatives confirmed their alibis. Other evidence against them was so flimsy that the grand jury refused to return an indictment.

Rumors about a quarrel between Lulu and Mellie Alledon, another girlfriend of Frank Eastman, were circulating at the same time Salmon and Wilson were being released. Alledon denied any jealously between them, but remembered a mysterious blonde woman who came to Lulu's house several times looking for her.

There was a bounty of tips about suspicious persons and rampant debauchery near the murder scene. Creepy Negroes, drunken white men, and loose women were parading through the thicket all night, if the mostly inebriated witnesses were to be believed.

Soon a teamsters' strike pushed Lulu Mueller's death off the front pages. But anxious Cumminsville residents would not enjoy a long reprieve from murder.

Rosy-cheeked Alma Steinway left her job on the evening of November 2, 1904, yet she never made it home. The next morning the switchboard operator's battered body was discovered in a vacant lot off Spring Grove Avenue, near the railroad tracks and close to where Mary McDonald had been found in May.

Alma was described as "a girl of eighteen innocent years," who attended church regularly and sang in the choir. The press assured readers that unlike the first two victims, Alma had not been carousing in bars with unsavory men.

But her skull was bashed in like the others, and the gash on her forehead was so deep that it penetrated the brain. The coroner noted that "the chop" could have been made by a hatchet—many hobos who prowled the railroad yards carried small axes or hatchets with them.

Clutched in Alma's hand was a bloodstained streetcar transfer. Police theorized she was attacked around 9:40PM as she emerged from the Clark Street car, and then dragged 130 feet into the lot and dealt the fatal blows. Her ravaged corpse was left in plain view, alongside the murderer's footprints embossed in the thick mud.

Her coworker, Catherine Schlenker, always rode with Alma until she switched cars at Winton. Miss Schlenker was certain that her friend had no "engagement with any person" that night and said she'd never heard Alma "talk of any male friends."

Several suspects quickly surfaced, including "Jack the Pincher," a pervert with a penchant for grabbing women's buttocks. Most intriguing was the squat, bearded man roaming the crowd when the body was discovered, who witnesses remembered seeing at the Lulu Mueller scene a month before, wringing his hands and crying out, "It was an accident!"

Now his distraught behavior once again aroused suspicion, but he slithered away before police could detain him.

Three savage murders in seven months had stunned the community, especially "this latest atrocity against a young, devout girl." The press continued to cover this one differently—the spotless reputation of the newest victim provided a fresh slant.

Coroner Cameron lashed out, proclaiming that "the attack that resulted in the death of Alma Steinway was that of a fiend!" He quickly dispelled rumors that Alma had been hit by a train: "The theory of accident is absolutely untenable." He backed it up with gruesome details: Her skull had been crushed by a murderous blow—portions of the brain had oozed out through the crack.

The coroner clinched it with motive. Alma was murdered while "defending her honor," as microscopic evidence proved that she had been raped. He called the killer "a fiend of the worst possible description." Locking into the single killer theory, Dr. Cameron believed "the assassin is a degenerate who is also guilty of the two other murders in the same locality."

The term serial killer did not yet exist—but for the first time the specter of Jack the Ripper was haunting the harsh alleys and stark dwellings of Cumminsville.

Investigators soon identified their prime target as the unknown man who was stalking Alma on the night of her death. As the *Enquirer* noted: "Witnesses said he bore the general appearance of a degenerate or a man afflicted by partial dementia." He was around 40 years old, unshaven, about 5 feet 8 inches, 140 pounds and wearing a black slouch hat. Despite being "partially demented," he was "slovenly but not quite trampish in dress."

2009

Alma Steinway was attacked here on the corner of Winton and Spring Grove, and then dragged to this spot next to the Mill Creek.

His movements had aroused suspicion. At 7:40PM he tried to attack the wife of the Winton Place station manager, and he was seen twenty minutes later a few blocks from the murder scene. At 9PM he allegedly boarded a street car with Alma Steinway at Knowlton's Corner—an hour later he surfaced in a saloon on Spring Grove Avenue, "greatly excited and covered with dust." He pulled down his hat to hide his features, and inquired about "leaving town on an early freight train," before abruptly fleeing the bar.

This suspect was actually two different men. The bearded man on the same car as Alma turned out to be James Halliday, a respected Cumminsville resident who was hardly the "degenerate and demented" man described by witnesses. Halliday did not realize he was being sought until his wife told him. He immediately went to the police, telling them he had seen Alma Steinway as she alighted from the trolley car and walked toward the waiting room.

But Halliday was not the dusty, agitated saloon dweller trying to flee the area in a boxcar. That man remained at large.

On Saturday afternoon Alma Steinway was memorialized at the Methodist Church in Winton Place. She was buried in the white dress she had made for a party she didn't live to attend. Remembered as an excellent musician who often sang for the other girls at the telephone exchange, her family recalled that she was shy of strangers and content to "seek her companionship at home" rather than go out socially—a marked contrast to the other "fallen" victims of Cumminsville killer.

The Reverend Dr. Burdsall used this somber gathering to deliver some tough words for the Cincinnati police, chiding them for not investigating with their full manpower and calling their "cavalier attitude an assault upon the character of the dead girl."

Investigators were still sifting clues as Alma was buried. Her purse was missing, as was one of her gloves. Detectives had found an article of clothing they were certain belonged to the killer, but would not identify it.

The fact that Alma was found within ten feet of Mill Creek suggested the killer had intended to throw her body into the

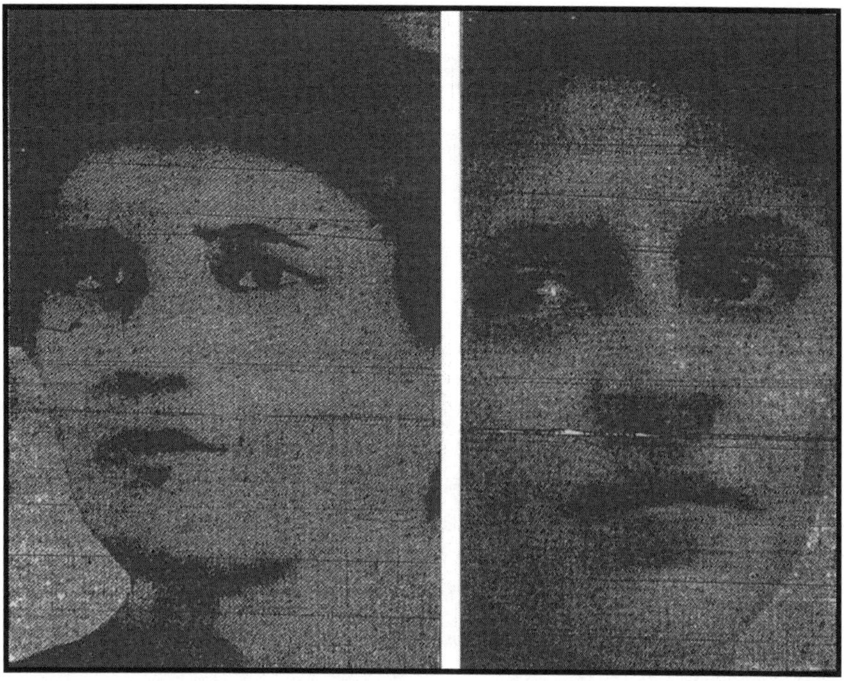

Lulu Mueller (left) and Alma Steinway were murdered within a month of each other in 1904.

water. Based on the flurry of muddy footprints, cops assumed that he panicked and dropped her instead.

A female companion of Miss Steinway soon came forward to tell investigators that Alma had quarreled with an unknown man a few days before her death. While the two were walking on Spring Grove Avenue, this man caught up with Alma and sneered, "You are getting awfully popular, aren't you?" They were offended by the man's tone. Alma explained that he was merely "an acquaintance," and by no means a rejected suitor. Still, this "fine humored, vivacious girl" had seemed visibly upset by the incident.

Another woman emerged to tell of her own narrow escape the night of the murder. Miss Dorothy Hannaford, daughter of the Winton Place mayor, was accosted by a "heavyset man in a slouch hat" just minutes before Alma Steinway got off her trolley car. He startled her by rushing from the shadows, but was scared away when another man approached.

Alma's brothers soon thrust themselves into the case. Ed Steinway tarnished the investigation, saying police "have not developed one single fact of any consequence." He vowed to spend the rest of his life bringing his sister's killer to justice.

Charles Steinway was a different story. Considered Alma's favorite of four brothers, he became haunted by vivid dreams of his sister's murder. He claimed to see a "Jack the Pincher creep" stealthily approaching her from behind and striking her on the head. He saw "the murderer bending over the body, his eyes gleaming with lust. He seizes her by the ankles and drags her from the tracks, down the embankment, and the thick fog envelops them, the monster and his victim."

His dramatic imagination propelled him into the spotlight. Charles was "sweated" by a team of detectives about his habit of following Alma when she went out. He declared that he was only watching out for her—police concluded they were "much attached to each other." Ed Steinway claimed there was nothing more than "a brotherly affection" between them, insisting that Charles was not jealous of Alma and only concerned for her welfare. The grieving brother was finally released.

Investigators were certain of one thing. The location of Alma's facial wounds pointed to a left-handed killer, as did the evidence in the Lulu Mueller murder. This was strong corroboration that both women were killed by the same man.

They now believed that the killer wasn't on the streetcar with Alma, but lurking in the dark waiting room for an opportune victim. A witness had seen a man in the kiosk that night yet didn't get a good look at him.

With no progress to report, newspapers ran every episode with the slightest connection. This was in the heyday of yellow journalism—in 1905, murder had become a form of tabloid entertainment, complete with histrionic headlines:

- **Woman Attacked Near Her Home—She Underwent Horrifying Experience.**

- **Farmers Chase a Heavy-Set Man.**
- **Walnut Hills Girls Panic Stricken.**
- **Nurse Mistaken for Alma Steinway.**
- **Another Cumminsville Girl Has Narrow Escape.**
- **Demented Man Has Been Haunting Winton Place.**

Within weeks a record number of assaults were reported against young women, along with several incidents of menacing and harassment. Two feminist organizations in Cumminsville were outraged, proclaiming that women were now "prisoners of fear." As rewards swelled and vigilantes gathered, newspapers were barraged with letters from women demanding beefed up police protection and better street lighting.

Residents braced for the next horror. But death took a holiday. Months passed with no new murders, and the answers grew remote as seasons spun into years.

More than five years later the killer stuck again—or did he?

Anna Lloyd was a 43-year-old secretary for a Cumminsville lumber company. A competent businesswoman, she left work at 5:30PM in the dim winter twilight of New Year's Eve, 1909.

Trudging through the gloomy darkness near Hopple Street, Anna met her assassin just hours before 1910 unfolded.

She was found lying in a gulley near the CH & D railroad yard. The killing bore the savage imprint of the Cumminsville slayer—a bashed-in head near railroad tracks. Yet this time the victim had been gagged with a muffler, and her throat was slashed. And unlike the 1904 women, defensive wounds proved that Anna Lloyd had engaged in a prolonged battle with her assailant.

Within days police developed a startling theory about the murder: Miss Lloyd had been slain by hired killers who were stalking her. A witness had seen two men outside the lumber office at around 5PM, pacing in the shadows, with Anna clearly visible inside working by the only light still burning.

A half hour later, engineer Tom Tehan was at the controls of his locomotive when his headlamps flared over three figures writhing in the ravine where Anna was later found. He saw two men forcing a woman to the ground—then the train roared past. "I saw what I thought was a fight about 100 feet from the lumber office," said the engineer. He described one of the men as being over 6 feet tall.

Two witnesses had bolstered the theory of premeditation. But if Anna's killer was a mercenary, then who had hired him—and why?

Miss Lloyd's mother told detectives that her daughter "feared a man." A forewarning overtook her on Friday night, about the time of Anna's murder. She told a neighbor, "I will never see her again," and soon afterward fell into a "daze."

Anna's sister lamented, "She was never afraid of anything—that was the trouble." When asked about discord at the office, the sister claimed, "She always spoke as though her business relations were most pleasant. Everyone seemed to like her." Police would learn there was one exception.

A coworker told them that New Year's Eve was "the first time in three months that Miss Lloyd left the office alone." Nellie Herancourt also believed "the murderer of Miss Lloyd knew her. I believe he was familiar with the premises and had perhaps been lying in wait for her for days." She and another woman left work just ten minutes before Anna and walked past the crime scene. "He must have been lurking behind the freight cars at the top of the embankment, and he must have been there when we passed . . . an easy matter in that lonely place."

The path Anna took was described as "very dark." Fire from a nearby factory chimney would sometimes light up the scene, and many women used it as a shortcut before the murder. Now they were vowing to never walk it again, "day or night."

The landscape allowed the murderer an easy getaway. The ravine was surrounded by stacks of lumber and dense underbrush—whatever direction the killer or killers fled provided a cloak of safety. Bloodhounds traced them across the Mill Creek from the railroad tracks, but the trail ended right where a bloody handkerchief was found.

Inevitably, the three 1904 murders were revived by the press. That all four crimes had occurred in the same district led many

This *Cincinnati Post* montage of the Anna Lloyd murder was typical of the sensational coverage spawned by the Cumminsville Killer.

citizens to start calling it "a murder zone." And despite the five-year gap between attacks, most investigators favored the notion that the murders were related.

Yet Police Chief Millikin broke ranks and declared this crime was "independent of Cincinnati's series of women murders in the same territory." Millikin did not believe Anna Lloyd's killer was a degenerate, but rather a cold-blooded stalker with "a desire for revenge."

Anna's fiancé supported this theory, relating the history of conflict between Anna and a male coworker. She had told Joseph Teague about her problems with bookkeeper C.H. Thomas, who resented working under Anna. She complained, "Thomas is getting unbearable, and I don't know what to do about it." Other workers agreed "there was no friendliness between them. Miss Lloyd thought he was too easy in a business way . . . she said he did not keep his accounts properly."

Detectives had puzzled over why several men still at work in the office had not heard a scream or sounds of a struggle only 100 feet away. Now they wondered if the men were covering for someone.

By January 3 they had a good suspect in custody. Henry "Dude" Cook, age 24, was enduring rough questioning after having been identified as one of the dudes who were skulking around the ravine on the night of the murder. And Cook had incriminated himself later at the crime scene. As onlookers watched the body being removed, he was heard to say, "They are trying to accuse me of doing this."

He was on the hot seat for several days, yet despite getting caught in some lies police were ready to release him. They had nothing but circumstantial evidence—Cook's face was scratched, but stains on his shoes turned out to be paint. They failed to link him to the black muffler used to gag Anna Lloyd.

Because of his conflicting statements, the cops kept Cook on ice a little longer. He continued to plead the standard Cumminsville defense—he was too drunk to remember what he had said and done.

Detective Crawford admitted to the press that they were "still up in the air . . . the motive has not been established. The weapon has not been located. Not a real clue has been turned up."

The mayor defended their investigation. He insisted the police were "straining every nerve in that endeavor" to bring the killer to justice. "The crime is so revolting," he implored, "that it strikes fear into every Cincinnati home in which there is a young

Dude Cook was identified by witnesses as the man they saw skulking around the ravine just before Anna Lloyd was killed.

woman. This latest crime cannot but make every father, mother, and brother tremble for the safety of their daughter or sister."

Frustrated by their lack of results, the cops fell back on an old tactic. They rousted a Negro tenement building at midnight and dished out some sharp questioning to the residents. The sweep generated publicity but little else.

Anna was laid to rest on January 4. The Enquirer reported that "grim faced men and half-hysterical, sorrowing women passed in a stream for half an hour past the coffin of murdered

Anna Lloyd." Alice Lloyd fainted at the sight of her sister in the casket.

Joseph Teague, the victim's fiancé, delivered this cryptic comment after the funeral: "There is more to this case than has ever been hinted at."

"Dude" Cook continued to proclaim his innocence even while subjected to the third degree. Detectives considered his statements about the murder night to be "untruthful and evasive." He was seen running from the crime scene with another man, and his lies blanketed him with suspicion. But he could not be linked to the murder itself. Cook was finally released after being held for a month.

As the Anna Lloyd case wasted away, police received an anonymous letter from someone signing himself S.D.M. He promised to "clear up matters" in the unsolved slayings.

All it did was muddy the waters—and Anna Lloyd was added to the murder zone list.

The killer concluded his macabre binge on October 25, 1910, when 26-year-old Mary Hackney was found beaten and slashed near the railroad tracks. Sometime during that sunny Tuesday morning she was attacked in her cottage on Canal Ridge near Dane Street. Her body was found at 6PM by her husband and a teenage boarder as they returned from work.

At first glance this crime didn't fit the pattern. The previous victims were all single women, and Mary was killed at her home in broad daylight, not ambushed in the shadows of Cumminsville. And there were instant suspects with motive and opportunity.

There was one glaring match to the other four slayings—the excessive brutality. The killer had left the stain of his ferocity at every murder scene.

The coroner released graphic details of this latest outrage. Mary had been struck down in her kitchen and dragged into the dining room, where her throat was cut from ear to ear, severing the jugular vein in a torrent of blood. There were ten deep gashes about her face and head, and her right cheek was

Blamed for Darkness in Murder Zone---Crime Is Nightly Invited

Coroner Examines Many Witnesses in Inquest Into Mystery--Employers of Anna Lloyd Say They Knew of No Enemies.

The poor lighting in Cumminsville was a hot topic, especially with so many "factory girls" walking home from work at night.

hacked open. For good measure the killer had fractured her skull with two vicious blows.

Mary was the wife of Harley Hackney, a former army private currently employed at a lumberyard. She was partially disabled, and the couple had no children. Police detained Hackney and several others, including the young boarder Charles Eckert, and a mulatto milk wagon driver whose route included the Hackney home.

Another Negro, Richard Finley, was arrested when a Hackney neighbor claimed he'd attacked her the previous Monday night. A Mrs. Hulbert identified Finley, and then surprised police by swearing that she saw Mary on her front porch at 8:05AM Tuesday morning. Since both Hackney and Eckert had arrived at work around 6:30AM that day, the husband's alibi appeared solid.

However, when a wife is murdered the spouse is scrutinized. It was known that Mary always seized his paycheck and doled out a quarter for spending money. Investigators wondered if Hackney knew about his wife's past—they learned she had given birth to an illegitimate child who'd died seven years earlier.

They puzzled over curious incidents on the morning of the murder. Mary always let the chickens out when Harley went to work, but they had remained penned up that day. Milk had been delivered around 6:30AM, but the bottle on their doorstep had not been taken in. And the Hackney dog was found roaming loose along the creek.

Even witnesses who placed Hackney at work that day commented that he was not his usual jovial self. One coworker said the husband's demeanor had attracted his attention several times that afternoon. Hackney himself made a puzzling statement that night: "I have had a presentment all day that I was going to meet with some kind of trouble."

He was arrested when it was found that some of his clothing was missing. As he languished in jail Hackney pleaded with detectives, "Let me out, and I'll help you find the murderer."

Yet investigators weren't finished with Mary's husband. They found some letters in the attic which provided insight into the past life of Hackney and his wife. They would not reveal the details, other than to say that "the family was a strange one."

The young Negro milk wagon driver told an interesting story during questioning. Herman Schwering had made his delivery to the Hackney home around 10AM. He said the doors were locked, yet Hackney had claimed they were ajar when he came home from work. Schwering insisted he saw a bloody broadax on the porch—he did not report this at the time, assuming someone had just killed a few chickens.

When Schwering was arrested he had a bloody handkerchief in his pocket. He had also made a habit of meeting a Cumminsville police officer while on his rounds. But Sgt. Otting could not alibi him. "I did not see the boy on Tuesday," said Otting. "It was the first time I had failed to see him for weeks."

Both Eckert (the boarder) and Schwering made no protest when asked to submit to Bertillion photographing and measuring. They were frail in appearance, and police considered this as favoring their innocence. Mrs. Hackney's killer had seemed to possess brute strength.

Detective Crawford speculated that whoever killed Anna Lloyd in January might also have slain Mary Hackney. "The cases are parallel in their brutality," he reasoned. "The throats

Husband of Mrs. Mary Hackney and Boarder Near Freedom as Negro Is Arrested on Woman's Charge.

THE HACKNEY MYSTERY

THE CRIME: Murder. Woman's head crushed and throat cut.

THE VICTIM: Mrs. Mary Hackney, aged 26, wife of Harley Hackney, a former private in the regular army and later employed as a lumber checker at the Farrin-Korn plant. No children. Woman crippled.

WEAPON: A short-handled broad-ax, which belongs to the Hackneys.

SCENE OF CRIME: Interior of Hackney home, on Canal Ridge, near Dane-st., in the "murder zone" of Cumminsville. Woman evidently had been struck down in the kitchen and her body dragged into the dining room, both on the first floor, where she was found dead.

TIME: During the day Tuesday. Body found at 6 p. m. Tuesday by her husband and Chas. Eckert, 16, a boarder, who lived in the house with the Hackneys and who was employed at the same place as Hackney.

MOTIVE: Not established. Mayor Schwab and alienists say the murder indicates the hand of an insane person—probably the type that experiences pleasure while committing crime and undergoes a change that robs him of all memory of the crime afterward

CHIEF CHARACTERISTICS OF THE CRIME: Excessive brutality, in which respect it is similar to the four other murders of women that have taken place within two miles of the Hackney home within six years. In all of these cases the chief characteristic was the evidence of the ferocity of the murderer. In none of the cases had the woman been criminally attacked before being killed.

ARRESTS: Husband and several others detained by police. Bloody finger print on door of Hackney home examined as clue. Police generally baffled by mystery.

OTHER VICTIMS OF MURDER ZONE: The Alma Steinigeweg murder occurred at Spring Grove-av. and Winton-rd.; the Lulu Mueller murder was committed at Spring Grove-av. and Fergus-st.; the Mary McDonald murder, at the C., H. & D. Railroad tracks and Dane-st., and the Anna Lloyd murder, in a hollow at Hopple-st. and the C., H. & D. Railroad.

Mary Hackney's husband Harley was the first suspect, but the murder timeline didn't fit his alibi—he was at work when she was killed.

of both women were cut by the same sort of weapon." None of the 1904 victims had their throats slashed.

Hackney neighbor Alice Steuting had talked with the slain woman about the peril in their desolate district: "This is a lonely neighborhood, and we discussed a number of times the danger confronting women left at home while their husbands were at work."

Mrs. Steuting insisted that the Hackneys "seemed an ideal young couple and deeply in love with each other."

Several days after the murder, a writer named Ruth Neely criticized the investigation, saying it lacked a system to seek clues. Her column in the *Enquirer* told of women frustrated that police could not solve any of the murder zone mysteries: "Women of Cumminsville say openly that something must be radically wrong with the methods of a protective system confessedly powerless to protect."

She was on the scene of the Hackney murder and observed officers not working together. "Each man seemed to follow his own initiative, which led him to duplicate the acts of his companions, while precious time was being lost and perhaps valuable clues being obscured by the very process." She herself had found Mrs. Hackney's purse containing $10 and handed it to police, thus eliminating robbery as a motive.

Ms. Neely closed with a final jab: "It may be the feminine rashness of justice to draw involuntary comparisons," she wrote. "Systematic effort brings results in newspaper work but in police work it seems to be considered futile."

Issues of gender and race would not stay buried.

The Hackney house was in a lonely part of Canal Ridge—the few houses nearby were occupied by poor blacks. "There are too many unemployed Negroes running loose around Cumminsville," complained one neighbor woman. "The police ought to watch them closer." The next day she reported being menaced by a black man who warned her to keep quiet or she "will be marked for the next one."

From his cell, Harley Hackney chimed in as the fear of violent black men inflamed the citizenry: "It is my belief that a Negro, crazed with whiskey or cocaine got into the house and killed her."

Detectives were still probing the strife in the Hackney marriage. They grilled Harley about their quarrels over money, and pounced on his statement that he was getting tired of his wife. But Hackney calmly answered all questions and was not evasive. One investigator called him "the coolest man I've seen for a long time."

With one exception—Hackney was astonished to learn that his wife had been engaged 10 years earlier and had given birth to an illegitimate child.

The coroner did his best to exonerate him. "It is my belief that the husband and the young boy are probably guiltless," he announced, citing coworkers who were talking with both men at the hour of Mary Hackney's death, and the neighbor who saw Mary alive on her porch at 8:15AM, after her husband had already gone to work.

The next day all those in custody were freed. Hackney immediately joined the hunt, telling the police chief, "I won't rest until I find the murderer." He later enacted his own theory for the press, claiming the weapon was a hatchet missing from their kitchen.

With all the suspects released, this latest murder fell into the gray area of the other slayings. "This is going to be a very difficult case to solve," proclaimed Coroner Coe, "because of the absence of clues indicating even a motive for the crime. Nothing was stolen, the woman was not assaulted, and the only reason seems to have been a lust for blood."

Eccentrics soon crawled out of the woodwork. There was a young woman who'd seen the murderer's face in a dream, and a spiritualist who held a fruitless séance. There were more letters from the mysterious "S.D.M.," who had written after the Anna Lloyd murder—he claimed knowledge of all the crimes, but investigators now dismissed it as a hoax.

Inevitably, the *Enquirer* ran a morbid comparison with the crimes of Jack the Ripper, the whore slasher of 1888 London. Still uncaught, Jack was dismissed as "a monster," yet opinion was divided about the railroad killer: "The Cumminsville murders have already reached the point of psychological controversy."

Several experts weighed in as well. Doctors Beebe and Kendig quoted Kraft-Ebbing in highlighting the killer's "peculiar mania for murder" when faced with an "imperative hallucination" or "a vision of blood." Another alienist called the killer "an insane person—probably the type that experiences pleasure while committing the crime and undergoes a change that robs him of all memory of the crime afterward."

Spurred on by Ruth Neely's writings and the impassioned oratory of the burgeoning suffragette movement, the women of Cumminsville were demanding better lighting and more protection. They became incensed when the police promised more lighting only "if there was another murder."

The Susan B. Anthony Club went so far as to recommend the hiring of female police officers, an unthinkable notion in 1910. "Women police would have found the Cumminsville murderer or murderers long ago," boasted the club's president, while pointing out that night shift factory girls were resigning their jobs in droves.

Better lighting was on the way—but a solution to the murder spree was lost in the looming darkness.

Several women were attacked in the "murder zone" toward the end of 1910. On July 18, 1911, a Black woman was beaten to death in Cumminsville, but police declined to link this crime to the white victims.

Fading memories revived in 1913 when a railroad conductor was implicated in the murder of Anna Lloyd. A threatening letter in his possession mentioned "persons who saw him in the act of Dec 31," and detectives investigated his connection to the three-year-old case.

Yet this last lead proved to be the final dead end.

POLICE SEEKING CLUES IN MURDER LACK SYSTEM THINKS WOMAN WRITER

BY RUTH NEELY.

Cumminsville's woman murder mystery No. 5 had on the fourth day after the discovery of the body of the victim, Mrs. Mary Hackney, reached the impenetrable stage, so no harm can be done by giving the impressions of a mere woman observer of the case.

With the weak logic of their sex, women conclude that something is lacking in a police and detective force that cannot solve even one of the murder zone mysteries.

Women of Cumminsville say openly that something must be radically wrong with the methods of a protective system confessedly powerless to protect.

Perhaps it was feminine rashness of judgment that caused me to draw involuntary comparisons between the methods adopted, say by a newspaper, in gathering information and those of the Cincinnati detective force when I visited the Hackney home at Canal Ridge Wednesday morning after the murder had been revealed.

SYSTEM IS APPARENT IN ONE CASE

To me the difference was striking, since on a newspaper such work is carefully systematized. I

RUTH NEELY

Enquirer **reporter Ruth Neely took the police force to task, and even suggested they hire a woman detective to solve the crimes.**

SUMMATION:

The Cumminsville murders remain unsolved. But how many killers were there?

Five years between crimes is not evocative of a serial killer, unless he was imprisoned for another offense during that time. Only incarceration could curtail such obsessive blood lust.

There are motives that suggest multiple killers.

Certainly Mary McDonald and Lulu Mueller consorted with a number of unsavory men, but Alma Steinway sang in the church choir. The killing of Anna Lloyd looks like a private vendetta—she told her mother that she "feared a man", and her slashed throat indicated a personal motive. Whoever murdered Mary Hackney in her home in broad daylight knew the rest of the family's movements. It is tempting to suspect Harley Hackney, but the timeline eliminates the husband.

It is possible the same man killed sweet Alma and saucy Lulu. If any of the five deaths are connected, it would be these two, occurring a month apart and within the same quarter mile. And the swarthy man acting creepy at the Mueller scene also was loitering in the crowd when Alma's body was found.

EPILOGUE:

When the fiend's rampage ended in 1910, the streets of Cumminsville were brightly lit, and women went on their way once more, without the fear of brutal death stalking from the darkness.

Like Jack the Ripper in London, the Cumminsville killer exposed the squalid and spiteful living conditions of the city's working poor, which led to improved social programs for the "murder zone" residents.

But who was Cincinnati's first serial killer—and why did he stop killing?

It's conceivable that the railroad stalker was an urban legend that cloaked five different killers and motives.

Or perhaps he was an obscure madman who lived to a ripe old age and died peacefully, leaving behind a legacy of doubt and despair.

POSTSCRIPT: AUGUST 2011

Further information about the "Cumminsville Ripper" has been brought to my attention since **QCG** was published in October 2009. With the glut of press coverage at the time, it was easy to overlook some of the angles.

This story appeared in the *Iowa Recorder* in November 1904, one month after Alma Steinway was slain: **GIRL REPELS THE RIPPER: Cincinnati Woman Uses Revolver and Puts Assailant to Flight.**

It seems that Miss Josephine Hewitt had a revolver concealed in the folds of her waist and did not hesitate to use it when confronted by "Cincinnati's Jack the Ripper." Miss Hewitt encountered a "rough looking man" who emerged from Spring Grove cemetery one night and made a grab for her throat. She whipped out her weapon, and as her assailant fled she "opened fire on him and continued blazing away until every chamber of her revolver was empty." Detectives found no trace of the man.

On March 18 1905, 15 year old Lottie Lucas was abducted from an orphanage in Xenia, Ohio and later found murdered. When her bloody dress and undergarments were found in Cumminsville, detectives initially feared "the Ripper" had killed the child, but were never able to connect this crime to the other victims.

The *Williamsport Sunday Grit* ran a story on September 3, 1905 headlined: **Jack the Ripper Still Active!** "Miss Elsie McGrath, aged 17, was struck down with a blunt instrument by a short heavy set man. Her injuries were not fatal."

Later that year, Dr. Oliver Haugh briefly became a suspect in the Cumminsville slayings. The Dayton, Ohio physician had poisoned his parents and brother, yet it wasn't clear why Cincinnati police were interested in him. They had hoped he might confess before his execution in 1907, but he went to the electric chair without making any statements. His obituary noted that "The felon was buried as he had lived and died, alone and unwept save by his wife."

In February of 2010, a startling confession to the three 1904 murders came out of Leavenworth Federal prison in Kansas. A 28-year-old convicted forger named John Hill had provided specific details of the crimes to his cellmate, a young boy who feared Hill and thus did not tell prison officials until after Hill had been released.

It seemed remote at best, yet Cincinnati detectives were impressed with the accuracy of the confession and initially believed it to be true. But Hill disappeared after his release, and efforts to find him were fruitless.

Eventually the local police discounted the second hand confession as hearsay. They could not verify that Hill had been in Cincinnati during the 1904 murders, and they noted that Hill was "one of those strange characters steeped in perversion who study the stories of atrocious crimes and retain them in memory."

I WITNESS:

Mary McDonald downs her fifth shot of whiskey—she is on a real bender. The murky bar is packed cheek to jowl.

Stagman plies her with drink all night long, hoping she'll come across for him. But her heart is empty, her body unwilling.

This pathetic moth is weary of life on the candle's fringe. The tawdry affair with her late sister's husband has steered her to the bottle. She knows that her fiancé, her one, final chance to win respectability, will soon discover her sordid past.

In the alley, Stagman gives her some morphine. Even through her alcoholic haze, the drug infests her with a lethal clarity.

Her upcoming marriage is already doomed. Love will once again turn to dust. All is lost.

She is the prodigal daughter, debauched and dissipated, back in the gutter. Wandering away from Stagman, she lurches along the grimy, deserted streets. Mary grabs a pole next to the railroad tracks and begins to sway, waiting for the heavens to plummet.

She collapses onto the tracks as the train's lights blind her. She scrambles to crawl away as the belching engine bears down—or does she?

They find her with a smashed skull and a severed leg, gasping for breath. In the hospital she rears up once, moaning, "Oh, girls, don't do that! Please don't!"

Then she sinks back down on the bed and dies.

This moth never even feels the warmth of the flame.

Lulu Mueller is a borrower of the night.

Comely and impetuous, on this evening she is furious with Frank. He's passing up a good time with her so he can drink with some slovenly horse traders. And Lulu really needs to talk to him.

Between beers at the corner tavern, she walks the tracks to Frank's house, hoping to run into him. That one-legged peddler is urging her to give it up—he and his friend want her to go to the lover's lane with them. But Lulu can only think about Frank's letter, which she carries in her pocket.

She knows her swain is a bit of a rake. But she is a brazen damsel, not about to be bridled by a hustler like Frank Eastman.

She dumps her shady companions sometime after nine, hearing them curse her as she sets off for Frank's once again. She will confront him tonight at all costs—she has to tell him. If he truly wants to marry her, he must give up the carousing, the gambling, and the womanizing.

This time she leaves the tracks and cuts through the whispering fields to her lover's house. There is no moon, only the ghostly white vapors drifting up from the creek that mingle with the soot. Yet the shadows are bereft, dark and heavy as liquid.

The killer catches her in a quivering thicket. She recognizes him, the burly, bearded man who always stands in the background, leering at her and making lurid suggestions. The smell of liquor on his breath is overwhelming.

After so many rejections, he has an evil urge to take her, and his frustration is a seething madness. He attacks her drunkenly, but with surprising power. Lulu has only a moment to cry out before her skull is shattered by the makeshift club he carries.

Coming out of his stupor, he tries to bury her body, but is spooked by the constant lover's lane traffic—night dwellers skulking across the land in romantic wanderings. The killer abandons her by the tracks and flees his handiwork.

They find Lulu as the sun slices the horizon; blades of grass are entwined in her tightly clenched fingers, along with that letter from Frank Eastman, which pledges his undying love.

The culprit lies doggo for a month, and then emerges again. He is the bewhiskered yard bird who slew Lulu only a week after being released from the local lockup.

Now he is stalking Alma. He knows her routine of changing streetcars at Winton and Spring Grove, having ridden the same car with her several times.

This time he picks the prettiest of them all.

Alma sees him lurking near the corner where she usually stands for her transfer. She retreats into the waiting room, but it is not the safe haven she prays for.

The beast traps her in the kiosk and deals her a wicked blow with the hatchet. He then drags the dying girl to a vacant lot where he can have his way with her.

Alma drifts in and out of consciousness, but feels no sense of panic, only a profound sadness. She is a good girl. She attends church. She has kind words for everyone she meets. Above all, she cherishes her good name—and her honor. Now this horrible, smelly gorilla is ripping at her undergarments, intent on stealing something she safeguards, a precious gift reserved for a husband. She can't even scream, not with this man's filthy hand clamped over her mouth. She can only cry silently.

Just before everything turns dark, she remembers the white dress she finished hemming just two nights earlier.

White stands for purity and innocence. She has no right to wear it now.

Once sated, the man dumps her ravaged body in plain view. All he leaves behind are his footprints in the thick mud.

By the following morning he is sober, and just as with Lulu, he visits the crime scene, mixing among the crowd and expressing his remorse. Several onlookers are alarmed by his behavior, but he once again slips away before police can question him.

Within months he is in another city and another jail for attacking another woman—he eventually dies in prison.

Dude Cook and his partner pace the shadows, sharing a cigarette. The men talk quietly, their speech scattered with long silences.

Thomas wants her killed tonight! New Year's Eve—just after the sun goes down.

Cook watches the final rays of daylight scurry into the winter evening. She'll be leaving work anytime now. Behind them the railroad tracks start to glow, illuminated by the fire blazing in an old factory chimney by the creek.

He muses to himself about why Thomas wants this done. Anna Lloyd must really have something on the bookkeeper, and Thomas is afraid she will talk. He also despises her—he wants the men to cut her throat! He is, in fact, insistent on that point.

So be it. All Dude Cook cares about is that the money will spend.

Two young women from the lumber office walk by, and they realize that Anna is the only one left working. The men lurk behind a boxcar near the ravine—within minutes, they see her walking toward the tracks.

When she passes by a lumber stack, they strike. They try to drag her into the dense underbrush, but Anna fights hard for her life. She recognizes these blackguards, and she knows exactly who sent them. She defends herself with a gusto that surprises her assassins. *No pansy-ass bookkeeper is going to enlist this pair of dolts to whale the tar out of me,* she thinks. *All three will be going to jail for a very long time.*

Dude tries to gag her with his muffler, but she breaks away and runs back toward the tracks. They catch up with her just as the train roars past. In the engine's glaring headlamp she is forced to the ground and her throat is gashed. As the cars clatter by, she lies there, convulsing like a fish. The killers bludgeon her several times for good measure, as the chimney fire throws decaying light up and down the railroad yard, like a giant, twisting lantern.

Dude and his tall minion rush across the creek and up the embankment to safety, leaving behind a bloody handkerchief as mute testimony to the contract killing of Anna Lloyd.

Mary Hackney is a woman of many secrets.

If Harley knew what she was doing, he would leave her for sure, she thinks. But nothing is happening—yet.

After her husband leaves for work, Mary waits again for her young caller. It started weeks earlier with the Negro doing some odd jobs around the Hackney place. He seemed more polite than the other blacks who lived in the shanties along the creek.

Yet on this bright autumn morning, Richard Finley is sullen and fidgety. Mary is unaware that Finley attacked her neighbor just ten hours before. She knows that he is a scavenger. She cannot know that he is about to become a predator.

She invites him in, as usual, to discuss today's chores. Harley would be furious if he knew she let this black man inside their home.

She becomes alarmed when Finley accuses her of leading him on. Mary has been friendly, even flirty. But what she considers cordial, he considers—what? Is the man daft? She has gone behind Harley's back before, but it would be unthinkable with a Negro!

When Finley tries to touch her, Mary recoils in disgust. Fuming now, she orders this lackey out of her house.

Finley explodes like a piece of machinery, cleaving her skull with a mighty whack from the hatchet he carries. His lurking bloodlust bursts opens, and he emerges from his rage only after pummeling her about the head and cutting her throat.

He is arrested that same day, along with Harley and two other suspects, but he has already tossed his weapons and bloody clothes into the creek. Detectives sweat him, but this smooth criminal has been interrogated before—he knows how to deny and deny.

As the cops become more interested in Harley Hackney, Finley is forgotten and eventually released. That night, he jumps the first available freight train, and leaves Cumminsville forever.

2009

Freda Hornberger vanished forever after leaving this bakery in 1921.

INTO THE WIND

THE VANISHINGS OF LIZ NOLTE, EMILY GUMP, AND FREDA HORNBERGER: 1915-1921

"What is your life? It is even a vapor that appears for a little while and then vanishes."

Corinthians

PROLOGUE:

Over a six-year period beginning in 1915, three little girls disappeared from the same quarter mile of the old Mohawk neighborhood of Cincinnati. They were not runaway urchins—they came from stable, loving families. The first was found ravaged and mutilated several days after her kidnapping. The other two vanished into thin air, as if carried from earth by giant eagles.

Were they all victims of the same fiendish slayer? Or was this just a cruel twist of fate, ensnaring a trio of angels who never grew up.

NARRATIVE:

The summer of 1915 saw the dawn of U.S. military and social upheaval. The First World War was escalating in the wake left by the Lusitania, the British passenger liner torpedoed by a German U Boat with the loss of 1200 lives (128 Americans). The fledgling

NAACP was flexing its muscle by protesting racial depictions in the controversial hit movie *The Birth of a Nation.* And birth control pioneer Margaret Sanger was facing an obscenity trial for referring to "contraception" in her magazine called *Woman Rebel.*

On several fronts, issues which had always been deemed unmentionable were suddenly taking center stage.

Perched atop the stone shoulders of the Queen City, Mohawk had its own bustling style and distinct aromas. The tight cross hatching of streets and the short urban blocks afforded a familiarity that made residents feel safe.

Yet Mohawk also had a murky quality that defied explanation. The district was teeming with undesirable men, many of whom harbored a furtive lust for young girls.

It began on Tuesday, June 15, when 11-year-old Elizabeth Nolte vanished a few blocks from her home. She had just returned from the butcher shop when her niece Bertha asked her to go to "an entertainment" at a nearby park, but Elizabeth said she was going somewhere else. Bertha saw her skip off in the direction of Hyman Alexander's stable in the alley behind her house right around 4:30PM.

She didn't come home that night, and went missing all day Wednesday.

On Thursday morning at 6AM, a worker noticed a bundle outside the Nolte residence at 1411 Central Avenue. He opened the door and summoned Mrs. Nolte, who reached into the bag and screamed, "My God! It's my baby!"

What was left of Elizabeth was ghastly. Her nude body had been violated, and her head was nearly severed.

That her body had been returned elicited a good deal of speculation. The *Cincinnati Enquirer* called this "an unusual feature" of the case and ascribed a noble motive to the murderer: "The degenerate slayer upset local criminal tradition by bringing home the body of his victim, that it might be given a proper burial."

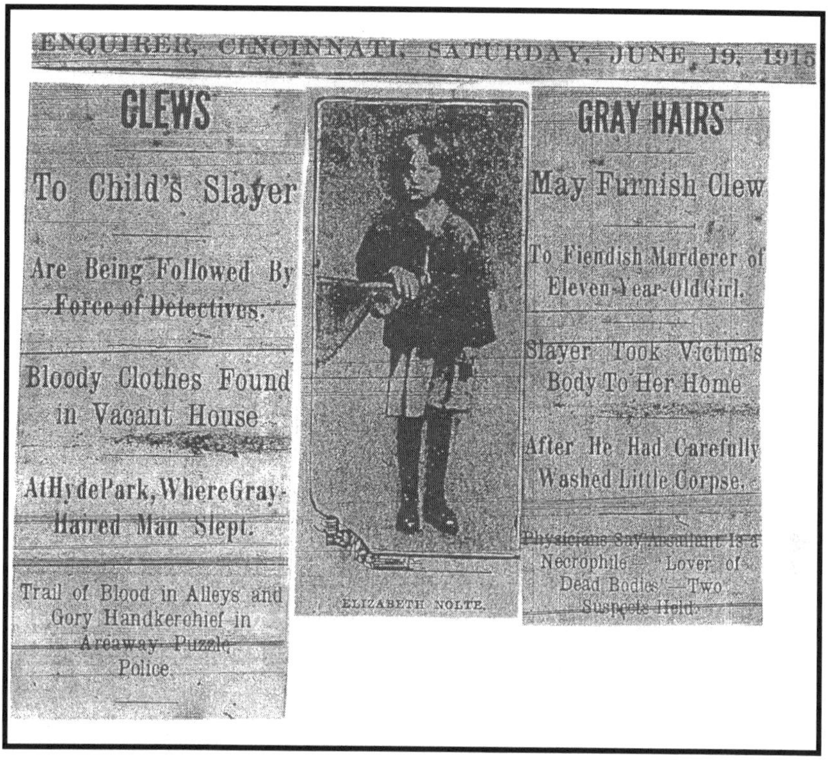

ENQUIRER, CINCINNATI, SATURDAY, JUNE 19, 1915

CLEWS

To Child's Slayer

Are Being Followed By Force of Detectives.

Bloody Clothes Found in Vacant House

At Hyde Park, Where Gray-Haired Man Slept.

Trail of Blood in Alleys and Gory Handkerchief in Areaway Puzzle Police.

ELIZABETH NOLTE.

GRAY HAIRS

May Furnish Clew

To Fiendish Murderer of Eleven-Year-Old Girl.

Slayer Took Victim's Body To Her Home

After He Had Carefully Washed Little Corpse.

Physicians Say Assailant Is a Necrophile — Lover of Dead Bodies — Two Suspects Held.

The savage murder of an 11 year old child shocked the city.

After confirming the coroner's verdict that Elizabeth had been sexually assaulted, the *Enquirer* noted, "Ordinary murderers either escape immediately or attempt to rid themselves of bodies by burying or burning. But this latest fiend, whether impelled by his conscience or some other impulse, risked the danger of capture by bearing the little form to the abode of its parents."

By dawn Thursday two men were already under arrest. William Dean and Noble Moore were taken into custody, despite their protests of innocence.

Moore was the ideal suspect. He was a black man, and his motive was strong—the murdered girl had been due in court that Thursday to testify that Moore had exposed himself to Elizabeth in an alley two weeks earlier. He was arrested that day and later freed when the charge was reduced to disorderly conduct.

Mrs. Nolte claimed that Elizabeth had "been kidnapped by a Negro" when she reported her missing on Tuesday night. Now in custody again, Moore was whisked to the crime scene. A sheet was removed from the corpse, and Moore was commanded to look into the dead child's face. The hulking black man betrayed visible emotion.

"Do you know her?" shouted Detective Knidel. "Ever see her before?"

"Yes," said Moore dejectedly. "I believe she's the little girl who lived here."

Knidel knew that Moore had killed another black man in self defense several years earlier and served a short jail term—and that fight had been over a young girl.

William Dean was being interrogated while Moore was viewing the body. The white man hung out at the same stable where Elizabeth was headed when last seen. If Moore had motive, then Dean had opportunity.

"I'm innocent, I tell you!" he exclaimed. "I liked that little girl as much as if she were my own. I gave her nickels and candy and took her to the moving picture shows." Such behavior seemed innocent to Dean but not to investigators, who agreed that his protests were agitated and awkward.

His undue attentions to Elizabeth had raised suspicion. A search of his residence revealed that his bed sheet from Tuesday night was missing, and numerous cherry stones were found on his doorstep—Elizabeth was known to be fond of cherries.

Dean was a rag dealer who had delivered 18 sacks of goods the day after the murder, but a quick search determined that none contained the dead girl's clothing. Detectives then tried to link him to the sack that contained Elizabeth's body. It was 4 by 5 feet with a drawstring, and looked like it was used to hold winter clothing—or rags.

Dean had been a frequent visitor at the Nolte residence. "He was good to my baby," said the mother. "Tell them to let him go!"

Elizabeth's father had a different take. "I don't like Dean, and he doesn't like me. He has good reason. I cut him some time ago in a fight, but just the same, I believe he's innocent."

The parents gave no such exemption to the Negro. "Moore has been watching my baby for months," said Mrs. Nolte. "We caught him hanging around several times after he got out on bond."

The noose began to tighten around Moore's neck. In the week before the murder, he had been observed spying on Elizabeth from a nearby alley. Early Wednesday morning, a Nolte neighbor witnessed two unidentified black men carrying a large basket in the direction of the Nolte home.

The *Enquirer* pointed out the similarities between this murder and the notorious killing of Mary Phagan in Atlanta several years before. A black man had been held in the Phagan case until Leo Frank, the Jewish superintendent of the factory where she worked, was convicted and condemned.

The Frank case became a national sensation. Many believed he was wrongfully convicted, based on the perjured testimony of Negro suspect Jim Conley. It was the first time in the South's memory that a black man's word was accepted against that of a white man. Frank was lynched after his death sentence was commuted, only to be posthumously pardoned in 1986, after an old man who'd worked at the factory as a boy finally came clean to incriminate Conley in the murder of Mary Phagan.

The Nolte case achieved only local notoriety. But the fervor to lynch Noble Moore was building—police beefed up security at the jail where both Moore and Dean were being held.

While tips regarding dubious black men were flooding police headquarters, investigators were taking a hard look at William Dean. They believed the murderer knew the Nolte family "intimately" and had kept close watch on their movements the week before the crime.

Late Thursday the coroner released his gruesome findings on the slaying of Elizabeth Nolte, already being called the most baffling child murder in Cincinnati history.

The girl's hands showed evidence of a fierce struggle. Both were tightly clenched and peppered with defensive wounds, cuts indicating she had grasped a double edged blade that was drawn from her fingers. Inside one hand the coroner found and preserved two gray hairs.

The cut in Elizabeth's throat was 5-1/2" long, deep enough to sever the spinal cord and nearly her head. The coroner speculated that the fatal wound was inflicted with either a ground razor or a large knife.

Her body was found nude, and there was evidence that "the fiend responsible for the crime had carefully bathed it after he had used his knife." But washing did not conceal the depravity. The *Enquirer* reported that "the child had been assaulted twice after death in a manner that indicated an advanced degree of degeneracy. Physicians stated that the man who'd committed the crime was afflicted with necrophilia. This type of degenerate is gifted with the greatest cunning and is seldom traced by the police."

Bloodstains were turning up all over Mohawk. Most had innocent explanations, but each finding was urgently reported as significant. A house where Elizabeth and a friend had played hide-and-seek contained a large pool of blood, later determined to be from a chicken.

Since only her shoes were returned with the child's ravaged corpse, the search for Elizabeth's clothing became a top priority. Police probed every house within four blocks of the congested borough where the family lived. They were also hoping to find the crime scene—the place where the victim's throat was cut could yield vital evidence.

The washing of the dead child perplexed detectives. They suspected that a woman was enlisted in the preparation of the corpse to destroy any trace evidence, and also to help the killer return the body. Did he just want to remove her from the crime scene, or did his conscience insist on offering Elizabeth a Christian burial? They concluded that only a family friend would have taken that kind of risk.

The connection between Elizabeth and William Dean was flourishing. His neighbor reported suspicious activity by the suspect shortly before the body was found. Dean was seen after midnight carrying a bucket, using a faucet, and sneaking around the alley near the Nolte residence. Dean denied these allegations, and pointed to his work alibi for the Tuesday of the disappearance, even as his partner insisted they had separated at 4:30PM, right around the time Elizabeth went missing.

Dean continued to trip over his own mouth. He had recently told Elizabeth's uncle that she was "his girl" and he "innocently" gave her candy and money, and he repeated an earlier claim that he loved her "like a daughter."

Celia Madden, Dean's neighbor and a firm believer in his innocence, nevertheless reported that she had seen "the girl" go often to his place. But she didn't see her on that fateful Tuesday.

Vigorous work by the undertaker prepared Elizabeth's mutilated body for burial on Friday morning. Her favorite doll was placed inside the casket with her.

During the second week investigators snared two new suspects.

Four young girls came forward, complaining of an elderly man who "annoyed" them in the local theater. Described as a flashy dresser who frequented the Mohawk nickel show, he would sit next to a girl and expose himself, often following her as she changed seats. Police checked out a 9th street address where the pervert supposedly lived, but no one there knew who he was.

The second suspect was no phantom. As the *Enquirer* reported: "A startling development in the Nolte murder case came yesterday when James Frond declared the child was in a lumber yard on Liberty Street last Monday evening with 62-year-old William Hoon. He is now being held on suspicion."

"Elizabeth sat on Hoon's lap on a pile of lumber," said Frond. "He was hugging her closely . . . I first saw them at 5:25PM Monday . . . They were still there at 7 o'clock . . . I also saw her in the lumber yard with the old man several weeks ago." The witness soon provided a positive identification of Hoon at the jail: "That's the man, all right!"

Hoon had gray hair, like those clutched in Liz's dead hand, and a search of his house turned up bloody handkerchiefs. When arrested he was in the company of two young girls, and was alleged to have taken other children into the lumber yard as well.

The children with Hoon admitted to police that they had a "date" with the old man. "The wee maids" tearfully recounted his improper advances once in the lumber yard. Hoon became "greatly excited" as he was being booked, while cops rushed to check out his alibi for the previous Tuesday.

William Hoon was a dirty old man—but he was no killer. After his release detectives became frustrated with the staggering number of dead end leads. A Kentucky boatman with a grudge against the family was looked at, but proved to be in Indiana on the day of the disappearance. A couple acting strangely in the vicinity of the Nolte home were unsuccessfully sought by police. Reports of perverts and Negroes giving money to little white girls continued to pour in, even as police finally released suspect Nobel Moore.

The failure to locate the crime scene hampered the investigation, and the sheer number of nefarious men roaming Mohawk was daunting. The *Enquirer* noted the area was indeed a ripe hunting ground for child predators: "In this cosmopolitan and congested neighborhood are numerous little girls who consort with men and whose actions cause comment."

Even the little victim was not immune from speculation. One newspaper noted her problem with truancy, and neighbors remarked how approachable Elizabeth was and how often she asked strange men for candy.

There was one positive upshot of the investigation. "The police are rounding up many men who are charged with acting improperly toward little girls, "proclaimed the *Enquirer.* "This crusade against the despoilers of childhood is one effective result of the Nolte investigation."

Yet the search for Liz Nolte's killer began to wither. William Dean still had the support of the Nolte family, even though detectives doubted his alibi for the day Elizabeth vanished, and were intrigued by the lingering animosity between Dean and Walter Nolte.

Eventually William Dean was released due to lack of evidence.

Elizabeth's mother vented her spleen as the trail grew cold. "I'd cut the murderer of my baby to pieces if I got hold of him," she exclaimed. "I'd start at his feet and chop his head off last."

As months expired, the furor receded amid the hustling, faceless throng. Yet somewhere in this dark knot of people walked a child killer.

Four years passed. Mohawk's fading memories of the shocking murder of Elizabeth Nolte were about to be revived.

On Sunday, November 9, 1919, Cincinnati was preparing to celebrate its first Armistice Day. Citizens were also breathing easier now that the Spanish influenza outbreak of last winter was finally abating. This flu pandemic had killed almost 40 million people worldwide, including 4100 victims in the Queen City.

Around 4PM, 9-year-old Emily Gump left St. John's Church after attending a play there. Blue-eyed Emily had short brown hair and wore a blue sailor dress with a black cap and black shoes. She was seen entering an alley between Republic and Vine Streets near from the school.

Emily crossed over the alley—and passed into oblivion.

The previous month she had visited her aunt without telling her mother. She was not there this time, and Mrs. Randolph Gump notified police on Monday that her daughter had met with harm. There was no reason to believe she had been kidnapped for ransom or revenge, because the family had neither wealth nor enemies.

Mrs. Gump was wracked with guilt. Before Emily left home on Sunday, she'd asked for ten cents to buy the ticket for the play and begged her mother to go along. But Mrs. Gump had to watch her other five children, all younger than Emily. The *Cincinnati Enquirer* offered this portrayal of the anguished mother:

> **She maintains constant vigil in the hope that the child will come back to her. She listens eagerly for a well-remembered step and watches for a familiar little face. The children in the neighborhood are legion and they come and go dancing through the narrow hallway, but there is not among them the little one whose absence is breaking the woman's heart . . . a hundred times since Sunday the despairing mother has gone through that alley.**

There was a glut of Emily Gump sightings around Mohawk the next few days.

Her friend Elsie saw Emily in the alley around 4PM, and they made plans to visit the nearby grocery. But Elsie was called into her home, and when she came back outside Emily was gone. Another schoolmate made plans with her for after the play. "Then Emily went up the alley alone, and I went to a picture show," he explained.

William Miller, manager of the local movie house, swore he saw Emily in front of his theater on Monday, about the time her disappearance was first reported. He remembered her as the same girl who on Saturday had accosted him by saying, "I'm Emily Gump, give me a nickel, mister, please."

By Tuesday rumors were on the wing: A stranger told Emily's mother that she was a prisoner in a house at 12th and Broadway;

2009

The alley where Emily Gump got into the wind remains unchanged today.

a retired cop saw her boarding a train for Dayton; someone had seen Emily hiding out in Burnet Woods. Other reports placed her in Detroit and on a train near Chattanooga, Tennessee. Police dismissed many of the "sightings" as bogus and publicity-fueled.

After Mrs. Gump urged a citywide search of cellars and vacant buildings, a careless reminder from a reporter brought her to the brink of despair. In 1911 two young brothers had vanished from their home on nearby Whiteman Street. After a massive search they were discovered in the box seat of an old baker's wagon rotting in a stable. The boys had smothered after crawling into the box and pulling down the lid so the hasp was engaged. A quick check of milk cars and bakers' trucks in the neighborhood revealed no trace of Emily Gump.

The only tangible clue in Emily's disappearance was the vestige of a stranger. Gottlieb Mueller, a baker on Mulberry

Street, recalled a suspicious customer who vanished right after Emily did. Mueller described this man as about 40 years old, wearing "clothing that was either immaculate or soiled." He frequently gave money to little girls in the bakery—a place Emily Gump knew well—and seemed highly nervous, frequently looking over his shoulder.

When the stranger returned several months later, the Gump case was already colder than the winter of 1920. Police neglected to interview him at that time, an oversight that would come back to haunt them two years later.

By the summer of 1921, Mohawk had bulged into a clanging district of breweries and taverns. Authorities had their hands full with the regular rotation of vagrants, drunks, and swindlers who crawled the neighborhood.

On Sunday afternoon, August 21, 9-year-old Freda Hornberger left her home at 204 East Clifton Avenue around 3:30PM. Her mother had sent her to the bakery of John Dierks on Liberty Street, where Freda bought a tea ring and three coffee cakes. She pranced out the door—and into the universe.

When she didn't come home for supper, her family notified police and sat up all night praying for her return. Mrs. Hornberger was adamant that Freda was not a street waif. She was a good child, a talented violinist who also sang in her church choir. Of the ten Hornberger children she was her mother's closest companion, and would perform any errand with extreme haste.

Unlike Gump case, authorities had an immediate lead. They started a citywide search for a swarthy man about 30 years old who had been following Freda for several weeks prior to her disappearance. Freda's father and several playmates had observed his odd stalking behavior—he would follow her to within a few doors of her house and then hurriedly depart.

This same man had been hanging around the dairy where Freda fetched milk for her family, and he had even given her a nckel several weeks ago. She accepted the money and immediately took it to her mother, expressing fear of this peculiar

GRIEF-STRICKEN MOTHER KEEPS CONSTANT VIGIL

GIRL MISSING SINCE SUNDAY

Emily Gump, 9, Previously Left Six Weeks Ago.

Waits and Longs in Vain for Return of Little Daughter.

MYSTERY IN CHILD'S ABSENCE DEEPENING

Detectives Fail to Obtain Clue to Her Where-abouts.

The *Enquirer* captured the despair of a mother of a missing child.

stranger. Her parents were requesting an investigation of the man when she vanished, yet he was not seen there after she went missing.

Several witnesses gave conflicting accounts of seeing Freda on Sunday, skewing the timeline and puzzling investigators. Martha Weber was certain she had seen Freda at the corner of Moore and Walnut Streets twice on that Sunday. She knew the girl, and first observed her at 3:30PM leaning against a wall as though waiting for someone. Mrs. Weber saw her in the same spot at 7PM, only this time Freda was eating a large ice cream cone.

Corrine Kenning, age 15, also saw Freda about 3:30PM that day on Walnut. Freda told her she was on her way to the bakery and "in a hurry." Yet 12-year-old Juanita Hall claimed to see Freda at 2:30PM on the corner of Central and Wade, standing with a man who was urging her to follow him.

Considering Mrs. Weber and Baker Dierks to be reliable adults, detectives connected their stories and sparked some questions. What happened to the cakes she bought for her family? And how did Freda buy an ice cream cone after spending all her money at the bakery? Detectives considered that a man, possibly the "swarthy stalker," had bought her the ice cream and asked her to wait for him on the corner.

Even while focusing on this thread, other tips began to pour in.

Investigators checked out a story that Freda had been abducted by a roving gypsy band—being carried off by gypsies was not a cliché in 1921. A group of Kentucky itinerants were questioned about a girl traveling with them who resembled Freda, but it was quickly established to be someone else.

Another witness claimed to have seen Freda early Monday morning with two men and a woman on Baymiller Street. In bed but awake, she looked out her window and saw a crying child who resembled Freda. She heard the woman tell the men, "Take this little girl down Gest Street. If you meet any cops, tell them you are taking her home to her mother."

Baker Gottlieb Mueller once again told police about his mysterious customer. This man had visited Mueller's shop daily for four months, but dropped from sight the day Freda Hornberger disappeared. He'd repeated the same pattern two years earlier when Emily Gump vanished, but police had failed to question him once he reappeared.

Mueller received a threatening note shortly thereafter: "You have said enough. Keep your trap shut." The baker was convinced his weird customer and the note writer were the same person.

Mueller didn't know his name or much about him. He again described the man as around 40—sometimes sporting a suit, other times in "rough, soiled clothes and a slouch hat." He wore glasses and kept his mustache highly waxed. In addition to his

"Old Man" May Have Known Girls' Fate

Neighbors Talk Of 30-Year-Old Disappearance

BY BETTY DONOVAN

An "eccentric old man, who seemed afraid to talk to people" might have carried to his grave the solution to the mysterious disappearance of two little girls who left home almost 30 years ago and never returned.

That's what some old-time Mohawk residents surmised Monday when they learned of the discovery of an abandoned cistern in the basement at 273 Mohawk street.

Police said the cistern might provide a clew about Freda Hornberger or Emily Gump, both of whom were nine years old when they vanished. The store room had been the home, many years ago, of an old man who "avoided people, but talked to the children who played in the yard," neighbors recalled.

Lived Alone.

"I remember the stories they told," said Frank Stenglin, 79, who has lived on Mohawk street all his life, "but I don't remember hearing about a well—or cistern under that house across the street."

He said a "crabby old man" had lived for years in the basement room where the cistern was found. The old man "kept to himself," said Mr. Stenglin, "and nobody seemed to know much about him.

"He wasn't like the rest of the people in the neighborhood. He didn't even belong to the Bauverein down at the corner, and he didn't join any of the marching clubs. I used to live at 270 Mohawk before I moved into 266, and I remember all the hullabaloo when those little girls disappeared. It was an awful thing—made me glad I was a bachelor and never had any little ones to grieve about."

Recalls Mystery

Another neighbor, Frank Nenninger, of 271 Mohawk street, said he'd only been in the neighborhood 20 years, but had lived "Over the Rhine" all his life, and remembered the stories about Freda and Emily "like it happened yesterday."

The Cincinnati Post in 1919 carried stories told by neighbors about a "mysterious stranger" who followed Emily Gump several times and gave her nickels. But intensive questioning by police failed to disclose a clew to the identity [illegible] stranger or the whereabouts of Emily. Similar stories about Freda Hornberger also were recalled.

May Have Fallen in Canal

Ferd Hengholt, whose family has operated a furniture store for over 40 years in the Mohawk area says that some neighbors believe the girls might have fallen into the old Canal which was being converted into a Rapid Transit system between 1919 and 1926.

"There have been all kinds of rumors, and some people think the children were trapped by falling dirt and never found. But since they disappeared two years apart that seems too much of a coincidence."

There are countless abandoned wells in the neighborhood, said Mr. Hengholt, including one on property his firm is now converting into a parking lot on Central Parkway near the intersection of Mohawk place. Any one of the abandoned wells or cisterns might

A *Cincinnati Post* depiction of the missing girls in 1948 after efforts to locate their bodies were renewed.

sometimes "foppish dress," he spoke with a "nasal twang" and often carried a satchel.

Mrs. Mueller was afraid of him. "There was something about the man that made us shiver with distrust," she said. "He was nervous and jumpy and always looking over his shoulder." She didn't like "the way he eyed little girls" and gave them money.

Police were kicking themselves for not checking him out after the Gump girl went missing. He had the gloss of a prime suspect.

Within the week rumors flying near the Hornberger house sparked a near riot. When word spread that Freda's body had been found, infuriated residents swarmed the streets with vigilante vengeance on their minds. As the hue and cry swelled, the mob flocked to Race Street, broke into the home of suspect Andrew Lieberman, and ransacked his cellar and attic.

Police quickly arrested the 42-year-old Lieberman and his nephew, 21-year-old Joseph Spilker—more for their own safety than anything else. Lieberman was a known "chicken hawk" who often bothered young children near the Hornberger residence. As they took him away he exclaimed, "You must be looking for Spilker!" His nephew tried to jump out a window when the cops cornered him.

Both men refused to answer any questions. Neighbors said that they drove a peddler's wagon together, and had been out all day on the Sunday in question. Further inquiries revealed that each had previous convictions for assault—Spilker had attacked a young woman in 1920 and served six months, while Lieberman had done twelve years in prison for molestation.

Witnesses who had seen Freda with a man on Sunday evening were called in to view the suspects but could not identify them. Breaking their silence, Lieberman and Spilker denied ever laying eyes on the girl before clamming up again.

While they cooled their heels in lockup, a letter was delivered to the Hornberger home. In handwriting similar to the Gottlieb

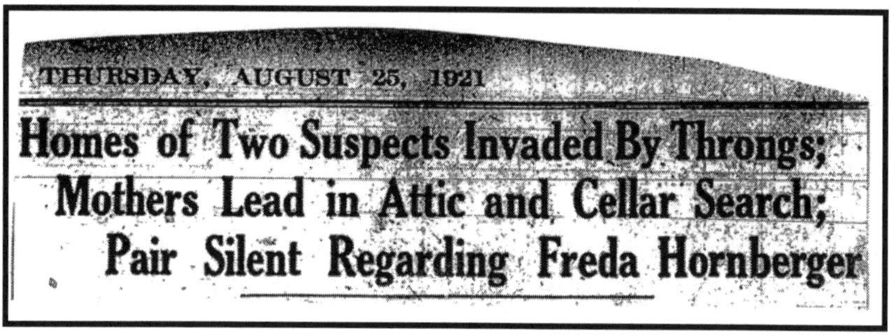
THURSDAY, AUGUST 25, 1921

Homes of Two Suspects Invaded By Throngs;
Mothers Lead in Attic and Cellar Search;
Pair Silent Regarding Freda Hornberger

Vigilantes went looking for suspects after sweet, innocent Freda Hornberger was snatched in 1921.

letter, the writer claimed to have "the missing girl" and that he intended to "keep her and marry her" when she was "of age." The note was signed "Rich Farmer."

The same day the family heard that Freda's body had been found in a trash can on nearby Dunlap Street. Mrs. Hornberger and her two sisters rushed to the site, but no trace of her daughter was found. The poor mother collapsed and had to be carried back to her home.

A massive building-by-building hunt was still ongoing. The fact that every man, woman, and child in the vicinity was involved in the search convinced police that Freda had been taken to another part of the city—or to another city.

One week after Freda's disappearance, detectives grudgingly admitted they'd made little progress. Lieberman and Spilker were released for lack of evidence, and none of the other countless leads bore fruit.

Yet just as the investigation began to sputter, a tantalizing suspect plunged right into the middle of it.

Will John Crane was a "sex moron"—as child molesters were called back then. The 47-year-old resided on McMicken Avenue, the same street where Emily Gump lived. Investigators grilled him over a four-day period and finally got him to admit he liked to "annoy young girls."

A search of his residence vaulted him to the pinnacle of suspicion. Police found over 200 photos of girls between the ages of 5 and 12, along with a diary containing details of "misconduct committed on scores of children he had under his control."

Crane protested that the pictures were of "nieces, cousins, and daughters," but under questioning admitted they were "friends"—he had over 100 names listed under the photographs. Soon he confessed to "mistreating" a number of young girls.

His diary exposed a tortured man obsessed with the young women of the streets. He collected clippings about the murder of Elizabeth Nolte and the vanishings of Gump and Hornberger, along with articles about girls running away and men seizing them in public, accompanied by some crude and obscene sketches.

Crane denied knowing Elizabeth Nolte or encountering the two missing girls, but detectives noted he became "visibly upset" when asked about them. He also admitted to serving a penitentiary term in 1910 for assaulting a child.

Crane persisted with evasive answers as witnesses came forward against him. A 16-year-old girl named Cohen identified Crane as the man who had "controlled" her for "nearly four years." Even though his gifts of money encouraged her to visit him, she feared him enough to withhold the details from her parents. Her picture was one of the first from Crane's diary to be traced back to a victim.

Police were anticipating a multitude of charges against Crane as more girls spoke up or were tracked down. Crane's own housekeeper corroborated their accounts, telling investigators that her employer always sent her on an errand whenever one of "his many little girls" came to visit.

Will Crane, clearly a decadent stalker of young children, could not be linked to the Nolte murder or the missing girls. But at least he would be on ice for awhile Crane was convicted on four counts of contributing to the delinquency of a minor and sentenced to a year in the county jail.

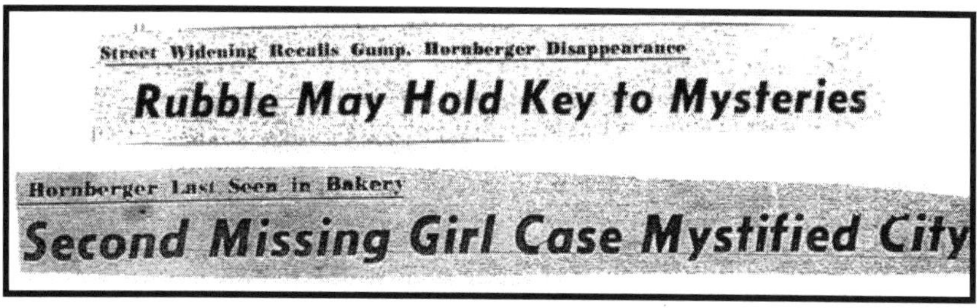

Street Widening Recalls Gump, Hornberger Disappearance

Rubble May Hold Key to Mysteries

Hornberger Last Seen in Bakery

Second Missing Girl Case Mystified City

30 years later Mohawk was still looking for their lost angels.

With their options dwindling, police launched another hunt and distributed Freda's picture throughout the county. Gottlieb Mueller's bakery was given a thorough inspection, and bloodstained shirts found in his attic caused momentary excitement before being discarded. Mueller was already tense—he had carried a gun since receiving the threatening letters.

His mysterious customer, the one who had disappeared after both the Gump and Hornberger abductions, was still lurking in the shadows and looming over the investigation.

In the stillness of remembering the vanished girls, years dashed by without an echo, the mystery still stealing into the minds of Mohawk residents decades later. This blue collar district near downtown Cincinnati had a heart of flint, but would not forget those they'd never buried.

In 1948 John Matacia, proprietor of the Mohawk Fruit Store, discovered an ancient cistern beneath his cellar—he nearly fell into it when some rotting floor boards gave way. He knew instantly what he had stumbled upon: "Right off I recalled the stories about an old well being under the building, and also the neighborhood gossip about the missing girls. I was told the little Gump girl was seen playing in this yard on the day she disappeared."

The misplaced children were once again front page news. So was Mohawk, described by the *Enquirer* as "now an area of abandoned breweries with cavernous cellars, rotting tenements, and debris-filled vacant lots." And decades before, three girls had been lost within these scarred, empty houses.

Matacia recalled some neighborhood gossip about a man who'd lived in the overhead room 30 years earlier. He was described as a grumpy, cadaverous, white-haired fellow who kept to himself, "an eccentric old man" who was "a little queer" and "seemed afraid to talk to people." He had been questioned during the original investigation, but police were unable to link him to the girls.

At the time they did not search the cistern under his room. Now firemen drained it to rake the muddy bottom for skeletal remains, noticing that the water was not stagnant, indicating natural drainage to some larger tributary. They found no trace of the girls.

Today there is still a vast network of derelict springs and forsaken channels prowling beneath Mohawk—with a bounty of unknown hiding places.

SUMMATION:

Three little girls—one slaughtered, two vanished. Three crimes taking place over six years. Were they connected, or just isolated episodes of opportunity?

Elizabeth Nolte was murdered by someone who knew her family. That is the only reason a killer would risk capture by returning his victim's body to her own doorstep.

William Dean fit the profile of the killer. Noble Moore and William Hoon are also good suspects and interchangeable in this scenario. But Dean's fixation with Elizabeth—a girl who seemed older than her 11 years—aroused his perverse instincts. He still remains the best suspect more than 90 years later.

Emily Gump and Freda Hornberger were taken by the same culprit. With all the glut of despicable men prowling the streets, there was one whose proximity and movements fit the timeline of both crimes—the daily visitor to Gottlieb Mueller's bakery. His undue attentions to young girls and his absence after the Gump child vanished were incriminating.

Dank Waters To Be Searched for Bodies Of Long-Lost Girls

BY RALPH BRADY

A 30-year-old mystery—of two little girls who disappeared, never to be seen again—was revived Saturday in a dank, cob-webbed basement at 273 Mohawk street.

Police sensed a possible lead to solution of the strange disappearances after John Matacia, operator of the Mohawk Fruit Store, discovered a forgotten cistern under the old brick tenament. He nearly fell into its dark depths when some rotten floor boards gave way under his weight.

His discovery came exactly 27 years after the disappearance of the second child, Freda Hornberger, 9, of 204 E. Clifton avenue. She was last seen at 7 p.m. Aug. 21, 1921. The first girl, Emily Gump, also 9, of 257 W. McMicken avenue, disappeared Nov. 9, 1919. She had lived only a few doors away from Mr. Matacia's fruit market.

EMILY GUMP
. . . missing since 1919

FREDA HORNBERGER
. . . missing since 1921

There was hope that the old canals and cisterns beneath Mohawk would finally give up their secrets.

EPILOGUE:

The fate of Elizabeth Nolte was no secret—the killer dumped her despoiled body on her mother's doorstep. Through this audacious display of such a grisly trophy, Mrs. Nolte was at least spared the uncertainty of never learning what had happened to her little girl.

But was the horrifying sight of Elizabeth's corpse better than not knowing?

Emily Gump and Freda Hornberger got into the wind as vapors of life, swallowed by slivers of darkness. Their parents spoke out in 1948 as the cistern was being checked.

"I think Freda's still alive," said Mrs. Hornberger. "I think somebody took her and just never gave her back to me."

Mrs. Gump was still hopeful. "Someday Emily may come back. But I don't suppose I would know Emily if she were to walk in this minute."

The deaths of their parents in the 1950s revived the mystery one final time, but then it fell dormant again beneath the months and years. It no longer seemed real; it carried the aura of another age.

And the underground canals still flow beneath the streets of Cincinnati's old Mohawk district, where the fate of the little girls remains locked in grim secrecy.

I WITNESS:

Liz—she doesn't want to be called Elizabeth anymore; Elizabeth is a baby's name—is a precocious, rebellious young girl who is becoming more streetwise with every passing day. Although only 11, she notices men's eyes following her. She has learned that if she smiles at them, she can sometimes get them to buy her things. Candy, gum. Occasionally a piece of cheap jewelry, which she must keep hidden from her mother.

The neighbors are gossiping. That little girl, they say, is always trying to wangle something. And she tends to attract unsavory men.

Liz is not concerned. There is obviously something these creepy old fellows want from her, but she isn't entirely certain what that might be. For now she's enjoying a strange, intoxicating surge of power. She's a child who can control grownups. Imagine.

Skulking around the alley after making his last delivery at about 4:30PM., rag picker William Dean watches Elizabeth enter Alexander's stable. He can't believe his good fortune—he's been looking for her all week. Knowing the stable is empty, he darts in after her, causing her to cry out in surprise.

She surveys him with a squinted eye—and then winks.

Unaware of the effect this has, she fuels his fire by asking, "What do you want? And what will you give me for it?"

He is instantly aroused. Her blend of childlike innocence and womanly wiles always spawns something sinister within him. He has favored her with little treats for over a year, but now she seems intent on infuriating him.

It's time for her to pay off.

The restless awakening of his own flesh stokes his ire. Liz sees the danger dancing in his eyes—she senses that everything has suddenly changed. They are no longer playing. As Dean advances, she gives a sad little murmur of surrender. Whatever he does to her, she will watch and listen—and learn. Because he will likely want it again and again.

And she's willing to bargain.

Later, when he is satiated, his anger collapses into fear. What in God's name has he done? Although obsessively fond of Elizabeth—he would marry her if she were of age and he had the means—he is deathly afraid of her father.

Reading his thoughts and her own opportunity for gain, Liz taunts him. It will take a lot of money, she declares, to keep her quiet. She is too young and brash to realize that she has just made a fatal error in judgment. Had she waited until she was safely home before issuing such an ultimatum, she might have saved her own life.

Panic grips with his realization that she won't protect him. She's looking out for herself. He must prevent her from exposing him. Tight jawed and trembling, he slits her throat.

For Dean, there's no turning back now. The stable has running water to wash away the blood, and he hides the body in the box seat of an old carriage. Later that night he moves Elizabeth's corpse to his room, wrapping it in his bed sheet only after he violates her once more.

By Wednesday his conscience is burning a hole inside him. The only way to prove his remorse—and his devotion—is to return the child to her parents for a Christian burial.

That night he lovingly washes "his" girl one last time, kisses her cold forehead and weeps as he gently stuffs her into the cloth sack, then waits until the streets are barren.

He takes her home and places the sack on the Nolte doorstep.

The man flashes a smile that never quite reaches his eyes. And his stealthy yet strident glances at young girls are unsettling—both the baker Mueller and his wife are wary of their mysterious customer.

Like all pedophiles, previous incarceration does not deter his desire to violate children. He is a "chicken hawk," a true molester. Back east they called him "short eyes," but he never went for the jaspers. Little girls are his fancy. He likes to shanghai them and make them his consorts for a few days. In his world, it's all according to Hoyle.

But this time he will not be identified after his pleasure is sated. He is ready to kill.

He waits for Emily Gump at the other end of the alley. He has watched her at the bakery, and she is just his type—part angel, part urchin.

He offers to buy her some ice cream, and then drops a nickel at his feet. As she stoops to pick it up, he checks both ends of the alley, and then the chloroform rag is over her mouth. Within a few moments she is tucked away in his canvas sack.

He stows her at his house for several days. Taking his time, the killer has his fill of perversion—he is gilding the lily. By nightfall he dumps her weighted-down body in an underground cistern near his building.

He goes back east for several months, returning to Mueller's bakery in the spring of 1920. Later that year, he sees Freda for the first time.

She's different from the last one. Obedient and respectful, yet tougher to lure. Little girls are generally so easy to bribe—but this one has been instructed not to interact with strangers. He strokes his finely waxed mustache as he ponders this new victim. She requires a well-formed plan. Once again, he can afford to take his time.

On the fateful day he wears his suit, eschewing the rough clothing and slouch hat he wore when taking Emily 18 months earlier. And this time he actually buys her an ice cream cone, making sure it is vanilla, her favorite.

It is getting late in the afternoon, and he insists on escorting her home. His voice is soft but assertive. He would never forgive himself, he says, if she met with any misfortune. Freda has been taught to heed well-dressed, well-bred gentlemen. He takes great care to walk ahead of her until he cuts through an alley, and ever docile, she follows. When the coast is clear, the chloroform does its job, and she crumples to the ground.

He takes less pleasure with her—Freda is no streetwise waif. Once awake, she is terrified, crying for her mother and trying to cover her modesty with her hands. He finds it more annoying than exciting. He won't keep this one. She's too cantankerous and she wails too much. He strangles her, and then tosses her corpse into a canal feeding the Ohio River.

After Freda, the killer flees the city and goes incognito for eternity. But his odd behavior ensures that this anonymous patron of little girls will remain a "person of interest" long after investigations go dark.

Living out his days on the east coast, this scoundrel resumes a life of desultory wandering and loathsome intrusion into the lives of children.

2009

Today the house where Frances Brady was killed looks much the same as it did in 1936.

THE BRIDE IN THE CASKET

FRANCES MARIE BRADY GUNNED DOWN AT HER FRONT DOOR: 1936

"If I must die, I will encounter darkness as a bride, and hug it in my arms."

William Shakespeare

PROLOGUE:

Impenetrable mystery still shrouds this classic unsolved murder—standing like the locked door which separated killer and prey. Was the shooting of Frances Marie Brady a botched burglary or cold-blooded murder?

That the pretty victim was to be married within the week only intensified the heartbreak. The young woman was gunned down as she arrived home from her bridal shower, shot through the heart in front of her devoted sisters, just days away from embarking on a new life.

NARRATIVE:

In the autumn of 1936, World War Two was looming. The German-Italian Axis had been formed earlier that year, when Mussolini cast his lot with Hitler. Yet Americans cheered as Jesse Owens triumphed at Berlin's Summer Olympics, shattering Hitler's claim of Aryan supremacy and causing the Fuhrer to snub the black sprinter at his gold medal ceremony.

Across the nation people were browsing a new photo magazine called *Life*, and reading Dale Carnegie's *How to Win Friends and Influence People*—destined to become the best-selling (after the Bible) nonfiction work of the century.

Covington, Kentucky hovered just across the Ohio River from downtown Cincinnati, and slithered along the west bank of the Licking River like a snake.

When the staid Queen City jettisoned its vice and corruption across the bridge during Prohibition, Covington and sister city Newport were happy to oblige the sin-seeking denizens of the night. Despite the Great Depression, the two towns thrived in the shadow of Cincinnati and its wretched refuse.

Yet Oakland Avenue was a historic and respectable street in Covington, and love was in the air on the hushed satin night of October 2, 1936.

The three Brady sisters had parked their car in the alley and were walking arm-in-arm toward their home. The street was quiet, and lights had long since gone dark in windows framing lean Victorian houses. A tiny breath of wind from the river rustled fallen leaves, as a vigilant moon hung low in the sky.

The sisters' happy laughter drifted over the fall air. Frances Marie Brady, age 37, was to be married in five days, and the raven-haired secretary had been the guest of honor at a bridal shower they'd just left. Ella Celine and Margaret later recalled that their sister was "supremely happy" that night.

Just before 1AM they stepped onto the porch of the house they'd inherited from their parents—their father was the late Mose Brady, a Covington policeman. The block looked like a row of taut Brooklyn brownstones hugging the street, burnished brick houses that were spartan and stalwart. There was no room for driveways, only an alley cutting through the middle of each block.

Margaret Brady tried her key in the front door. It wouldn't budge. She pushed several times, but something seemed to be holding it closed. "Give me the key; I'll open it," said Frances. She turned the lock effortlessly and opened the door.

Then she flipped on the light in the foyer.

Victim of Covington Slaying

SHOT IS FIRED AT SISTERS IN DOOR OF HOME

Victim Was to Have Been Married Next Week at St. Mary's Cathedral

A fatal shot from the darkened living room of her home cut short the wedding plans of Miss Frances Marie Brady early today.

Miss Brady and two sisters returned to their home at 2104 Oakland avenue, Covington about 12:50 a. m., to be greeted by two intruders—death and an unidentified man.

They had been attending their club's party for the bride-to-be.

Miss Brady unlocked the front door after another sister was unable to turn the key.

She stepped into the hall, flicked the light button, gasped, "Oh," started to scream.

A Gun Flash

A flash and the report of a gun came from the living room. Miss Brady staggered out the door, down the front steps and fell dead in the yard. Miss Brady was 34.

She was shot in the heart. Coroner James P. Riffe of Kenton county said the bullet has been removed. are Margaret and Ella Celine, saw the invader. Neither could say whether he was white or a Negro.

Police are baffled by the murder. Neither of the sisters, whose names are Margaret and Elasline, saw the invader. Neither could say whether he was white or a Negro.

Chief John Putthoff said "This is a mysterious case. I can't say yet whether burglary was the motive

Photo by Newman Studios.

Miss Frances Marie Brady, above, was shot to death in her Covington home today. A picture of the Oakland avenue residence appears on Page 1, second section.

Raven haired Frances Brady was coming home from her bridal shower when the assassin struck.

She had only a moment to utter a startled "Oh!" before fate came roaring at her from the muzzle of a .32-caliber revolver. A single bullet pierced her heart. The report of the shot resounded through the streets and echoed along the river.

Frances staggered backward and toppled off the porch, dead before she hit the ground. Her sisters fled the porch in terror. Margaret stumbled and sprained her ankle as Ella Celine screamed for help. Neighbors found them kneeling beside Frances in the yard, sobbing hysterically.

Walking his dog on the rear side of the block, Chester Lathrop heard the shot and ran toward the Brady home. Considering his location, the shooter must have barely missed him after fleeing out the Bradys' back door.

Next door neighbor Hugo Wachs rushed over and helped Lathrop carry Frances into Wachs' home. Only then were police called. When they arrived the crime scene was already tainted—Wachs and Lathrop had compromised it by removing the body. After Frances was placed in a police car, Lathrop drove her to the hospital where she was pronounced dead on arrival. The last rites were administered in the lobby.

Officers quickly cordoned off the neighborhood, but there was no sign of the slayer. They combed the area until dawn, seeking clues, rousting sleeping neighbors, and firing off questions.

After giving tearful statements about seeing the flash of the gun, Margaret and Ella were taken to a nearby hospital and treated for shock. Neither got a good look at the shooter. When they were released later that morning their doctor wouldn't allow them to be interviewed further.

The sisters managed to tell police about the impending nuptials for Frances. She was to have been married the following Wednesday to John J. O'Donnell, a 46-year-old assistant city passenger agent for the Louisville & Nashville Railroad.

Around 3AM, several detectives went to the hospital to question Frances Brady's fiancé. O'Donnell, who shared a home with his mother, had been awakened at 1AM by Mrs.

The Kentucky Post

HOME EDITION

PRICE TWO CENTS

SECTION ONE—TWO PARTS

BRIDE-TO-BE SLAIN IN COVINGTON

GRAND JURY RETURNS ARSON INDICTMENT IN FIRE FROM WHICH FIVE WERE RESCUED

Mrs. Pearl Mildenberger, Covington Grocery Operator, Accused; 65 Defendants Are Named in 84 True Bills

BUSINESS UP IN COVINGTON

Singer Will Be Queen Candidate

LUDLOW BOARD HALTS MERGER BY 5-4 VOTE

Victim of Covington Slaying

SHOT IS FIRED AT SISTERS IN DOOR OF HOME

MAN, 60, KILLED IN TRUCK TRAGEDY

Both Kentucky Senators

From the beginning, the murder of the pretty secretary on her own porch mystified citizens on both sides of the Ohio River.

Hugo Wachs, calling to tell him that Frances had been "hurt in an accident." Arriving at the hospital, he became distraught upon learning that his longtime sweetheart had been murdered at her own front door.

"Who could have done it?" he wailed repeatedly. Finally regaining his composure, he quietly lamented the loss of his "Fanny." They had known each other for ten years, and had finally become engaged the previous Christmas. Earlier that evening, the couple had gone apartment hunting in nearby Fort Mitchell before going to confession at St. Mary's Cathedral, where they were to be married.

And in a chilling coincidence, they also stopped by a funeral home to pay their last respects to a deceased friend.

At 9PM they parted. Frances joined her sisters to attend her bridal shower, while O'Donnell went to a café and had a few beers. He was home and in bed by 11PM.

Detectives got what they needed in this early morning interview. They established that the fiancé was sleeping when the victim was killed, and confirmed the couple had no known enemies. O'Donnell was quickly eliminated as a suspect.

At dawn, Covington police chief John Putthoff gave his first official statement to reporters swarming the station house: "This is a mysterious case. I can't say yet whether burglary was the motive. It looks funny. Though drawers in the house had been opened, apparently nothing was ransacked. Nothing was reported stolen."

Kenton County coroner James P. Riffe declared it to be "one of the most baffling murders in the police annals of Covington, and then hurled the first plot twist at the eager press: Amid speculation about the killer's race, Riffe alleged uncertainty about whether the shooter was a man or a woman. The surviving sisters had distinguished only the vague outline of a "figure" running toward the back door.

Reporters dashed out to call in this sensational spin—a headline in that morning's *Kentucky Times Star* asserted that the **"Sex of Intruder Also Offers Police Mystery,"** while the story noted that the killer had "concealed himself or herself in the house."

By midday on Friday, Covington police were calling the Brady shooting "one of the most mysterious cases within memory."

Their two best witnesses were in seclusion, horrified from watching their sister murdered. Their family doctor informed detectives that he found a grain of gunpowder over the left eye of Ella Celine, who had been standing behind Margaret as Frances unlocked the front door. There were no powder burns on the body or clothes of Frances Brady.

Investigators working the crime scene grew more bewildered as the day wore on. Their gut instinct about a bungled burglary wasn't gaining ground. Several drawers were open, but the

MURDERER

Kept Vigil, Theory

As Police Scan Scene At Brady Residence.

Lighted Porch Offered Clear View For Person Hidden In Darkness Indoors.

Admittedly baffled by the peculiar circumstances in the case, Covington police last night pondered anew the question, "Who killed Frances Brady and why?" They found no logical answers in any of various theories.

They discarded a burglary theory because no valuables were disturbed and because the killer, amply warned that Miss Brady and her two sisters were returning to their house at 2104 Oakland Avenue, apparently made no effort to flee until he fired the fatal shot.

"We're about where we were yesterday," said Police Chief John Puthoff. "There's nothing new to give out."

Miss Brady was shot and killed about 1 o'clock Friday morning, five days before her scheduled wedding to John J. O'Connell, railroad passenger agent.

2009

Frances Brady was shot to death at this front door 73 years ago.

contents were intact, and the wedding presents on the dining room table were not disturbed. Also, the killer had ample warning that the Brady sisters were returning home. The delay at the front door had provided time for escape, yet the intruder apparently made no effort to flee before firing the fatal shot.

Late Friday Chief Puthoff and Coroner Riffe told reporters they "did not believe burglary was the motive for murder."

Riffe speculated that the shooter kept vigil inside the house, using the lighted porch to view the sisters' return. "I believe the killer either watched from an upstairs window or from the stairway landing. He had plenty of warning," the coroner reasoned. "There was nothing to halt his flight. He could have run toward the back door from the stairway landing if he stood there. He could have seen any movement the girls took. If he knew them, he wouldn't have to wait for Frances to turn on the light. He could have peered out the glass in the front door and identified the girls easily."

When asked if the exclamation Frances uttered just before the shot indicated she recognized the killer, Riffe waffled: "Not necessarily, although the sisters got the impression that Frances had recognized someone."

Puthoff announced that they hadn't found any fingerprints in the Brady home or footprints in the yard. "The killer left us nothing to work on," he said, while also declining to speculate on a possible motive. But he agreed with Riffe that "no ordinary prowler had killed Miss Brady."

The only evidence in the case was the fatal bullet, fired from a .32-caliber revolver. It was a lead slug, minus the steel jacket used on automatic pistols, and was being sent across the river to be tested by the Cincinnati homicide squad.

To break through the veil of mystery covering the investigation, Coroner Riffe announced his plans to schedule an inquest for the following Wednesday—the same day as Frances Brady's now forsaken wedding.

By the weekend two opposing theories had evolved.

Brady family members were convinced the murderer was a panicked burglar. John O'Donnell, still bereft over losing his fiancée, was unwavering that a stranger had killed Frances. Other relatives pointed out that Margaret would have been the gunman's target had she been able to open the front door first.

The sisters' physician reported that both girls "repudiated any jealousy theory in the slaying," and insisted Frances and O'Donnell were "only sweethearts who were supremely happy . . . neither had any rivals for their affections."

But detectives could not overlook several stiff facts: There was no forced entry, nothing was stolen, and the killer did not to leave any fingerprints or footprints. A thief could have escaped while the sisters struggled with the front door.

"Murder That Blocked Wedding Plans Keeps Authorities Baffled" headlined the Sunday papers. "We do not know which way to turn," Chief Puthoff admitted. "We have chased down every clue, but they have led us nowhere." Yet rumors of a female shooter were prodding the investigation away from the prowler theory.

Both Covington and the Queen City were buzzing over the sensational murder of the lovely bride-to-be. In a scathing editorial, the *Kentucky Times Star* called the killer a "cowardly wretch," while the *Cincinnati Post* lamented that "A splendid woman enjoying the respect of hundreds of friends was shot in cold blood and on her own premises."

The crime was attracting nationwide interest as well. On Saturday, a reporter and a cameraman from New York arrived by plane, while two Chicago newspapermen appeared at the scene on Sunday.

The Brady tragedy had aroused citizens both near and far.

On Monday October 5th, Frances Brady was laid to rest. *Kentucky Post* reporter William Hagedorn captured the somber occasion:

> **Up the aisle of St. Mary's Cathedral, the same church in which she was to have taken her wedding vows Wednesday, all that was mortal of Frances Marie Brady moved today to the solemn strains of her funeral requiem in contrast to the joyous cadences of nuptial music . . . Miss Brady was dressed in the wedding gown she was to have worn on her wedding day.**

"You know not the day or the hour" was the sermon chosen by the pastor. An estimated crowd of 800 jammed the church, with several hundred more remaining outside. Scattered among the mourners were detectives looking for someone who didn't belong. But if Miss Brady's killer was in attendance, he (or she) did not reveal themselves.

Early Tuesday police detained three Negroes found wandering the streets, one of whom had a previous burglary conviction. In fact, there had been a rash of recent break-ins by black prowlers in Covington, and a report of suspicious noises near the Brady home two nights before the murder was being rechecked.

Yet most investigators still discounted the sneak-thief scenario. The locked doors, the lack of fingerprints, and the killer's movement through the house had them stumped. Why did they pause on the stair landing instead of bolting for the back door?

The sisters' delay with the front door lock was also puzzling. A duplicate key could have skewed the tumblers, but Margaret had told police it felt as though someone on the inside was holding the knob of the lock.

Buried beneath this front page speculation was a forgotten item: "A negro woman who cleans the Brady house was questioned about a missing key." Police had learned that two front door keys were missing—one had been lost two years earlier and the other disappeared in August.

On the eve of the inquest, a grieving John O'Donnell offered a $500 reward for the apprehension of his fiancée's slayer. "My whole ambition in life from now on will be to solve this dastardly crime," he declared, while also announcing that Judge Joseph Goodenough would represent him and both sisters at the inquest.

The girls' uncle was skeptical about how much help they would be: "We are at a total loss to give any reason whatsoever for the murder. Neither Frances nor her sisters had any enemies. They were the finest kind of girls and could not have anyone who would want to deliberately kill them." He also tried to dispel the swirling rumors. "Mr. O'Donnell was the only sweetheart Frances ever had. He is a splendid man and has been like a big brother to the two sisters of Frances."

While some of his men wondered why the family required a judge to stand for up them, Chief Puthoff expressed hope that the sisters' inquest testimony would shed some light on a case that was swiftly going dark.

On Wednesday, October 7, Frances Brady's life was exhumed on what should have been her happiest day. Coroner Riffe impaneled his jury at 10AM—one hour after she would have become Mrs. John O'Donnell.

Between the gavels the proceeding was packed with emotional testimony.

KENTUCKY EDITION OF CINCINNATI TIMES-STAR

"MAKES YOUR DAY COMPLETE"

FRIDAY, OCTOBER 2, 1936 — SIXTY PAGES — HOME

BRIDE-TO-BE'S MURDER BAFFLES POLICE

Covington Woman Was to Have Been Married Next Week to L. & N. Passenger Agent.

SISTERS AT HER SIDE WHEN KILLED

Gunman Escapes Through Rear Door; House Apparently Had Been Rifled by Him.

DRUGGIST FIRST TO REACH BRADY HOME AFTER SHOT STARTLES HIM AND HIS WIFE

He Aids Police in Removal of Victim to Hospital

Victim of Intruder and Scene of Covington Crime

Grand Jury Ignores Charge of Murder Against Marshal

No Indictment in Case of T. W. Roach, Elsmere.

GAMBLING ALLEGED

Two Covington Youths Are Cleared in Attack Case.

FEE OF LAWYER PAID BY COUNCIL

Bellevue Officials Allow City Attorney's Claim.

LENGTHY DISCUSSION

Caucus on Lower Street Car Fares Is Deferred.

NOTHING DISTURBED

LUDLOW COUNCIL REJECTS BROMLEY

Ordinance to Annex Defeated by 5-to-4 Vote.

MAYOR BREAKS TIE

Petitions Signed by More Than 700 Citizens Unavailing

TO WALK DOG

DAYTON'S OLDEST RESIDENT IS TAKEN

Father of Former Police Chief Ortlieb Succumbs.

93 YEARS OF AGE

Fine Garden He Cultivated Was Show Place.

The complete lack of clues was frustrating to detectives working the Brady case.

Ella Celine and Margaret Brady made their first public appearance since seeing their sister shot down. Together with O'Donnell, they continued to hush the whispers that there was more to this crime than burglary.

O'Donnell recounted his movements with "Fanny" on the fateful night, which included inspecting an apartment and viewing a friend's body at her wake. After she went to the bridal shower he had several beers at a café and went home to bed, where he was awakened by a call telling him that "Fanny met with an accident." Upon arriving at the hospital he learned the truth.

Replying to questions from his attorney Judge Goodenough, he testified that he had known Frances for ten years, and they had become engaged the previous December. Her fiancé insisted there was no love triangle.

"Have you ever gone or associated with any other girl in those ten years?" Goodenough asked.

"No," O'Donnell replied, choking back tears. "Fanny was my only girl."

"Did you know of any enemies, yours or Fanny's?"

"I never knew of any, and I know of none now."

"Did you know any male or female who was jealous of you or Fanny?"

"No."

"Do you know of any motive anyone might have had for shooting her?"

"It's all beyond me," O'Donnell sighed. Before leaving the stand he vowed again that he "would not rest" until he found the murderer.

Ella Celine was next, and the "star witness" struggled to maintain her composure. Gently questioned by Judge Goodenough, her halting testimony was crucial to the investigation.

She reiterated that Frances and O'Donnell were "supremely happy and deeply in love. There was no one who knew this better than I . . . and there were no enemies who wished to break them up." She admitted Frances had gone out with another man since she knew O'Donnell, but that had been seven years earlier. She was certain she locked the front door and the kitchen door before they left for the bridal shower.

At the shower the sisters played cards with other guests. Ella recalled that the conversation was lively and mostly about the upcoming wedding. She said Frances was "unusually happy" at the party.

Ella became anguished when describing the murder—several times her doctor emerged from the audience to console her. She recounted the difficulty Margaret had unlocking the door, and the ease with which Frances opened it. She saw Frances hand the keys back to Margaret, who had moved to the left. Faltering, she told how Frances opened the door at arm's length and flipped on the light switch to the right.

Principals in Murder Mystery at Inquest
Left to right, Miss Esaline Brady and Miss Margaret Brady, sisters of Miss Frances Brady, who was slain mysteriously, and John J. O'Donnell, fiance of the murdered woman.

Ella Celine Brady (left) and her sister Margaret sit with John O'Donnell prior to giving testimony at the inquest.

As the light blazed "Frances screamed and shuddered," followed by the deafening report of the gunshot. Ella saw a flash which appeared to come from the living room, but since she was holding the screen door her view was limited.

"Whoever fired the shot must have had the gun pointed at the door as Fanny opened it," Ella wept.

"Did you see who fired the shot?" Goodenough asked quietly.

"No, not even a shadow—only the flash of the gun."

"Could you see into the living room from the door? Were there any other lights in the house?"

"No, just in the hall."

"Then the living room was dark?"

"Yes." Ella began sobbing.

All three sisters had turned to flee the porch, but then Frances "staggered down the steps and collapsed on the lawn." Ella's tears flowed again. Moving on, Goodenough asked her about looking in the mirror the day after the shooting, when she saw powder burns on her forehead. The family physician would testify that the particle he removed was a grain of gunpowder.

After a short break, she responded to questions from Cornoner Riffe by confirming that the front door could not be unlocked if someone inside was holding the latch—this was based on a test that she and Judge Goodenough had performed. She agreed that the full moon provided good illumination, and that anyone on the porch could be seen clearly from inside the house.

Margaret Brady took the stand with more restraint than her younger sister. Her testimony matched Ella's: She saw the flare of the gun, caught no glimpse of the killer, and believed the shot came from the living room. She did admit that the murder night was the first time she'd ever had trouble opening their door.

That ended the morning testimony. As reporters dashed out to call in their stories, the three people who most loved Frances sat in their own private silence.

In the afternoon session, Coroner James Riffe testified about the autopsy. Based on the trajectory, he was certain the shot was fired from the staircase directly opposite the door. The bullet had entered the left side of Frances' chest about four

The Kentucky Post

HOME EDITION

PRICE TWO CENTS

SECTION ONE—TWO PAPERS

WEDNESDAY, OCTOBER 7, 1936

JEALOUSY DENIED IN MURDER QUIZ; NO OTHER GIRL, O'DONNELL SAYS

PLANT STRIKE HELD UP WHILE GROUPS MEET

BULLETIN

TOSSES HAT IN

CHRISMAN IN CITY CONTEST

MORE ARRESTS MADE IN SIFT OF AUTO RING

State and Federal Officers Continue to Push Investigation in Case

DEFENDANTS' BONDS SET

Hearings for Accused Set for Oct. 13 Before U. S. Commissioner Here

Principals in Murder Mystery at Inquest

POWDER BURN COMPLICATES INVESTIGATION

Doctor Finds Grain Imbedded in Forehead of Third Girl in Line; Groom-To-Be Traces Actions on Night of Tragedy

BULLETIN

Despite O'Donnell's denial of a love triangle, rumors persisted that the killer had a motive to stop the wedding.

inches below the shoulder, tore a ragged path down through her heart, and veered right to lodge in her liver.

Then Riffe dropped a bombshell. Briefly called out of the hearing, he returned to tell the jury that he had just received new information: A neighbor came forward who had seen a man and a woman running from the direction of the Brady home immediately after the gunshot. The *Times Star* headline that afternoon blared, **"Man and Woman Fled Murder Scene, Coroner Told."**

Chester Lathrop had a unique vantage point to witness the killer's escape. While walking his dog on the back side of the block he heard the shot, and rounding the corner he could see the Brady back door illuminated by the moon. He believed it was open, because the gun's report was loud, yet he saw no one racing through their backyard. He also testified that the house was dark ten minutes before the shooting, and that the foyer light was the only one burning when he arrived after the gunshot.

Lathrop was followed by a parade of policemen who admitted sullenly that they were no closer to a solution than they were four days ago. Their findings had already saturated the press coverage:

- No fingerprints or footprints were recovered from the crime scene.
- Drawers in the living room buffet were pulled open with nothing disturbed.
- Drawers were open in two upstairs bedrooms yet nothing was taken.
- Detectives believed the disorder "looked staged."
- The window over the porch and a bedroom window were open "about a foot."
- There was no sign of forced entry on either door or any window.
- Two front door keys had been missing for several months.

Two patrolmen did testify about an episode that had never made the papers. When they arrived at the murder scene, Officer Behringer had encountered a stranger standing on the Brady front lawn who told them, "A man has been shot." They entered the Wachs home and found the female victim, yet when they went back outside the man was gone.

Detectives had been searching for this "mystery man" since Friday morning.

Judge Joseph Goodenough, speaking for the friends and family of Frances Brady, delivered an impassioned closing statement:

"A fiendish beast has perpetrated a most horrible crime in our city," he began. "Today, at this very hour, Miss Brady was to have been married to Mr. O'Donnell. These sisters of the dead girl and Mr. O'Donnell, instead of participating in the ceremonies of a blessed wedding, are here to give you any and all facts pertaining to the death of the bride."

Goodenough continued: "My clients are here to help solve this crime. They will leave nothing undone to reach the true and just solution of the crime."

The he unleashed his rancor against the rumors whirling around the case: "My clients know, and I know, that many tongues in the community are wagging. We know that some individuals are wont in this case to spread the scandal that this or that individual may have perpetrated this cowardly offense. We must not indulge in theories that would mar the unblemished reputation of good Covington citizens."

By day's end the jury rejected the burglary theory. "There being no proof that burglary was the motive," they demanded that police "find the motive!"

This verdict was guaranteed to keep those tongues wagging.

On Thursday, the *Kentucky Post* ran an editorial titled, **"Let's Not Jump at Conclusions."** Calling the slaying of Frances Brady a "dastardly crime," the writer urged citizens to take the coroner's verdict with a grain of salt: "We must be calm in our curiosity, for we are right where we were the day the killing took place. The burglary theory is as feasible as any."

As the reward fund increased to $2500, amateur sleuths were out in force, highlighted by a spiritualist who claimed to have seen a vision of the killer. His crew inundated by information, Chief Puthoff offered a hollow promise: "We will continue to sift every clue given us, however slight, in hope of catching Miss Brady's murderer."

But the press was not optimistic. Articles headlined, **"Detectives at Blind Wall in Murder Probe,"** and **"Is Brady Killing To Be Listed As Perfect Crime?"** appeared on Friday. Another editorial was titled, **"Hope for Solution Is Fading as Inquest Proves Fruitless."**

The police had some good leads. There was a report of a man having a key made the night of the murder, a key similar to the type used on the Brady door. A Covington man was grilled for parking his car near the Brady home that night. And a disorderly youth was arrested in the railroad yard with a .32-caliber revolver in his possession.

The witness who saw a man and a woman fleeing the murder scene was Frank Armstrong, whose house was behind the Brady home. Even though he was late with his story, it was considered significant in light of testimony about the unknown man on the Brady front lawn minutes after the shooting.

After seven days, the investigation was bogged down by three diverse scenarios:

- An addict looting the house killed Frances while in a heroin haze.
- A novice burglar fired the shot during a panic after being discovered.
- A mentally unhinged "person" murdered her to halt the wedding.

This last scenario still had legs. Could such a creature harbor a secret desire for Frances without her or anyone else knowing about it? Did he (or she) hold the latch on the front door and look through the glass until Frances finally took the key?

The *Post* summed up the challenges smothering the investigation:

> **For whom shall the police hunt? They do not know whether the killer is a burglar, a child, a man or a woman or whether the assassin was white or black. No one but Frances saw the murderer and she was killed instantly.**

During the investigation's second week, a group of Covington businessmen hired a private detective to help the police, a "widely known sleuth" who had solved a number of national cases. He agreed to take on the case only if he received an "official request" and was assured cooperation.

Chief Puthoff had no objection to a new pair of eyes—the Brady family had already retained a Cincinnati detective to act as their liaison with the Covington police. But the chief reminded these imported operatives that the killer did not leave a single clue other than the bullet.

In December there was a spark. Covington police arrested a 16-year-old Newport youth who had bragged to friends that he was at the Brady house on the murder night. He also had a .32-caliber revolver in his possession. Yet during interrogation he denied any knowledge of the crime, and ballistic tests soon proved his gun wasn't the murder weapon. The boastful delinquent was sent off to the reformatory.

During Christmas, Kentucky Governor A.B. Chandler offered a $1000 reward. But with motive gone astray, 1937 arrived as the case limped inexorably toward the unsolved file.

Months passed. Suddenly on December 1, detectives caught the break they had been praying for. From Kenton County death row, a condemned man spun a desperate tale that thrust the Brady murder out of the shadows and into the harsh light of day.

Harold Van Venison, described by Cincinnati newspapers as "the Covington Negro sentenced to be hanged for a criminal attack on a white woman," was bargaining for his life.

The previous August he and another man had hijacked a young couple at gunpoint and driven them to a lonely country road, where Venison assaulted the man and raped the woman.

Venison's conviction and death sentence in November had launched a rash of activity by the Ku Klux Klan. A cross was burned on a hilltop in Covington, followed by a letter to the *Kentucky Post* which lauded the verdict and called the fiery cross "a warning to all other criminals."

Racial fervor erupted again after Venison began talking about the Brady killing. White citizens of this Depression-era river town were incensed that black men may have been responsible for the pretty bride's death.

According to Venison, he and three other men had planned to rob the Brady home, but he had missed the caper because of a singing engagement in Springfield, Ohio. The convicted rapist implicated two associates, Willie Bradshaw, age 37, and Rudolph Haynes, age 31, in the murder. Covington native Bradshaw and Cincinnatian Haynes were linked to a third suspect—this quartet of black men was part of a burglary ring working the Brady neighborhood.

Venison continued to run his mouth from his cell next to the gallows, fingering Haynes as the shooter while using Bradshaw's gun. Before leaving for Springfield, he had asked the others how the "little job" at the Brady house was going down. Haynes told him they had "a bunch of keys." The next day Haynes allegedly told Venison he "had to use the trigger" and that "she won't talk."

The condemned man also gave up the former Brady maid, who he claimed was friendly with the robbery gang. She had already been questioned about the missing keys early in the investigation. Now confronted by Venison's allegations, the black woman denied any acquaintance with the suspects, but detectives could feel the pieces falling into place.

Bradshaw and Haynes were arrested after tests on Bradshaw's gun seemed to indicate it was the weapon that killed Frances Brady. As the pair were arraigned on murder charges, Chief Putthoff told the press, "We are satisfied that we have solved the murder. Both men have talked, but not enough."

Reporters speculated about third-degree tactics being used on the two suspects. According to the Cincinnati Enquirer, Puthoff, two Covington detectives, the Kenton county sheriff, and the city prosecutor all "participated in the grilling of the Negroes."

Bradshaw and Haynes vehemently protested their innocence. Bradshaw pointed out that he was the witness who "dropped the dime on Venison" for the rape of the white girl, and that he was seeking the reward for the singer's arrest. He admitted owning the revolver, but said he often pawned it or loaned it to Venison—who responded by admitting he had carried it on "several occasions."

Ben Rowe, another Covington Negro, testified at the preliminary hearing that he had loaned his automobile to Bradshaw the night of the Brady slaying, and had seen Haynes enter the car as well. Rowe would die before the trial, but his statement was the final link in the prosecution's chain of evidence.

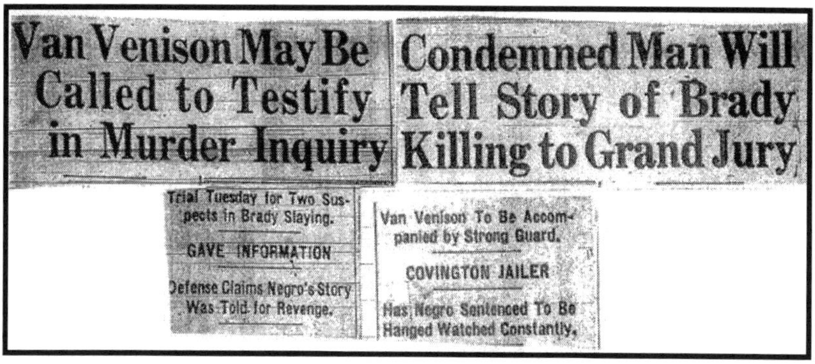

Van Venison May Be Called to Testify in Murder Inquiry

Trial Tuesday for Two Suspects in Brady Slaying.

GAVE INFORMATION

Defense Claims Negro's Story Was Told for Revenge.

Condemned Man Will Tell Story of Brady Killing to Grand Jury

Van Venison To Be Accompanied by Strong Guard.

COVINGTON JAILER

Has Negro Sentenced To Be Hanged Watched Constantly.

From his death row cell, Harold Van Venison broke the Brady case wide open.

The grand jury returned murder indictments against Bradshaw and Haynes, with Commonwealth attorney Ulie J. Howard promising the state would seek the death penalty. Held without bond, Haynes consulted with two Cincinnati attorneys, while Bradshaw retained former State Senator John T. Murphy to defend him.

It was a wise choice. Murphy had a reputation as a wicked cross examiner who fought like he himself was facing punishment.

Willie Bradshaw's trial for the murder of Frances Brady began on March 16, 1938. The state's star witness was former radio singer Harold Van Venison, whose date with the hangman was on hold.

Prosecutor Howard opened with the Brady sisters reliving the events of the night in question. Their narratives from the inquest were intact, but Margaret insisted on referring to the shooting of Frances as "the accident."

When Venison took the stand, he immediately implicated Bradshaw. He testified that the defendant had invited him to "crack a crib" in October of 1936—he explained that this meant to commit a robbery. The next day, Rudolph Haynes spoke of the failed burglary and told Venison he "had to do it the straight way" to escape the Brady home.

Venison claimed Haynes and another man named Melvin Jones entered the Brady home with a key, while Bradshaw waited in the car. The unexpected return of the Brady sisters prevented them from looting the house—Jones escaped, but Haynes "did not get away in time." Venison added that Jones had died in Louisville five months before the trial.

Trying to address potential trouble, Howard asked Venison about his motivation to accuse Bradshaw and Haynes of murder. John Murphy objected just as Venison pulled a small Bible from his pocket and waved it in the air. The objection was sustained, and the question went unanswered.

As Murphy rose to question Venison, spectators leaned forward, anticipating that this confrontation would be critical to the trial's outcome. During his opening remarks Murphy had thrown down the gauntlet, declaring, "Before this trial is over, I will be able to point to the man who killed Miss Brady. If you prove that the gun killed her, I will prove that Venison killed her."

Murphy waded in, conducting some of the cross examination at the top of his lungs. He attacked Venison's credibility with a blistering onslaught.

First Question—Murphy: "Didn't you fire the shot that killed Miss Brady?"

Venison: "No, Sir, I did not."

With elegant contempt, Murphy calmly led Venison through his movements since coming to Covington and being arrested for rape. He allowed the former singer to restate his alibi that he was performing in Springfield on the night of the slaying. Then, with swift and violent indignation, Murphy charged that Venison and Melvin Jones had killed Frances Brady. Another denial from the witness, but it was clear that Murphy was rattling him.

Venison denied he had fingered the men because of Bradshaw's "snitch" to the cops on the rape charge. When Murphy insisted his "story" was concocted for revenge, Venison's defiance became less convincing. As he left the stand, not only was his credibility compromised, but Venison was suddenly a viable suspect for the murder.

"FEED, THEN HANG ME," IS PLEA OF VENISON

Man, Facing Trial on Capital Charges, Big Eater.

IN COVINGTON JAIL

Accused of Criminal Attack and Armed Robbery.

Harold Van Venison was in the Covington jail Thursday awaiting arraignment before Judge Johnst Northcutt in Kenton Circuit Court to plead to indictments charging him with criminal attack on a Covington white woman and the armed robbery of her escort.

Under guard of officers in four police cruisers, the 36-year-old Negro was taken to Covington police headquarters after arriving at the Ludlow railroad station Thursday at 8 a. m. The time and point of arrival had been kept secret by the police as a precaution against any possible violence.

After recovering from his fear of being mobbed, Venison asked that he "be fed and hanged as soon as possible."

He refused to say whether he was guilty of the attack, adding:

"I don't remember doing anything like that because I was drunk. But if the white folks say I done it, I done it. I want to get it over with. Give me something to eat and then hang me."

AMAZED AT APPETITE

Chief George E. Langley and Patrolman Otto Frolicher and Covington Detective James Higgins who returned the prisoner from Aiken, S. C., where he was arrested Sunday, were amazed at the appetite of the prisoner. "Every time we ate a meal, he ate two," Chief Langley said.

Harold Van Venison, 36, Negro night club entertainer, indicted in Kenton County for criminal assault upon a Covington white woman, is shown seated in the center of a group of Covington and Kenton County police officers as he was being questioned in the office of Covington Police Chief John Pulthoff Thursday morning. The officers were part of an escort of police who guarded Van Venison from the Southern Railroad station at Ludlow to the Covington City Building. He was captured Sunday at Aiken, S. C.

Standing left to right behind Van Venison are Covington Detective James Higgins, Covington Police Chief John Pulthoff, Covington Patrolman Robert Spanton, Kenton County Patrolman Otto Frolicher and Kenton County Police Chief George E. Langley.

Harold Van Venison had already shown his flair for the dramatic after his 1937 arrest for assault and rape.

The trial's second day was highlighted by Murphy's questioning of Lieutenant John Messmer, ballistics expert of the Louisville Police Department. To discredit this key piece of evidence, Murphy attacked the procedures used to link Bradshaw's gun to the Brady shooting, establishing that Messmer found only 12 similarities between the murder bullet and a test bullet. Dramatically holding the two bullets up for the jury to see, Murphy counted five similarities that "could be seen with the naked eye" and which "are found in the average bullet."

The state ended by reading Ben Rowe's preliminary hearing testimony into the record. Rowe had sworn he lent his car to

Bradshaw and Haynes on the fatal night—but like the mysterious Melvin Jones, Mr. Rowe was also dead.

On March 18, John T. Murphy presented his case for acquittal, beginning with Willie Bradshaw as the first witness in his own defense. He testified he had given the revolver to Harold Venison as security for a loan, and that Venison still kept it weeks after the murder. He also denied that Rudolph Haynes, awaiting trial as the "triggerman," was with him anytime during the week of the shooting.

Bradshaw swore he was at home on the night of the murder, because he had to get up early to work at a Covington café—work records confirmed that he was at his job the morning after the slaying. Murphy also elicited that Bradshaw had turned letters from Venison over to the police. The singer had fled to South Carolina to escape the Kentucky rape charge, yet wrote incriminating statements in his letters to Bradshaw.

After a tepid cross examination by Prosecutor Howard, Murphy called on Henry "Buster" Walters to smash Venison's alibi for the murder night. Walters was the manager of the quartet that included Venison, and he was positive they were not singing in Springfield on the night of October 1-2, 1936.

Murphy also introduced a portion of Ben Rowe's preliminary hearing statement, where the now deceased Rowe had testified about seeing Venison enter Bradshaw's house a few hours after the Brady murder.

Virginia Cunningham testified that Bradshaw stayed at her Covington home in the fall of 1936, following an argument with his wife. Mrs. Cunningham then stunned the prosecution by confirming that the murder weapon was in Venison's possession during September and October of 1936. She had witnessed Bradshaw pawning the weapon to Venison in mid-September, and remembered this clearly because Bradshaw immediately gave her the money for his overdue rent. She recalled that Venison returned the gun "about the middle of October." Anticipating future pawns, she placed it in a trunk for safekeeping.

On cross examination, Mrs. Cunningham said she believed that "Bradshaw was probably at my home the night Miss Brady was murdered."

The mother and sister of accused triggerman Rudolph Haynes testified that Haynes had remained at their Cincinnati home every night during September and October, caring for a niece with tuberculosis. Both women worked nights, and they were adamant that Rudolph was a devoted caregiver who wouldn't abandon the girl for even one night.

Murphy then rested his masterful defense. Spectators and reporters were whispering about the beating absorbed by the prosecution, the weakness of their case exposed by Murphy's probing needles and thundering bombast.

Closing arguments began that afternoon. Judge John Northcutt, a no-nonsense jurist, allowed Murphy and Howard just 45 minutes each to sway the jury.

Murphy came out swinging, hammering home the reasonable doubt that surrounded his client. He recalled the witnesses who debunked Harold Venison's alibi for the murder night. He reviewed the inconsistencies in the ballistic report, and reminded the jury that "a religious woman like Mrs. Cunningham would not lie to protect Bradshaw."

Then he zeroed in on the state's star witness. Murphy told the jury that Venison's story implicating Bradshaw and Haynes was "fabricated for purposes of revenge," based on the letters Bradshaw gave police that incriminated Venison.

His voice echoing through the courthouse, Murphy charged that Venison himself was the triggerman, reminding the jury that he was already a condemned rapist. "He is a sex killer!" the attorney bellowed. "I believe that he killed Miss Brady. I believe he went to the Brady home that night on a mission other than burglary!"

Murphy didn't have to back up his speculations. Just by conjuring up the image of Negroes stalking white women for sex, he got this Covington jury's full attention.

Prosecutor Howard closed with a short address where he contended the evidence showed conclusively that Bradshaw was connected to the case. But the eradication of Venison's credibility, faulty ballistics, and hearsay testimony from a dead man were all weak links in the state's chain of evidence.

A jury of six men and six women received the case late that day. After weighing the evidence against William Bradshaw for 52 minutes, they returned a verdict of not guilty.

It was a remarkable event—an all-white jury deliberated less than an hour before acquitting Bradshaw, an extraordinarily quick vindication for a black defendant in Kentucky charged with killing a white woman. Yet the verdict surprised no one.

After several delays, Rudolph Haynes was released on bail. He was never brought to trial, probably because his accuser was dead.

Harold Venison became the last man ever hanged in the state of Kentucky on June 3, 1938. The convicted rapist walked to the gallows while singing hymns with his ministers. As the trap was sprung, Venison's rich baritone still echoed throughout the execution chamber.

The former radio singer denied to the end any involvement in the Brady slaying.

SUMMATION:

Despite the verdict in the Bradshaw case and the lack of evidence regarding the robbery theory, it is a better fit than any personal motive against Frances Brady. The most likely scenario remains a combination of crooks who wanted to "crack a crib." Whether it was Bradshaw/Haynes, Venison/Jones or someone else, this remains the best explanation for the chain of events that ended with Miss Brady murdered at her own front door.

Regardless of the rumors surrounding Brady's death, the love triangle theory never got traction. When the coroner's jury rejected the burglary motive, detectives had a year to make their case for a vendetta against Frances, yet never harvested even the slimmest of leads.

It's possible a rejected suitor killed Frances to prevent her marriage to John O'Donnell. But he never surfaced during the most intense investigation in Covington police history.

Frances got a good look at her killer. If it was someone she knew standing there, the exclamation would have been surprise. Yet the fear described by her sisters was more consistent with the shocking tableau in the foyer—a Negro violating their home, with a gun leveled at her.

The home invasion scenario still has some kinks in it. Yet it is the most probable cause for the death of Frances Marie Brady.

EPILOGUE:

The Brady tragedy destroyed the lives of the three people who loved Frances.

Fiancé John O'Donnell never married and died eleven years later, still disconsolate over his shattering loss. Ella Celine and Margaret Brady both died in the 1950s, neither having ever recovered from the shock of seeing their sister killed.

A vagrant rumor floated for years that Frances had been having an affair with "a neighbor" at the time of the slaying. More recently, a Falmouth, Kentucky psychic claimed a raven-haired ghost in a bridal gown was haunting the Wachs house where the body had been carried.

More than 70 years later, the case remains a paradox: Was it a botched burglary or a cold-blooded murder? Or both?

One thing is certain. Whoever gunned down Frances Marie Brady in the shadow of her wedding day took the secret to their grave.

I WITNESS:

Harold Venison was looking to pull a heist. And a chance conversation with the former Brady maid set this crime in motion.

The maid knew about the sisters' plans to attend the bridal shower. She told Venison about the cache of jewelry hidden in one of the Brady bedrooms. Then she clinched the caper by handing him the spare key she had palmed two months earlier, when Frances Brady had dismissed her for stealing.

She assured Venison that this job would be a walkover. He had already jawboned the revolver from Bradshaw. Now all he had to do was select the right cohort from his crew of "midnighters"—this was a two-man job.

On the night in question, Venison and his associate arrive late—it is after midnight when they enter the Brady home. Some failed attempts to scavenge other houses nearby have delayed them.

Shrouded in darkness, the two criminals go to work. His friend heads upstairs while Venison rummages through the ground floor, both of them looking for small items of value. The wedding gifts are a last resort.

Yet somehow, within minutes the Brady girls arrive on the front porch. Venison buckles into a blind panic. He hisses to his partner that the jig is up—they have to get out of there now! Without waiting, he flies out the back door.

The other crook, still upstairs, is petrified. As the sisters struggle with the front door lock, the robber opens a window and considers jumping. But there is only one escape from the second floor.

Quickly lurching down the stairway in total darkness, Venison's partner tumbles onto the landing, standing up just as the front door swings open, and the light blazes on.

For one eternal moment, the burglar locks eyes with Frances Marie Brady. This chance juncture of their lives freezes into a stark montage—the white bride and the black thief are now companions in peril.

Frances makes a startled sound, an exclamation of recognition. The thief knows she can make a positive identification in any lineup.

In sheer terror, Venison's partner quickly brings the revolver upward and squeezes off a round.

And in an everlasting instant, the bride is "gone glimmering". Her dreams of marital bliss spark off into the darkness, as a divine wind washes the autumn trees with her last breath.

The shooter rushes out the back door and into the October night. The gunsel is certain that neither of the Brady sisters will ever learn what Frances witnessed in her last moment:

That her killer, the person in cahoots with Venison from the start, is their former maid.

2009

The Georgian Apartments where Willard Armstrong died still have an ominous aura today.

TO BE OR NOT TO BE

THE LONELY DEATH OF WILLARD ARMSTRONG: 1939

"Give us long rest or death, dark death or dreamful ease."
Alfred Tennyson

PROLOGUE:

It was a crime—or was it?

Riddled with contradiction and irony, investigators were divided from the start: Was the young executive they found trussed up inside a bag murdered, or did he take his own life?

The case would prove more baffling with age. Armchair detectives have whetted their appetites for years on the Willard Armstrong case, and their conclusions are still locked in conflict.

This strange death was too close to call—only a coin flip could resolve it.

NARRATIVE:

"I can't help feeling something is wrong with Willard," sighed the attractive brunette. Jessie Armstrong was referring to her husband, and her tone was beyond a wife's normal intuition.

"There's nothing wrong, believe me," assured her friend Don Arnette as they entered the fourth floor hallway of the Georgian Apartments in Norwood. The stately building at the corner of

Ida and Smith Roads was a respectable house that had never suffered a hint of scandal.

"I don't know," Jessie replied. "He should have been at the depot to meet me. He's always shown up before." They arrived at her door as she fumbled nervously for the key.

"He's probably asleep," offered Arnette, whose wife was waiting in the car outside. "We'll get him up and then go have dinner somewhere."

Jessie opened the door and stepped into her apartment. A sudden, inexplicable chill gripped her heart like an icy hand.

Arnette followed her inside. As their eyes adjusted to the darkness, they both saw it—a man's legs protruding from a large bag lying on the floor. Jessie Armstrong rushed over and frantically ripped it open, only to find the lifeless face of her husband staring up at her.

It was 7:30PM on Sunday, February 5, 1939. And thus began one of the strangest crimes in Cincinnati history.

Norwood is an island municipality, surrounded by, but not part of Cincinnati. It was incorporated in 1903 and matured into an industrial breeding ground with a working-class citizenry. Factories and foundries were the community's lifeblood, and the opening of the Ford Motor plant in the early 1930s cemented Norwood's financial future.

As 1939 began, Adolf Hitler was eying Poland for an invasion in the fall. Yet Hollywood kept Americans oblivious to the rumblings of war by delivering a miracle year for motion pictures, including an astonishing number of instant movie classics—*Gone with the Wind, The Wizard of Oz, Wuthering Heights, Of Mice and Men, Stagecoach* and *Goodbye, Mr. Chips*. The Depression was still a cloud over everyone's head, with the economy showing few signs of rallying. Escapism was the only reliable moneymaker.

That year Norwood's population had reached 40,000. Led by Police Chief Thomas Jenike, law enforcement was dealing with the influx of immigrants and non-whites looking for work—a major concern for the steadfast Caucasian community.

Chief Jenike, Coroner Frank Coppock and Detectives Flower and Kiley responded to the Armstrong residence that evening. They found 38-year-old Willard Armstrong, chief clerk of the CC & St. L Railroad, trussed up in a giant cloth bag with his wrists lashed to his ankles. Flower commented that the knots looked as if they had been tied "by an expert."

Norwood detectives had never confronted a more bewildering array of conflicting clues. A runner hose ran from the kitchen stove to the sack, and there was a faint smell of gas in the apartment. Someone had struck Armstrong twice over the right eye, bound him, put the bag over his head, and placed the hose near his mouth. It appeared the victim had been asphyxiated.

Coroner Coppock certified he had been dead for several hours, and concluded immediately that it was a case of homicide committed during a robbery. But he was begging the question, and his judgment proved both premature and controversial.

Friends would tell police that Willard Armstrong and his pretty wife Jessie were "a devoted and happy couple." They were planning the construction of their new home. Armstrong was in line for a promotion, and by all accounts led an exemplary life.

Yet details about their marriage would soon turn this assumption inside out.

Mrs. Armstrong made some hasty comments about $250 missing from the chest where they kept their cash. Then she became so distressed that she was placed under a physician's care, and could not be questioned further.

Don Arnette had telephoned Armstrong Saturday evening and learned his friend had an appointment that night to discuss the new house. Arnette called him on Sunday, but got no answer. He and his wife stopped at the apartment Sunday evening to pick up Armstrong on their way to the train station to fetch Jessie. Still no answer.

By Monday the police inventory of the scene added to the confusion. It was a collage of incompatible evidence:

- The victim's billfold and $31 on the kitchen table were intact.
- Contents in the fronts of dresser drawers had been rifled, but items in the rear were undisturbed.
- Several books had been thrown on the floor, while others remained on the shelves.
- A pint bottle half full of expensive liquor was found in the kitchen—Armstrong did not drink, according to Arnette.
- The $250 Jessie Armstrong thought was missing was found in place.
- Numerous stocks and bonds were found undisturbed in a bedroom chest.
- Several pieces of jewelry were in plain view on a dresser.
- An alarm clock near Armstrong's bed was still running, indicating it had been wound on Saturday night.
- Despite the odor of gas, Arnette was certain it was turned off when he entered the apartment with Mrs. Armstrong.

Detectives discounted robbery as a motive—even the disorder appeared staged. By Monday afternoon they were digging into the victim's outwardly ordinary life, and scrutinizing his last day on earth.

A young woman who knew Armstrong from church rode the bus with him on Saturday afternoon, and expressed surprise when he missed his normal stop. He told her his wife was away for the weekend and that he needed some groceries. Armstrong did buy cube steak and butter, yet his refrigerator was already full of food. The steak was not found, and the autopsy confirmed he had not eaten it.

The dead man was last seen alive Saturday night about 8PM by his neighbor across the hall, dressed in the same clothes he would be found in. Arnette called Armstrong a few minutes after that.

Kerman Wardell, who lived directly below the young couple, told police Armstrong came home about 12:30AM Sunday morning. He divulged a friendly signal they shared—whenever he heard Armstrong enter his apartment he knocked on the ceiling, and Armstrong answered by stomping on the floor.

HUNT VISITOR TO MAN SLAIN IN MOTH BAG

GAS VICTIM'S $4000 SAVINGS ARE INTACT

Police Told by Armstrong's Friend Of Appointment

A man who had an appointment with Willard H. Armstrong, railway chief clerk, shortly before he was clubbed, trussed, thrust into a paper moth bag and asphyxiated with gas, was sought Monday by Norwood police for aid in their investigation of the killing.

Never had the police been confronted with a more bewildering array of conflicting clews than by this strange slaying in the Georgian apartments, Ida and Smith roads.

Mr. Armstrong was found late Sunday by his wife, who just had returned from a week-end in Indianapolis.

Slain Norwood Man

Willard H. Armstrong

The enigmatic Mr. Armstrong and his puzzling death were big news in 1939.

Wardell was having a lively party that night, yet he heard Armstrong's door slam and the customary three stomps to indicate his neighbor was home.

Who was the mystery man Armstrong was meeting with on Saturday night? Police contacted all construction people with whom the victim had dealings, yet none of them had an appointment with him. Armstrong also told Arnette that he was going to withdraw $4000 as a down payment for the meeting, yet the bank confirmed he didn't make any withdrawals that weekend.

Chief Jenike speculated to the press that someone had posed as a builder to gain an audience with Armstrong.

The autopsy did verify one thing—Coroner Coppock reported Armstrong died due to asphyxiation. His blood contained 90% illuminating gas. "Death by gas poisoning in an undetermined manner" was the official verdict, "occurring sometime between 1AM and 9AM Sunday morning." Coppock carefully refrained from designating either murder or suicide, but his personal viewpoint was homicide.

Jenike wasn't convinced. He was starting to believe that this was a counterfeit murder choreographed by a suicidal man.

The detachment of Jessie Armstrong was already an investigational burden. Prostrate with grief, she remained in seclusion with her parents in Indiana, under the strict care of her doctor.

Cops weren't buying it. The behavior of the attractive widow was not consistent with normal grief—there was a consciousness of blame that flirted with guilt. They would just have to wait her out.

The matter of whether the gas was on or off when the body was discovered had become paramount. If the gas was off that meant murder. If it was still on, then suicide was more likely.

Don Arnette was certain it was off. He had carried a lighted cigar into the apartment, and felt that "the odor of gas was not so strong." But neighbors Abner and Harry Ownes, who entered the apartment shortly after the body was discovered, claimed the smell was so overpowering that they opened a window before turning off the gas.

Yet did they turn it off? The Norwood Fire Chief maintained that his men turned the gas off sometime after 9PM. Police had to ponder whether the Ownes brothers had actually flipped the gas back on instead of shutting it off.

Captain Jenike was still following the victim. Background checks confirmed Armstrong had no enemies, and no suicidal tendencies. Several of his men believed the crime scene photos "indicated the victim had been murdered," and they favored "a robbery based on opportunity."

Yet Jenike would not abandon the suicide theory. He was convinced Armstrong's meeting was either a ruse for someone to gain entrance or a lie told to mislead Arnette. Jenike didn't see how a stranger killer could know that Mrs. Armstrong would be away for the weekend.

The day of Armstrong's funeral, the *Cincinnati Post* reported that Coppock and Jenike "had a long and animated argument over the matter, the chief contending suicide was possible and Coroner Coppock saying it was impossible."

The *Cincinnati Enquirer* laid out a compelling rationale for each theory—confirming that the known facts in the Armstrong death only intensified the mystery.

THE MURDER THEORY:

- The blow to Armstrong's temple was strong enough to render him unconscious.
- The ropes binding him were too tight to have been self-inflicted.
- The Armstrongs were apparently a happy and devoted couple.
- Armstrong exhibited no suicidal inclinations—he was in line for a promotion and was actively planning to build a new house.

THE SUICIDE THEORY:

- The bruise over Armstrong's right eye was small with no swelling.
- There was no sign of a struggle—a frontal blow should have resulted in a fight.
- The scene was staged to give the appearance of a robbery—a distraught man was more likely to make such obvious mistakes than a killer.
- No valuables of any kind were taken.

- The knots tying Armstrong could have been tightened after he had slipped into them—one was identical to a clothesline knot he had tied for his wife.
- The death bag was large enough that he could have squirmed into it.
- The bag was open—a killer would have put him all the way in and closed it.

As Willard Armstrong was laid to rest in Indianapolis, investigators were growing impatient with the widow.

Mrs. Jessie Armstrong, still ensconced in Indiana, insisted through Don Arnette that her husband must have been murdered, even though she was baffled by the motive. She did finally confirm that the cord and safety pins used to bind her husband came from her own clothesline.

Back in Norwood, Willard Armstrong's spotless reputation was unraveling like the rope that had bound him. A garage mechanic told detectives Armstrong had offered him a drink from the mysterious whiskey bottle on Friday night. That was odd behavior for a church-going man known for his abstinence.

The young woman who rode the bus with Armstrong on Saturday reluctantly submitted to a longer interview. What she revealed drove this case further into the sand.

Mrs. Fay Sonnycalb of Norwood told investigators Armstrong did not seem depressed that day, but that his behavior was out of character. She claimed he offered to pick her up and take her to Sunday school the next morning. Fay declined the invitation when he told her Jessie was out of town—she thought this was peculiar, since only both Armstrongs had taken her to church before.

Armstrong had seemed bothered by her refusal. But they talked of bowling and other subjects during the bus ride, and his normal mood soon returned.

Rumors that Mrs. Sonnycalb was with Armstrong Saturday night were groundless, set off by her statement about riding with

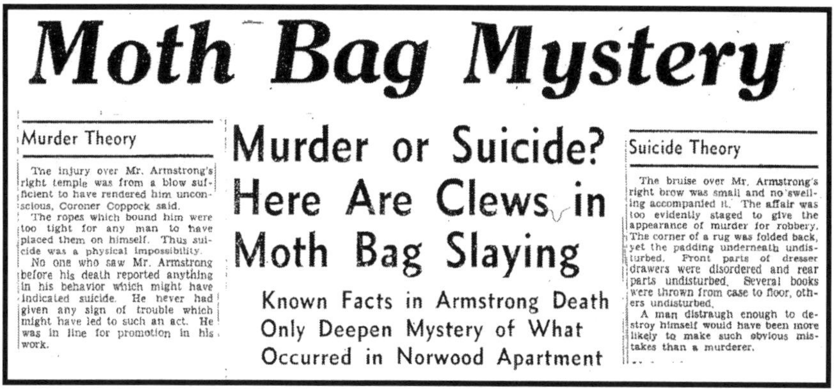

Moth Bag Mystery

Murder or Suicide? Here Are Clews in Moth Bag Slaying

Known Facts in Armstrong Death Only Deepen Mystery of What Occurred in Norwood Apartment

Murder Theory

The injury over Mr. Armstrong's right temple was from a blow sufficient to have rendered him unconscious, Coroner Coppock said.

The ropes which bound him were too tight for any man to have placed them on himself. Thus suicide was a physical impossibility.

No one who saw Mr. Armstrong before his death reported anything in his behavior which might have indicated suicide. He never had given any sign of trouble which might have led to such an act. He was in line for promotion in his work.

Suicide Theory

The bruise over Mr. Armstrong's right brow was small and no swelling accompanied it. The affair was too evidently staged to give the appearance of murder for robbery. The corner of a rug was folded back, yet the padding underneath undisturbed. Front parts of dresser drawers were disordered and rear parts undisturbed. Several books were thrown from case to floor, others undisturbed.

A man distraugh enough to destroy himself would have been more likely to make such obvious mistakes than a murderer.

This *Post* Headline exposed the rift among Norwood detectives over their competing theories.

him on Saturday afternoon. Still, the young and attractive wife was under scrutiny.

On the same day, two anonymous letters arrived at Norwood Police Headquarters addressed to Chief Jenike. The first was typewritten, urging the chief to seek the murderer among Armstrong's friends. The second was written in ink, and advised searching among his acquaintances at the Sunday school and the Masonic temple.

Chief Jenike urged more citizens to open up: "I welcome any suggestions from anybody for clues in the case. I will hold confidential any communication, but I prefer personal visits."

The next day he received one from Elmer Arnold, the proprietor of Arnold's Grill in downtown Cincinnati. His interview uncovered a tarnishing implication about Willard Armstrong's personal life.

Armstrong ate there every Saturday afternoon, including the day before his death. Because he visited the restaurant alone and always ate in the same booth, waitresses jokingly referred to the young executive as "the lone wolf." Arnold revealed that Armstrong posed as an unmarried man when chatting with his "girls." He only learned of the victim's marital status after reading accounts of his bizarre death in the newspapers.

Armstrong was regarded by Grill employees as "sober and hardworking"—but his flirtatious conduct had raised some eyebrows.

Upon learning that the Sunday school superintendent had pretended to be unmarried, Chief Jenike refused to engage in innuendo. His official position was that Armstrong's ploy shed no light on the investigation. Yet reporters grasped that a tinge of scandal now colored the case.

Several days of salacious copy did not rouse Jessie Armstrong to defend her husband. Still cloistered with her parents, she showed no inclination to purify any gossip. Police lamented that "there are several little points that only she can clear up for us," and now were forced to wait for her return before ascertaining any "facts on the personal life of the victim."

As the delay lingered, Chief Jenike asked Hamilton County Prosecutor Carl W. Rich to step in and help the Norwood prosecutor. Those familiar with Rich knew he would take an active role in the investigation, especially in expediting the overdue interview with Mrs. Armstrong.

But the new widow had sentenced herself to everlasting grief—as if sorrow would staunch her unavenged tears.

With the impasse between murder and suicide hampering the investigation, Chief Jenike reviewed the imperative questions that had to be answered:

Was the gas on or off? There were conflicting statements here. The Arnettes and Jesse claimed the smell of gas was insignificant, while other residents felt it was overwhelming. Brothers who claimed they turned it off might have turned it back on—Norwood firemen believed they had turned it off later.

Coroner Coppock believed the gas was turned off. He said the odor was faint when he entered the apartment soon after the body was found. But if Armstrong had been murdered 12-16 hours before (according to Coppock), any lingering gas would have dissipated if the killer turned it off.

If the gas was off, this ruled out suicide. If it was on, Armstrong ending his own life was the more likely scenario.

Evidence leaned toward the gas being on—although not conclusively.

Were the lights on or off? Both Arnette and Jessie were uncertain, but felt the lights were off when they found the body. This question related to time of death and in determining whether Armstrong had gone out.

In the end it was questionable.

Who set the alarm clock? A clock near the bed was set for 6:00, and the alarm had run down. Coppock bolstered his murder theory by insisting Armstrong had intended to rise early Sunday morning, yet was already dead when the alarm sounded.

But the alarm clock could have been a red herring to conceal suicide, with Armstrong killing himself sometime after 6AM. The clock was still running when it was found, indicating a recent winding. Armstrong was known to take naps—the 6:00 setting could have been for the evening.

This answer remained elusive.

Did Armstrong leave the apartment Saturday night? When seen at 8:30PM Armstrong was dressed as he was found on Sunday night. It had rained Saturday evening, yet his shoes showed no sign of dampness, and he had not changed his shirt. He seemed to be in for the night and waiting for his meeting.

However, downstairs neighbor Waddell heard his door slam about 12:30AM Sunday morning, followed by the prearranged signals that Armstrong was safely home. Waddell heard no movements or noise from above between 8:30PM and the loud entry after midnight.

If he left then where did he go? Any destination or rendezvous would be vital in determining the motive for his death. But no one came forward who saw him during that crucial four hour period.

Why did Armstrong not accompany his wife to Indianapolis? He usually traveled with her. Was he contemplating suicide, or was his unexplained Saturday night appointment legitimate? And did this assignation end with his death?

This question remained unanswered. Yet Mrs. Armstrong's anxiety regarding his failure to meet her at the depot was jarringly prophetic.

Did the elaborate robbery staging indicate murder or suicide? If Armstrong intended to conceal his suicide, his anguished state of mind might have hampered the ruse. Yet a murderer with a motive other than robbery could have ransacked the place to confound the police.

The staging pointed both ways.

Could Armstrong have trussed himself up and then wiggled into the bag? This was the pivotal question, the bone of contention dividing investigators and creating discord down at headquarters. Despite Coppock's insistence that the bindings were too tight to self inflict, two Norwood patrolmen replicated the same slip knots and were able to crawl into the bag and then tighten them.

Coppock assured reporters that his upcoming inquest would answer these questions and put the investigation back on track. Yet nothing could be scheduled without the still absent Jessie Armstrong.

Tired of the delay, the investigative team flew to Indianapolis to interview the widow. They would return later the same day, floundering in a state of confusion.

Prosecutor Rich tried to be charitable: "Mrs. Armstrong gave us nothing new which would establish one way or another a suicide or a murder theory. She kept asking me what I thought about the case. She believes that her husband was murdered."

Rich explained the difficulty in questioning Armstrong's wife. "She is a very sick woman . . . frequently she suffered coughing spells and had to take long rests. She gradually pieced her story together, repeating the same facts she had given when the body was first discovered . . . she identified the cloth bag, the hose and the rope used to bind Mr. Armstrong."

The prosecutor hinted at discrepancies in her story: "Mrs. Armstrong said she tore the moth bag cover from her husband's body" (life squad members claimed they did this). She said there

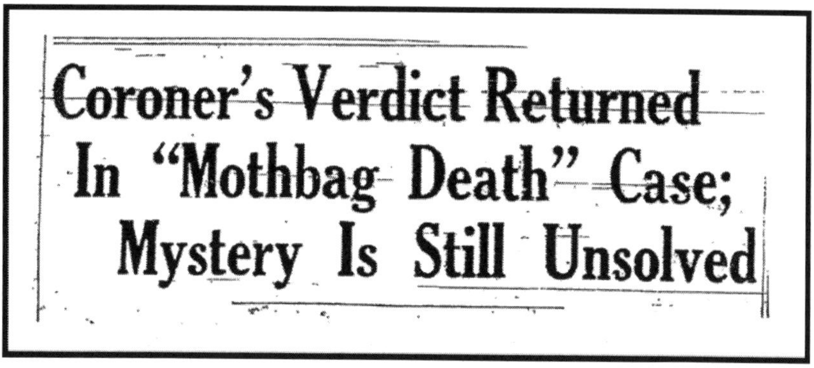

Coroner's Verdict Returned
In "Mothbag Death" Case;
Mystery Is Still Unsolved

The coroner's verdict only deepened the mystery.

was but little gas odor in the apartment (disputed by others), and she insisted that $250 was missing from a vanity drawer" (but it was found in another location).

Slowly the realization came that detectives did not possess a solitary clue in the inexplicable demise of the puzzling Mr. Armstrong.

Within days Coppock announced that lack of evidence had stalled any plans for a grand jury probe or a coroner's inquest. Chief Jenike's belief in the suicide theory remained unshaken, even after he read a newspaper article that claimed "the case would be set down as the perfect crime."

"The longer the case goes without any clues, the stronger the suicide theory gets," Jenike decreed to the press.

On February 28, Jessie Armstrong finally came home to her shattered life. She returned to her secretarial job at a Norwood plant, and refused all interview requests.

On April 5, Coroner Coppock confirmed his earlier verdict of "death by gas poisoning in an undetermined manner."

"I feel as strongly today as I did on February 5th that the case is murder," insisted Coppock. "I purposely listed the cause as 'undetermined' so that if anything develops the case can be reopened." He vowed to remain on the assignment until proving that Willard Armstrong had been murdered.

SUMMATION:

This is a tough nut to crack.

The evidence twists in a tortuous path, every lead merging into gridlock. A murder judgment would bring clarity, but the lack of motive sweeps it back into the shadows.

If there was a killer, they moved like a phantom, leaving no trace and taking nothing with them.

If you can't follow the money, then look for the woman. And the manner of death suggests a woman was involved. Somehow.

Men can lie, but behavior is never untruthful. Willard Armstrong was preoccupied with something during the final weekend of his life.

EPILOGUE:

The bizarre death of Willard Armstrong was finally given an official designation. But it did not close the book.

Coroner Coppick's "undetermined" ruling cemented the impasse, but his personal belief was always murder. Chief Jenike never wavered from his suicide theory, while prosecutor Rich remained on the fence.

Jessie Armstrong would become the second victim in the case, dying prematurely in 1956. She never recovered from the shock of seeing her husband's ghostly white face.

Willard Armstrong has stepped into the twilight zone. And the gray areas of his life secure the mystery that still keeps armchair detectives riveted today.

POSTSCRIPT:

There was a glimmer of the Armstrong case in July, 1951. Fred C. Nuetzel, age 53, was found dead in his Beekman Street home with strange mutilations on his naked body.

The man had been castrated, and the coroner felt that cutting had been skilled. But police developed an alternate theory—Nuetzel had died of a heart attack and was maimed afterward by his pet fox terrier! Yet an autopsy of the unfortunate dog revealed no human flesh.

Nuetzel had complained of feeling unwell that night, and since there were no signs of violence in the house, the coroner tentatively listed the cause of death as "hemorrhage and shock" due to groin mutilation with a sharp instrument.

Detectives called it The Beekman Street Mystery. Others called it one of the weirdest cases in memory. Nuetzel's death was ruled a homicide until "that theory is disproved"—a most unusual verdict, unless one remembers Willard Armstrong.

I WITNESS:

He was having an affair. They were deeply in love. Then she discovered he was married.

She ended it just before Armstrong's wife left for Indiana, but he was hoping to reconcile with her while Jessie was gone.

We just need to get a second wind, he thought. *Perhaps if I get divorced? Will she take me back? No, I can't abandon Jessie. But what else can I do?*

Does Fay Sonnycalb feel his anguished melancholy while riding the bus alongside him? Armstrong's casual but clumsy overture does not mask his cloak of sadness. As he studies the lovely young woman whose arm rests softly against his own, his eyes are wistful, then yearning, then desperate. He shifts his gaze toward the window.

Do the waitresses at Arnold's wonder what has become of their lone wolf? This shell of a man sitting in Armstrong's booth has no appetite for flirting now. His heart is barren, leaving only the ache of exile.

Does his wife have misgivings about leaving him at home alone? Okay, so their marriage is rocky—whose isn't? But Jessie is spending more and more time away with her parents. When he doesn't appear at the station, a dreadful awareness suddenly floats through her mind. He wouldn't have forgotten to fetch her. Has he finally stepped beyond the margins of his life into betrayal?

Saturday night. *Cherchez La Femme*—look for the woman.

She sees him one last time. He is bitter, distraught that she will not relent, despite his impassioned pleas for another chance. She is determined that their tawdry business be swallowed into a crevice of darkness—and ultimately a complete memory loss. *It never happened,* she tells him.

The final blow. Not only does she want nothing more to do with him. She wants to wipe out all awareness of everything they were and said and did. All of the soft murmurs during those heady, naked afternoons of stolen love. She wants to obliterate them—by erasing *him*.

He arrives home after midnight, fatigue and apathy converging with his toxic thoughts. He once fancied himself the master of his own personal legend, a great lover, however uncelebrated, but known and cherished by the only other human being who mattered. Now he is the king of nothing, ruling only a fool's paradise.

And he has hurt Jessie in ways that he hopes she never knows. *Will she know? Of course she will. Women always do.*

The constant abrasion of living magnifies his depression, until he is left with a profound sense of loss, untouched and untouchable by anyone. He cannot face Jessie; she can read him like a book. He cannot face another morning, either, when he awakes, doomed to live again.

He has no choice—in order to conquer this despair, he must flee.

With languid alacrity, he fashions a harness of slip knots, sets up his rubber hose, turns on the gas, and then stands there, mentally surveying the ashes of his weary life. At least this way, they'll never suspect that he ended his own miserable, forlorn, loveless existence himself.

Then he crawls inside the bag, a majestic despot in his vain kill jar, lying there until all he hears is a hollow, hissing echo.

Sophia Baird as a high school senior—one year before she embarked on her fateful journey to Cincinnati

CAUGHT IN A WHIRLWIND TAILSPIN

THE SOPHIA BAIRD BILTMORE HOTEL SLAYING: 1943

"You will put on a dress of guilt and shoes with broken high ideals."

Roger McGough

PROLOGUE:

Sliced up in a cheap hotel and left to die thrashing in her own blood, Sophia Baird's murder exposed the vile underbelly and racist overtones of downtown street life in Cincinnati. Her tragic odyssey is the Queen City's answer to Hollywood's infamous Black Dahlia case, where a pretty yet naïve girl wanders into an urban jungle looking for a better life, only to fall victim to the sordid night.

Questionable eyewitness accounts fingered "a Negro" for the crime, but as years passed the riddle of Sophia's death hinted at a more ominous truth.

And 30 years later, the reappearance of her long-missing corpse in a Tennessee cemetery only deepened the mystery.

NARRATIVE:

It was 1943, and The War dominated the headlines. From the Allies trouncing Rommel in North Africa, through the Warsaw Ghetto uprising in Poland, to Montgomery and Patton teaming up to invade Italy, this global conflict overshadowed all aspects of daily life in America.

Women were flooding depleted factory workforces across the nation. In Cincinnati, young female residents of the Biltmore were boosting the bustling war economy, as U.S. military mobilization left the Great Depression in the dust. It was a tremendous time of opportunity for callow and eager girls. Leaving home, finding jobs, and earning their own money, unthinkable a generation earlier, gave them a sense of freedom and exhilaration.

The Biltmore Hotel was a four-floor walkup on 9th Street in the sleazy heart of Cincinnati. Whoever said old buildings and whores eventually become respectable had this edifice in mind on both counts.

The Biltmore displayed a grand exterior, guarded by an iron gate and sporting brass rails leading to the front door. But the location was pure guilt by association.

The two city blocks wedged between Vine and Walnut were a freewheeling maelstrom laced with pimps, bookies, prostitutes, and thugs. Cops who didn't steer clear took their girlfriends up to the empty rooms in the Biltmore for free. Politicians and judges consorted there with strippers and hookers, confident that the proprietors were paid well enough to keep quiet.

The Biltmore was controlled by gray-haired 62-year-old Ella Bezenah, known as "Ma." She was a charming owner and a salty, street smart operator. Ma Bezenah also owned the Drake Hotel down the block, even more of a dive than the Biltmore and next door to a strip club known as The Gayety. Vice squads would use the club's fire escape to spy on activity at the Drake, yet few arrests were made.

The Biltmore was a gathering place for a motley crew of minions and moles. An after-hours bar in the back alley hosted a small bookie operation. Ma ran untaxed liquor through it, and if a cop wandered in tally sheets were taken down and the officer was set up with drinks.

The hotel could be just as accommodating to the city's toughest hoods. Pimps regularly took strippers there and often imprisoned them for days. Hopped-up Negroes and boozy "crackers" seemed to infest the area.

It was a squalid district, where inhabitants sputtered and squirmed in the streets, a river of changing faces ceaselessly swirling as the eccentric rubbed elbows with the deranged.

It was that kind of place—and Sophia Baird would land right in the middle of it.

She arrived in Cincinnati with Mildred Sharpe on July 4, 1942, leaving a different world behind. The girls had migrated from Elk Valley, Tennessee, a remotely peaceful spot flanked by the Cumberland Mountains. Sophia came from rural stock. Her parents were hardworking, God-fearing people who raised their eleven children with a firm hand.

Young Sophia was the town belle. At age 19, she was a honey-haired blonde with blue eyes and a graceful figure. Boys told her she was pretty, and Sophia was starting to believe them. Tired of the labor and loneliness of farm life, she was suffocating in the boredom of the thin mountain air. She wanted so much more—city lights, fine shops, places to go, and people to meet.

She wanted to be where the world could notice her.

For Sophia that place was Cincinnati, the big city she had read so much about. After much pleading, her parents finally gave their blessing, relieved that her best friend Mildred was traveling with her.

When they boarded the bus on Independence Day, Sophia's beau Melvin urged her not to go. He was leaving for the War soon, but his insistence annoyed her. She kissed his cheek and promised to write.

The last thing her mother told her was, "Always stay with Mildred, and don't ever go out at night alone."

As they said goodbye, her parents could never have imagined that their daughter would become the central figure in one of Cincinnati's most brutal and sensational murder cases.

Mildred Sharpe knew people in Cincinnati who were hiring waitresses, and both girls found work immediately. Within a few months they moved to the Purple Cow, a home-cooking place in the hub of downtown, and made plans to go after high-paying jobs at an aircraft assembly plant sometime in 1943.

For now, being a waitress was perfect for Sophia. It provided what she had been craving—contact with people far away from the mountains of Elk Valley.

Their first place was a rundown rooming house crawling with bugs, and the girls soon tired of sitting up all night, smashing insects with their shoes. One of Sophia's coworkers suggested a clean and pest-free hotel for women called The Biltmore, which let rooms for $25 per month.

After working hours, they hung out at Krause's Café, a bar notable for its black boogie-woogie band. Although she had been raised on gospel and country music, Sophia quickly became a jazz devotee. She and Mildred would sit at a table drinking 2% beer and tapping their feet. "This is the only kind of music, "Sophia would say. "It really drives me wild."

Sophia got to know Curley Shearer, a Negro horn player in the band, and would often make special music requests after tipping him a quarter. Sometimes she would dance, and she cut a striking figure on the floor, with her smooth, ivory skin and golden hair cascading down her back like fire in the wind.

She was young and pretty, and she liked a good time. She attracted male admirers, but Sophia was no lady of jelly virtue. She hadn't "been around"—only nearby. Nor did it seem she caused any problems with her after-hours cavorting.

But those who flee temptation often leave a forwarding address.

By April, 1943, both girls were dating men they had met at Krause's. Mildred had just become engaged to Butch Bowling, and Sophia was keeping company with Butch's roommate Jack Helton.

The four of them took a trip to Flemingsburg, Kentucky, in mid-April. Springtime in the mountains reminded the girls that it was almost a year since they had left Elk Valley. Sophia told

Sophia Baird, Cumberland Falls, Kentucky—1942

Sophia relaxes at Cumberland Falls, just weeks moving to the Queen City's urban jungle.

Mildred she was having a wonderful time. "I love it here," she gushed. "I could stay here forever."

On the way back to Cincinnati, Sophia turned gloomy. She confided to Mildred that she didn't want to return to the Biltmore. When asked why, Sophia blurted, "I'm afraid!"

Mildred had never heard her friend talk this way. Sophia always made jokes rather than discuss her problems. "Tell me," Mildred demanded. "What are you afraid of?"

"I don't know," was Sophia's puzzling response. "I'm just afraid."

After returning to their room, Sophia became ill. Pale and shaking, she lay on the bed, moaning, "I feel sick." Then she uttered words that got Mildred's attention: "Something's going to happen," Sophia sobbed. "I'm not going to live very long."

Sophia finally quieted down and went to sleep. The next morning she felt fine.

But Mildred later recalled a disturbing detail from their trip. During a sing along at the home of Butch Bowling's parents, Sophia had repeatedly requested one song: "Death, Oh Death."

On Saturday, April 24 Sophia worked the breakfast shift at the Purple Cow. It was the day before Easter, and she was looking forward to a Sunday off.

Mildred lay in bed while Sophia dressed for work. "I envy you," she said to her roommate. "You get to stay in bed and sleep."

Shafts of daylight worked their way across the bare floor, marking the sun's progress on a beautiful spring morning. Mildred opened her eyes to slits and saw Sophia looking at her before she walked out the door.

She would always remember her last glimpse of Sophia's face. Her friend's girlish charm had evolved into a profound beauty, yet her eyes seemed to be pleading for something beyond her reach.

Mildred took the evening shift at the Purple Cow. When she started work at 5PM, Sophia had already left. The restaurant was packed with folks not bothering to cook on Easter Eve. At about 7PM, the manager asked Mildred to call Sophia and persuade her to return to work.

Sophia's voice was languid. "I'm so tired. I'm drinking a Coke. I'm going to finish it, and then I'm going to bed." She lay on her bed fully dressed, and was sound asleep by 10:30PM.

Her neighbor across the hall came over at around 11PM. Ruth Combs needed to borrow an iron to press her Sunday best and knew Sophia well enough to wake her. Sophia found the iron and then fell face first back onto the bed. When Ruth returned around 11:15PM, she didn't wake Sophia. She set the iron down softly and borrowed some ink to write a letter. As she left she turned out the light, but didn't close the open door.

It was nearly midnight in downtown Cincinnati. The din of the city had receded into the darkness, letting the night sounds take over—muted laughter from the cafes, a cool breeze wafting across the violet sky. The moon shimmered like a thin, white wheel.

In a few moments it would be Easter Sunday.

Just after 12:00, screams erupted from the Biltmore's third floor. When police arrived minutes later, they confronted an appalling scene.

Detective Bob Meldon later described what he saw. Sophia was lying in the hallway, her body leaning against the wall but sliding downward. He heard her ragged last gasp of life and saw the light fade from her eyes.

Blood was everywhere—it had exploded from her body like a geyser, the force rupturing her neck. Meldon said it was so thick the girl's features were unrecognizable. Spatters on the wall gave mute testimony to the furious struggle that had taken place.

Another cop at the scene wavered on wobbly legs as he stood above the dead girl. "I know her," he croaked. "She goes with the Negroes at Krause's café."

Cincinnati would learn of Sophia Baird's slaying on Monday morning, April 26, 1943. The *Enquirer's* lead was inflammatory: "A pretty blonde waitress was brutally stabbed and slashed to death by a Negro in a downtown hotel yesterday." From the start, the search for the shadowy black man would overwhelm the investigation.

Two witnesses saw the trespasser, whose presence in a white hotel at that hour should have raised alarm. The first was Fred Proctor, an ex-convict who lived on the Biltmore's fourth floor and was employed as a handyman. At 11:45PM he heard heavy footsteps on the stairway. Proctor was surprised, for only he and the maintenance man lived on the top floor.

He opened his door and peered over the banister. "A Negro man was coming up the steps. He was copper-colored and had a full-lip mustache." Proctor described him as about 35 years old, 5 feet 10 inches and 140 pounds, wearing a gray topcoat with black checks and a dark hat.

He demanded to know what the man wanted. "I want to see Miss Beard (sic). They want to know about getting a job at Wright's." Proctor knew Sophia and Mildred hoped to get high-paying jobs at the military plant. The man said the landlady sent him up there to find them.

That didn't ring true with Proctor. He said, "No one is up here," and sent him back down to the front desk. Proctor was puzzled over why a black man would be looking for a white girl in the middle of the night. He went down to the office and roused Ma Bezenah, but neither she nor her daughter-in-law Mary had seen the visitor.

Scratching his head, Fred Proctor went back to bed just as the clock struck midnight. "I was lying there for about ten minutes when I heard the screams." He rushed down to the third floor and encountered Sophia Baird lying against the wall outside her room. "She was flailing her arms, and I could see the blood. I knew it was a matter for the law. I telephoned police."

The second witness was Mary Bezenah. She told police the early edition of the Sunday paper had arrived just after midnight, and she was starting to read it when she heard the screams. Ma Bezenah was not alarmed. "I thought at first it was some of the girls joking or having a party. Then I said to Mary, 'Someone is screaming. It sounds like screams of terror to me.'"

They raced up the stairs, only to recoil in horror when they saw Sophia drowning in her own blood. "Mary was ahead of me," explained Ma. "I heard her shout, 'It's a Negro, Mom. A Negro is running down the back steps.'"

Mary woke her husband, Ma's son Lou, a former boxer and current heroin addict who bankrolled his habit through confidence schemes and pimping. They both pursued the prowler, yet the black man had vanished like a phantom.

Based on their eyewitnesses, investigators were running with the black intruder theory. But a woman emerged on Tuesday who gave them a different slant. Lucy Thomas was a Biltmore

MONDAY, APRIL 26, 1943. PRICE THREE CENTS

EASTER SLAYER LEAVES TRAIL OF FINGERPRINTS IN WILD FLIGHT

Fred Proctor . . . he saw the slayer.

Jack Helton, boy friend of the victim.

The hotel room where pretty Sophia Baird met death.

Sophia Baird, the Victim

Mildred Sharpe, Friend of Victim

Suspect Wearing Zoot Trousers Sought in Attack

A Negro wearing "jitterbug pants" and a green sweater was hunted Monday as the slayer of pretty Sophia Baird.

Police linked him with the brutal Biltmore Hotel Easter-morning killing after he had beaten a Mt. Auburn housewife in her home.

Both the slayer and the housewife's assailant were "copper colored" and had dark mustaches, police said.

The Mt. Auburn victim was Mrs. May McKinney, 26, of 2448 Highland avenue.

She was telephoning in her bedroom when she saw the Negro enter the door. He leered at her.

"Don't come near me," she screamed. He walked cautiously toward her, then lunged at her. She fought to the kitchen. She screamed again and he fled.

May Be Killer

"It may be the killer," police said as they checked new developments in the brutal hotel stabbing.

These included a bloody fingerprint leading from Miss Baird's hotel room.

The fingerprints showed plainly the slayer's path of escape after he slashed the blond, 20-year-old waitress to death.

They extended down the hall on the third floor of the ... building through a series of doors which led to an alley exit.

Police will match the prints with those of three other Negro suspects taken in custody Monday.

The picture of one of the suspects, whom police described as a "numbers racket figure," was identified tentatively by Fred Proctor, hotel handyman, who saw the killer flee.

The slashing death of the pretty blonde by the "Negro intruder" was a front page sensation for weeks.

guest staying in the room next to Sophia's, and she heard a man with a raspy voice arguing with Sophia just after midnight.

"The words were mumbled, and I couldn't hear what the quarrel was about," she told detectives. "They argued for about ten minutes. Finally I heard a woman's voice say, 'You bastard!' This was two seconds before I heard the first scream. I went to my door and looked out. Miss Baird was huddled in the hallway. I closed my door and heard her door slam. I heard no more."

She didn't recognize the voice, nor could she distinguish it as a white or black man. Her lack of concern for Sophia might have been fear—her statement that Sophia's door slammed indicated that the killer remained in the room for several minutes.

Despite having provided critical timeline evidence, Lucy Thomas just faded away. Nothing from her turned up in the case file or follow-up newspaper articles.

Yet grisly details of Sophia's murder continued to emerge on the front pages. The fatal blow was a savage knife thrust to the neck which severed her jugular vein. There was a deep wound at the base of her skull, her face was slashed, and she had defensive wounds on both hands. Her bed was drenched with blood.

The coroner conjectured that the killer may have been a sadist, wielding a razor that he took with him. He had strewn the contents of her purse across the bed, ransacked her bureau, and had even taken the time to carve the letter "M" on her hand.

The blood trail began on the bed, smeared the door, and spattered the hallway. Bloody fingerprints dappled the slayer's escape route. They extended down the third floor hallway, smudged the staircase banister, and left a curious path through winding hallways and empty rooms to the back exit.

What about the Biltmore's back exit? The rear stairway could be reached only through one of the apartments. This passage was not marked, and only Biltmore staff knew about it. Even after finding it, someone would have to get past an unmarked shed door before reaching the alley.

That maze of doors leading to the back exit was a problem for Detective Walter Hart. He was a smart cop—the logistics of the rear door told him the killer knew the Biltmore quite well.

Within days Sophia's lifestyle became the hub of the investigation and her links to black men were the spokes. How did the Negro know her name and address? How could he know she had a roommate? Proctor stressed that the man seemed familiar with the girls and their job-hunting at Wright's.

Mildred Sharpe confirmed that Sophia often "chatted" with Negro musicians and tipped them to play special tunes, although

Woman Tells Of Talk Heard In Room Next To Slain Girl's

An argument in the hotel room of Miss Sophia Baird, 20 years old, preceded the murder early Sunday of the pretty blond Elk Valley, Tenn., farm girl at the Biltmore Hotel, 24 East Eighth Street, detectives told Chief Clem Merz yesterday.

Key witness Lucy Thomas was ignored after her initial interview with police.

she denied knowing of any who ever leered at Sophia or made improper advances. Other waitresses were asked if they saw Sophia do anything "which might have caused a Negro to believe that the girl had no qualms about racial barriers."

There was also the phone call Sophia received on the evening of her murder. Maintenance man Leroy Hall called her to the phone, but the party hung up before she took the call. Hall, a black man, was certain the caller was a Negro.

A man named Puckett had seen three black men loitering near the Biltmore hotel late Saturday night, all well-dressed with full mustaches, just as Fred Proctor had described the intruder. When they suddenly left in an automobile, Puckett followed their car until he lost it in the suburbs.

Black musicians, white boyfriends, and street dwellers were rounded up for questioning, yet the witnesses failed to identify anyone. Police could not connect any of the suspects to Sophia's murder.

On Tuesday, another woman was attacked near downtown, and detectives tentatively linked it to the Baird slaying. Mrs. May McKinney was in her home when a black man walked in the door and glowered at her. “Don’t come near me!” she screamed, and when he lunged at her she fought back. He began tearing her clothing as they battled, and as she continued to scream he broke off the attack and fled through her back yard.

She described him as between 35-40 years old, with a light complexion and full mustache, wearing a green sweater and “jitterbug” pants. The description tallied with that of the Biltmore assailant. There was apprehension that a Negro maniac might be loose in Cincinnati, but within days Baird investigators concluded that McKinney’s attacker was not Sophia’s killer.

Both Fred Proctor and May McKinney looked at several black suspects and failed to identify them. This was becoming a habit with the abruptly cautious Proctor.

As hordes of black men were rousted and paraded in lineups, Sophia Baird’s family quietly claimed her body. Her father told police that he had eleven children, and none of them had ever caused him any problems. He and his wife were devastated by the violent fate of their daughter after only ten months in the big city.

They took her back to Elk Valley for burial.

The case lay dormant for a week before detectives landed their first challenging suspect—a light skinned 23-year-old black man who claimed to be part Cherokee. He lived across the street from the Biltmore, he had worked at the Purple Cow when Sophia first started there, and he was now an instructor at Wright’s Aeronautical, where Sophia and Mildred were looking to work.

The circumstantial evidence was compelling. The man was seen with Sophia in a Walnut Hills café the night before her death, and a hat found in the alley behind the hotel was a perfect fit. When a switchblade was found during a search of his room, he was arrested on suspicion and held for questioning.

Detectives noted his reputation for becoming abusive when drunk and his inability to remember things he’d done after sobering up. Waitresses at the Purple Cow said that he acted "fresh" with them and would grab their hands or pinch them.

The suspect's landlady came forward, telling police that he had bragged about visiting Sophia often. One of her friends at the hotel confirmed she had dated this man, "but Sophia broke up with him a few weeks ago and he was pretty mad about the whole thing." The suspect even admitted that he was angry when Sophia "gave him the gate." Yet he denied slashing her to death.

A check with Charleston, West Virginia, authorities revealed his violent background. While living there he'd threatened two women, telling one he would "cut her head off" if she went with any other man. The other said he had flashed a knife several times and promised to cut her throat.

"The murder has not been solved," Detective Hart stressed, denying rumors of a confession. "I wish it were true."

Proctor and Mary Bezenah said he "resembled" the mysterious intruder, but neither of them would positively identify him. This unnamed suspect was eventually released.

In July the case appeared to crack wide open.

A Negro musician, Earnest "Curley" Shearer, was arrested after forcing a white girl into his hotel room. He was the former drummer for the Krause Café jazz band, and had been overly attentive to Sophia Baird.

The girl, 19-year-old waitress Peggy Freeland, said that Shearer followed her one day and harassed her. "Under threats he made me follow him to the Seventh Street hotel," she recounted. "I was forced to stay all night, but resisted his advances. Saturday morning he met me again on the street and made me go to the room again. He locked me in both times."

It looked bad for "Curley" Shearer when the reluctant Fred Proctor fingered him as the Biltmore intruder. Mary Bezenah waffled: "That looks like him, but I'm not sure."

Shearer denied any involvement in the Baird slaying, and vehemently disputed the girl's account of her "abduction," swearing that she came there voluntarily.

Peggy Freeland had reason to be untruthful. After receiving a report of a white woman walking into a Negro hotel, the responding officer found Peggy in the room attired in a "play suit." She blurted out that she had been kidnapped, which sounded better than the truth. Shearer was arrested when he came back to the room with a bucket of beer.

It all came to nothing, because Earnest Shearer had a rock-solid alibi. Employees of Krause's Café swore that none of the band members left between midnight and the 2AM closing time—Sophia was slain shortly after midnight.

Proctor eventually backed off his ID of Shearer, and he was never able to identify any of the dozens of Negroes the cops rounded up. A former bank robber who had been paroled to the Biltmore, Proctor may have been reluctant to snitch, even though the suspects were black.

As the summer of 1943 came to a close, Baird investigators drained their parched leads and simmered in the heat of their exasperation.

A decade passed. In 1953 the *Post Times Star* published a ten-year anniversary article on the Baird case that was rampant with speculation. "The Murder in Room 29" still languished in mystery, yet police were certain Sophia Baird knew her assailant, and they believed some of her friends did too.

They never believed the ransacking of her room to be robbery—it was as if the killer was looking for something incriminating. He also knew his way around the Biltmore. Investigators could not overlook his quick disappearance through the maze of hallways leading to the back door.

In 1956 the *Cincinnati Enquirer* included the Baird case in a series called **"Murders and Manhunts—Killer Struck in 1943 But Escaped Justice."** In an interview, one veteran cop swore that the murderer was hidden among the scores of released suspects. "It's one thing to feel certain yourself and another thing to prove it in court," he lamented.

Later that year, detectives traveled to Elk Valley upon hearing that a dying woman had confessed to the slaying. Yet the "confession" turned out to be errant gossip, and the woman had no intention of dying either.

Mildred Sharpe had mentioned her early in the 1943 investigation. This woman was from Elk Valley, and had confronted Sophia on a Cincinnati Street weeks before the murder. Apparently the man Sophia had been dating was the woman's philandering husband, and there had been a brief scuffle. But the wronged wife could prove she was not in Cincinnati on the night of the murder, and investigators had eliminated her at that time.

This episode looked like the end of the line. Yet detectives did not bury the Baird file. They yearned for that day when a flash of temper or a thirst for revenge would cause a witness to give up the killer's identity.

They could not envision that the final act would unfold two decades later.

It took one of Sophia Baird's ten siblings to revive this lifeless case in 1972.

Adrion Baird was eleven when news of his sister's murder reached their farm in Elk Valley. He remembered "the shock and pain to my family, but the message didn't come through as to the brutality of the murder itself."

There were bad memories of Sophia's wake. Adrion could still see his sister's stone face, her blonde hair styled for an Easter service that never was. He couldn't understand the stillness in the living room, the adults whispering as if they were in the presence of some great and terrible truth.

He preferred recalling the good times with Sophia: her singing when washing the dishes; her laughter while walking with friends; her kindness as she helped him with school lessons.

The last words of her eulogy still echoed in his mind: "Like the fragrance of a spring rose, her memory will permeate our lives on and on and on . . ."

Now in his forties, Adrion heard a bizarre revelation at a family reunion picnic. Sophia's body had disappeared from its grave.

In 1964, the Baird family had arranged for Sophia's remains to be moved from Elk Grove cemetery and placed beside her mother at the family plot in La Follette. They were notified in November that the relocation had been completed—and Sophia's headstone now stood beside her mother's.

When her father died in 1972 his request to be buried in his daughter's former grave was honored. The diggers were toiling when a sharp crack ripped the day to shreds. They were staring into a shattered coffin at the flawlessly preserved face of Sophia Baird, dead for 29 years. Her skin was white with deep tones of marble. Most astounding was her blonde hair, coifed and shining just as the undertaker had laid her out.

The gravediggers fled in panic. As word spread about the body in the supposedly empty grave, curious onlookers arrived to see for themselves. Legend has it that someone cut large portions of Sophia's golden hair and kept it for the "angelic power" it possessed.

As neighbors and kin gazed at her petrified face, they saw something in Sophia's frozen features—her soul was not at peace. And when the funeral home sent a crew the next morning to deal with the situation, her casket had vanished!

Upon hearing this, Adrion Baird guessed that the original burial team from 1964 had moved the body to avoid liability for failing to transport his sister's remains the first time. He vowed to begin an investigation to locate not only Sophia, but also her killer. Baird hired two retired FBI agents and retained a private detective, and he would eventually spend $20,000 and travel more than 10,000 miles in his quest.

As he delved deeper into the case, Adrion recalled how his family had fractured following Sophia's death. He had watched his parents drift apart, each blaming the other for letting their young daughter run off to Cincinnati, even though there was nothing they could have done to stop her.

Five years after the murder the questions and whispers had ceased. No one spoke of Sophia again. His parents separated, and the siblings scattered across the country, with Adrion moving to Washington State.

Murders and Manhunts--No. 3

Killer Struck in 1943, But Escaped Justice

BY PAUL LUNSFORD

It was nearly midnight in downtown Cincinnati. The night sounds of a city had taken over.

The soft swish of tires through silent streets. Too bright laughter from cafes. A shrill quarreling voice, and then a quick calming one. The scratching sweep of a street broom over concrete. The slosh of water against a curb.

It was Saturday night and in a few more minutes it would be Easter Sunday.

FRED PROCTOR wound his clock and set the alarm before getting ready for bed in his fourth floor room at the Biltmore Hotel, 24 E. Eighth street.

The hands on the clock pointed to 11:45 p. m. He put the clock beside his bed. The hotel had settled down

SOPHIA BAIRD
slain in hotel

MILDRED SHARPE
friend of victim

The *Enquirer* series "Murders and Manhunts" profiled the Baird case in 1956.

In October, 1979, Adrion received a package from Cincinnati containing the old newspaper clippings about his sister's death. Reviewing the press coverage convinced him that the original investigation had been tarnished. In 1943, encountering a black man in a white hotel at midnight should have caused an uproar. Yet Ma Bezenah and daughter-in-law Mary reacted to Proctor's report of a Negro prowler by going back to their Sunday paper. It didn't ring true.

During a visit to Cincinnati, Adrion realized just how sinister his sister's environment had been. Besides Ma's association with gambling and racketeering, her son Lou was also connected to illegal activity at the Biltmore. And he had never been officially questioned—the Bezenahs left Cincinnati the day after Sophia's murder and stayed in Kentucky for two weeks.

It all seemed shady to Adrion: The bloody trail leading to the unmarked rear exit; the reluctance of Fred Proctor and Mary Bezenah to identify any suspects; the police handling the Ma's family with kid gloves. As he investigated the Bezenahs, Adrion realized that some people were still uneasy when discussing the clan.

Within days Baird received a strange phone call at his Maryland residence. The anonymous caller asked him if he was looking into Sophia's death. When Adrion explained that he was just gathering facts, the voice warned him: "You'd better stop, because you're not going to finish it."

This threat was the last straw—perhaps he was really on to something. He thought again about how his sister's murder had destroyed his family.

Adrion Baird had suffered for 37 years. Now he wanted a reckoning, and he wouldn't stop searching until he found it.

Bob Meldon was a retired Cincinnati cop who killed three men in the line of duty and kept their morgue photos as souvenirs.

When Adrion Baird asked him to find Mary Bezenah, horrifying images flooded back of Sophia flopping like a fish as she bled out. Meldon knew Sophia by sight in 1943, and as the first officer on the scene had watched her die. He immediately agreed to help Baird.

Lead detectives Walter Hart and Tom Farager were both dead. Ma Bezenah and Fred Proctor were long gone, and Lou Bezenah had died in 1970. That left Lou's wife Mary as the last known living witness.

Notes from the case file showed that Hart regretted their early obsession with the Negro prowler—he had become convinced that Sophia was no random victim. She was an unlikely robbery target, and her clothing wasn't disturbed. And like Adrion, Hart suspected some of the hotel witnesses were less than truthful.

Hart's questions peppered the yellowing file pages. Why would a thief or rapist ask directions to his victim's room? Why would Sophia engage in a loud argument with a stranger who surprised her at midnight? Why not just yell for help? To Hart this had suggested personal motivations like vengeance or jealousy.

As he read the file, Adrion wondered about the kind of life Sophia was leading in Cincinnati. His wife warned that he might not like what he uncovered.

In late 1979 Adrion found Mildred Sharpe, running a diner in Indiana with her second husband. She had been Sophia's closest companion, yet she never contacted the family following the murder. It was obvious to Adrion that she still blamed herself for not having prevented her friend's murder.

She insisted that Sophia would not go with men for money or favors. Mildred didn't think she even had a serious boyfriend, and claimed she was a light drinker who never took anything stronger than beer.

Upon arriving at the murder scene, she recalled how detectives spewed loathsome things about Sophia and accused Mildred of despicable actions. As she stared at Sophia's blood splashed across the walls, she became convinced that the killer would now come after her.

As Adrion pressed for details concerning his sister's last days, Mildred suddenly became hazy, declaring, "I just don't remember like I should." He was certain she was repressing something only a close friend could know.

He offered to pay for a session with a hypnotist. To his surprise Mildred agreed.

While Adrion worked with Mildred, Bob Meldon struck gold. On a trail that had been cold for 37 years, Meldon unearthed a forgotten witness.

Morey Zaidins was the manager of the Gayety burlesque theater in 1943, which was right across the alley from the Biltmore. He was now close to 80, but still had his wits about him. In his day, no one was better connected than Morey. He knew everyone, and his big ears heard everything that went on for miles.

He told Meldon a story about Lou Bezenah, the junkie who managed the Biltmore for his mother. On the evening of the murder, Zaidins was standing in the alley around midnight. He had a clear view of the Biltmore's back entrance, but there was no crazed black man bolting out the door.

Instead, he saw Lou Bezenah, sauntering out and moving briskly down the alley toward Vine Street.

When he learned about the murder minutes later, Zaidins began to panic. He went to the cops and was greeted with shrugs. He told Meldon that after a few days the investigation went "hush-hush." But Morey heard enough to draw some conclusions. "There was a lot of beefing because they didn't take Lou and question him. A detective made a crack that Lou was so full of junk, they'd only have to hold him 24 hours, and he would tell them anything to get a fix."

Zaidins also remembered what other Biltmore women had been saying in the weeks before the murder—that Lou was crazy about the little country girl named Sophia.

Mildred Sharpe's hypnosis sessions had indeed unlocked her memory, throwing a harsh light on Sophia Baird. When Adrion first asked if Sophia might be involved in prostitution, Mildred was positive that she was "not that kind of girl." Yet certain aspects of her suppressed recall suggested otherwise.

Sophia sometimes stayed out late, saying she'd been "with some friends." Mildred observed that she often had new leather shoes and fashionable clothing that were hard to acquire in wartime. Sophia would say, "A friend got them for me."

Once while they were walking, a carload of men accosted Sophia and called her over to their automobile. They spoke for a few minutes, and as Sophia walked away one of the men yelled, "You'd better be there!" When Mildred asked what they wanted, Sophia said they were "just some friends."

Mildred then told another disturbing story, a tale so weird and murky that it seemed more dream than remembrance.

While waiting for Sophia at a cafe one evening, a couple walked in and told her that "Sophia couldn't make it." They claimed she was fine, and invited Mildred back to their apartment.

There they gave her a drink, and a dazzling light ignited behind her eyes. Just before she passed out, she heard the man say, "She wouldn't be any good at it."

When Mildred awoke it was morning. The strange couple was gone.

Sophia's forewarning of her own death still haunted Mildred. Adrion asked her if someone had assaulted Sophia in the hotel. Could it have been Lou Bezenah? Sophia had complained to several girls that Lou was bothering her, and his unwanted attentions were increasing.

Without pointing directly to Bezenah, Sophia admitted to Mildred that she was afraid of "someone."

Bob Meldon was not expecting Mary Bezenah to cooperate.

No longer a slender beauty, Mary was now a fat old lady still living in Cincinnati. She'd married Lou when she was 15 and he was 35. Although he'd been dead nine years, her loyalty never wavered.

Meldon told her about Adrion's quest. He urged her to "tell me the story on it." Mary knew where he was going. She stood up and yelled, "There is no story on it! There never was!"

Meldon left her tiny apartment convinced she was a liar.

Over the next few months in 1980 he returned a dozen times, usually with a six-pack. Unaware of the small cassette recorder in his pocket, after a few beers Mary would become more talkative. But she always stuck to her story of the Negro intruder.

Contradictions to her 1943 statement began to surface. Instead of her and Ma running up the stairs, Mary now said the portly Ma "couldn't run if her life depended on it." She also claimed she and Proctor searched for the intruder before hearing the screams—Meldon wondered why they hadn't they started with Sophia's room?

Baird and Meldon pored over their taped transcripts, looking for any strand that might unravel Mary's story. According to her, Lou had slept through the entire episode, whereas in 1943 he had supposedly pursued the black man out the back entrance.

Time can erode even a good memory. But whether Mary was rehashing her original account or challenging it, her confidence was unshakable.

Meldon was certain he could exploit her coolness under pressure. He visited Mary one more time and went for broke.

He told her about Adrion's $10,000 reward, and he promised that no one could be prosecuted at this late date.

Mary cut to the chase: "Lou was a good con man. But even if I'd seen him do it, I wouldn't tell."

"How much would you tell it for?" Meldon taunted. "$500,000?"

"Not for anything," Mary replied. "I will never tell it."

She died two years later of natural causes. Her lawyer stated, "With her death, the final chapter of the Sophia Baird matter seems to have been written." Adrion refused to accept this. He was certain Mary had been lying, and he believed the hotel workers had conspired to protect the killer. But the motive still eluded him—why had his sister been slain?

He would later tell his story to *Enquirer* reporter Tom Shroder, who ran a five-part serial on the case entitled, "Visions of Sophia." Yet even that provided no closure. Adrion's last image of his sister was the marbled hue of her face during the wake.

Her body and her soul were still wandering.

SUMMATION:

In his autobiography, *My Long Journey Home,* Adrion Baird had this to say about his sister's murder: "I concluded that someone living in the hotel committed the murder. However, I could not establish a motive."

The obscure black prowler who bluffed his way into a white hotel to cut a blonde girl's throat is the stuff of legend. It was

Chapter 1: Visions Of Sophia

Sophia Baird, a pretty 20-year-old waitress, was murdered in Cincinnati on Easter Sunday 41 years ago. The murder was never solved. For a time the case claimed the avid attention of the press, but when police were unable to solve the puzzle of her final days, Sophia Baird was all but forgotten. Until 1978. Spurred by the mysterious reappearance of Sophia Baird's corpse in a Tennessee cemetery, Adrion Baird set out to answer the questions that had plagued his family for 36 years. The story of Sophia's life and death, and her brother's search for the truth, have been reconstructed from contemporary newspaper accounts, documents, letters, and the memories of those still living. The memories of one particularly important source had been committed to tape shortly before her death. Enquirer reporter Tom Shroder has drawn on detail provided by these sources to describe the scenes.

Elk Fork Cemetery,
Elk Valley, Tenn., 1972

TWO HUNDRED MILES southeast of Cincinnati, in a level clearing carved from an old pine grove, the gravediggers began to sweat. The sun was hot for May, and the joking subsided as they bent to their work, filling the silence with the ringing crunch of shovels breaking limestone and the thud of heavy soil.

The hole bored into the secret darkness, then, with a sharp crack, ripped the afternoon to splinters.

The unfortunate man wielding the shovel dropped it as if it had come alive in his hands. Instead of further darkness, he found himself staring into a shattered casket at the perfectly preserved face of a young woman, dead for 28 years.

Her skin was white touched with deep tones of gray, like marble. Later, when one of the curious cautiously touched the corpse, it was found to be hard, petrified by the leaching limestone. But the most astonishing thing was the blonde hair, bright and coiffed as it had been on the undertaker's table.

THE GRAVEDIGGERS, an inexperienced crew of roustabouts, threw down their tools and scrambled out of the hole across the grass to a battered pickup truck. They left in a hurry, their wheels spewing blue gravel toward the exposed remains of Sophia Baird.

All day the curious and concerned, and eventually some of Sophia's relatives, came to see for themselves whether the fantastic story was true. Local lore has it that someone invaded the grave that day, hacked large portions of golden hair from the corpse, then encased the locks in glass for the "angelic power" they contained.

In 1984, the *Enquirer* ran a 5 part series on the Baird mystery and Adrion's quest called "Visions of Sophia

spawned by the street life around the Biltmore and two witnesses with something to hide.

Mary Bezenah's interviews with Bob Meldon oozed with guilt. She had changed her story significantly from the 1943 version. Even with the passage of time a truthful person wouldn't need to recreate what had been said before. But a liar would have to remember the finer points of previous falsehoods.

Lou Bezenah was the motive, means, and opportunity perpetrator of this crime. He skulked under the radar during the entire investigation, and never even reached suspect status. Police reluctance to question him is still a stain on the case file.

Lou was a con man and a pimp took advantage of his mother's vast network. Ma Bezenah enjoyed a special status with some of Cincinnati's police and politicians. In 1943 it was easy to look the other way when your palm was being greased.

Bezenah was also a career criminal who grew up on New York's mean streets. Carrying a switchblade would have been second nature to him—and cutting up a troublesome call girl was just business.

Sophia was entangled in some sort of clandestine activity, based on the buried memories of Mildred Sharpe. Her bizarre recollection of being drugged by the couple who knew Sophia sounded like a botched hooker audition.

The fetid undertow of the Biltmore dragged many women into prostitution. Sophia was living well on her waitress's tips. The fancy clothes, the new shoes, and the late hours—she was at best a paid escort for discerning clients.

Lou went to Sophia's room that night looking for sexual favors. Sophia had confided to several friends that he had been "bothering" her, and others saw that Lou was "crazy about his country girl."

The Bezenah clan fled the Biltmore the day after the murder and stayed away for two weeks. Yet no one questioned this lax supervision of three material witnesses. By the time they returned, the hunt for the Negro prowler had overwhelmed the investigation.

Fred Proctor and Mary Bezenah didn't have time to jell their stories, and these discrepancies would puzzle investigators. Their failure to identify any of the legions of black men paraded before them was significant—they wouldn't even finger a Negro on false pretense for this crime.

EPILOGUE:

The Biltmore Hotel is long gone—the Cincinnati Public Library now occupies the entire downtown block between 8th and 9th street.

But the nightmare of Sophia's death remained, resounding through a sprawling city of displaced persons. She was enchanted and tortured by what lay just beyond her reach. She wanted far more than what she had out of life—coveting bright lights, hopping jazz, fine dresses, delicious dinners, and happy laughter.

Her fairy tale had a tragic ending—a pale, drained girl lying on a slab in the city morgue, her pretty face and soft blonde hair drenched with her own blood.

Sophia Baird was taken back to peaceful Elk Valley and buried in the tiny family plot. She returned to the home she had so desperately wanted to leave. But in death, her restless soul and petrified body conspired to escape the grave.

Her killer eluded justice—at least from this earthly court.

POSTSCRIPT: OCTOBER 2009

When contacted by the author earlier this year, Adrion Baird was eager to talk about his sister's murder. The case still curves and meanders through his mind's eye, abounding with episodes of police conspiracy and sinister transgression.

Here is just a sampling of his cryptic commentary:

"I have been told by several sources that James Baird (no relation) killed Sophia—He died last month at the age of 89 . . . James Baird was arrested by the Cincinnati Police and interrogated. He was released due to lack of evidence. But the rumors persisted and still do."

"The murder was covered up from the beginning . . . Any fool would conclude, given the social position of Negroes at that time, that handyman would have gone ballistic at the sight of a Negro in any hotel, especially the Biltmore since it was billed as a place for women to live during the War."

"Sophia was not involved in any escort service or the like. The autopsy report reported she was a virgin."

"Many merchants told me Sophia would come into their stores and browse. One elderly man told me: 'When she would come into my store, I could not keep my eyes off her; her beautiful blond hair, blue eyes and fair skin just knocked me winding.'"

"Two of the black band members called me and told me that all that 'shit' the police put together about a 'Negro' killing Sophia was all wrong. They told me Sophia was a perfect lady who liked to listen to their band and would tip them on occasions.

"The Cincinnati Police were totally uncooperative. They treated me as if I was a fly on their lapels: 'Go away—the case is too old and you are wasting our time.'"

"It was absolutely crazy to allow Lou, Mary and others to go on vacations while no solid leads could be found. Ma Bezenah made sure no members of her hotel staff would be implicated."

"Mildred put out those stories about Sophia in an attempt to take suspicion away from her because she was afraid for her life if she told the truth . . . I am convinced that Mildred Sharpe knew who killed Sophia. The investigators told me they were sure that Mildred knew much more than she would tell them."

Adrion Baird is an elite investigator who knows more about this case than anyone alive (unless the killer is still with us). Yet even he cannot navigate the blind alleys of Sophia's murder maze.

And as a man of strong faith, he will admit that his sister's death became an irreparable crack in the foundation of his soul.

I asked him one final question: Was Sophia's body ever found?

The pain of 65 years was engraved into his reply: "Beneath her gravestone there are only a few unidentified bones. There was no skull. The mystery remains."

I WITNESS:

Lou inserts the spike into his vein. He'd shot some horse earlier that night, but the junk wasn't pure. He scrounged it from some spade hophead in the back alley—they usually had good shit. Now he needs to double tap just to take the edge off. A shot in the arm in both a literal and a figurative sense.

He's still strung out. Sweating buckets, with tiny bugs festering under his skin. Almost midnight—yet he's too wired to sleep.

His thoughts drift to Sophia. That's one filly he'd love to parlay. The little country girl is bona fide whistle bait. Watching her sashay around the hotel really puts him into a twist. And seeing the way those "eight balls" eye her on the street infuriates him.

Lou leaves his first floor room and heads for the stairway. Ma and Mary are in the office, poring over the racing forms in the paper. He knows they'll be at it for a while.

He's going to pay that little gal a visit. Show her who runs this place. As Lou mounts the stairs toward the third floor, he pats the switchblade in his pocket.

Sophia is sound asleep, dreaming. She's walking the bluffs of Elk Valley, its cool, fresh mountain breezes ruffling her hair. The sun casts a shower of vivid golden dust, painting the meadows with a blaze of summer.

Melvin is standing there, his smile as easy and familiar as on the July day they said farewell. He extends his hand to her, and Sophia can see the promise of deliverance in his eyes.

Suddenly, the sky goes dark as a massive shadow douses the landscape, and the air turns muggy and fetid. Melvin becomes a grotesque, smirking goblin.

Sophia jolts awake to find Lou's face inches from hers. He is on the bed, straddling her, his eyes wild yet remote. "What are you doing here?" she hisses, instinctively sliding away from him.

The heroin is kicking in—Lou feels both dazed and agitated. "I want what those juke joint niggers get," he flares back at her, "and I ain't paying for it!"

Her shrill laughter unnerves him. He can feel his energy leaking through his feet, his power over her ebbing like the ocean's tide.

When Sophia rejects his advances and threatens to tell Mary, Lou explodes into a quivering rage. Jealousy, fear of exposure, and a desire for revenge all converge. He pulls out the knife.

"You bastard!" Her shriek sparks the haze of his mind into flame. The blade carving up her alabaster flesh is just another mirage—her screams sound as if she is underneath a waterfall. Her body is swollen, sunken, her great, gaping wounds spouting crimson geysers. Somehow she manages to stagger into the hallway, where she slumps to the hardwood floor.

Lou snaps out of his fog and begins to search her room, ransacking her purse and dresser, looking for anything and nothing. Knowing the Biltmore like the back of his hand, he calmly navigates the tricky rear exit, oblivious to the bloody trail oozing in his wake.

And unaware that his wife Mary and Fred Proctor see him leaving the third floor hallway, where Sophia now lies propped against the wall, dying.

2009

56 years ago, Apple was killed after leaving this corner drugstore and passing the church.

THE MAN WHO KNEW TOO MUCH

ODA APPLE SHOT DOWN NEAR HIS HOME: 1953

"It is worse than a crime, it is a blunder."

Antoine Boulay de la Meurthe

PROLOGUE:

The gunshot that killed Oda Apple left a ringing in the city's ears that never faded. No man could ever again take his son for an evening stroll without wondering: "Is it safe?"

This motiveless slaying of a husband and father, gunned down a few doors from his own home, echoed with the random temperament of fate. But for Oda, a man who encountered his own grim premonition the week before, it was simply destiny.

NARRATIVE:

The harbinger of death was hovering over 45-year-old Oda K. Apple.

It began one day at work in the late winter of 1951. As his boss looked on in disbelief, Oda started to repair an adding machine backwards. The once reliable typewriter repairman could not explain his sudden stupor.

Assuming Apple was ill, the boss sent him home, where Oda threw himself into bed and slept for twenty hours. His wife Mabel became alarmed. When Oda finally awoke, a dreadful confusion grappled with his mind, and his vision began to swim.

His life of quiet desperation was now unbearably noisy. Time lost all meaning. Oda watched as the wanton hours flew by, his eyes rapt yet remote.

He was riding the wings of madness.

Oda became a stranger to his own family, as his increasingly irrational behavior defied logic and flouted reality. He would sit in front of the TV for hours, sunken in a deepening despair. He didn't seem to know his 3-year-old son Kenny, and Mabel began to worry that Oda might actually harm the boy.

For the next year and a half he was in and out of the hospital, being treated for "nervousness." Mabel Apple soon became impatient with the pace of the treatment, and after consulting with her husband's doctors, she made the heartrending decision to have Oda committed to Longview Mental Hospital.

At first he became more depressed, resenting the doctors and ignoring the nurses. Yet when he realized they were his only hope, he shed his hostility and embraced his rehabilitation.

Every time the icy fingers of anguish began to squeeze, he recalled the uplifting words of the hospital psychiatrist: "Oda, you have responded well to treatment. We are satisfied, and you should be too. Others have resumed normal life, and there's no reason why you can't."

Finally the day arrived that Oda had waited for. He took a last walk around Ward 64, his address for the past four months. He was jubilant that his wife was taking him home for the weekend, and if things went well, he could go home for good the following week.

But was he ready for the coarse, seething world of the city, away from the comfortable routine of Longview?

Something in the darkness was stalking him, the terror magnified by a relentless foreboding. Just a week before, Oda Apple had told another patient he'd seen a vision of his own death.

It was the summer of 1953. The Korean War armistice had been signed in late July. Earlier that spring, Russia had both grieved and celebrated the death of despot Josef Stalin. On the home front, Americans were enjoying the advent of color

TV, and American men were enjoying a new magazine called *Playboy*, featuring Marilyn Monroe on its first cover.

Decades later, this era would be dubbed an all-too-brief age of innocence—unless one remembered a murder which left everyone in Cincinnati shaking their heads.

Oda Apple returned home on Thursday night, August 6, to 3123 Hackberry Street in Walnut Hills. While he played with Kenny, a bouncing, blue-eyed tot, Mabel prepared his favorite meal of veal cutlets. Oda ate like a man possessed, and afterwards he and Kenny watched TV. It was a normal family evening.

Oda was self-conscious about his illness. He was doing well, but felt more at ease away from curious stares, so on Friday and Saturday he stayed in and caught up on his reading. He still had fleeting thoughts of the nameless thing lurking behind him.

On Saturday night, August 8, the Apple family enjoyed another splendid dinner. They talked about going to the movies, but Oda preferred to stay home and watch TV. He was thinking about returning to Longview early Monday, hopefully for the last time.

Mabel was washing dishes around 9PM when her head began to throb. She gave her husband a dollar and asked him to go to the drug store for some aspirin. Kenny jumped up, eager to tag along, and soon father and son were walking down Hackberry Street, hand in hand beneath an evening sky of dying violet.

They turned left on Fairfax Avenue and entered Wolliver's corner drug store. Oda bought a bottle of Anacin and pocketed the change. He said goodnight to the clerks and walked out. Outside the door was a penny weight machine, so Oda lifted Kenny onto it, and his son laughed delightedly as the big needle swung around to mark his weight. "Big boy!" he declared proudly.

It was now dark, except where street lights spread their amber pools across the parched pavement. On the sidewalk shadows hung like curtains. Kenny clung to his father's hand, still chattering about the penny scale.

A few autos were parked in the street, but none of the residents were on their porches—a recent break in the heat wave sent folks back inside to watch their television sets in comfort.

They were almost home, passing 3133 Hackberry where the Reverend Steinman lived, when a single gunshot pierced the neighborhood stillness. Oda staggered, tried to regain his footing, and then pitched forward onto the sidewalk. A bullet had severed his spinal cord.

Kenny screamed in terror, and ran home panting and sobbing. Mabel heard his cries and rushed outside. "Where's Daddy? What happened?" she demanded, hugging Kenny to her chest.

"The firecrackers got Daddy." And with this innocent pronouncement, the strange case of Oda Apple waylaid the city of Cincinnati.

Mabel ran to her fallen husband and lifted his head. His neck was soaked with blood—she knew he was dead. Within minutes cops flooded the scene, confronted by "a murder without motive" that would become one of the Queen City's most unfathomable mysteries.

It was a night of unhinged emotion. Detectives pulverized the pavement, hammered on doors, and flung questions at sleepy residents until dawn.

Several people had heard the shot but dismissed it as an automobile's backfire. The best ear witness proved to be Jane Breen of 3127 Hackberry. Senses sharpened by a long bout of invalidism, she gave this account: "When I heard the bang I knew it was a shot. Then I heard the sound of feet running past the house. I can still hear them running—it was a man, I'm sure. Then I heard Kenny scream."

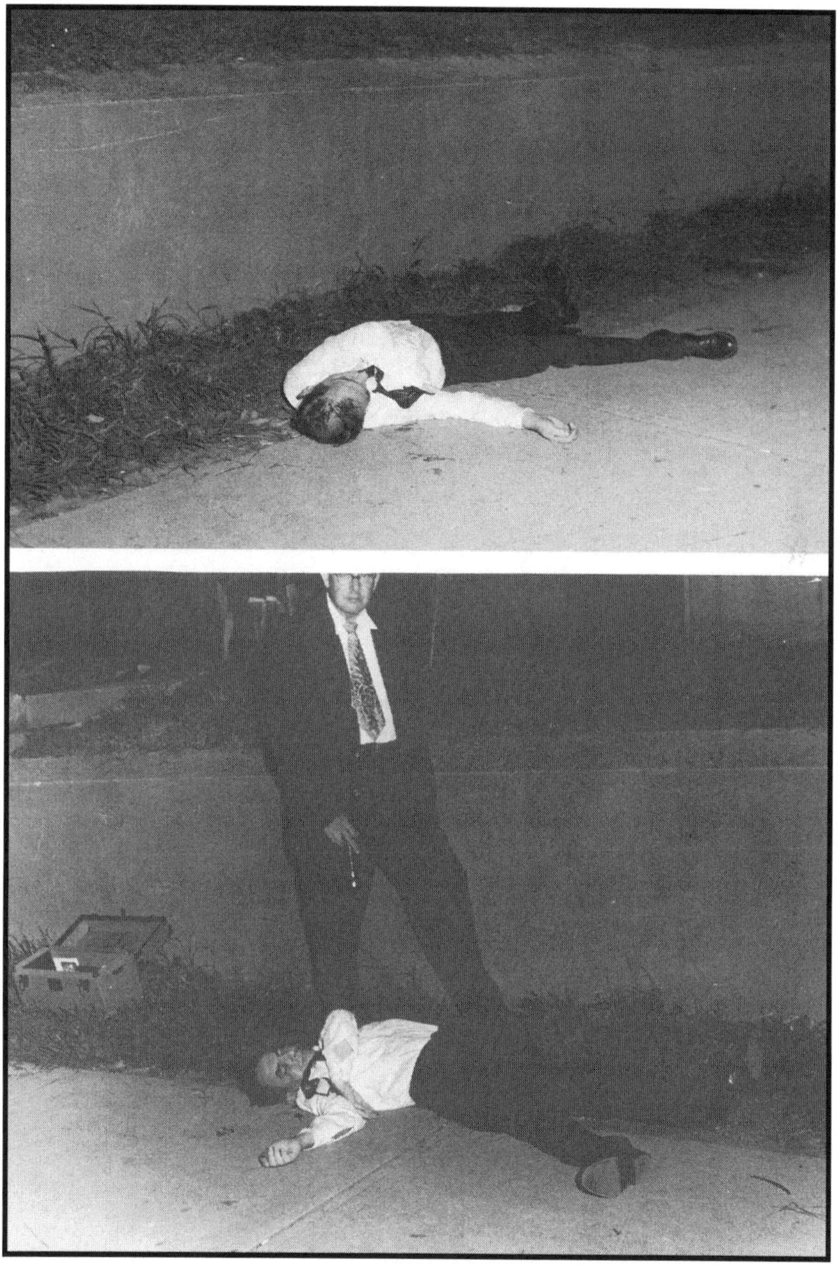

Dead before he hit the ground, Oda was shot through the neck just two doors away from his home.

Between fits of crying, young Kenny was able to say that his father didn't meet or talk with anyone going to and from the drugstore. Police weren't ready to draw that conclusion. As one veteran cop said that night, "A conclusion is where you get tired of thinking."

Neighbors described Oda as a likable guy "who minded his own business and seemed a devoted family man." Mabel Apple, fighting for composure, assured police that her husband had no enemies—she was certain the shooting was accidental.

By noon Sunday detectives fleshed out a trio of scenarios:

- Apple was murdered intentionally from ambush.
- He was the victim of a mistaken identity slaying.
- He was killed by a random gunshot.

Ballistic and coroner reports were inconclusive. The fatal slug was a .38 caliber fired from an ancient gun with an indistinct rifling pattern. A zip gun or another homemade weapon was not ruled out.

There were no powder burns, suggesting the killer was at least three feet away and possibly farther. Yet tests showed "the bullet had a significant amount of force," indicating a close range shooting. Detectives believed the shot came from one of three locations: between two trees at 3133 Hackberry, from behind a parked car, or from the rear of the church at the corner.

The coroner discounted a rumor that the bullet ricocheted, because the wound was not consistent with the ragged hole a glancing bullet would have left. This bullet tore an upward course from the neck before lodging in the victim's brain. Oda Apple died before he hit the pavement.

Investigators were left with a vexing question: Did the silent war inside Oda's head somehow contribute toward his death? They were doubtful, but several went to Longview hospital anyway, trying to dig up one of the usual motives for murder.

Hackberry Avenue in 1953—the killer targeted Oda from somewhere within the photo at top. He had just passed the car in both photos when he was shot.

The bigger question: How could a man living in virtual obscurity be shot down two doors from his home for no apparent reason?

Within days the Oda Apple case assumed a hazy hue. There was no buzz on the street, and even police informants were clueless. The Longview visit was a dead end—Apple was a model patient with no enemies there. One man claimed Oda was having trouble with a fellow inmate just before he left, but the story didn't pan out.

The rumor about Apple's death omen, however, had substance. Just days before his release, Oda told a patient, "Something is going to happen to me." He was acting nervous, but refused to say who or what he feared. This man had forgotten the conversation until reading about the murder.

The psychiatric evaluation described Apple as one "who wears a fixed somber expression on his face. At times he appeared apprehensive and at other times relatively unconcerned. His stream of speech was marked by occasional confusion and distortion."

Investigators had learned other details from the report that they didn't share with the press. Most startling was the initial diagnosis: paresis, also known as a long bout of untreated syphilis. Oda had a gut feeling about his condition for many years, but declined treatment until his mind started to deteriorate.

While they winnowed down their three theories, people on Hackberry Street left no doubt about their feelings. Residents feared that a wolf was loose. Doors were suddenly locked, porch lights blazed, and children fled to their homes at dusk.

On Tuesday Coroner Hebert P. Lyle labeled the Oda Apple shooting a homicide. He qualified this by insisting the unknown identity of the shooter made homicide a mandatory ruling. If police later proved Apple's killing was not intentional, Lyle had the authority to change the verdict to accidental death. When asked about his personal belief, Lyle opined that Apple was slain in a close range ambush that was the result of mistaken identity.

Page 4 — THE CINCINNATI POST, WEDNESDAY, AUGUST 26, 1953.

Mystery Deepens as Slaying Is Studied

ODA K. APPLE
. . . victim of bullet

"THERE"
. . . Don Roney, Kenny Apple

APPLE HOME, 3123 HACKBERRY STREET
. . . death was a visitor here

—Post Photos by Robert Stigers.

SLAYINNG SCENE ON HACKBERRY STREET
. . . the shadows were deep here

MABEL APPLE
. . . life shattered

WOLIVER'S DRUG STORE
. . . last stop

The *Post* tried to roust some clues with this montage of the people and places during the second week of the investigation.

Several early leads seemed to back this up. George Lindsay claimed his wife was "running around with some fellow" and they "had trouble about it." Lindsay lived in the neighborhood and had a small child—he thought "the fellow" had mistakenly shot Apple while really trying to kill him.

The wife of a Cincinnati cop dished some juicy hearsay. A friend of hers named Mrs. Justice had confided that Mr. Justice believed Oda Apple was "fooling around" with their teenage daughter. Her father's .38 caliber revolver disappeared around the time of the killing, and she "believed her husband might have shot Apple."

The Justice family had lived one block over on Hackberry, and they suddenly moved away weeks after the murder. But detectives couldn't place Mr. Justice at the murder scene, and this promising tip fizzled.

Anthony Pandilidis, another neighbor on Hackberry, saw a suspicious man cross his driveway on the night of the murder. He said the stranger climbed his fence and headed towards the drugstore about 20 minutes before the shooting.

Oda's 20-year-old daughter Mary described a weird man who came to their house after the murder. He claimed to be a Seventh Day Adventist, yet Mary said he "acted funny about her father's death."

Mary also wondered aloud if her husband might be involved. He was a marine stationed in California, and their marriage was wavering. She speculated that he was on leave and had shot her father to get even with her.

On Wednesday a woman injected herself into the case. She had seen the shooting from her car, and watched Oda Apple stagger and fall. Detectives were elated—they now had an eyewitness to the murder.

Mrs. Rocky Carmosina was a Columbus resident who had been visiting her family on nearby Dexter Street. They were engaged in a drunken party, and she eventually left in disgust to get something to eat. Nearly running the traffic signal at Hackberry and Fairfax, she braked and looked sharply south on Hackberry for approaching traffic.

"I looked up Hackberry Street, where I saw a man and a boy." Mrs. Carmosina described how "the man suddenly whirled and fell" and how Kenny ran to fetch his mother. She did not hear the shot fired, but she did confirm there were no other pedestrians nearby or cars speeding away from the scene.

Within days the excitement over this witness would wane, because Carmosina had skeletons in her own closet. She was returned to Cincinnati under arrest, and was indicted on charges of stealing TV sets and furniture valued at over $2000.

Cops were already wary of her story. She claimed to be sober, but everyone at her family's house was drunk when the shooting went down. Her polygraph test was deemed inconclusive—

Slain Man Had Premonition Of Danger, Enquirer Learns

Police Lack Clue And Motive In Fatal Shooting Of Apple; Lean To Stray Bullet Theory

Lack of clues and a motive for the slaying Saturday night of Oda K. Apple, 45, 3123 Hackberry St., led officials last night to a theory that the victim may have been struck by a wild shot from a passing automobile, or even shot by mistake.

Mr. Apple was killed when a .38 caliber bullet struck him in the nape of his neck as he walked with his son, Kenneth, 3, in front of 3133 Hackberry St. They were returning home from a trip to a nearby Woodburn Avenue drugstore when the shot was fired.

Police said a careful check of the man's friends and associates failed to reveal a motive for a slaying. Officials at Longview Hospital, where he had been an inmate for a short time, said Mr. Apple was a model patient and had no known enemies there.

Detectives confirmed Oda's prediction of his own death when they interviewed fellow patients at Longview Mental Hospital.

among the questions asked were, "Did your husband Rocky shoot Mr. Apple?" and "Was he shooting at you instead?" After considering her sworn statement, investigators cut her loose, realizing she had nothing more to give them.

They were at odds over the case. Some favored the mistaken identity killing over the accidental shooting scenario. By Thursday, two distinct theories were locked in:

- Oda Apple was murdered by "a teenage gunman" who "had it in for another neighborhood resident," someone who would ordinarily walk Hackberry around 9PM on most nights.
- Apple was killed accidentally by a "stray or wild" bullet fired from a makeshift "pistol range" two doors down from the shooting.

Jane Breen had heard "a man" run past her house immediately after the shot, and she remained certain the footsteps were those of an adult. Her account dovetailed nicely with the mistaken ambush supposition.

Yet a wave of vandalism along Hackberry buttressed the accidental shooting premise. There were complaints about a gang of boys firing cap pistols and firecrackers after dark. Two false alarms were turned in from a nearby firebox, "Hot-rodder's" were racing up and down the street, and some parked cars had been tampered with. Detectives canvassed the neighborhood to root out this "bad gang of juveniles."

Some arrests were made, but that basement pistol range was never found.

Mabel Apple kept close tabs on the investigation. Convinced that her husband was murdered but baffled by the motive, she kept Kenny near her at all times. "We are watching the boy very closely," she wept. "Maybe he might recognize the slayer, and some harm might come to him."

Several psychiatrists from General Hospital interviewed Kenny, hoping to unlock his three-year-old mind. But he just repeated what he said earlier: No one spoke to them during their walk, and that "the firecrackers got Daddy."

As the investigation trudged into its second week, detectives were still split on whether the slaying was a tragic accident or a malevolent crime.

They had learned early on that Oda Apple was not someone to be marked for murder. He appeared to be a quiet and inoffensive man, not one who inspired the brand of passion required for killing.

Yet further information from his psychiatric report seemed to contradict this.

In a memorandum to detective Eugene Moore, the reason given for Oda's admission to the mental hospital was "because of a family situation that had arisen." His daughter Mary was pregnant by her husband in California, and she became quite ill and needed her mother's help. The memo also referred to a "violent quarrel" between Oda and his daughter in May of 1952. Both of them had been injured during the altercation.

But it was the final paragraph that astonished detectives: "There is no indication he had any recent affairs with women. In his talks with the psychologist he stated that many years ago when he worked at a West Virginia bakery he had some fifty girls under him and he had intercourse with forty of them. However, he does not list any recent infidelities."

Oda Apple may have been delusional about the number of women he slept with. Nevertheless, the green eyes of adultery glimmered for investigators straining to find a motive.

For most of 1954, police received tips almost daily, but gradually they dwindled to nothing. A reward fund started after the murder was abandoned, with the money returned to donors or given to charity.

Two years later the case flickered to life in dramatic fashion.

A 20-year-old man strolled into the District Six police station, plopped into a chair and announced, "I think you want me for murder." When asked to be more specific, David Poole said, "You know, the one on Hackberry Street, something Apple."

"I guess everyone knows about the Oda Apple murder," the sergeant on duty replied, trying to remain calm. He quickly summoned two detectives to take a statement.

"His story sounded pretty good at first," said Captain Williard Elbert. "He claimed he had 'got religion' and thought he better confess it." Poole correctly placed the murder in August—he bragged that he stole a car that night and found a gun in the glove box.

But soon his story began to disintegrate. As Elbert recounted, "He told us he was driving along toying with the gun when it went off. The next day he read about the murder and threw the gun away. But then he said it happened in 1950, and three years is a big difference. Then we found out there was no report of a stolen car or gun on the murder night."

Poole readily recanted his confession. "It's all a hoax," he admitted. Elbert finished him off by saying, "There were too many discrepancies in his confession. He couldn't have done it."

Poole had been under indictment for armed robbery. While in the county jail talking to other inmates, he got a brilliant idea: "I would rather be electrocuted than spend 25 years in the pen—I'd sooner have a murder rap against me."

As he was taken downtown for a polygraph to officially eliminate him as a suspect, David Poole still had murder on his mind. Eyeing the reporters who'd gathered on hearing of the confession, he snarled, "Why don't you guys go to hell!"

His 15 minutes of fame were up.

Years passed, but the police had not forgotten Oda K. Apple. His file was thick with persistent memory.

"There might be a break someday when we least expect it," predicted prosecutor Donald Roney. "But we can't afford to pass up a single lead." Another detective agreed, "If the case was an accident—a stray shot—it will be solved someday."

Mrs. Mabel Apple would not expunge her husband's mystifying death. In 1959, she was still calling the homicide squad every three months, hoping they'd found something new. Oda's spoken fear of his imminent demise continued to puzzle her—she could not reconcile this bizarre twist to the case.

Yet Mabel never wavered in her view of the crime. Until her death in 1982, she believed her husband was the victim of an accident, because no one had a reason to kill him.

Oda Apple is buried in a little cemetery near Cherry Grove. His grave is well tended and green, yet surrenders no secrets regarding the final date on the headstone.

SUMMATION:

There are three conflicting theories concerning the death of Oda K. Apple.

He was killed intentionally from ambush: Apple was in the hospital four months prior to his fatal furlough. Who would know

Murder Or Accident?

Oda Apple's Death Is Mystery 6 Years After Found Shot

By Frank Weikel
Enquirer Reporter

"It's one of the most puzzling cases we've ever worked on," declared homicide detectives as they discussed the Oda Apple case.

Apple, a 45-year-old Longview Hospital patient, home on a weekend pass, was shot to death six years ago yesterday as he walked near his home at 3123 Hackberry St.

The case started to unfold at 9 p.m. on August 8, 1953. Apple and his son, Kenneth 3, left the house and walked to a nearby drug store. Oda purchased some headache tablets and started home.

It was a few minutes after 9 p. m. when Kenny ran into the house and screamed, "The firecrackers got Daddy."

Apple's wife, Mabel, then 42 years old, ran from the house and found her husband lying dead in front of 3133 Hackberry St. Homicide detectives responded to the scene and started an investigation.

It was learned during the investigation that Apple was killed by a .38 caliber bullet that passed through the nape of his neck.

The bullet had traveled at least three feet. There were no powder burns.

Several neighbors heard what they thought sounded like a shot.

Apparently no one was on the street when Apple was killed.

Apple had no known enemies and no motive could be found.

Lab tests showed that the bullet taken from Apple had indistict rifling marks. This led police to theorize that the bullet was fired from "an old gun, a zip gun, or propelled by a sling shot or even tossed against a wall causing it to discharge."

Although the case is labeled a homicide by both police and the Coroner, detectives still wonder if the death could not have been accidental.

Homicide detectives hav

The shot that took Oda Apple's life still echoed through the city six years later.

he was coming home and then stalk him for two days when he never left the house? And what lucky assassin just happened to be on the street when Oda took a spontaneous trip to the drug store with his son?

Only rumor and innuendo support this opinion. Logistically it doesn't add up.

He was the victim of mistaken identity: Neighbor George Lindsey speculated that he had been the intended victim, and he often walked to the drug store with his young son. Could a hired gun have been prowling those safe streets looking to finalize a vendetta? It's more plausible than if Oda himself had been the target.

Yet this hypothesis has problems. Plus someone would have eventually talked if Oda was gunned down by mistake.

He was killed by a random gunshot: Some youngster, with a stolen pistol, fired an inadvertent shot which struck the victim. Police questioned scores of teenagers and parents in the neighborhood, but they never uncovered anything to back up this theory.

This murder has all the earmarks of an intentional shooting—and a colossal blunder.

EPILOGUE:

The Apple question reverberated through Cincinnati for decades: Was it safe to walk the streets at night? Peace of mind while strolling near one's home was the other casualty of this case.

"The firecrackers got Daddy!" The simple words of three-year-old Kenny Apple cloaked the secret still locked in his childish awareness. As he grew older, Mrs. Apple tried to shield him from the disturbing memories: "I don't want him to remember the bad part and get scared. Sometimes he has nightmares, but he never remembers what frightens him."

Mabel Apple never believed her husband's death was intentional. "Someone had a gun—he got scared and ran," she said. "He was afraid to admit it. He should give himself up and ease his conscience."

Then she added, "I would give anything on earth to find out."

But the final piece of Oda Apple's puzzle is still missing.

POSTSCRIPT: SEPTEMBER 2011

I was recently contacted by Sara Apple, granddaughter of Oda Apple and daughter of Kenny, the only witness to his father's killing. Like other victim's relatives who contacted me since ***Queen City Gothic*** came out, she was startled by the previously unpublished information I had gleaned from the cold case files.

And like anyone living with a mysterious legacy, she surrendered secrets that were part of private family lore.

In his first interview with police the day after the shooting, young Kenneth Apple was asked if his mother had a gun. He

2009

Oda Apple left this house one summer night in 1953 for a short walk—but he never made it back.

told them that HE did. But after they pulled a toy gun from the child's toy box, they made Mabel Apple take a lie detector test about owning a gun, even though she was still distraught over her husband's death.

As the victim's spouse who was just two houses away from the murder scene, poor Mabel could not elude that compelling combination of motive and opportunity, even though she had nothing to do with the Oda's death.

According to Sara, her father "was interviewed many times as a child, and even put under hypnosis." It was eventually determined that the 3 year old could remember nothing that would shed light on this baffling crime.

Yet it was an overlooked fragment locked in the memory of the child witness that glimmers for this writer.

Sara says her father "mentioned something to me about remembering red and yellow", as if he saw a blaze of those colors just before the shooting. He later speculated that it was a "high school jersey or letterman jacket".

The former Purcell High School (now Purcell Marian) is located at 2935 Hackberry Street, just two blocks from the Apple murder scene. And a check of their website confirms that the school colors are "crimson and gold".

This dovetails with the prevailing theory in 1953—Oda Apple was shot deliberately or inadvertently by a teenage gunman from the Hackberry neighborhood.

My communication with Sara Apple endorses what I already know about the family members of unsolved murder victims—their sinister inheritance is confronted by curiosity and doubt yet veiled by secrets and shame. Everyone reacts differently to this unwanted heirloom.

Imagine a grandfather who only exists in faded photographs. Picture your father haunted by harrowing visions of his father's murder.

And consider loved ones whispering unanswered questions about unsolved episodes that echo into their dreams.

I WITNESS:

Concealed in the green darkness between tall houses, the youth waits, his fingers intently busy as they caress the gun. Confidence courses through his body. He is bored with just shooting at paper targets—tonight is his chance for a righteous kill.

He steals across the yard and takes a position between two trees at 3133 Hackberry. The moon mingles with the streetlights to cast grotesque shadows along the sidewalk.

His resolve is tested for one moment, when he glances back at the church steeple across from the drug store. The youth has nothing against George Lindsay. Yet he believes what Mrs. Lindsay's lover has told him—that her husband is threatening to kill her for "fooling around."

The man promises him $100 if he'll take a shot at Lindsay—$50 up front and the rest when the deed is done. And he informs him that Lindsay often walks to the corner store with his young son to buy ice cream.

But can this teenager really bushwhack some child's father?

Outside the store, Oda Apple lifts little Kenny off the penny scale, and they amble back down the street toward home. As Kenny chatters, holding his father's hand, Oda reflects on his own fragile state of mind.

The bizarre episodes haunting him for the past two years are arriving farther apart now, and not lingering nearly as long. His legacy of terror is receding backward into the shadows. This sudden gift of premonition, if indeed that's what it was, is too disconcerting to be welcome. *Take it back,* he thinks. *I don't want it. Insight makes a lousy bed partner!* He shakes his head, almost laughing.

Oda feels strangely lighthearted as they pass the church. Summer is passing by, and he's looking forward to autumn's cool nights. He gazes up at the steeple—death still hovers and is with him always, but he no longer dreads it. He understands now that the fear was his real Achilles heel. *Everyone dies eventually; so what?* All he needs to do is let it go; stop dwelling on it.

The young gunman watches Oda and Kenny approach the tree where he's hiding. Assuming this is Lindsay and his son, his mind races in the August heat, balancing opportunity against risk. His breathing becomes shallow. His finger is on the trigger.

The guy never said he wanted Lindsay killed—only scared. OK, then he'll squeeze off one round. He's a scant five feet away as he brings the weapon to bear on his human target. Yes, just a warning shot. That's plenty. But his gaze rests on the boy. He must be careful to point the gun high off Lindsay's left side, not his right.

Yet before he can take conscious aim, the gun bucks in his trembling grasp. The shot whines like a skittish mare, and he watches in horror as the man pitches face-first onto the ground.

A spasm of panic blots out everything. He can only think with his legs, and as the shooter runs for his life, he is chased by a terrifying army of echoes—and the frightened wailing of a three-year-old child.

This crime is the equivalent of a sudden lightning strike. It comes, it crackles, and then departs without explanation, leaving all observers shaking their heads.

Yet Oda Apple knew far more about his impending death than his killer did.

2009

The front of the Pugh house has been extensively remodeled from the way it looked in 1956.

THE MATRON AND THE METER MAN

THE MURDER OF AUDREY PUGH AND THE TRIAL OF ROBERT LYONS: 1956

"It looked as if a dark intent was coming . . . Someone had better be prepared for rage."

Robert Frost

PROLOGUE:

Robert Lyons was destined to be strapped into Ohio's electric chair. He had confessed to a homicide, and even reenacted the crime in front of police movie cameras. The veteran meter reader was absolutely guilty of killing a young housewife in the city's upscale Hyde Park district.

But when he recanted his confession and hired a prominent Cincinnati lawyer to defend him, the stage was set for the Queen City's murder trial of the century.

NARRATIVE:

Spring was on the move in 1956. The fragrance of flowers meshing with auto exhaust was an obvious sign. Other subtle changes persisted—green tree buds bursting open, faint breezes giving chase.

These were halcyon days for mushrooming suburbs throughout the nation, even as the Cold War chilled the air.

The cocktail party set was getting its news from the recently launched *Huntley-Brinkley Report*. But there were plenty of distractions for a culture striving for normalcy and conformity: Elvis Presley had exploded onto the music scene, while French film star Brigitte Bardot had emerged as the latest sex symbol in *And God Created Woman.*

For one working man, just hearing that movie's title could ruin his day.

Wednesday, April 11, awoke in Cincinnati with a somber face and a sky of endless gray clouds. By the time the chilly twilight rolled in, the Queen City had been jolted out of its skin.

The case broke just after 6PM, when a calm-voiced husband notified police he'd arrived home to find his wife unconscious. "This is William Worthington Pugh speaking," he intoned. "Send the life squad . . . I just got home; my wife passed out. I don't know what's the matter."

Patrolmen responded to the residence on Hill and Hollow Lane, a secluded cul-de-sac in Hyde Park. Mr. Pugh had underestimated his wife's condition.

Audrey Evers Pugh was sprawled in a hallway near the front door, dead of multiple stab wounds to the neck and chest. The 34-year-old housewife was wearing a pajama top and a robe—several buttons were torn off during the struggle. Defensive wounds on her hands and forearms told the silent story of Mrs. Pugh's futile resistance against the killer's frenzied slashing.

After making a note to collect her fingernail scrapings, arriving detectives determined that there was no sign of forced entry or burglary, and their quick search of the house did not turn up the murder weapon.

A sheet pulled from her bed suggested that the victim had risen to answer the doorbell. Pugh admitted his wife hadn't been feeling well that week and was probably menstruating. The breakfast dishes were still on the table, as if she'd gone back to bed immediately after he left for work.

William Worthington Pugh was president of the A.H. Pugh Printing Company. His wife was described as "an attractive

34-year-old society matron." Pugh was an old-money name in Cincinnati, but this couple spent their evenings at home rather than consorting with the Queen City's elite.

Detectives swiftly eliminated Pugh as a suspect. His secretary placed him at work all day—except for the lunch hour, when he ran several errands.

As darkness fell, the husband became emotional. He told milling reporters that his wife was "a wonderful woman. I can't understand why, or who, would do a thing like this. The last thing she said to me this morning was, 'See you this evening.'"

Apparently not. As police swarmed over the house at the end of the lane, William Worthington Pugh retired to his study.

As word of the high profile murder spread, Hyde Park residents were stunned by this violation of their exclusive neighborhood.

Hill and Hollow Lane branched off Grandin Road, the turn of the century address for the city's wealthy patriarchs. Former Speaker of the House Nicholas Longworth brought his bride Alice Roosevelt, daughter of President Theodore Roosevelt, home to his mansion on Grandin in 1907. Other eminent names have since graced the street, including the Tafts, Krogers, Wilshires, Wallingfords, and Graydons.

Hill and Hollow was a narrow street that twisted like a devil's backbone and ended in front of the Pugh home, which lay below street level. To the left was heavy brush, to the right a thicket of trees. Their backyard dipped into a wooded ravine.

Police were soon deluged with calls regarding shifty looking salesmen and suspicious workers. Housewives were terrorized, locking their doors to peddlers and other strangers. "What will we do when the police leave?" one asked. They needn't have worried—the cops were obsessed.

Chief Stanley Schrotel defended their zeal: "This case is not more important than others because of the neighborhood or family." Yet he called the slaying "a threat to the community,"

THE CINCINNATI ENQUIRER

116th YEAR NO. 3—DAILY THURSDAY MORNING, APRIL 12, 1956

HYDE PARK MATRON MURDERED

This brutal crime in an elite neighborhood was the top newspaper story for months.

and took the extraordinary step of putting himself in charge of the investigation.

The morning after the murder, her friends eulogized Audrey Pugh. The last night of her life had been a happy one. She'd attended a club party in Price Hill and reunited with classmates from her college days, with whom she spoke excitedly of an upcoming vacation she and her husband were taking to Europe. "It will be good for him," she told them. "He works so hard."

A classmate called her "a very gentle person and always very dignified. I don't know a soul in the world who didn't like her." Others remembered the accomplished cellist as a shy woman who didn't like to attract attention. She attended Mass almost daily and taught a weekly class for adults who had converted to the Catholic faith. One friend speculated that someone from the class may have been attracted to her, and visited her home on Wednesday when he knew she would be alone.

They were all steadfast about one thing: Audrey was a devout woman who would not have answered the door in her pajamas, not even to admit a workman.

Her neighbors were left grasping for an explanation. One told reporters, "This is a private street, and it seems impossible such a thing could have happened."

Their privileged neighborhood was not immune from murder.

Within days a revolving door of oddball suspects swung in and out of police headquarters. A *Cincinnati Enquirer* sidebar

THE SOCIETY BEAUTY AND THE WOMAN-HATER

Had an uncanny resemblance propelled the killer when she snapped angrily, "Don't make a fool of yourself!"?

BY D.L.CHAMPION

True Detective Magazine **called Audrey Pugh a "society beauty" in their June 1956 feature article.**

titled, **"Weird Characters on the Loose"** closed with this ominous paragraph:

> **The next worst thing to the fears instilled in residents of Hill and Hollow Lane by an uncaught murderer, especially one who seemed mentally unbalanced, is the disquiet caused in the whole community by the number of strange individuals who have slipped through the rather wide net of our law enforcement agencies and mental institutions.**

In the first week police detained several of these "characters."

Mansiel Hagerty was a roving silver polish salesman and former mental patient who volunteered for questioning, only to become a real headache. He had been working the Grandin Road area, and police learned that he became incensed when turned down by customers, often cursing and breaking bottles on their doorsteps. They soon filed a lunacy affidavit against the 52-year-old Hagerty, who fought with officers on the way to the institution and was admitted as "abusive and threatening."

Paul Holden, age 24, had recently posed as a narcotics agent in Hyde Park to boost his criminal record, which already included several rapes. He gained admittance to victims' houses under the guise of a counselor for young girls using drugs. Holden was arrested in possession of a switchblade and was held for questioning.

Dan Von Siglock was arrested after he was spotted burning clothes in Clermont County. He was driving a green Studebaker, similar to one seen parked outside the Pugh residence on the day of the murder. Like Hagerty, he was a recent mental patient, released despite a report labeling him "too dangerous." His car trunk contained dozens of nude photos and "pennant-shaped felt strips emblazoned with swastikas." Siglock was sent to the psychiatric ward for evaluation.

An intoxicated man named Pat Ryan left a "dagger type knife" with a downtown waitress the day after the murder. He "got real upset" when a customer talked about the Pugh case, shouting, "I don't want to hear anything more about it!"

"Why would anyone want to kill her?" asks victim's husband
As body is removed, police continue to search for evidence

William Worthington Pugh is questioned by detectives as his wife's body is carried out. He was immediately eliminated as a suspect.

Investigators determined he was the victim of his own alcohol fueled imagination.

Pugh neighbor Harry Ranier was sporting strange abrasions on his arms and legs the morning after the crime. Police took several photos of the baleful Ranier displaying his bruised flesh, but soon discounted him as a suspect.

Police arrested a laborer who lived less than half a mile from Audrey Pugh. 37-year-old Ambrose Johnson had been convicted in a 1940 attack on a wealthy Hyde Park woman in her home, and a routine check of cases similar to Pugh had unearthed him. He was locked up on an open charge and grilled repeatedly.

City water meter reader Robert Lyons had entered the Pugh home on the murder day while on his route. He had limited interaction with Mrs. Pugh and had seen nothing unusual. Police noted during questioning that he liked to drink beer and had an "undisclosed sexual deviation."

As the only verified visitor to the murder house, Lyons was examined closely. A discrepancy in his log book was cleared up, and he was released that same day.

However, investigators were not yet finished with Robert Lyons.

The coroner's report wasn't released until the case was a week old—it answered some questions and raised several more.

Based on the position of the 23 wounds, Dr. Frank Cleveland concluded that the killer was right-handed and taller than the victim. The 14 critical stab wounds were at a downward angle: one on the left side of the neck, eight in the left side of the chest, and five on the left side of the back. There were two superficial chest wounds and seven defensive wounds on Audrey Pugh's arms and hands.

Official cause of death was "internal and external hemorrhage resulting from multiple stab wounds to the neck and chest." The fatal thrusts had penetrated her lungs and heart, severing her jugular vein. Cleveland's report concluded that the killer could not have avoided getting his clothing stained with the victim's blood.

Chief of Detectives Henry Sandman studied the findings and began looking for clarification on some points. Was Mrs. Pugh face-to-face with the killer when first stabbed? Were the back wounds inflicted as she turned to flee or while she was on the floor? And at what time did death occur?

Some detectives speculated that Audrey unwittingly opened her door to the killer, thinking he was there to see about a gardener's job. But had the intruder actually gained entrance or struck her down in the doorway. If he entered the house, did he stay long enough to clean himself up? And what did he do with the murder weapon?

City Safety Director Oris E. Hamilton decided to weigh in with the press, and he tried to lower expectations. He declared the Pugh case to be "the most baffling murder in Cincinnati's history,"

Det. Eckler dusts front door for prints

Audrey Pugh's body was found just behind this front door in the foyer.

adding that "Ellery Queen and Mary Roberts Rinehart together couldn't have written a greater mystery than this one."

Hamilton referred to the investigation as "methodical," but to the cops he was damning them with faint praise. This was in the days of no specialists, and responding detectives had to work in teams of three. One was the spotter, another was the pickup man, and the third was the photographer. They were trained to approach murder cautiously, protecting the scene while rotating in fresh eyes to spot the clues.

"We aren't being stampeded or rushed," assured Hamilton. "These things are very unpredictable. It took the FBI three years to solve the Brink's robbery. Some crimes are never solved."

Not exactly a vote of confidence from the Safety Director.

Investigators had ruled out the victim's husband—William Worthington Pugh was at work on the day of the murder. He ran some errands during lunch, leaving critical time unaccounted for, but his status shielded him. A middle class spouse would not have been handled so delicately.

Even then, one detective noted in the file that "his secretary's story was too pat."

Pugh was starting to show the strain. When asked by a *Post* reporter if he was willing to take a lie detector test, he snapped, "That's a leading question—like being asked 'have you stopped beating your wife'? It's none of your business!" The next day he reconsidered and said "Certainly" when asked again, probably taking his lawyer's advice.

That left two theories for the Pugh murder, and detectives were divided: Was Audrey slain by someone she recognized or did she fall victim to a psychopath who picked her house at random?

The motives for a stranger killing were not there. She had not been sexually assaulted, and simple robbery seemed unlikely to inspire such violence, even though Audrey's wallet was missing and some coins had been removed from a dresser.

Several suspects, including the meter reader, were eliminated after passing polygraph tests. As days passed with no arrest, two retired detectives were called in as advisors. George Percy and Patrick Hayes had served a total of 86 years between them—Hayes had arrested lonely hearts killer Anna Marie Hahn back in 1937.

Hayes felt the violence involved indicated that Mrs. Pugh had recognized her assailant: "It follows a pattern of a crime of rage." Many detectives concurred, calling it unlikely that an intruder would strike 23 knife wounds. A surprised prowler would stab once and then flee.

Robert Lyons, the city meter man quizzed in the initial batch of suspects, was picked up a second time for questioning after minor discrepancies were found in his original statement. He cleared them up and was again released the same day.

Lyons insisted that he'd never left the basement of the Pugh home during his meter call. He told police Mrs. Pugh was alive and cheerful when he entered the residence at about noon. She had reminded him to use the side door near the garage instead of the basement door, and this wasn't the first time she'd made this request of him.

Pugh Recognize Slayer? Or Was He Sadist?

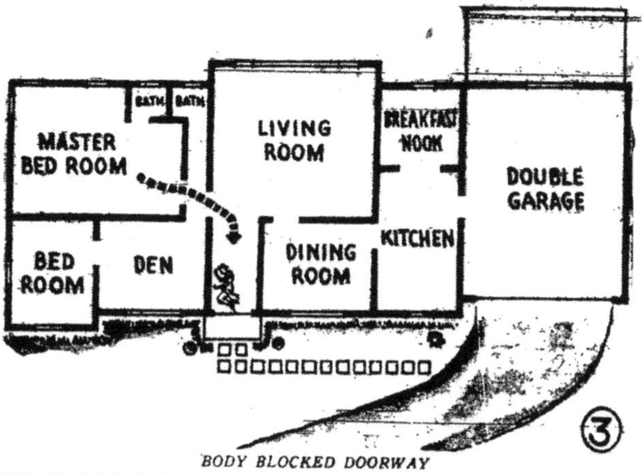

Press speculation was rampant during the first weeks of the investigation

Soon weeks became a month, and the media grew impatient with the lack of progress. Henry Sandman was not encouraging: "We're right back where we started," he told the *Cincinnati Enquirer.* "We've worked hundreds of thousands of hours. We've run down every possible clue. We've questioned hundreds of people, and we just haven't got a thing . . . We're still digging, and we'll keep on."

All through Hyde Park there was unrelenting anxiety. And Cincinnati's reputation for old-fashioned hospitality had taken on a frosty edge among housewives waiting for the Pugh murder to be solved. Tradesman and doorbell-ringing salesmen were getting the cold shoulder. Even mailmen and milkmen were reporting added scrutiny from the other side of the door. Women living alone were advised by one editorial to look out the window: "And if you don't know who it is, don't go near the door!"

A special inspector from the gas company received a chilly reception while checking meter types along a Hyde Park route. When interviewed, he was thankful for one thing. "I'm sure glad the water meter reader was cleared in the case, else it would have made it tough on all of us."

The very next day, Robert Lyons was arrested after confessing to the murder of Audrey Pugh.

"The Meter Reader Did It!" screamed the *Cincinnati Post's* front page, while an editorial inside proclaimed **"Cased Closed!"** In the early morning hours of May 26, Robert Lyons finally came clean.

The *Post's* lead said it all:

> **Robert Lyons, 43, a water works employee, admitted with a smile at dawn Saturday that he had stabbed Mrs. Audrey Pugh to death April 11th in her home . . . He said he did it because of a 'bawling out' she gave him for entering the house through a basement door instead of the service entrance, as she had asked. 'She got pretty nasty with me down there (in the basement). I just ain't used to that,' he told police. Lyons said the murder weapon was a paring knife.**

Though Lyons had already been questioned three previous times, he'd finally spilled his guts after an exhaustive interrogation by a team of detectives. The *Enquirer* ran a photo of him calmly puffing on a cigarette just after confessing, while their headline boasted, **"Nearly Perfect Crime! It's Cracked by Police After 3000 Interviews!"**

The article also alluded to the unnamed "sexual deviation" in Lyons and revealed that Audrey Pugh bore a "striking resemblance to his ex-wife."

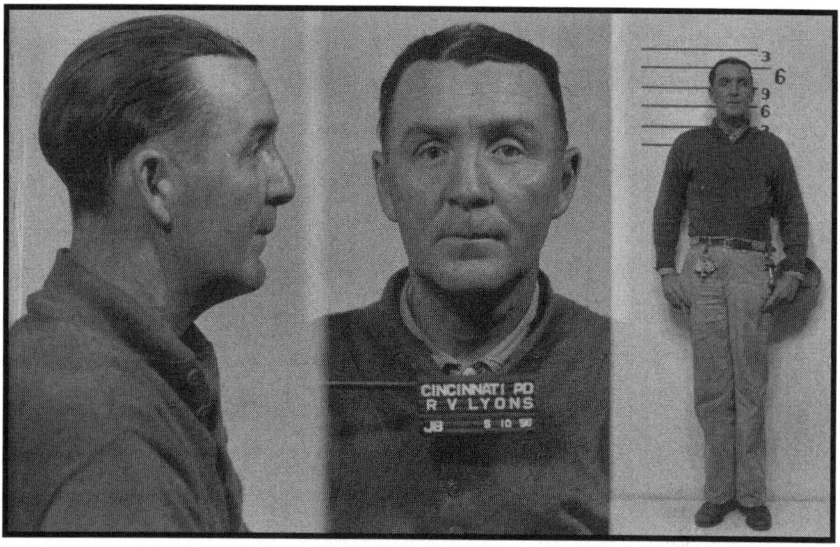

This was meter reader Robert Lyons' first mug shot, several weeks before his arrest for murder.

The confession struck to the heart of his motive—fear that Mrs. Pugh's complaints would get him fired. Having spent 20 years at the water department with a spotless record, the divorced Lyons' job had become his life. Audrey's attitude had angered him, and he'd followed her upstairs for an explanation. He claimed she grabbed a paring knife, and during a brief struggle he stabbed her several times.

After his 38-page statement was transcribed, he was immediately taken to the Pugh residence at 4:30AM to reenact the crime for police movie cameras. William Pugh declined to view his wife's killer and remained in his study.

Robert Lyons had been the prime suspect from the beginning. "Our investigation was directed toward the meter reader since early after the murder," Chief Schrotel admitted.

"He was a likely suspect—probably the last man to see Mrs. Pugh alive."

Other witnesses had cast suspicion on Lyons. Some neighbors disputed his log sheet times for reading their meters. A maid on his next stop after the Pugh house claimed he'd acted strangely and had altered his clothing when he left that house. And in a telltale coincidence, Lyons had failed to read the Pugh meter, writing down that the dial was "sweaty" even though it wasn't.

Pugh had told police about an altercation between his wife and Lyons the previous year, when she became upset with him for entering the wrong door and making too much noise.

"There's that water meter man making a fool out of himself again," Audrey had remarked to her husband.

The catalyst for murder was his insistence on once again coming to the basement entry of the Pugh home. At about 1PM he'd knocked on that door long and loud, because he'd been unable to gain access for his reading the previous month, and didn't want to make another estimate.

He said Mrs. Pugh came downstairs with a remark about "that screaming water man." Then she scolded Lyons. "You are the most insistent of all the people who come to the door. Why are you making a fool of yourself?"

He was "burned up" by the remark, but let it pass. He heard Audrey make several comments after she went upstairs, and he was afraid she was going to protest to the water department. He climbed the basement stairs, his mind racing.

According to Lyons, she was in the kitchen peeling potatoes. He claimed she advanced upon him with the knife and cornered him in the alcove near the front door. He turned and grappled with her. When he wrestled the knife from her hand, she slapped his face.

The meter man flew into a rage and began stabbing her, yet he did not remember inflicting 23 wounds. "When I stopped stabbing her, I knew she was dead," Lyons said during the filmed reenactment, while standing on the exact spot where the body was found. Detectives could accept that she was holding a knife, but they discounted Lyons' claim that Audrey intimidated him. They were certain she was the one who fled.

He said he washed the knife and laid it somewhere in the kitchen, yet both Lyons and the police were unable to identify it.

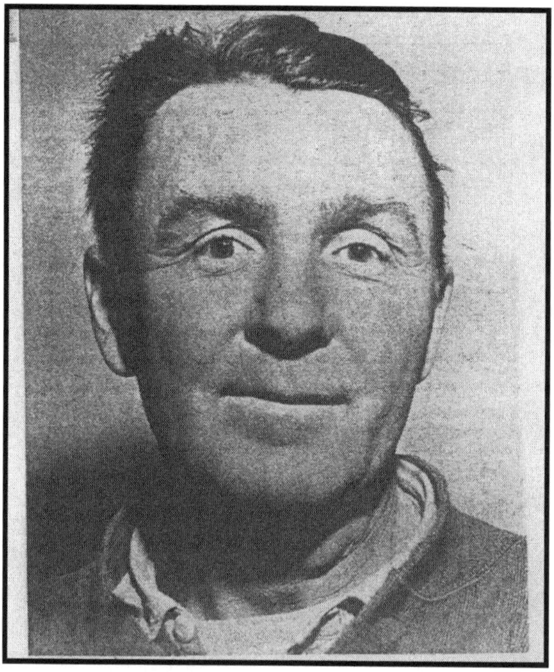

Robert Lyons smiling face gazed out from countless newspapers sold after the Pugh case was finally broken.

He then grabbed his meter book and left by the rear door, but not before marking the Pugh water dial as "sweaty"—this was the first time he had failed to take a reading at their house once inside.

Lyons continued on his route and admitted turning his jacket inside out when he noticed bloodstains on the sleeve. He said he burned the jacket that night in his fireplace, leaving only the buttons in the grate.

Mrs. Ethel Hanson was at work in the home of Dr. and Mrs. Oliver Ramey, next door to the Pugh house, when Lyons knocked on the door. From the moment the Negro maid saw him, she feared him. She told police he had a "wild look" in his eyes while standing outside the door.

"I told him I wouldn't admit him until he proved he was the meter reader," Mrs. Hanson recalled. "He looked funny to me . . . sort of tense."

Lyons took an unusually long time to read their meter, and when he finally came back up she noticed he had turned his jacket inside out and was carrying his sweater. She also disputed his time sheet for the call at the Ramey home.

"When he went out the door, he stood still for a minute and gave a great big sigh," she concluded. Ethel Hanson was about to become the star witness for the state.

There were holes in Lyons' confession that did not correlate with the facts. But investigators were so giddy over the arrest that they overlooked these contradictions.

When asked what cracked the Pugh case, Detective Chief Sandman could barely contain himself: "Constant work, team effort, vacations pushed aside, days off forgotten, magnificent cooperation from the public, the press, everyone—that's what broke the case!"

With the spotlight on Robert Vernon Lyons, cops found a way to push his buttons and bust him wide open.

It came as no surprise that the early morning confession was sparked by the only thing Lyons cared about. "His job was his very life—he lived for it," said Sandman. "We tried everything under the sun in our earlier questioning—God, mother, and family. But when he talked of his job, tears actually came into his eyes."

Sandman also confirmed the rumor that Lyons' ex-wife bore a striking facial resemblance to Audrey Pugh. When photos of the two women were placed side-by-side, most detectives could not tell the difference. Yet Sandman insisted that "there was no sex or passion in this murder case."

He then outlined how they'd unraveled the truth while grilling Robert Lyons. In the end four lies had trapped the water meter reader.

Lie #1: Lyons claimed he did not learn of the murder until the next afternoon. But he actually read about it that morning and discussed it with a coworker, who kidded him about the victim being on his route.

Nearly Perfect Crime! It's Cracked By Police After 3000 Interviews

BY PAUL LUGANNANI

Cincinnati police yesterday gave the public the prayed-for answer to the question of who killed Mrs. Audrey Evers Pugh, 35, Hyde Park society matron. The "near-perfect crime" was cracked.

"It was the meter reader!" came the electrifying news that spread rapidly about the city, over the state and through the nation.

At 2 a. m. Robert Vernon Lyons, 43, 240 Setchell Ave., admitted the first blemish on his spotless 20-year record as

Lyons' confession bared cunning methods he used to cover up his ghastly crime—how he washed the blood off the murder weapon, how he put on his jacket inside-out to conceal the blood stains on the left sleeve.

MAID "STAR WITNESS"

▸ Mrs. Hanson's entire story as originally told to Capt. Willard Elbert, District 6 commander. It will undoubtedly make her one of, if not "the" "state's star" witnesses. She knew about the jacket "reverse," which Lyons admitted, took place in the furnace room of the Ramey home.

▸ The unlocked rear basement door.

▸ What Detective Lytle Young described as "an overwhelming accumulation of facts, data and discrepancies—lies which he admitted telling—that built up to

Lyons arrest was the result of a vigilant investigation by the Cincinnati Homicide squad.

Lie #2: Lyons said the murder day was the first time Mrs. Pugh told him to use the service entrance. This was a windowed door near the garage, installed because of her fear of being home alone. Lyons had a notation in his meter book about using the service entrance, but he had attempted to erase it.

Lie #3: Lyons claimed he read the Pugh meter around noon. When asked how he knew that, he said he checked a wall clock in the house right before the Pugh residence. Yet police found no wall clock in that house. Also, the Ramey maid placed Lyons at her house after 1PM.

Lie #4: Lyons' meter sheet revealed he hadn't read the Pugh meter, instead marking "sweaty dial" on his trip report. But sweat won't dissipate unless the glass is removed. Investigators saw no sweat on the glass, and no one had removed it.

Lyons' meter sheets had been sent to the FBI for examination. The Pugh sheet and the ones before and after it showed erasures. Based on this, they picked up Lyons for the final time and gave him yet another polygraph. This time it showed deception on several points, and detectives hunkered down for a marathon interrogation.

Thirteen hours later Lyons signed the confession, threw up his hands, and laughed, an astounding climax to the most painstaking police investigation in Cincinnati's history. He was arraigned for first-degree murder a half hour afterward and ordered held without bond for the next grand jury session.

The prosecutor was in no hurry. Watson Hover admitted, "Loose ends must be gathered before completing the picture." He didn't say that they also had to reconcile some gaping holes in Lyons' confession.

While in jail Lyons seemed calm and relaxed, never becoming distressed or even interested in his plight. He showed no emotion when questioned except for his strange laugh, which was described by one investigator as "unconcerned."

In the cell next to him stood Robert Jackson, awaiting death in the electric chair for the slaying of detective Walter Hart, the chief investigator for the Sophia Baird slaying in 1943 (Chapter 5). But even sharing space with a man who was "going to burn" did not faze Robert Lyons.

Detectives searched the home Lyons shared with his father and daughter, a weathered bungalow on Setchel Street near the Ohio River. They came up empty on the murder weapon, but they did confiscate a pair of long underwear that would emerge during the trial.

After several days in jail Lyons' spirits began to sag. He worried about his 16-year-old daughter and the gossip at her high school. Images of the murder loomed in his head. "I can't talk about it," he pleaded to reporters. "I still don't understand it. Twenty years of reading meters . . . and now this."

Meanwhile, housewives around the city exhaled. Officials from both the Waterworks and the Gas Company assured their customers that Lyons was an aberration. "If a housewife is afraid of the meter reader, she might as well be afraid of the milkman, the laundry man, and the TV repairman," proclaimed C, G & E president William Zimmer.

Lyons' boss at the City Water Department was mystified. "He was one of our best readers, never caused any trouble," said Daniel Laurence, while agreeing that "this man had personal problems." Laurence also stressed that this was the first time in their history a meter reader was accused of harming someone.

Inevitably, there was a media debate about whether meter readers should be licensed, and given psychological testing to weed out "murder in the human heart."

A Water Works official countered that some meter readers had complained about the way housewives dressed. "You'd be surprised how many women come to the door in nightgowns, even in the middle of the day," he insisted. "Some of them invite our men into the house for a drink—our men are instructed in such cases to get out fast."

Even the people along Lyons' routes were surprised by the arrest. He had checked 3400 meters since the day of the murder without incident. Lyons was described as "a perfect gentleman" by the many housewives who had admitted him to their homes in the weeks following the Pugh slaying.

As the city began to settle down, investigators were puzzling over certain aspects of Lyons' confession.

Lieutenant Charles Martin leveled with the press: "The confession leaves many questions unanswered and in some instances doesn't ring true." He acknowledged that it was Lyons' story and slanted in his favor wherever possible.

Their list of questions was extensive:

- Why did Lyons disobey the instructions in his code book by going to the back door? And why did he erase those instructions and write his own?
- Why did he write that the Pugh dial was "sweaty," erase it, and then write it again?
- Were his known sexual deviations a motive for the brutal murder?
- Did the strong resemblance between Audrey Pugh and Lyons' ex-wife trigger violence in this otherwise passive man?

- What prompted Mrs. Pugh to admonish Lyons three times about "making a fool" of himself? Why was he so vague on this key point?
- What happened to Mrs. Pugh's missing wallet? Lyons never mentioned robbery.
- What happened to the murder weapon? Lyons said he placed the knife on the kitchen counter after rinsing it off.

This dissension about Lyons delayed the prosecutor in filing for first degree murder, since there was no evidence of premeditation. The "feud" between the housewife and the meter reader over using the wrong entrance was not enough to support the charge.

Police were certain of one thing—whatever happened between Lyons and Audrey Pugh was "the point of no return. Whatever he did, Lyons felt that he had gone over the brink," explained detective Eugene Moore. "If it got back to Waterworks, it meant his job."

Despite their public rejection of the sex angle, investigators had been probing the seedy side of Robert Lyons since his first interview in April. They had learned he was divorced 14 years and "had rejected all women" since then.

The transcript of his April 16 interrogation revealed the fascination with the meter reader's "unnatural sex acts."

Q: So you have had a desire for a sexual outlet?
A: Yes. That's right.
Q: So it's not directed to women. You said you hate women. So what do you do?
A: I hold it (a brassiere) over my penis.
Q: Have you ever done it with other garments?
A: No.
Q: You've got a face like a lie detector. The minute you lie your face changes.
A: Okay.
Q: Do you ever feel badly after you've finished masturbating?

A: No.
Q: You're not ashamed of it?
A: No.
Q: Then it's a perfectly normal thing?
A: No, it's not normal.
Q: You've masturbated since you were in high school, is that true?
A: I did it in the army.
Q: Why do you hold it back then?
A: Well, I am ashamed of it.

Among other questions hurled at him were: "Do you ever masturbate on the job—expose yourself to women—engage in oral sex?" He denied these particular activities, but did admit masturbating into a large brassiere found in his shed. He also told investigators that he only had coffee for breakfast, usually skipped lunch, and got "pretty well loaded" on weekends.

His former wife couldn't believe that Lyons was a killer. However, she agreed her ex-husband might have become upset because "Mrs. Pugh and I looked an awful lot alike."

As he stewed in the lockup, even Robert Lyons became confused by his own confession. On May 27 he was fired by Waterworks for "discourtesy to the public." That same day he told his brother Bill he wanted to recant his admission of guilt.

Lyons also informed his brother he wanted "Foss" Hopkins to defend him.

William Foster Hopkins has been described in many ways. In his engaging and enlightening memoir, *Murder is My Business*, he admitted having been called "old fashioned, evil minded, irritating, corrupt, sentimental, dignified, dogmatic, and a free spirit."

He was also called something else—the best criminal defense attorney in Cincinnati.

Hopkins' entry into the Pugh case changed the dynamic entirely. The prosecutor's office had been up against him before, and they witnessed him defending clients with dexterity and precision. He was an expert at navigating the twists and turns of justice.

He knew the law, yet he was also trained in dramatics. Hopkins was a tall man in his mid-50s who cut a striking figure in the courtroom, and he used this to full advantage. The Pugh case would permanently secure his status as a local legend.

His description of that first meeting with Lyons is worth quoting here:

> **He was taller than I imagined. He seemed more rawboned. He was rangy physically. But there emanated from him a universal meekness, a lifetime of unsaid but implied pardon-me's, and the sense that the moment your gaze was averted, he would fade into the scenery. He was the sort who would forever be at the end of every line that ever formed. He was the face in the faceless crowd, blending until lost among the other faces . . .**

Hopkins was skeptical upon hearing that Lyons wanted to renounce his confession, and had to be convinced to visit the meter reader in jail. The lawyer accused him of insanity for confessing to a crime he now denied. But after hearing the ordeal of Lyons' epic interrogation, he decided to take the case.

Lyons had already been questioned several times before detectives picked him up after work on May 25. Captain Charles Martin was the "good cop"—he knew Lyons from playing softball against him, and the two enjoyed a friendly rapport. The "bad cop" was played by Prosecutor Donald Roney.

They dragged Lyons down a dizzying 13 hour journey into his psyche.

After they wined and dined him at a local restaurant, they hustled him off for yet another series of polygraph tests and interviews. Martin exploited their friendship while coaxing the meter reader that they "were all city employees" and that he "should cooperate." At the same time Roney hammered Lyons, threatening him with the electric chair and swearing that the test results had already confirmed he was lying.

The cooperative meter reader shows (*l. to r.*) Dets. Stagenhorst. Martin, Moore, Young, Col. Sandman where he entered house

Lyons verifies details of his "confession" while touring the murder scene with the chief investigators.

Then Roney launched the haymaker: He told Lyons they had lifted his fingerprints from a piece of furniture near where Mrs. Pugh's body was found. Roney goaded him that "fingerprints don't lie," insisting that Lyons was "a cinch for the hot seat" if he didn't "play ball."

Hopkins made a note on hearing this—there was no mention by the press of fingerprints recovered from the scene.

He asked his client why he'd caved in. Lyons explained, "I kept telling them I didn't kill Mrs. Pugh, but they just wouldn't listen. I got so punch drunk and groggy I believe I would have confessed that I killed my own mother to get them off my back." And Roney had deceived Lyons with a bogus deal, promising to send him to a veterans' hospital for a few years if he confessed.

By then it was 4AM, and Lyons was exhausted. "It looked like I was a dead pigeon and didn't have a chance . . . I was scared, tired, and sick. As I look back now, it's hard to believe, but that morning it looked like the only way I could save myself. So, like a damn fool, I told them I did it."

Then Lyons shared an interesting detail with the still skeptical Hopkins. He was adamant that during the filmed recreation of the murder, he turned the wrong way coming up from the basement, and a detective had to push him in the direction of the kitchen. Lyons was certain this would show up on the police movie.

On June 2 Robert Lyons officially recanted. The meter reader maintained that he had admitted guilt only under intense pressure from Don Roney, who had threatened him with the death penalty. "If I didn't play ball with him they were going to fry me", was how Lyons remembered it to the press.

He closed with this jarring pronouncement: "Whoever killed Mrs. Pugh is still at large . . . I did not do it."

The city was furious that Robert Lyons had withdrawn his confession. Hopkins received numerous telephone threats, including a promise "to burn down the courthouse again" if Lyons was acquitted, this in reference to the 1884 riot when an enraged mob torched the county courthouse after a murderer was set free.

Hopkins' assistant summed up their challenge: "I think our client is already in the electric chair." Presumption of innocence was lost—the defendant had confessed and had even reenacted the murder.

Hopkins agreed: "They're waiting to turn on the juice."

William Foster Hopkins was undaunted—he believed in his client and prepared a brilliant defense. As the trial began on November 1, 1956, his opening statement characterized Lyons' interrogation as "a 13-hour brainwashing by police that included deliberate chicanery, subterfuge and outright lies."

Hopkins won the trial earlier during jury selection. He had hand-picked working class people who understood what it meant to toil their lives away for someone else. These were regular folks who unwound by drinking beer at the corner pub, folks just like Bob Lyons. This jury of eight men and four women had seen the downside of life, and Hopkins had perceived some anti-police sentiment among these 12 random citizens.

Prosecutor Watson Hover's opening statement painted Lyons as an odd duck: "The evidence will show Lyons is a peculiar sort of person. He has some distinctions which psychologists would call definite personality defects. His social life was restricted." Hover seized on the defendant's fear of losing his job, and threw in the "erotic interest in a woman who is slightly disheveled from lying in bed and dressed in a bathrobe."

Hopkins' opening remarks portrayed his client as an average working man. He pointed out that Lyons had read meters in 7000 homes without a single complaint registered against him, and that he was awarded custody of his minor child following his divorce.

Then he played his ace. When Hover failed to mention the incriminating fingerprints in his opening, Hopkins realized they didn't exist. Now he told the jury how the interrogation team had dangled this spurious evidence to close the deal on Lyons' confession, and he could see that this tactic did not sit well with them.

Hopkins drove it home by illuminating the torment of Robert Lyons: "They told him he was going to the chair if he didn't cooperate . . . he had been without sleep for 24 hours. He was physically exhausted and completely demoralized . . . he became befuddled in his thinking, and he no longer cared. He had been brainwashed."

The prosecution's case was circumstantially compelling.

Police had found a bloodstained shirt in Lyons' home, and his log book showed erasures where he tried to change the time for reading the Pugh meter. His previous dispute with Mrs. Pugh was detailed—even Lyons had admitted to a confrontation on the day of the murder.

Most damaging was the testimony from the neighbor's maid, who said Lyons "acted strange" and changed his jacket after reading her meter. Ethel Hanson was the first person to interact with Lyons after he left the Pugh house, and his demeanor was consistent with someone who had just suffered a shocking episode.

Throughout his cross examination of the state's witnesses, Hopkins asked police officers and forensic analysts if they had found anything of a "foreign nature" on the scene. The prosecution couldn't help but wonder: Did he have another ace up his sleeve?

Hopkins had already scored points when he skewered the faulty forensic testing of Lyons' bloody shirt. Then he embarrassed the police by revealing that the rug on which Mrs. Pugh was found had been laundered several days after the crime, thus destroying possible evidence.

When the murder movie was shown, Hopkins saw what Lyons had referred to—an officer did indeed show him where to turn once he came upstairs. Lyons had denied ever being up there. On cross examination Hopkins pointed out that his client was being coached during the filming. Detectives denied it, but the jury could see it for themselves.

While cross examining lead investigator Henry Sandman, Hopkins exposed his misconduct during Lyons' lengthy interrogation. He hounded him over their "big lie" that the meter man's fingerprints were recovered near the body. "Do you call that good police work?" Hopkins thundered. Detective Sandman claimed it was a standard interrogation tactic, but the jury sat tightlipped.

Hopkins later wrote: "This was, I felt, the first murder case on record where a defendant's confession would prove his innocence."

Foss Hopkins opened his defense with the usual array of character witnesses, all swearing to Lyons' reputation for peace and quiet in his neighborhood and at work. He then called a series of timeline witnesses from along Lyons' route. Their collective testimony accounted for the meter reader's location during the critical hours between 12:45 and 2:30PM, and placed him far away from the Pugh residence.

The coroner had already established the time of death as between 1 and 2PM. Lyons' confession had him entering the Pugh house at noon.

Ever the cunning tactician, Hopkins then recalled prosecution witness William Worthington Pugh to the stand. He later wrote that the victim's husband was "cold, remote, and beyond what was going on."

He questioned why Pugh did not notice his wife's stab wounds, even as he tried to "revive" her. He got him to admit she wasn't wearing slippers—in his confession Lyons had placed her at the kitchen sink wearing slippers. And Hopkins confirmed that Pugh himself had laundered the rug upon which his wife's body was found.

Yet the real "Perry Mason" moment came when Robert Lyons testified.

Hopkins first guided him through the confession ordeal, and wrote of it later: "I saw, and the jury saw, everything relived in his eyes: the shock, the exhaustion, the indignation, the fright, the desperation, and the hopelessness."

Then Hopkins stood him atop the witness chair and raised his pants legs for the jury. Lyons suffered from ichthycosis, also called fish skin, which caused him to shed flakes of skin wherever he went. The jury watched skin flakes fall on the chair as he stood there—Hopkins described it as "a snowfall."

No skin scales, Hopkins announced, were found anywhere near Audrey Pugh's body. Police witnesses had established that no "foreign material" was found at the crime scene, and that the rug had been cleaned.

This was the courtroom drama king at his best.

Rebuttal witnesses quickly claimed that Lyons wore long underwear tucked into his socks to eliminate the shedding, and pointed out that police had even confiscated a pair during a search of his house. But prosecutors were embarrassed when they produced it in court. The underwear was six sizes too small to fit the defendant!

During closing arguments the prosecution pleaded for a first degree murder conviction and the death penalty. Hover dismissed the skin flake demonstration as "courtroom shenanigans" and called Hopkins' defense "a deliberate attempt by one of the most capable criminal attorneys in this section of the country to lead you down a cold trail."

They were "asking for the moon—and hoping for a piece of cheese," according to Hopkins.

The defense attorney delivered a masterful closing argument, with variations on a theme of "sinister interpretations the police had made in this case." They had not produced the murder weapon or the jacket given to them by Lyons. And Hopkins would never let the jury forget the bogus fingerprints.

It took them seven hours to find Robert Lyons not guilty. Both reasonable doubt and disgust over police tactics had swayed them toward acquittal, though several said later they would have convicted on manslaughter had they been given the option.

Robert Vernon Lyons returned to his favorite tavern on Eastern Avenue, a free man welcomed back by all of his friends. He later called it the "happiest moment of my life."

It seemed to be a popular verdict around town. But once the shouting died down, the finger pointing began.

One juror, interviewed on promise of anonymity, claimed, "There were some anti-police minds on that jury—definitely. More than half, I would say. I don't see how some of them got on the jury."

The failure to produce the murder weapon, the time element on Lyons' route, and the duplicity with the "fingerprints" weighed heavily on the jury. "We all had reasonable doubt," the juror concluded. "We thought we did the right thing."

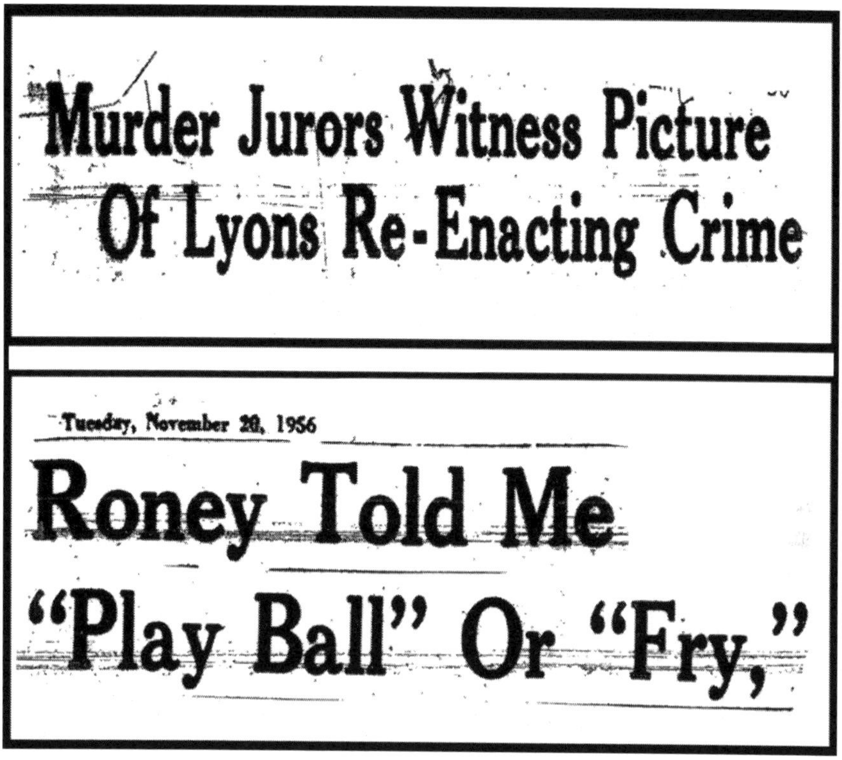

Murder Jurors Witness Picture Of Lyons Re-Enacting Crime

Tuesday, November 20, 1956

Roney Told Me "Play Ball" Or "Fry,"

Foss Hopkins put Lyons on the stand to rebut the police movie of the meter reader recreating the murder.

Prosecutor Hover continued to vent over his defeat: "It is almost impossible for me to understand how a jury will give more credence to the self-serving declaration of a man accused of a crime than it will to police officers who are doing their duty."

Chief Stanley Schrotel promised an internal investigation into "alleged police misconduct," which would eventually exonerate his detectives from any malfeasance. Schrotel maintained they were completely justified in charging Lyons with murder, and that no physical force was used while extracting the confession.

The former chief was still bitter about the acquittal 40 years later. In a 1997 interview with this author, he lamented the verdict: "Imagine a jury ignoring a 38-page confession and a movie where the killer acted out the murder!" But he admitted that Hopkin's tactics had worked, calling him "a histrionic fellow, but a good lawyer."

After the verdict, a *Cincinnati Post* writer cast a new slant on the case:

> **Suppose the victim of this murder had been some Mrs. Smith who lived in a tenement house on Race Street, instead of one whom the newspapers described as being a socialite? The trial would have no more than a few paragraphs a day, and wouldn't have lasted as long as it did.**

And what about Robert Lyons? After the trial he expressed hope that the real murderer would be brought to justice. Asked if he would pursue his old job, Lyons said he did not want to read meters "until the killer is found." He eventually returned to the Waterworks at a desk job.

He married a neighbor woman in a private ceremony three years after the trial. Reporters who crashed the reception were rudely rebuffed by Lyons. The *Enquirer* commented that "Lyons' aversion to newsmen was understandable: No Cincinnati suspect since mass murderer Anna Marie Hahn (1937) had received more publicity."

He surfaced two years later when his wife charged him with spousal abuse. Lyons told police he came home drunk and raised a "lot of hell," but he denied striking her. The matter was dropped when Mrs. Lyons failed to show up at a hearing.

Robert Vernon Lyons faded into obscurity, living out his days in the deep shade of vanishing notoriety.

SUMMATION:

Robert Lyons remains the prime suspect in the murder of Audrey Pugh:

- He was the only person who could be placed inside the home with the victim.
- He had a history of animosity with her, including an argument that day.

- He lied to police on several occasions, and his polygraphs showed deception.
- He had questionable bloodstains of uncertain origin on his shirt and pants.
- He made erasures in his meter book and failed to read the Pugh meter.

His demeanor with the next door maid was compelling. If Lyons had just murdered Audrey Pugh, then Ethel Hanson was the first person to encounter him. From his "wild look" to his change of clothing, his actions were incriminating. He behaved like a man who'd just weathered a traumatic event—and the maid had no reason to lie about his strange conduct.

The cops had him pegged from the beginning and just wore him down. Knowing his confession contained phony details, he decided to try and save his life after spending a week in lockup. Hiring Foss Hopkins was a master stroke. Getting Hopkins to believe him innocent was pure genius.

EPILOGUE:

Eventually, the characters in the 1956 meter-man murder drama began to leave the stage. Prosecutor Hover and Foss Hopkins both passed away in the 1970s.

Lyons returned to the Waterworks and retired in 1976. A year later he was found dead in the hallway outside his apartment, with a bag containing $10,000 nearby. He had told several people about the money, but no one knew why he was carrying so much cash. There were no signs of foul play—cause of death was liver failure.

Assistant prosecutor Donald Roney, the villain of the trial, summed up Lyons' passing with admirable restraint: "This was an incident that happened a long time ago. This man was accused, investigated, tried, and acquitted by his peers. I think the whole question should be laid to rest with him."

The riddle of his death only aggravated the enigma of Robert Lyons. Even being lifted out of the electric chair to freedom never reconciled the lingering questions: Did he kill Audrey Pugh? And if not, who did?

POSTSCRIPT: SEPTEMBER 2011

Police investigators do not believe in coincidence.

Yet this armchair detective was recently ambushed by a concurrence of events that defies imagination! It began with a routine doctor visit and ended with a lost manuscript about the Pugh case resurfacing in my custody.

Mary Anna DuSablon was the daughter of Lieutenant Charles Martin, head of the Cincinnati Homicide Squad in 1956 and the lead investigator in the Pugh case. Martin brought the triumph and frustration of this high profile homicide home with him, along with notebooks and personal files that his daughter inherited after his death in 1965.

An accomplished culinary author, Mary Anna tackled the Pugh case in 1998 and churned out "Who Killed Audrey Pugh", a book length treatment she completed in 2000. Yet she would die of colon cancer the following year, and her manuscript apparently went missing.

In March 2007 this author was diagnosed with stage 2 colon cancer. Now cancer free almost five years later, a follow-up visit with my surgeon unleashed an uncanny connection to the murder of Audrey Pugh.

After learning that I was the author of *Queen City Gothic*, my surgeon informed me that she had once LIVED in the Pugh house! And during that time she had a patient named Mary Anna DuSablon. And just before her untimely death, Ms. DuSablon gave her Pugh manuscript to my surgeon!

And now my surgeon, who I credit with saving my life, has given the manuscript to me . . .

Mary Anna DuSablon's unfinished book delivers a level of detail about the murder of Audrey Pugh not attainable to me through normal channels. The previously unpublished material from her father's file probes and prods this infamous case into uncharted territory, given Lt. Martin's status as chief investigator and his prior acquaintance with prime suspect Robert Lyons.

Among the areas of inquiry that were new to me:

William Pugh was NOT immediately exonerated and remained a suspect for longer than press indicated.

Audrey Pugh told friends in the months before the murder that she was being stalked while running errands and that someone was watching her from the woods behind her house.

Despite Lyon's confession, the murder weapon was NOT a paring knife from the Pugh kitchen.

Lyons interrogation was not a brutal brainwashing—DuSablon depicts it as a sympathetic negotiation, with investigators supplying food, drink, and cigarettes.

Lyons downed a single shot of "Crab Orchard" whiskey at his corner pub every morning before work.

After leaving the Pugh home, Lyons asked a woman on his route if he could use her bathroom.

The flakes of skin Lyons shed on the witness stand were actually ground cornflakes from a hole in his pants pocket—orchestrated by Foss Hopkins.

Hopkins created a timeline that put Lyons farther away from the Pugh house at 12:30PM by convincing the jury that the meter reader was working his route backwards.

Foss Hopkins is depicted as an unethical charlatan who knew his client was guilty yet focused on sullying the reputations of the Pugh case investigators.

Indeed, DuSablon's account of the trial reads like a forerunner of the O.J. Simpson case, as Hopkins disputed every facet of the Pugh investigation and questioned every detective as if they were the defendants themselves.

But the most fascinating aspect of the manuscript was DuSablon's speculation that Robert Lyons was the watcher from the woods feared by Audrey Pugh, and that the catalyst for the murder was Lyons being caught by Audrey masturbating in the basement while reading her meter!

I WITNESS:

Wednesday dawns gray and drizzly. Except for a sporadic moan of wind, the world is crisp and silent.

Bob Lyons really tied one on Tuesday night. Walking his route through a driving mist, he stabs a cigarette between his lips and instinctively coughs, a raspy hack punctuated by a wave of nausea surging through his grousing gut.

But there is nothing to heave up—Lyons never eats breakfast.

Such a crappy day. Cold, damp. Miserable.

All morning long, the meter reader conceals an irritable edge beneath his calm veneer, barely tolerating the bleak weather while strung out on lousy coffee and stale cigarettes. His hangovers are lingering these days—he doesn't bounce back so fast anymore. *The older I get, the better I used to be,* Lyons muses to himself.

Some mornings he thinks he'll need to rally just to die—his head thick and throbbing, the smell of beer still oozing through his skin. But at least he never misses work. As long as he keeps doing his job, how can there be a problem?

Striding down the driveway leading to the Pugh house, he flashes backward and is instantly wary. This place again. What a hassle. All because he once came in the rear door and announced himself—that was what he'd been doing for twenty years! Mrs. Pugh really bitched at him that time—muttered under her breath and called him a lummox.

What is a lummox, anyway, he wonders. Whatever it is, it can't be good. Women. So high and mighty. Their words are jackboots to the ego.

His decision to use the basement entry this time is pure stubborn tenacity—he is going to read this meter *his* way. The day this woman tells him how to do his job is the day he drinks hot piss and croaks.

So his incessant knocking and yelling, both deliberate acts, rouse the sleeping Audrey Pugh, still hazy from her own late night and the onset of menstrual cramps. She comes to the top of the stairs, looming over him like some vile harpy, berating him several times for "making a fool" of himself.

The insults clatter through his mind like billiard balls, and Lyons begins to percolate. Sure, she's pretty, in a high-society kind of way—but with such a damn mouth on her. Why do attractive women think they have the right to browbeat service men? This one needs a hefty smack in the chops. That would shut her up for good.

"What's so goddamn foolish about doing my fuckin' job?" He spits reflexively in anger, not even realizing he just cussed her. They stand separated by the stairway, as Audrey looks down at his saliva staining the basement floor.

As he turns toward the meter, Audrey's bile collides with his ire over an irretrievable issue—his continued employment. "I'm going to call your supervisor," she yells down the stairs. Then she retreats into the kitchen.

Lyons cannot let this pass. If he gets fired, that means two decades of hard work down the drain. He'll forfeit his pension, his dignity, his very identity. He really loves this job. It gives him status, the right to enter anyone's home on his route at will and without question.

It gives him the right not to be harassed.

Seething now, he mounts the basement stairs like a prowling panther and confronts Audrey, who is standing at the sink, furiously peeling potatoes. She doesn't back down, the bitch. She continues to taunt and bait him with more threats. Her voice becomes shrill as she grips the paring knife.

Suddenly Lyons notices the striking resemblance to his ex-wife. Why did he never see that before? He lived this same scene many times throughout his marriage—being chewed out for stupid things, minor infractions like forgetting to wipe his feet. He stares at Audrey with black, reptilian eyes, as vengeful yearnings from the past flood his present.

This time she isn't going to get away with it.

In a near ecstasy of rage, he approaches her. As she reaches for the phone, her final slur sparks a swift eruption of violence. And once unleashed, no prayer can save her.

He tries to grab the knife. The room is swimming in a choppy sea of motion. They grapple, and then she lunges toward the front door, trying to escape. But Lyons has the knife now, and he catches her in the foyer, yanking her backward by one arm. She emits a startled yelp. It arouses him further, almost like when he's about to jack off. Mouthing one filthy oath after another, he stabs her over and over with a ferocity meant for his ex-wife. Viciously vindictive, he doesn't stop until the final mortal thud of the blade cuts through bone.

As he stands over her bleeding body, Lyons is down to smoke and ash, wishing the world would just swallow him up. *Oh, shit. Shit, shit, shit.* Now he will lose his job for sure. Unless . . .

He gathers himself, knowing his demeanor at the next house is critical. Yet he cannot quite regain his composure for Ethel Hansen. He's sweating salty bullets, and his heart is hammering.

All that is left in his mind is the frozen horror on Audrey Pugh's face.

2009

Today, the spot where Patty Rebholz was killed (center) is more overgrown than it was in 1963.

THE WHISTLING SHADOW

THE BLUDGEONING OF CHEERLEADER PATTY REBHOLZ: 1963

"Kill then, and bliss me—but first come kiss me."
Thomas Morley

PROLOGUE:

A pretty blonde cheerleader is ambushed and savagely beaten while walking to her boyfriend's home following a teenage dance.

Innocence meets Evil in a suburban enclave.

The murder stunned the serene village of Greenhills and seized front page headlines throughout the summer and fall of 1963. It was a crime reporter's dream.

The victim's 15-year-old boyfriend became the prime suspect, until a friendly judge halted his unremitting interrogations by making him a ward of the court. Yet public opinion had already tried and convicted him.

Investigators chaffed as justice languished for 36 years. But in 2001 this long-running mystery spawned a dramatic second act—when the now 53-year-old boyfriend stood trial for a youthful crime of passion.

NARRATIVE:

Growing up around Greenhills in the 1960s, it was impossible to escape the speculation surrounding the brutal death of 15-year-old cheerleader Patricia Ann Rebholz. The case rivals that of the Bricca family murders (chapter 10) in breeding rumor and gossip.

It began on the muggy Thursday evening of August 8, 1963, so hot that the street stuck to your shoes. The Cincinnati summer swelter was in full force.

Teenagers were turning out for the American Legion Hall dance on Winton Road. Ticket taker Margaret Boyle had counted over 100 kids in attendance, including some boys who were not from Greenhills. Sophomore Bob Hatfield observed "quite a few" strangers there, a "rougher crowd" by his estimation.

Beth Upton was there with her best friend Patty Rebholz. As the girls danced, Beth noticed "pretty many boys" she did not recognize, and watched several of them make "suggestive eye movements" toward her friend.

Patty was too busy dancing to notice. The feisty and popular cheerleader was enjoying herself. Even though she had a steady boyfriend, she was an outgoing girl known as a friendly flirt. The blonde teenager radiated a sense of freedom to those who knew her.

Her boyfriend was 15-year-old Michael Wehrung, a tall youth who lifted weights and was getting ready to play on the freshman football team. They had been dating about four months. He had forbidden her to attend the dances and glowered when she talked with other boys.

And on this night in question, Patty confided to several friends that she wanted to break up with Michael and start dating another boy.

Several months earlier, Michael had given her an onyx ring that had belonged to his grandmother. Patty was wearing it as she left for the dance, but when she hit the floor the ring was inside her purse. Her friends assumed she didn't want other boys to know she was going steady.

This 1963 photo shows the final corner of Patty's last walk.

Patty would not break up over the phone—she wanted to talk to Michael in person. According to Beth, she spent "her last dime" and called the Wehrung home at around 9:30PM, telling Michael's sister that she would walk to their house.

As she hung up the phone, Patty was invited to a trampoline party with Beth. It sounded like fun, but she didn't have any shorts to change into, so she decided to go to Mike's house instead. Beth saw her leave at 9:35PM. She said later that it was the first time Patty ever left her alone at a dance.

A few minutes later, resident Gordon Massey recognized Patty walking on Ingram Road near Ireland. He did not see anyone following her.

Patty strolled down Ingram under yawning shadows as evening faded. She turned left on Jennings Street and was just a short block from Michael's house on Illona Drive.

Her life was down to minutes.

Around 9:40PM, 15-year-old Craig Smith left his job at the Greenhills shopping center and headed home. He was walking the same route Patty Rebholz had taken five minutes earlier.

As he turned onto Jennings, he became aware of two persons in the backyard of the house across from the Wehrung home. It was too dark to recognize either of them, but Craig could see one lying prone and the other kneeling. Thinking it was some couple making out, he continued on his way.

Yet he was unnerved. He later said he felt the eyes of the kneeling person "burning into" him.

When Craig reached the corner of Jennings and Illona, he saw a car packed with teens leaving the Wehrung driveway. Some of Michael's friends and his sister Cheryl were going to pick up hamburgers. They recognized Craig Smith standing at the corner and waved to him.

Michael would later say he became concerned when Patty didn't show up. Around 9:45 he went out to look for her and walked past the lot where Craig Smith had seen the two people. He then returned home and played cards until about 12:40AM.

Meanwhile, Patty's older brother was growing anxious. Mel Rebholz was supposed to pick her up at midnight—he had his own car and spent much of that summer ferrying his sister and her friends.

Now he was parked near the Legion Hall—waiting. Sweating.

When Patty didn't appear by 1AM, he drove home and told his parents. They instantly called the police to report her missing, and then phoned Michael to ask if he had seen Patty. With 45 minutes Mr. Rebholz and Mel arrived at the Wehrung home to talk with Michael.

At 2:30AM Greenhills police put out all points bulletin, unusual since she hadn't been gone for 24 hours. Mel went back out to hunt for Patty, and Michael joined him for a short time. They searched yards east of the Legion Hall before Mike went home to sleep. Mel did not give up so easily. Accompanied by several friends and some police officers, they spent the early morning hours scouring the neighborhood and retracing her route.

Not until the sun was bleeding the horizon did they find her.

Patty Rebholz's battered body was discovered by patrolman Jack Leach at 5:07AM in the rear yard of 1 Illona Drive, which was directly across the street from the Wehrung home. She was found in the exact spot where Craig Smith had seen two persons on the ground—the same backyard Michael had walked through while looking for her.

Officer Leach noted on his report that her body "was cold to the touch with stiffening of the limbs . . . the dew covering the surrounding grassy area had not been disturbed with mine being the first footprints toward the victim." Leach observed that her clothing was disarrayed, but he saw no sign of sexual assault.

She was sprawled on her left side, her feet against the fence at the rear of the lot. Throat bruises indicated her assailant had throttled her into semi-consciousness. Her purse was still wrapped around her right shoulder, contents intact.

Jack Leach fought to keep his composure as he recorded the cause of death:

> **"The victim had been brutally beaten about the face and head by a blunt instrument, apparently a small log 18 inches by 6 inches found at the head of the victim, covered with dark stains, hair, and particles of what I believe to be flesh. There were two lacerations of the right side of the face which was exposed to my view. The right side of the skull was depressed over an area approximately the size of the log. A large amount of blood was on the ground beneath the mouth and nose of the victim . . . removal of body exposed a depression in the ground beneath the skull where skull of victim had been forcibly driven downward."**

Mr. Rebholz was brought to the scene and identified the victim as his daughter. He was seen moments later pounding the hood of a police car as the sun rose behind him.

The question of why she wasn't located earlier was the first of many to be raised. Patty was wearing mostly white clothing, and her body was only 20 feet away from the sidewalk. Yet it had been a cloudy night with sporadic moonlight, and the nearest street lamp was 100 yards from the spot.

During the search, Officer Leach had gone to the Wehrung house to speak with Michael. His report would note that he "observed a fresh scratch on the right wrist of Mike as well as scratches on the left wrist and apparent bruise on left forehead."

And the ring Michael gave Patty was still in her purse.

The county coroner estimated the time of death between 9:30PM and 10:15PM Thursday night, yet people less than 100 feet away were unaware of the crime.

Alphonse Udry and his family were home from 7:45 until they went to bed at 1AM. Although Patty was slain in their backyard, they heard nothing and their dog did not bark at any time.

Mrs. June Minard, whose property abuts the fence where the body was found, was visiting her next door neighbor. They were on the patio with a clear view of the Udry backyard, but neither saw anything suspicious. Mrs. Minard did say she heard "a dull, thudding sound" between 9:15-10:00PM, but thought nothing of it.

Another witness told police he saw several "strange boys" loitering on the Jennings Road sidewalk around 1AM, about 40 feet from where Patty's body lay. He knew most of the neighborhood kids but didn't recognize anyone in this group.

Two potential witnesses to the murder were interviewed around noon on Friday.

Harry Eckstein's headlights had swept over the crime scene as he turned onto Jennings at around 9:45PM. He saw Craig Smith walking and then two figures on the ground near where Patty would be found.

Q: Describe what you saw the objects doing.
A: I saw the object on top straddling the one on the ground—as two teenagers wrestling—the conqueror straddling the one on the ground.
Q: Where did it appear the arms of that party were?

The bludgeoned body of the cheerleader was found just before sunrise.

A: They seemed to be outstretched in a manner holding the victim's arms in place . . . I'm positive the one on top was a boy.
Q: Did it turn and look at you?
A: Yes, the one on top looked in my direction.

Eckstein described the boy as wearing a white shirt and dark pants, but could not identify him as Michael Wehrung.

Craig Smith had been even closer than Eckstein, only 15-20 feet away. But in the muted light of Jennings, he couldn't really be sure what he had seen.

Q: What were they doing?
A: They didn't do anything. One of them was just looking at me, and I just looked at him, or it, and kept on going.
Q: And the person that was kneeling looked up at you?
A: He stared at me as I walked by. Just looked at me, he or she . . . I was positive I didn't know the person.

Smith described the boy as wearing dark pants, and placed the couple "near the middle of the yard, not by the fence." But he stumbled when asked if the person he saw was Michael Wehrung:

Q: Do you think it was him?
A: No, I don't. I couldn't tell who it was.
Q: You don't seem quite sure. Is there something that bothers you about that statement, Craig?
A: I guess it could have been him just as well as it could have been anyone. No, that doesn't sound right either . . . it looked like someone I have never seen before."

Several days later Craig Smith took a polygraph. In the opinion of the examiner, he told "substantially the truth" except for "a slight reaction to the question regarding having seen Mike Wehrung in the lot" where Patty was found.

Less than 24 hours after the crime, two witnesses were being questioned about the victim's boyfriend, whose demeanor had already drawn attention. Michael had been awakened at 5:30AM by police and told that Patty was lying dead across the street. Rather than rush to the scene of his girlfriend's murder, he went back to sleep.

The officers took note—the boyfriend was acting strange and should be considered a suspect.

Greenhills was born as a government subsidized district in the late 1930s, and when World War II escalated, military-style housing barracks lined the streets. The suburb suffered growing pains in the 1950s—Greenhills was entirely surrounded by Winton Woods Park and had no space for expansion. So it remained a charming and cozy village.

In 1963 Greenhills was a bedroom community of 5000 middle-class residents. It was a turbulent year: the Cold War was simmering, federal troops suppressed race riots in the South, and JFK would be assassinated in Dallas.

But in Greenhills, the murder of Patricia Rebholz dominated every conversation. The wicked bludgeoning of the perky blonde cheerleader struck the town with the force of a lightning bolt. Cookouts and cocktail parties were abandoned. Parents wondered: "Could this happen to my daughter? Could my son be involved?"

Mayor Theodore Lindner told the *Enquirer*: "This pricks the bubble that nothing bad can happen in Greenhills . . . The horror of it overwhelms me. You wonder how this can happen in a community like this."

Mrs. Raymond Shirer, whose backyard bordered the murder scene, voiced a strong sentiment: "This won't change our village unless it goes unsolved. When we find out who did it, things will be OK again."

A classmate of Patty's had a different perspective: "She is the first one in our class to die. I've been spending all day trying to figure out why." Greenhill's students were caught in the middle. They were curious about the investigation but afraid of what they might learn. Could one of their friends be the killer?

Years later, Carolyn Udry finally spoke about the murder that occurred in her backyard. "It was hot, and those windows were open, so why didn't we hear anything?" Her German shepherd "would bark if a stranger came into the yard, but on this night he just stood at the door and simply whined."

Carolyn went into her backyard around 11PM, only to be called back inside by her mother. "Many times I've thought how close I must have been standing to Patty. A few feet away? That's how dark it was."

She said that the night of August 8, 1963 had banished her innocence and sentenced her to a life of sinister memories—a legacy shared by the lovely village of Greenhills, Ohio.

Hamilton County investigator Donald Roney tried to diminish the fear factor. "It was an unfortunate murder," he told the *Enquirer.* "I don't feel there's a madman loose in the community." He confirmed the initial report that Patty was not sexually assaulted or the "victim of a deviate."

By Friday afternoon Jennings Road and the Udry backyard had become a carnival for the ghoulish. The neighborhood was gridlocked for several days—cars with Michigan, Indiana, and Kentucky license plates were seen prowling the streets. A cop directing traffic estimated that 600 cars each hour had been passing the crime scene.

Onlookers watched as Coroner Frank Cleveland took a mold of the area by the fence, hoping it would isolate footprints and illuminate the struggle between Patty and her killer. He also took a sample of dark red spots splattered on a patio next door to the Wehrung home.

His work was sent out for lab analysis, along with the victim's clothing and the murder weapon. Mr. Udry said the 2-foot by 5-inch post section wielded by the killer had been leaning against a tree in his backyard for several years.

Motive Is Sought In Bludgeoning Of Greenhills Teen

Fear Discounted That 'Madman' Is In Greenhills

The shocking crime sent waves of dread through the serene village of Greenhills.

Dr. Cleveland announced that Patty had suffered "severe muscular strangulation" before death, indicating prior intent. The killer had not just bashed her in anger—he got personal by using his hands on her throat. The coroner believed Patty was alive but unconscious when the blows were struck, which explained why she hadn't cried out. The force of the beating had left indentations in the ground, yet there were no other injuries on her body besides the head wounds.

By the weekend, Greenhills police insisted they had not established a motive or identified a suspect. But privately, they were fixed on Michael Wehrung. He had been their target from the start, and now a pipeline to the press had thrust the juvenile onto the front page.

Roney himself interrogated Michael the day after the crime. Excerpts from the interview show a confused teenager trying his best to help.

> Q: Did you leave the house between 9:30 and 10PM?
>
> A: Oh, yes, I forgot to tell you . . . I just cut across Udry's grass, you know, where she was found, but more sort of diagonal. So I walked over there and looked both ways and I didn't see her, and I whistled.
>
> Q: How close did you come to the area where Patty was found?

A: About 20 feet. That's why I don't see how she could be there, because I don't think I could have missed her.
Q: When you walked through the lot, was there much light there?
A: No, not too much. I wasn't paying any attention . . . I didn't have anything on my mind.

Wehrung had placed himself at the scene near the time of the murder, but did not seem concerned about it.

Roney now had the means and the opportunity—he pressed Michael for the motive:

Q: Did you mind her going to the dance without you?
A: We had an argument, and I told her I didn't want her to go. After it was all over, though, I told her that if that was what she wanted to do, she can do it.
Q: How many arguments did you have in the course of the four months?
A: You mean just small things?
Q: Right.
A: I guess about 50 of 'em.

It was hard to reconcile a teenage spat with the battered girl now lying in the morgue. Roney began to play the "good cop:"

Q: Why would you be scared, Mike?
A: I don't know.
Q. You are just a young lad . . . No matter what—if you did it—still nothing could happen to you because you are only a boy.
A: Yes.
Q: There's no reason to be upset or shaky. We're just trying to figure out how the girl came to an end.
A: I understand.

X marks the spot where Patty was found in this 1963 police photo.

But then Roney pounced on Mike's inconsistent statements about his clothing:

Q: Why this sudden tidiness, that the shirt would be in the laundry hamper?
A: Because I was downstairs when I changed to my swimming suit.
Q: How did the shirt get down to the hamper with the levis upstairs?
A: I don't know. I don't know what I'm talking about.
Q: Mike, we're in a very serious position here.
A: I know we are. You have me so confused I don't know what I'm doing.

Young Wehrung had shown remarkable composure during this first of many interviews. But by asking the same questions in different ways, Donald Roney had uncovered contradictions regarding Mike's clothing, his cut wrist, and his movements between 9:30 and 10PM.

Less than 24 hours into the investigation, the lanky teenager was in the crosshairs.

Other friends of Michael and Patty were interviewed over the weekend. Soon investigators had doubts about just how "steady" their relationship really was.

Tom Stonefield, age 16, had recently asked Patty to break up with Mike and go steady with him. After kissing her in the backseat of a car, she told him she "had to think about it." Stonefield also claimed that Patty never wore Mike's ring and "didn't act like a girl going steady."

Lois Schuehler, age 17, had casually dated Mike and wasn't friendly with Patty. "He didn't act too broke up about it (the murder) . . . I don't think he was so crazy about her." She also mentioned that Mrs. Wehrung "allowed her children to drink" in the house.

Mike's sister Cheryl admitted that he had been drinking beer in the basement while playing Ping Pong, and she found it strange that her brother had changed his pants in the basement: "Mike usually doesn't worry how his clothes look."

Ray St. Clair was Michael's best friend. He had driven the group for hamburgers, and when they returned he saw Mike lying on the couch, watching TV with his mother. When they played cards later, Ray saw the cut on Mike's wrist that he hadn't noticed when they played Ping Pong earlier.

And there was this telling exchange after Ray said that Cheryl was scared.

> Q: Scared about what?
> A: She is scared of Mike.
> Q: Why?
> A: Well, I guess she thinks he did it; I don't know.
> Q: Was this the first time she ever discussed this?

1963 photos show just how out in the open the murder scene was. The Wehrung home is on the left in the picture below.

> A: She told me already that he could have went out of his mind . . . and she seems serious about it, you know, like it is something that could happen.

But when Ray asked Cheryl if she thought her brother did it, "she said no." Ray himself thought that "anybody could have done it."

On the Monday after the crime, Michael was taken to Norwood by Greenhills police and "grilled for nine hours," according to the Enquirer headline.

This interrogation "generated a carnival air," with over 100 people keeping vigil outside the station. When Donald Roney emerged during a break, someone yelled, "What are you trying to do, brainwash that boy?"

Roney claimed they were handling Michael with kid gloves. "We have been dealing with a young boy, and every consideration must be shown for his youth and well—being . . . Mike is not in custody and never has been in custody . . . We realize that there is no place for a punitive attitude toward the boy under investigation."

Roney declared that Wehrung's parents "had no problem" with the prolonged questioning of their son. He said they were so certain of Michael's innocence that they didn't request a lawyer, even though he had encouraged them to retain one.

He also denied the investigation had "bogged down. We've got a ton of circumstantial evidence now," he crowed to reporters, but would not elaborate.

County prosecutor Ray Shannon made this statement to the press after a conference with his investigators: "The lie detector tests which we have been administrating yesterday and today led us to conclude that Michael Wehrung is attempting deception." He refused to answer questions, walking out as shouted queries echoed down the hall.

On the morning after the murder, Michael Wehrung was already the prime suspect.

The next day Shannon announced that blood spots were found on the white pants Mike wore the night of the murder. They were type B blood, matching Patty Rebholz—Wehrung had type O blood. The teenager could not explain how the stains got there. Shannon also complained that Michael had given them a dark shirt he claimed to have worn that night, yet witnesses said he wore a white t-shirt.

When Wehrung left the police station with his parents after yet another "interview," several people shouted, "There he is!" and Michael smiled briefly. The crowd was neither hostile nor friendly.

"Son, did you tell them the truth?" Mrs. Wehrung asked.

The boy cried, "Yes, Mom, I told them the truth, but they won't believe me."

Speaking to a reporter, the teenager seemed as bewildered as everyone else. "I know the bloodstains don't lie. I know the lie detector doesn't lie. I know I don't lie . . . I don't understand it."

Michael denied any involvement in Patty's death, insisting, "Kids know that when you like a girl, you'd not even slap her. Unless a boy is crazy, he would never kill her." Then he added, "I'm sure I'll be in the clear soon."

Prosecutors would press the teenage suspect for the next two weeks, putting him through an exhausting agenda of interrogation. At the same time, an apparently friendly reporter began to hang around the Wehrung house.

Investigators honed in on their man. Except that their man was a 15-year-old boy.

On Monday night there was a closed casket visitation for Patty. A mostly teenage crowd estimated at 1500 thronged to the Hodapp Funeral Home. "She was just about the most popular freshman at school," sniffed one classmate, fighting back tears.

A Greenhills mother pointed out a group of girls sobbing into their handkerchiefs. "Look at them. Last week they were thinking about dates and clothes. Now they know the hard reality of life and death."

Cincinnati Enquirer reporter Margaret Josten kept her eyes on Patty's boyfriend:

> **Michael Wehrung might have been watching a bad movie as he sat stiff and straight in the parlor of the funeral home. Not once during the brief last rites for Patricia Ann Rebholz, his girlfriend of four months, did a sign of emotion touch his handsome face . . . And Mike's flowers were there, a dozen red roses, standing on a little table near the casket.**

Slain Girl's Beau Given Tests To Determine Type Of Blood

Michael Grilled For Nine Hours But Keeps Calm

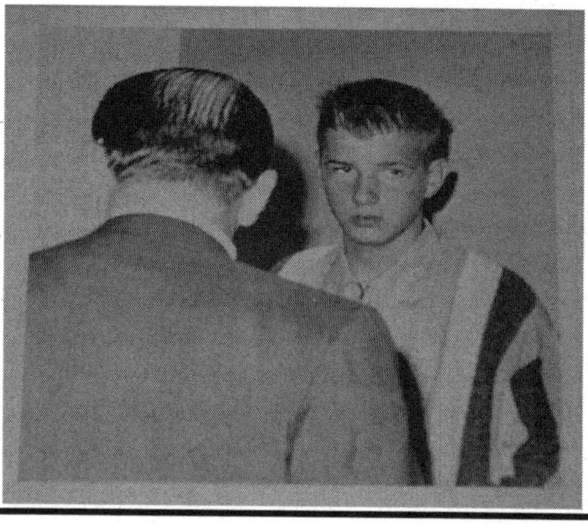

Questioning of Michael Wehrung will resume Thursday in Greenhills after a day-long session in Norwood Wednesday.

Donald Roney, chief investigator for the prosecutor's office, said late Wednesday that others would also be questioned in efforts to trace the movements of Patrica Ann Rebholz last Thursday night.

Mr. Roney said that in questioning Michael "we have been dealing with a young boy, and every consideration must be shown for his youth and well being."

The teenager is beginning to show the strain of the relentless interrogations.

As Patty was laid to rest the next morning, County investigators met with Greenhills police to compare notes.

They agreed that Wehrung's version of events on the murder night remained essentially the same during the prolonged interrogation sessions, with some minor discrepancies.

At around 9:30 that Thursday night, Wehrung's sister Cheryl had taken the phone call from Patty while Michael was in the basement playing Ping Pong. Cheryl told him Patty would stop by shortly. Mike told her to tell Patty he would be expecting her.

Patty's parents had told the police that it was unusual for her to visit Mike at that hour—and the last time she did was to discuss a problem with him.

At about 9:45, several of Mike's friends left the Wehrung home to get hamburgers. They took Cheryl with them, and she bought a hamburger for Patty.

Just before 10PM, Mike sauntered up Jennings Road to Ingram to see if Patty was still coming over. He said he walked through the backyard where she was later found. The timing was close to the coroner's death estimate, and Wehrung had placed himself at the murder scene.

Thinking her brother had picked her up, Mike returned home at 10:05 to wait for her call. Friends on the hamburger run returned with Cheryl at around 10:45. He played cards and watched television until 12:40PM, when Mrs. Rebholz called. Then Mr. Rebholz arrived at 1:15PM, looking for his daughter.

Mike made a cursory search with Patty's brother and then went to sleep on the living room couch at about 2AM. He did not normally sleep on the sofa.

One week after the murder, Prosecutor Shannon announced that his office would cease questioning Michael Wehrung unless there was a new development. At the same time, he outlined the reasons they were pursuing Wehrung.

- Michael's polygraph results: Shannon said the tests showed Wehrung was "attempting deception." Testing methods would later be called into question.
- Michael gave them the wrong shirt: Witnesses said he was wearing a white t-shirt, yet he gave investigators a dark button-down shirt.
- Blood stains on his pants matched Patty's blood type: Small stains were found on the knees of the pants. Wehrung could not say how they got there.
- Michael's alibi could not be verified: Neither friend nor family could account for his whereabouts during the crucial period between 9:30 and 10:00PM.
- Patty was ready to break up with Michael: She had taken the ring off at the dance and was not wearing it when she was found.

Donald Roney also revealed some new evidence—Officer Jack Leach had found a tooth fragment 20 feet from where the body was found. Leach came across it on Saturday after the murder, but Roney had held it back to blindside suspects during questioning. The tooth nailed down the point of attack, confirming that Patty had been choked and then dragged to the spot where she was fatally beaten with the fence post.

Asked about the motive, Roney answered, "Jealousy is a possible motive in this. It's one reason people kill people."

It was just a matter of time before Michael Wehrung was charged with the murder of Patricia Rebholz. But time was one commodity the police could not hoard.

The *Enquirer* profiled the beleaguered family on August 17, with an article headlined **"Wehrung's Composure Frays under Heavy Burden."** Included was a group portrait right out of the TV show "Father Knows Best," showing a smiling Art Wehrung with an arm around his sheepishly grinning teenager.

Michael's father told reporters that his son wanted to cooperate, but that the constant interviews were taking a toll: "I don't like this grilling. I don't want the interrogations to go on endlessly."

Mrs. Dawn Wehrung complained about the bad publicity and then went off on the reporter: "I'm tired of cooperating!" She claimed photographers were making Michael "look like a criminal."

Michael was more composed. "People seem to be with me. The publicity hasn't bothered me. I know I am telling the truth in my own heart."

The next day, the Cincinnati chapter of the ACLU made a formal protest to Prosecutor Shannon about their "treatment of the Wehrung boy and the unfortunate spectacular publicity." They considered the questioning "abusive and harmful" and were concerned about "the ruin of a young man's reputation."

Today, a juvenile suspect could not be identified in a Cincinnati newspaper. But in 1963, the name Michael Wehrung was out there every day. The TV news portrayed him as the likely killer, ignoring the fact that he wasn't even 16 yet, much less 18.

As days turned into weeks, Wehrung was being probed and prodded without letup. His parents accompanied him to these sessions, but they were not in the room during the grueling interrogations and tedious polygraphs.

A juvenile court judge named Benjamin Schwartz had been following the inquiry with great interest. Judge Schwartz, a staunch children's rights advocate, was concerned about the relentless questioning. He considered the media blitz and law enforcement pressure damaging to the boy's well being, and he believed that Michael's rights were being violated.

Schwartz recalled that lead investigator Donald Roney was caught fabricating evidence in the 1956 Pugh murder (Chapter 7). Roney had initiated a confession from meter reader Robert Lyons by falsely claiming police had found his fingerprint near the murder scene. The judge was afraid the boy would be fed phony details to force a confession, which was a standard interrogation technique at the time.

Michael Wehrung was legally still a child—a child being roasted by the media and hammered by the police.

Three weeks after the murder Schwartz took action. On September 1, the judge met with the Wehrung family, and the parents initiated a petition which was immediately granted. Schwartz officially made Michael Wehrung a ward of the court, thus protecting him from further questioning about the murder of Patricia Rebholz. He was convinced any statement the boy made during hours of "intense interrogation and lie detector tests . . . would be illegal and contrary to law."

It was a devastating blow to Greenhills police and Hamilton County authorities, who needed more time to investigate a crime of this magnitude. They were now constrained in their access to their suspect.

A WCPO-TV news editorial summed up their frustration: "Whatever the explanation, the transferal of Michael Wehrung from the status of free and fifteen . . . to dependent of the Juvenile Court . . . without any official elaboration . . . has certainly clouded the murder investigation in the public mind, more than it has cleared it."

Yet those who knew Schwartz were not surprised by his intervention. He often brandished his judgeship as a mandate to help problem teenagers, using a constructive approach instead of punitive measures.

Two weeks after granting the petition, Schwartz sent Michael to a private military school in Georgia. His actions were lauded by some as benevolent, but police were vocal with their exasperation. This juvenile court encroachment had effectively chilled the investigation.

On October 6, Arthur Wehrung died of pneumonia. Michael's father had been unwavering in his support of this son—perhaps the media crush had finally worn him down. His doctor assured the press that the death was "not in the least mysterious."

With Michael out of the state, the investigation went dark for more than a year, before the case fluttered back to life in 1965.

A witness who drove by the murder scene at 9:45 that night finally came forward. His headlights had swept the lot, and he saw a "youth" kneeling near a prostrate person. The boy froze in the glare and the driver got an excellent look at him.

This man was not from Greenhills and quickly forgot the incident. Only when reading an article about the case two years later did he make the connection, and he believed the kneeling youth "strongly resembled" a picture he saw in the article. It was a photo of Michael Wehrung.

Detectives wanted to question the now 17-year-old Wehrung, but were hesitant about getting Judge Schwartz's permission. The judge finally agreed that they could question the teenager, but only in court and with a lawyer present.

This new lead withered inside the file jacket, and detectives pulled the plug on the active investigation. Early in 1966 Michael Wehrung was granted re-admission to Greenhills High School. Though some tried to dissuade him, he was back in class by early February for his senior year.

It was either an act of defiance or innocence. Because this case could never go cold—it would simmer and seethe for the next three decades.

Those who grew up in Greenhills during this time were caught up in the rumors roiling around Patty's murder. Their memories are still vivid.

Screenwriter Richard Kuhlman was an eight-year-old resident in 1963. Returning to his hometown as an adult in 1995, he was astounded to discover that the Rebholz case still had a persistent pulse.

"Whenever you sit around with a group of people from Greenhills, somebody will bring up Patty Rebholz. Everyone will compare notes," explained Kuhlman. "And then, as you grow older, it kind of becomes a ghost story."

"The slaying didn't cause panic in the streets," he told the Enquirer. "But at the very least it was sacrilegious to her. Here was a beautiful 15-year-old girl who had her life ahead of her, and all she was doing was apparently changing boyfriends."

The local obsession resonated with Kuhlman, and inspired him to write a play called, "Confessions of a Lady-Killer," which opened in Hollywood in 1995.

While rummaging through the police document room in 1993, Kuhlman uncovered some peculiar witness statements. A Greenhills resident suspected "a guy who has power tools in his garage that he never uses" and "handed out pencils for Halloween." Another man was suspicious of his neighbor because his garage was locked on the murder night: "There was something going on in there that night."

Hidden among the minutiae was a long buried coroner's report, with a margin note indicating that "the boyfriend" had said "his other self" could have committed the crime.

Kuhlman's venture into the case jacket and ensuing publicity about his research revived interest in the Rebholz case. And in a harsh coincidence, a parallel mystery from the East Coast was heating up and receiving national attention.

Kennedy family cousin Michael Skakel had just been indicted for the 1975 murder of Martha Moxley in upscale Greenwich, Connecticut. As in the Rebholz case, a teenage girl had been bludgeoned, and the prime suspect was a 15-year-old boy who had placed himself near the crime scene. Other similarities included suspects named Michael and cities that began with Green. The TV news show "48 Hours" would eventually air an episode profiling both cases.

Inevitably, a reporter contacted Patty's brother Mel, who now lived out of state. He was still bitter about the decision of Judge Schwartz to intervene and make Michael Wehrung a ward of the court. "Everything just stopped at that point, the police investigations, the reporting, everything else," said Mel. "We were never given any full explanation of why he wasn't charged at the time, and basically it was kept pretty much of a secret where he went."

Mel talked of the devastation to his family because of the Schwartz decision. His parents were "deeply religious," and they "tried to work out what happened in terms of their beliefs, but they couldn't do it. They basically lost their religion." Going further, Rebholz insisted that "the people in the community all of a sudden realized there was evil out there and that it did exist . . . . it changed everybody in that area."

The renewed interest in the case stirred up painful memories for Patty's brother. Before she became the tragic victim of a murder mystery, Mel's kid sister "was friends to everybody. She was very much an ideal person."

These remarks by the only surviving member of the Rebholz family did not go unnoticed. The case was rumbling back to life, and rolling toward a resolution.

In November of 1999, Hamilton County Prosecutor Mike Allen announced he was launching a new investigation. "Whoever killed Patty Rebholz has gotten away with murder for 36 years," he declared. "We're going to do everything in our power to bring this person to justice."

Allen said his investigators had started digging in the spring of 1998. "We received information that the Greenhills Police Department was gathering some information about the case . . . we decided there was significant evidence and a justification to reopen the case."

His office had sent letters to Patty's former classmates and 40 responded—none of them had been consulted in 1963. Believing that the clothing and other physical evidence were in good condition, Allen shipped them off for DNA testing, only to learn the unsealed boxes revealed water damage that might compromise testing.

A stack of old tape recordings was found with the case jacket. Without explanation, Allen asserted that "we have reason to believe there could be a confession" on the tapes. The recordings were too old to play on a modern tape recorder, so a service was being hired to transcribe them.

Mike Allen refused to say how many suspects there were, but admitted Michael Wehrung was one of them. "He is a suspect," was the prosecutor's terse response, "but I'm not ruling anybody out."

Longtime Greenhills residents were aroused.

Craig Hammond said the murder had haunted the neighborhood for years because there was no closure: "Being from the area, I've always heard about it . . . If Wehrung is innocent, he needs to come forward and clear himself. They must have something more than DNA to drag this up again."

WEDNESDAY, DECEMBER 20, 2000

Report sheds light on 1963 slaying

'Other self' could have killed
Patty Rebholz, suspect said then

Many sealed documents and confidential files were released when the investigation was reopened in 1999.

Greenhills postmistress Carol Kuhlman heard the chatter among her customers. It was her son Richard who had delved into the evidence locker and emerged with incriminating data against Wehrung. "I'm probably the only one in town who doesn't think the boyfriend is guilty," she admitted, instead pointing the finger at the "mysterious handyman" whom she claimed was a suspect in 1963. She added that "bringing it up now is going to hurt a lot of people."

Indeed, most residents were against a trial for Wehrung. It was as if the town wanted to shelter its private shame.

Michael Wehrung was still living in the area. A vice-president for a local roofing company, he had led a relatively quiet life since returning to the area in 1966. Wehrung refused comment and deflected all questions to his attorney, who gave this statement to reporters: "He has always professed his innocence, and he stands by that."

Eventually Mike Allen leaked a tantalizing scenario from the long buried coroner's report uncovered by Richard Kuhlman six years earlier. Wehrung had told an investigator in 1963 that there was a possibility he was the killer. "The real me would not strike a girl," the report quoted Michael, but he couldn't help feeling that his "other self" had committed the crime.

In January of 2000, newsman Tom Schell revisited the murder scene with a *Cincinnati Enquirer* journalist. Schell was the WCPO-TV reporter who covered the case in 1963, and he had information that could help investigators.

He had spent the weeks after the murder supporting the Wehrung family while pumping Michael for information—he was the "friendly reporter." Schell "hung out" with the teenager, playing Ping Pong, shooting baskets, and just talking.

"He had incredible access," Mike Allen pointed out. "He is someone who could be a very valuable witness for us." Schell was scheduled to give a sworn statement during his visit. Living in California and in poor health, he wanted to get this off his chest while there was still time.

He had been close with both the Wehrung and Rebholz families, an unusual position for a newsman. "It was emotionally draining," he sighed to the reporter while standing at the murder scene, his weary melancholy drifting over the backyard where Patty died.

In March of 2000, Mike Allen sought an indictment to try Michael Wehrung as an adult. On May 2 he was indicted for the murder of Patty Rebholz—new evidence from the 40 classmates Allen interviewed had swayed the Grand Jury.

Wehrung was arrested, booked, bonded, and released after pleading not guilty.

His lawyers immediately sought to transfer the case to juvenile court, arguing that it wasn't his fault charges weren't filed in 1963. Had he been convicted as a juvenile, Wehrung would have been incarcerated until he was 21, yet as an adult he was now facing the rest of his life behind bars.

It was a persuasive argument. However, their appeal was denied and started a trend—the defense lost every legal maneuver they attempted for the next two years. Their challenge to remove Patrick Dinkelacker as the trial judge failed. They appealed the juvenile vs. adult question to the Ohio State Supreme Court, but a 1997 law had cleared the way to try Wehrung in adult court.

His lawyers then argued it was unfair to retroactively apply a new law to a 1963 crime, but the high court decision was upheld. Their ruling put "justice in a time warp," according to one *Enquirer* editorial.

That same week Tom Schell returned to Cincinnati to give his deposition. It made the defense team squirm, because he was the first person to link Michael Wehrung to the crime scene. Schell confirmed that in 1963 some of Wehrung's relatives had begun to question his innocence. Michael's father asked Schell to find out if his son was involved in the slaying, so they could "get him help."

Schell recalled that the teenager told him he saw Patty walking toward his house, and admitted to slapping her when she made some remark. Michael didn't remember killing her but wondered if it might have been "his other self."

Wehrung's attorney challenged Schell's testimony, peppering him with questions. Earl Maiman had limited criminal trial experience, but he was a bulldog on behalf of his client. Now he voiced astonishment that the veteran TV reporter had not taken notes and had failed to broadcast this stunning revelation in 1963!

Schell said he was protecting Wehrung's juvenile status, but Maiman pointed out that Michael's name had already been splashed across countless front pages by local media. Schell claimed he gave Judge Schwartz a memo regarding Wehrung's comments, yet within days the judge declared him off limits to police. "It was nothing but a political mess," Schell decided.

In December, 2000, the infamous coroner's report from 1965 was exhumed during pretrial motions. In it, deceased investigator Wilbert Stagenhorst had compiled a startling dossier against Michael Wehrung.

After first telling police he was home all night, Wehrung admitted to going out and confronting Patty. "When he saw her, he softly whistled to her and she came walking towards him," the report stated. When she made a "smart remark" he knocked her to the ground. Wehrung even remembered Craig Smith walking by the lot, and described the two of them locking eyes with a "burning stare," confirming Smith's 1963 description.

The report also exposed Michael's lack of concern for his girlfriend. Upon learning of her death, he had gone back to sleep rather than going to the scene. "He thought he was mentally sick," Stagenhorst wrote. "He knew whose body was on the stretcher. In his mind, this was Pat on the stretcher."

Most incriminating was Stagenhorst's interview with Norwood Police Captain Harry Schlie, the man who had administered Michael's polygraph tests. According to Schlie, "after each test there was a rest period given to Mike, in which we sat around and just talked and smoked cigarettes . . . in order to give the boy plenty of rest."

It was during these informal chats that Michael opened up to Schlie: "the boy practically pleaded with me to assist him to get over his mental block." At one point Schlie asked Mike if he had "a split personality . . . he was continuously saying that there were two Mike Wehrungs . . . and he feels, in his own mind, that the other Mike Wehrung probably killed Pat Rebholz."

As damaging as the report was, some of it was strictly hearsay, and Wehrung's lawyers were confident that most of it would be ruled inadmissible at trial.

In February, 2001, Earl Maiman sought to have his client's statements thrown out and the charges dismissed. He argued that Wehrung's parents were forced in 1963 to make their son the court's ward. "It was a gun-to-the-head deal," Maiman told judge Dinkelacker. "You folks either send him away, or we're going to charge him."

Prosecutor Allen countered with another surprise witness. Diane Fisher Blackburn was Patty's close friend in 1963. Over 37 years later, she testified that the cheerleader was planning to break up with her football player boyfriend. Speaking on the phone just hours before Patty died, Blackburn recalled that she wanted to end her relationship with Wehrung before dating the "other boy," and that she wanted to do it in person.

Wehrung's lawyers countered by demanding why she hadn't come forward in 1963, and suggesting the passage of time had clouded her memory.

But Allen had put the motive out there. He later claimed Blackburn's story had been the pivotal evidence for getting the

Suspect on trial – 38 years later

Proceedings begin Monday in slaying of Greenhills teen

By Marie McCain
The Cincinnati Enquirer

The president was John F. Kennedy. The Angels' "My Boyfriend's Back" was a top hit. Pete Rose was in his debut season as a second baseman with the Cincinnati Reds.

It was August 1963, a time imbued with a sense of innocence – a time when Cincinnati teens could walk home from a dance in the dark without fear of danger.

Then Patty Rebholz, a pretty 15-year-old cheerleader, was found beaten to death in a vacant Greenhills lot.

The first incident of its kind in thissuburban community 20 miles northwest of Cincinnati, her homicide shocked Greenhills residents almost as much as news that police suspected her boyfriend, 15-year-old Michael Wehrung.

Investigators questioned him for weeks and learned from the girl's friends that Patty intended to break up with Michael. But a juvenile-court judge intervened and sent the boy out of state to military school.

Rebholz

The investigation into Patty's death stalled, her family anguished, and the tragic story became part of Greenhills history, rehashed at dinner parties, school reunions and in anniversary media reports.

It wasn't until last year, following a new investigation into one of Hamilton County's oldest unsolved murder cases, that someone was finally charged with killing the popular teen.

On Monday, Mr. Wehrung – now a 54-year-old grandfather and executive with a suburban roofing company – goes to trial charged with second-degree murder.

Some hope the trial brings closure to a case that changed the middle-class community of 5,000 people forever.

"It was like living on a pillow," Richard Kuhlman, a Greenhills native who now lives in Los Angeles, said of the village in 1963. "It was easy. It was sweet. It was sunshine all the time. ... Greenhills was about as Americana as some of those novels can spin it. It was

Legal arguments
Effort to get case tried in juvenile court has been controversial. B5

See SUSPECT, Page B5

Decades later, county prosecutors finally tried to expedite justice for Patty Rebholz.

charges filed. "Why would a 15-year-old boy lose his temper?" asked Assistant Prosecutor Mark Piepmeier. "It's because of what happens with teenagers every day. She broke up with him."

In August, 2000, Dinkelacker released more documents in response to yet another appeal. Most damaging was the statement of a friend who saw fresh cuts on Michael's wrists at 10:30 on the murder night. Another report painted Wehrung as a jealous liar who was upset when Patty pressured him to improve his grades—Michael had been held back and was going to have to repeat his freshman year.

Earl Maiman kept trying to get Wehrung classified as a juvenile, but three more courts turned him down. A flurry of other pretrial motions went nowhere. So on a cold day just after Thanksgiving in 2001, Michael Wehrung took a seat where many thought he should have sat decades ago—in the defendant's chair.

The trial of Michael Wehrung should never have taken place.

The Ohio Supreme Court had used twisted logic to apply a 1997 law to the 1963 case. They ruled Michael was not "apprehended" until after his 21st birthday and must therefore be tried as an adult, ignoring the fact he was in semi-custody during his endless interrogations, and that Judge Schwartz took control of his life and banished him to a military school.

Mike Allen pursued the indictment as if he had no other choice under the no statute of limitations clause. Yet he was convinced that Wehrung had gotten away with murder. The case was revived not because of a DNA finding, but because Mike Allen didn't like the way it had played out in 1963.

To many observers this trial seemed like a vendetta. In an *Enquirer* editorial titled, **"A Case that Never Died"**, David Wells wrote that "taking this man to trial now, as an adult, somehow seems more like an attempt to rewrite history than to correct an injustice." Wells pointed out that "Mr. Wehrung didn't beat the system in 1963. The system simply sent him off for a couple of years and then spit him out."

The trial began on Monday, November 26, with Judge Dinkelacker ruling that prosecutors could not use some statements from four dead witnesses. But he decided that notes from a deceased police officer containing details of Wehrung's "alleged confession" were admissible.

It took three hours to select a jury of seven women and five men, and they were given a tour of the crime scene later that day. After opening arguments on Tuesday, the prosecution called Mel Rebholz as its first witness.

Mel had returned to Cincinnati from his Florida home to seek justice for Patty. "It's almost surreal," he told reporters. "After 38 years I'm finally standing in a courtroom to have somebody answer to my sister's murder . . . hopefully we'll be able to get some closure out of this."

Mel was 17 the night his sister didn't show up for a ride home from the dance. He told of going the Wehrungs' house to look for her, and Michael had agreed to join the search. But Mel said he only stayed out for 30 minutes, claiming his mother wanted him home. "He didn't seem too concerned," Rebholz testified. "He was very quiet."

Craig Smith was the closest eyewitness to the murder. Now 54 years old, he recounted his 1963 statements about passing a young couple on the ground at the murder scene. He watched them briefly, and then quickly moved on from what he assumed was a romantic encounter.

He confirmed that a car driving past swept its headlights across the two figures. But to the exasperation of prosecutors,

Friend testifies about breakup

Prosecutors say girl killed in 1963 over split

By Dan Horn
The Cincinnati Enquirer

Wehrung

Rebholz

Patricia Rebholz told a high-school friend 38 years ago that she wanted to meet with her boyfriend one last time so she could break up with him.

Prosecutors say the meeting ended with Patricia's murder.

"Why would a 15-year-old boy lose his temper?" asked assistant prosecutor Mark Piepmeier. "It's because of what happens with teen-agers every day. She broke up with him."

Evidence of motive was introduced at the trial—Patty was walking to Michael's house to end their relationship.

he still would not identify Michael Wehrung as the youth kneeling in the Udry backyard.

Allen introduced part of the Stagenhorst report at this time. In 1965 the deceased investigator had written that Mike recognized Craig Smith walking by. "The one thing he remembers and that worries him more than anything else is that he could feel Smitty's eyes burning into his eyes, and his eyes burning into Smitty's eyes."

The trial's first day of testimony wrapped up with ten more prosecution witnesses, many testifying that Patty was ready to break up with Wehrung face-to-face. One ear witness near the crime scene told of hearing voices followed by the sound of someone "slapping a football." Prosecutors believed this was the sound of Wehrung bashing in Patty's skull.

Throughout this parade to the witness stand, Michael Wehrung showed no visible emotion.

Former Hamilton County Coroner Frank Cleveland painted a grisly picture via his videotaped testimony on Wednesday, with details far worse than what had been printed in 1963. Patty had been throttled, dragged by her feet, and bludgeoned so ferociously that two teeth were knocked out and pieces of her skull were driven into her brain. Yet she had no defensive wounds on her body—the strangulation had rendered her incapable of resisting or crying out.

Wehrung again had no reaction as photos of Patty's battered body flashed onto the video screen.

The last prosecution witness was a reluctant one. Ray St. Clair was Wehrung's employer, best friend, and former brother-in-law. Mike Allen showed him transcripts of his 1963 interview when St. Clair gave conflicting statements from the witness stand.

When confronted with his original statement that Michael was "always hurting Pat," St. Clair tried to back peddle: "He would say mean things to hurt her feelings and not pay attention to her." He added that Wehrung often wrestled with Patty but did "not really hurt her." He said Wehrung's temper was "no different from anyone else's."

St. Clair insisted he didn't see Wehrung leave the house before he drove to get hamburgers with the other kids. Upon returning, he did spot a scratch on Wehrung's wrist that he hadn't noticed earlier.

Michael Wehrung had so far listened stoically as others portrayed his actions on the night his girlfriend was murdered. On Friday of the trial's first week, the most damaging witness of all spoke to the court—the defendant himself. Over vigorous objections, prosecutors introduced notes from his 1963 interview with police officer Chris Waldeck.

Waldeck obtained this "confession" after conferring with TV reporter Tom Schell about Wehrung's "other self" knocking Patty down in the lot. The now deceased cop had prodded Michael and eventually wrote, "He thought it was him that killed Pat. In fact, he was sure he did, but he couldn't remember anything about it."

Wehrung's 1963 statements were conflicting and damaging. Michael had initially told detectives he never left the house that night, only to admit later that he had crossed the lot where Patty was found. And he made an astounding statement when he was asked how he missed seeing Patty's body during his search. She was wearing light clothes under a half moon, yet Wehrung said at the time that he "wasn't paying much attention."

He also speculated about luring Patty to the lot with a soft whistle, where his "other self" may have killed her. This statement had already been introduced, but not in Michael's own words.

This tallied three separate "confessions" introduced as evidence—from Schell, Stagenhorst, and Waldeck. The defense termed them "psycho babble" and reminded everyone of what Michael had endured: "What the media and public were doing to him was way out of control."

Yet Michael Wehrung had been a devastating witness against himself.

The prosecution was closing strong. Tom Schell would be their last witness. Because of rapidly declining health, the former TV reporter's testimony from the pretrial hearings the previous March had been videotaped.

Wehrung had made several incriminating statements to Schell during the period when the newsman was hanging out with the family. He said he spotted Patty walking toward his house, then grabbed her and knocked her down. The "other self" remark came up again, with Schell saying, "I never heard anything like that before. I thought maybe he just forgot about the killing."

As the prosecution rested its case, Patty's murder was once again the talk of the village. "It is a cloud hanging over Greenhills," sighed the mayor.

The defense case was short and to the point. Michael Wehrung did not testify, and his lawyers called only five witnesses.

Tom Stonefield was the boy Patty kissed in a car weeks before her death. Now in his 50s, Stonefield testified he asked her to break up with Wehrung and go steady with him. But she had refused, saying Michael would not take back the ring he gave her. Stonefield did a nice job of casting doubt on the "breakup" theory.

Wehrung's sister Cheryl testified that she saw a stranger cross the street near their house on the night Patty was slain. She also claimed that a Greenhills police officer caused her to be afraid of Michael. "He told me over and over again that Mike had killed Patty, and that he'd buried the memory, and I had to help him," Cheryl explained. "I knew Mike did not do this. He would never do anything like this."

Barry Hatfield was an 11-year-old who saw Patty on her final walk in 1963. He said hello to her as she walked by—the last person to speak to her other than the killer. He testified about seeing an odd teenager following Patty. "He wore taps on his shoes," said Hatfield. "He was average height with slicked back hair and Buddy Holly-type black-rimmed glasses. The ear pieces were chrome. His pants were dark."

Barry did not recognize the boy. "He didn't speak to me, he didn't look at me. He appeared focused on her . . . It wasn't Michael Wehrung . . . I don't know who it was."

Bonnie Armstrong corroborated Hatfield's testimony as she described a terrifying encounter she had on the night of the murder. Only 15 at the time, Armstrong had been at the Legion Hall dance and left at 9:30PM, walking the same route Patty would traverse minutes later.

Bonnie testified that someone was following her. As she quickened her pace, they caught up to her and grabbed her shoulder, but she broke free and ran all the way home. She had recognized the stalker as 16-year-old Robert Goodballett, and after hearing of Patty's murder she told her parents about him. Bonnie's mother called police, but they never got back to her.

Barry Hatfield also told his story to the Greenhills police, but was met with a shrug. They had already passed judgment on Wehrung. Plus Hatfield could not identify the boy he saw following Patty as Goodballet.

Goodballet, a Los Angeles resident now known as Robin Conrad, was the final defense witness. He admitted he enjoyed sneaking up on people because "it was fun," yet he denied sneaking up on either Bonnie or Patty that night. Conrad had walked past the spot where the body was later found, which had unnerved him: "My God, I must have walked right by her." Conrad also testified that he was never questioned during the 1963 investigation.

The defense rested having identified two possible killers—Goodballet and the boy seen by Hatfield—but accomplishing little else. They had not addressed the glut of circumstantial evidence weighing down the defendant.

Motive, means, and opportunity remained in the sole possession of Michael Wehrung.

During closing arguments, defense attorney Earl Maiman implored jurors to ignore "Mike's white lie." Apparently the "naïve, embarrassed, and foolish" teenager told police he'd left the house and cut through the murder scene because he hadn't searched for Patty when she didn't show. "He felt lousy that he didn't go out to look for her," Maiman explained. "This is not the kind of story that a guilty person would tell."

Maiman questioned why Wehrung hadn't been arrested 38 years earlier. He even hinted that authorities waited almost four decades so key witnesses would die, thereby improving their chance of a conviction.

The prosecution took offense with this aspersion in their summation. "To think that this was delayed 38 years for an advantage is insulting," Mike Allen protested.

He centered on three points of Wehrung's guilt:

- His statement placing himself at the murder scene.
- Patty's type B blood on his pants—even though this evidence had since deteriorated.
- His confessions to both a reporter and a policeman.

Assistant Prosecutor Piepmeier ridiculed defense efforts to portray Robert Goodballet as the killer because he liked to sneak up on people: "He's goofy, I agree . . . we call him goofball . . . But he wouldn't harm a mouse."

Piepmeier concluded by demonstrating how Michael might have incurred that cut on his wrist. He held the murder weapon and struck the floor with it three times—the jury saw that the edge of the post sliced his right wrist. "Who had the means and the opportunity and the motive? The same person who had blood on his pants and an unexplained cut on his wrist!" Piepmeier exclaimed. "He was guilty in 1963, and he's just as guilty today."

But the jury didn't see it that way. After deliberating 14 hours over two days, they returned a verdict of not guilty.

As Mel Rebholz slumped in this chair, the Wehrung family erupted in a celebration that was cut short by the judge. Someone asked Mel if the verdict changed his mind about Wehrung's guilt. "Absolutely not," he said, adding, "There's a higher court than Hamilton County out there."

Mike Allen admitted the odds had been stacked against the prosecution: "Presenting a case 38 years after the fact presents unique circumstances." Noting that most jurors had tears in their eyes, Allen commented, "The ones who were crying were obviously struggling with their decision."

Would a verdict four decades in the making provide redemption for Michael Wehrung?

Immediately after the jury had spoken, both sides tried to control the spin.

Even with the acquittal, Mike Allen wouldn't let go. Hours after the verdict, he released inflammatory notes from the 1963 investigation that Judge Dinkelacker had ruled inadmissible at trial.

Wehrung not guilty in 1963 slaying

Who killed Patty Rebholz still a mystery

Rebholz

By Marie McCain
The Cincinnati Enquirer

A 38-year-old murder mystery is still a mystery.

A Hamilton County jury found Michael Wehrung not guilty Thursday of second-degree murder in the 1963 beating death of his then-girlfriend, Greenhills cheerleader Patricia Ann Rebholz.

The passage of 40 years and reasonable doubt for the jury combined to exonerate Michael Wehrung.

These reports branded Michael Wehrung as "a cruel boyfriend who drank heavily." and "was jealous of Pat but didn't want her to know it. Even Wehrung's best friend Ray St. Clair described him as "a mean boyfriend . . . whenever Mike took Pat out, he tried to belittle her and would usually embarrass her in front of other kids."

Wehrung's sister Cheryl thought it was odd that he went back to sleep after Patty was found instead of rushing outside. His only comment to her was, "Is she dead?" Not the demeanor one would expect from a boyfriend who should be worried about his missing girlfriend.

Deceased officer Chris Waldeck had portrayed Wehrung as a volatile wild child whose family couldn't control him: "Subject was drunk the night before with friends and was told to leave a drive-in theater . . . might have set fire to barns." Waldeck also wrote: "Subject would not look at a picture taken of the (slaying) scene."

But most revealing was Wehrung's response to a question about Patty. His chilling reply: "I don't worry about her anymore. All I think about is myself."

None of these "dead cop's tales" had been heard by the jury. And the negative slant certainly blunted the joy of vindication felt by the Wehrung family.

So Michael's supporters fired back, blasting the media for printing the excluded reports. "The person that committed this horrible crime is walking around out there and has probably since done it again," one e-mail read. "You don't do something like that with your head screwed on properly. (Wehrung) is a wonderful person, husband, father, grandfather, and friend."

Mike Allen was restrained in his personal comments. "What I feel about his guilt or innocence is irrelevant. In the eyes of the law he's not guilty." Allen agreed that after 38 years it had been far easier for the defense to create reasonable doubt.

Former Greenhills police officer Larry Zettler praised the defense for establishing that doubt, especially with the blood evidence. "They arrived at the only verdict they could," Zettler said. "I don't fault the jury at all." Earle Maiman had convinced the jury there was no blood on Michael's pants when tested in 1999, without mentioning the blood from 1963 that had been corrupted by moisture or already cut away for testing.

Four jurors did hold out for second degree murder. None of the twelve had found the defense witnesses credible, and they didn't swallow the testimony about the two other suspects. Yet they chose not to convict Michael Wehrung.

"It was emotional. I feel for both families, but the evidence wasn't there to convict him," said Kevin Anderson, who like most jurors had tears in his eyes after the verdict.

Earl Maiman went on the offensive for his client, tackling the perception that Wehrung had not really been exonerated. In an April 2002 feature article in *Cincinnati Magazine,* Maiman recalled his first meeting with Wehrung, who looked him in the eye and said: "There are a couple of things I want to tell you. Number one, I am innocent. I did not do this. And second, I will not accept any kind of plea bargain."

Maiman took the case and was shocked after his first look at the files: there was no record of the blood tests on Wehrung's pants, nor was there any documentation of the polygraphs where he allegedly attempted deception. The lawyer became convinced that Michael had been "gaslighted"—barraged with false information to force a confession. "It's a standard technique," Maiman declared after the trial. "But this time it got out of hand, because it got into the press."

In his opinion, the testimony of two prosecution witnesses may have been the key to securing Wehrung's freedom.

Steve Tillett, then age 14, was at the Wehrung house on the murder night, playing Ping Pong with Michael and other friends. Tillett left with the group going for hamburgers, and had testified that Wehrung was sitting in the living room as the car pulled out. He also saw Craig Smith standing at the corner as they drove by.

Smith had earlier testified about seeing a car filled with teens leaving the Wehrung home—moments after he saw two persons on the ground at the murder scene.

This juxtaposition resonated with the jury. During their hours of deliberation, they asked to rehear the testimony from only two witnesses: Steve Tillett and Craig Smith. Jurors had grasped the significance of this crucial timeline evidence. If Tillett saw Wehrung in his house as the car pulled out, and then moments later saw Craig Smith just moments after Smith had witnessed the murder, it was physically impossible for Michael Wehrung to have killed Patty Rebholz!

Steve Tillett's testimony had been ignored by the media—no TV station or newspaper gave him a mention. Prosecutor Allen countered that Tillett's timeline was confusing and open to interpretation, and therefore did not provide Wehrung an alibi.

Yet in reality, this small connection between two witnesses was the linchpin of reasonable doubt, keeping Wehrung from serving a life sentence.

SUMMATION:

Michael Wehrung lives in the heart of the motive, means, and opportunity matrix.

His relationship with Patty had deteriorated badly over that last month. And if even half the hearsay about the teenager is false, he still comes across as a spiteful and arrogant liar with a drinking problem.

The timeline evidence offered by Smith and Tillett is intriguing, but either could have been mistaken on the timing. Or was Tillett belatedly covering for a friend? No one else in that car full of hungry teens ever testified about seeing Wehrung just before they left—or about seeing Craig Smith on the corner.

EPILOGUE:

The verdict may have cleared Michael Wehrung in the legal sense, but it can never exonerate him. He will forever remain the prime suspect in the murder of Patricia Ann Rebholz.

But his acquittal has earned him one thing—the presumption of innocence. That right evaporated in 1963 when he was a teenager, grilled by cops who were obsessed with yet overwhelmed by the biggest case of their careers.

If he did it, can we presume to judge him by the worst day of his adolescence? And if he didn't, should we continue nearly five decades later to stew the meat of hearsay?

Michael Wehrung deserves his peace and privacy.

And Patty Rebholz still drifts as a restless ghost, hovering in the long sleep that outlasts love.

I WITNESS:

He drinks several beers that night—part of a final binge before summer ends and football practice begins.

The night before, he and the guys grew rowdy enough to get kicked out of the Drive-In. Now he needs to play it cool, act contented to slam a few Ping Pong balls between furtive sips from a can. Then another. And another.

But when Patty calls about coming by, cool is gone, and tension creeps in. She's walking over from the dance. He hates the dances—and the people there. She acts differently around them. She wears lipstick, the ultimate deception. And he told her not to go!

Patty was becoming a real pain in the ass—treating him like a messy room, riding him about his buddies and his grades. Also, doing the opposite of whatever he says. Yes, her visit following the dance wafts of betrayal. She flirts with other boys, while he sits, waiting, unblinking, his beer growing warm.

Agitated and impatient, he slips out of the house without anyone noticing. Once outside in the sweltering night, his mind races in frantic fits and jackrabbit starts, his scalp crawling with sweat as his irritated gaze sweeps the streets.

Where the hell *is* she?

As Patty approaches Jennings, the sultry breaths of wind make the moonlight swim, painting the trees pale against a horizon empty of stars. She's drifting on a heart full of sky, confident in her decision, relieved that it's nearly over. They've been dating four months; it seems only right to break up in person. Besides, she knows he wants to start seeing someone else too.

She cannot feel the green serpents of jealousy slithering closer.

From the Udrys' backyard, he watches her turn the corner. He whistles softly. Patty sees him and approaches.

Face-to-face, he tries to smile, but it becomes a grimace. She recognizes his familiar, frosty indignation—his eyes are glittering chips of ice.

She is suddenly on edge. This confrontation could get stormy. Fighting to keep her voice steady, wanting it finished, done, Patty blurts out her message.

He spots her barren finger where his ring should have been, and an evil urge to break her spirit takes hold. Sparks sputter inside his brain. Clenching and unclenching his fists, he surrenders to the violence churning within.

Patty smells the rapid, pungent odor of danger, and sees that his face is now a mask of twitches and snarls.

Quaking with rage, he slams her with his fist, knocking out her tooth. He begins to throttle her, dragging her deeper into the yard. Silently mouthing obscenities and consumed by a dreadful power, he tightens his hands around her throat. He drops her limp form to the ground and trips over a fence post. On furious impulse, he grabs it and swings a hard arc against her skull. He keeps hitting her, oblivious to the small cut opening on his wrist as she convulses beneath him.

Abruptly, he stops. Patty is motionless. He resurfaces into a shocked, embalmed stillness.

Returning home, he changes his blood-spattered clothes in the basement and gradually recovers his composure. Then he goes upstairs to watch TV. The memory of his "other self" is already fading.

But when he rises from the sofa, goes into the bathroom and looks in the mirror, he cannot evade the ugly laceration on his soul.

2009

The Coby house still sits perched above the garage where Dennis and Evelyn were found shot to death in 1964.

LESS THAN MEETS THE EYE

THE SHOOTING OF DENNIS AND EVELYN COBY: 1964

"It is a riddle wrapped in a mystery inside an enigma."
Winston Churchill

PROLOGUE:

Nothing haunts like an unsolved murder—especially one that was dead solid perfect.

The shooting of Dennis and Evelyn Coby endures 45 years later as a classic Cincinnati whodunit. And "who" isn't the only question that goes begging—the "when," "where," "why," and even "how" cannot be answered.

This crime became an intricate impasse, a puzzle authored by cunning ingenuity or diabolical luck. The killer's trail never thawed, because detectives were working on a mystery without any clues.

NARRATIVE:

A year after JFK's assassination, Americans were questioning the findings of the Warren Commission, thereby planting seeds for a deluge of conspiracy theories. Kennedy's successor Lyndon Johnson managed to get the landmark Civil Rights Act passed by Congress. And cigarettes finally lost their allure when the Surgeon General implicated them as a cause of lung cancer and heart disease.

So many previously unassailable assumptions—that government explanations were trustworthy, that segregation was acceptable, and that smoking was harmless—were now being challenged.

And one more assumption—that middle class neighborhoods were insulated from violence.

November 25, 1964 was a bleak Wednesday before Thanksgiving on Marshall Avenue, a bustling street cut into a jagged hill that connected Camp Washington to the University of Cincinnati campus. Despite hectic traffic and hurried pedestrians, Marshall was an aloof road where people minded their own business.

Slanting showers pelted the neighborhood all morning, and the falling mercury was whipping up some cold-blooded weather. A brisk wind lashed the rooftops as black clouds throbbed across the sky, and trees shivered in lonely corners.

A steep bank rises on the north side of Marshall, blanketed with small frame houses perched above the street and linked by sheer columns of narrow steps. Below them, garages dug into the hillside resemble earthen caves.

One resident would later say they reminded her of a tomb.

At 2853 Marshall, Dennis Edward Coby, age 33, and his 29-year-old wife Evelyn Louise were having lunch with their eight-year-old son Tommy. Married eleven years, they were a devoted couple. Dennis had worked at St. Mary Hospital before taking a position at the VA in 1961. Evelyn was a lifelong Cincinnati resident and a contented housewife.

Around 1PM Tommy went back to Sacred Heart School where he was a third grader. Dennis was scheduled to start a 3PM shift at Veterans Hospital in Clifton that afternoon.

As young Tommy returned to school, a killer was already stalking Marshall Avenue.

The Cobys' movements during the next four hours would become the subject of intense debate.

At 2:15 they walked down the steps leading to their garage. Neighbor Emma Bertsch noticed them sharing an umbrella, but didn't see their station wagon leave.

Tommy Coby came home at 3:15PM to an empty house. The door was open and the TV set was on, yet there was no sign of his mother. His parents' lunch dishes hadn't been cleared either. Tommy went to his grandmother's house to wait.

Both newspapers would report that he told police his father's car was not in the garage. Meanwhile, Dennis Coby, described as "a conscientious and punctual employee," did not report for work at 3PM, nor did he call to say he'd be late.

At 4:45PM, 18-year-old neighbor Dave Grosser saw a couple he thought were the Cobys sitting in their car in front of the garage. Thinking nothing of it, Grosser passed by fifteen minutes later and saw the car inside the garage, but without any occupants.

At 5:05PM brother-in-law Ray Temke showed up in response to the grandmother's anxious phone call. The Cobys' garage had no doors, and Temke could see their car parked inside. Glancing in the window, he saw the couple lying on the floor of their car.

Assuming they were victims of carbon monoxide, Temke quickly called the Life Squad, and the paramedics carried the couple onto the sidewalk in an attempt to revive them. Unknowingly, they had just compromised a crime scene.

Mouth-to-mouth resuscitation was started on both victims with no response. When a fireman pushed on Mrs. Coby's chest, her blood-soaked sweater stained his hands. Captain Roland Hulley then made a stunning discovery. "I opened the man's shirt and saw that he had a hole in the center of his chest. Then I examined the woman and found that she had a hole in the lower right side of her chest."

"Neither had bled very much," explained Hulley, trying to defend why two murder victims had been moved. "There was no blood on the man's jacket, but there was a little on his shirt. The woman had no blood on her dress."

The Reverend Robert Schaffer had shown up to assist paramedics. Now he found himself giving the last rites to a couple he had known well from church.

Tommy Coby was sent to his room as investigators ascended to the little house on the hill. A quick search eliminated it as the crime scene. Evelyn had never returned after walking her husband to the garage.

Tommy was taken back to his grandmother's house that night. He was told of his parents' death the following day—Thanksgiving morning.

There was nothing to be grateful for around the Coby table.

Despite the holiday, autopsies were rushed through the coroner's office. By late Thursday afternoon detectives sifted through the specifics and drew some conclusions:

- Bloodstains and bullet holes confirmed that Dennis and Evelyn Coby were shot to death inside their car.
- Their bodies had no trauma other than the wounds. Coby was seated on the floor behind the passenger seat with his wife was lying across his feet.
- Coby was shot twice and Evelyn three times with a .38-caliber revolver. Bullets lodged in their chests passed through arms and elbows first, suggesting they tried to fend off attack—there were eight separate wounds on Evelyn's body.
- The killer fired from point blank range and to the left, as if sitting in the driver's seat.
- Both victims had heavy internal bleeding despite a lack of external bloodstains.
- Food in the victims' stomachs showed they had eaten a meal just before dying.
- The coroner speculated they could have lived up to an hour after being shot.
- No fingerprints were recovered from the car. The doors were unlocked, the key was in the ignition, and the engine was still warm.

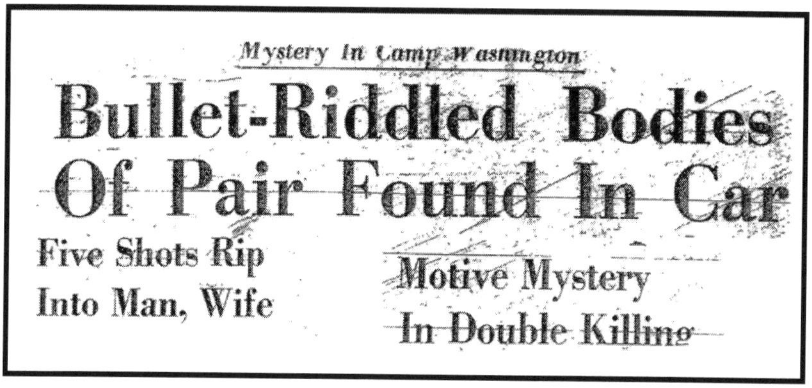

Mystery In Camp Washington

Bullet-Riddled Bodies Of Pair Found In Car

Five Shots Rip Into Man, Wife

Motive Mystery In Double Killing

The Coby shootings were a riddle from the start, with scarce clues and a hazy timeline.

- Coby's wallet containing $3 was still inside his pocket.
- The umbrella Evelyn was seen carrying could not be found.
- A neighbor claimed to hear a sharp report sounding like a shot at 4:55PM but did not investigate.
- There was no sign of a struggle and nothing was missing from the house perched above the garage. Apparently Evelyn Coby expected to return to her TV program after walking her husband to the car.
- Paraffin tests on the victims' hands indicated neither had recently fired a gun. Yet a rumor was already spreading that this was a murder/suicide, with someone swiping the gun during the confusion when the bodies were discovered.

Cincinnati detectives would miss their own Thanksgiving dinners—24 hours after the crime, they were running a gauntlet of uncompromising questions:

- **Who** had the motive, means, and opportunity to kill them?
- **What** was the reason for the lack of blood in the car?
- **When** were they killed—right after 2PM, or just before they were found?

- **Where** were they slain—in the garage, or at another location?
- **Why** didn't neighbors hear the five gunshots between 2 and 5PM?
- **How** could the killer kidnap and/or kill them without being seen?

Investigators floated several theories over the long holiday weekend. The case was brimming with contradiction, and not everyone was in agreement. As they worked the scene and canvassed the neighborhood, witness statements were skewing the timeline even further.

Tommy Coby had lunch with his parents and left at 1PM to return to school. Though he had already eaten, his parents were just sitting down to their meal. Based on their digestion, the coroner believed they were killed an hour afterward, which set time of death at around 2:15PM.

The neighbor from across the street had seen the couple around 2:15PM on the steep steps to the garage. Emma Bertsch confirmed that "it was raining, and they had an umbrella. She had on a sweater, and I thought it was pretty cold for that. I got the impression she was taking him down to their auto. I went on with my housework and didn't see them drive away."

Evelyn Coby had left the door unlocked and the TV on—there was no indication that she ever returned to the house after walking her husband to the garage. Yet there were no sightings of the couple between 2:15 and 4:45 that afternoon. Coby's work shift started at 3PM, but he did not call to say he would be late.

Tommy Coby arrived home at 3:15PM, along with a young neighbor girl Evelyn had asked to baby sit Tommy that weekend. The house was curiously empty, and both children thought the garage was also empty. But they could not be certain.

David Grosser, who lived two doors up on Marshall Avenue, arrived home at 4:45PM and observed a car halted in the Coby driveway with the couple still in it. "There were a man and a

Dennis and Evelyn were champion ballroom dancers. Here they are leaving for a competition just 3 months before their deaths.

woman in the front seat," said Grosser. "I guess it was the Cobys, but I didn't pay any particular attention. Then I went back past the house around 5 o'clock and I saw the auto in the garage. I didn't see if anyone was in it."

Believing the Cobys were shot around 2:30PM, some investigators assumed Grosser saw another car with a different couple—they had identified a husband and wife on Marshall with a similar station wagon to the victim's car. The report of a loud gun shot at 4:55PM was also being discounted.

Yet that still didn't explain where the Coby car was at 4:45PM. The engine was still warm when Ray Temke discovered the bodies just before 5PM. If they were killed between Grosser's two sightings, the shooter had a ten minute window of opportunity before Temke's arrival.

Crucial questions hung in the investigation's stale air: Were the Cobys murdered around 2:15 or closer to 4:45? And if they were killed later, where were they for those missing 2-1/2 hours?

Irreconcilable evidence began to pile up. Medical reports maintained the Cobys were killed an hour after their lunch, when Emma Bertsch last saw them. Yet coroner Frank Cleveland reversed himself, now insisting the couple "did not die before 4PM."

To further blur their vision, a few cops still favored the "murder-suicide" theory, with a third person, most likely Ray Temke, removing the gun. Even after paraffin tests on the victims' hands ruled this out, rumors persisted that the weapon had been lifted.

When a *Cincinnati Enquirer* headline declared **"Many Unknowns Persist in Killings,"** Chief of Detectives Henry Sandman agreed: "It could have happened while the car was in the garage or somewhere else . . . we don't know where or at what time the murder occurred . . . we have found no reason why anyone would want to kill them."

What Was Motive?

Seek Murder Clues

Police investigation into the slaying of Mr. and Mrs. Dennis E. Coby of Camp Washington evolved into a routine, methodical checking of relatives, friends and neighbors Friday.

Detective Chief Henry Sandman said there were no dramatic new leads or developments in the case.

The Cobys were found shot to death in their station wagon parked in the garage of their home, 2853 Marshall Ave., Wednesday. Ray Tompke, 29, 230 Hartwell Ave., husband of Mr. Coby's sister, found the couple slumped in the back

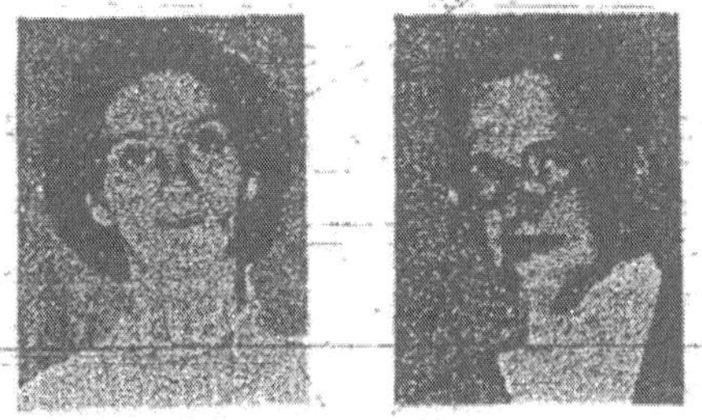

First Pictures Of Slain Couple

Evelyn and Dennis Edward Coby

Many Unknowns Persist In Killings

Who, When, Where, Why? The slaying of the young couple was a puzzle with many missing pieces.

Then with a sigh of frustration, Sandman muttered, "everything we have checked so far seems to lead nowhere."

By Sunday police had questioned over 100 people, focusing on three groups: neighbors, Veterans Hospital patients, and patrons of the Arthur Murray dance studio, because most of the Coby's social life revolved around activities there.

Residents of Marshall Avenue were on the verge—many were calling the murderer "a maniac." Some whispered that the killer walked among them, waiting to prey on another victim.

That Sunday a steady stream of cars crawled past the Coby house, as Tommy's dog Lassie barked a despondent greeting from his backyard kennel. Mrs. Luther Baker, the Cobys' next store neighbor, was feeding the dog. "It's an awful thing to happen next door to your home, but you just can't pick up and leave as much as you might like to," she lamented to a reporter.

"My husband and I both work and seldom saw them," she continued, even though the Bakers had shared the stairway down to the street with the murdered couple. "This isn't the sort of neighborhood where the women do a lot of visiting back and forth."

Two doors away, Bernard Bess said his wife was terrified. "We keep the doors locked now. We knew the Cobys as neighbors and attended the same church."

Witness Emma Bertsch, the last known person to see the Cobys alive, waved the milling reporters away from her house. "I've said enough already," she declared. "We are afraid and will be until they find out who did it." Bertsch wished she had "watched more closely" as the couple descended toward their garage—she might have seen the killing or at least the abduction.

Movie cameras were rolling during the Coby funeral on Monday morning. Suspicious mourners and anonymous flower senders were checked out by the investigators in attendance, who continued interviewing relatives of the slain couple right after the service was over.

"Anything to come up with a lead," sighed Sergeant Russell Jackson. He implored witnesses to come forward and help pinpoint the Cobys' movements, describing their car as "a black four-door, 1963 Falcon station wagon, with simulated wood panel sides and a luggage carrier on top."

By now Jackson had sent the fatal bullets to the FBI laboratory in Washington, along with another slug recovered from a Cumminsville man who had been wounded by an intruder hiding in his basement.

The roving lunatic theory suddenly looked promising. A former patient on Coby's ward had attended the wake and returned

Neighbors Fear Killer Of Couple May Lurk Nearby

Marshall Avenue residents are uneasy these days. They lock their doors. They view callers with suspicion in the wake of a double murder on the street.

Dennis and Evelyn Louise Coby, 2853 Marshal Ave., were found slain in the back seat of their station wagon in the garage in front of their home Wednesday afternoon.

The logistics of the murder seemed to indicate someone with prior knowledge of the Coby's schedule that day.

to the hospital eager to discuss the double killing. Another outpatient requested admission the day before the slaying, claiming he had a premonition that he would kill someone.

Dale Frary, the talkative one from the funeral, gave the *Enquirer* an exclusive interview about Dennis Coby, calling him "extremely popular among most patients at the hospital." He described Coby as "a semi-huge man who stood over 6 feet tall . . . he often smiled, but more as if inwardly amused over his own private joke. And the victim was an unhurried man."

Frary had his own theory. "Perhaps it is obvious to you that the victim was murdered by a 'kook' whom once he had wronged at work," he reasoned, "and his wife joined him in eternity simply because she was with him when the deed was perpetrated."

Then he waxed cryptic: "It has been told to me that among some personnel after 'lights out' patients were sometimes *persona non grata*. I do not mean to insinuate the victim was ever involved in such behavior. But if he were, could you not assume such incidents would create a motive?"

The abuse excuse was now in play.

Frary concluded by saying, "I realize that by stating the above I may create a cloud of suspicion over myself, but I knew the victim personally and enjoyed his company. He was a fine man."

One week after the murders, Russ Jackson issued a terse update: "No suspects. No clues. Little progress."

Sergeant Jackson was not optimistic: "We have talked to more than 150 persons. Some have been discounted as suspects. We have a lot more people to talk to." His tone was weary, and there was no spark in the swollen case file.

By early December jaded leads began to bottleneck the investigation.

A teenage girl from down the block was questioned. She was a habitual runaway with some unsavory connections. Her former boyfriend owned several guns—yet none was a .38-caliber.

A bullet fired by an unknown sniper into a door on Liberty Street was compared to the Coby bullets. Though it was a .38-caliber, ballistics confirmed it was not fired by the murder weapon.

A man who'd robbed several homes on Marshall died before he could be questioned—several detectives had "liked him" as a suspect in the Coby shootings.

One hopeful lead still had legs. A neighborhood woman driving home from work on the murder day saw a young man running down Marshall just before 5PM. This coincided with Grosser's statement about seeing the Cobys in their car at 4:45 and his report of a gunshot ten minutes later.

Yet as December rolled toward Christmas, one detective admitted to a reporter that the investigation was "stymied."

Police did possess one piece of symbolic evidence—a key found inside the death car. Several tips were phoned in after

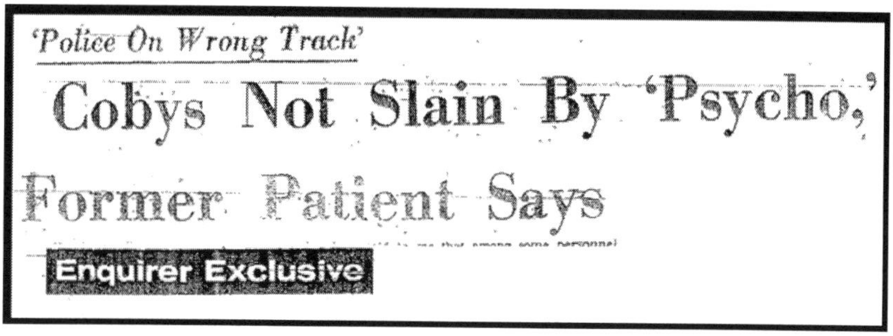
'Police On Wrong Track'

Cobys Not Slain By 'Psycho,'

Former Patient Says

Enquirer Exclusive

The first suspect had been a patient on Dennis Coby's ward. He said Coby was well liked by his charges.

Jackson revealed that it was discovered on the floor next to the murdered couple.

One relative thought it might belong to Tommy Coby. But the eight-year-old denied it: "It's not my key, and it's not my mommy's and not my daddy's. I never saw it before in my life." Others suggested it had been left there when the Cobys moved in two years earlier, or perhaps it was for the dance club they belonged to, or maybe it was for a room the couple may have rented the previous year.

The key was traced to Yale & Towne Mfg. of Stamford, Connecticut, who verified that it was made before World War Two and was either for a door or a safe deposit box. They said it would fit thousands of locks and would be "almost impossible to trace."

Police did not disclose this evidence until December 11th, almost three weeks after the crime. If they withheld it to weed out false confessions the strategy failed. It's likely that any connections to the key drifted after the first week.

Just before Christmas, the FBI lab identified the type of weapon used in the shootings. It was a 38-caliber Spanish revolver that "should be easy to trace." Yet December slipped into January with the murder weapon still out of pocket.

On January 14 a rift developed between police and the firemen who had responded to the crime scene. The problem was the missing gun. Detectives suspected that a fireman had picked it up as a souvenir and was reluctant to admit it. And now all firemen were refusing to take lie detector tests in connection with the Coby shooting.

The "murder-suicide" hypothesis was hovering. Speculation still thrived that Dennis Coby had shot his wife and then turned the gun on himself—several cops felt it was as plausible as any other theory.

Legendary Police Chief Stanley Schrotel jumped into the middle of the dispute: "The police division is using every technique possible to solve this case . . . even to using polygraph tests in the hopes that something noticed subconsciously and not recalled by memory might be developed into evidence bearing on the case."

Captain James Hunt, president of the firefighters' union, responded dismissively: "We don't think a mechanical gismo can reveal anything in the subconscious mind. Sodium Pentothal or even hypnotism would be better," he added with a straight face.

"We're willing to cooperate," Hunt continued. "Our men have given written statements to police. We have submitted all records they have asked for. We don't think lie detector tests are necessary."

In the end they did not take the polygraphs. Hunt cited a city ruling against such tests for municipal employees, and noted that the firemen's union had voted years earlier that its members "could not take lie tests under any circumstances."

As winter shuddered into the Queen City, the Coby murder trail was justifiably frozen.

In late February, the *Cincinnati Enquirer* ran an update on the case headlined: **"After 90 Days—Unsolved Mystery."** According to the front page exclusive, "Ninety days, a thousand interrogations, and many sleepless nights later, the killing of Dennis and Evelyn Coby remains a mystery to Cincinnati police,"

Sergeant Russell Jackson ran down what the cops knew and what they didn't.

He reviewed the exhaustive search of the Marshall Street area, an inch by inch hunt that included a wooded lot and nearby Coy Field. A city crew with large electromagnets had scoured the sewers in hopes of retrieving the murder weapon. But all searches proved fruitless, including ballistics checks of over 1500 .38-caliber pistols.

Suspects were divided into three categories: a psychotic from Coby's ward, a car thief caught in the act, or someone thinking the couple carried a lot of money. Each potential assassin had a respective origin: the hospital, the neighborhood, and the couple's social life.

Yet Jackson couldn't deny the quandary staring them in the face. There was no gun, no fingerprints, no witnesses, and no evidence.

Detective Chief Sandman was also pessimistic: "This is one of those peculiar cases where the intangible elements have fallen in favor of the killer."

"But the murderer can't have covered everything," Sandman insisted. "Something always turns up to furnish a key to every crime." He quashed the ridiculous rumor that it was a murder/suicide, citing the trajectory, number of shots, and the lack of gunpowder residue. And he admitted that two former mental patients were "being checked out and have not yet been eliminated as suspects."

Dale Frary had attended the Coby funeral, returned to the hospital to discuss the murders, and had given an interview to the press. His interrogation was "inconclusive," and he was eventually committed to a state hospital.

According to Sandman, the other man was a better suspect, and sometimes "slept over" at the VA hospital. The day before the murders, he'd requested admission because of a premonition that he was "going to kill someone."

This unidentified man, a former Trappist monk, was given lodging for the night and slept in the ward where Dennis Coby worked his last shift. In the morning he received a bus ticket home to Chillicothe, but instead skipped the ride and went on a drinking spree the afternoon of the murders.

He turned up in Chillicothe late that night, unable to account for his time between 2-5PM. He claimed to have been at the bus terminal, yet there was no one there to back him up. He was returned to Cincinnati, questioned for two days, and then released.

"We had to let him go because we had no evidence," explained Sandman. "But if we come up with some there will be no problem getting him back."

The most tantalizing lead remained the young man seen bolting down Marshall Avenue just before 5PM. Since many detectives believed that the killer was inexperienced but "got lucky," this unidentified teenager was a "definite person of interest."

In November 1965, the brother of a man jailed in the county workhouse finally passed along an interesting bit of hearsay. Six months before the murders, the prisoner had overheard another inmate threaten to shoot "a woman and her husband" when he got out, and claimed he took a shot at the woman once before. Russell Jackson admitted his men had learned that the Coby station wagon "had been fired upon before the killings." He would not elaborate.

But this tip washed away. "The suspect had shot a woman when he got out, but it was not Mrs. Coby," Jackson explained. "He is in jail on another charge."

Detectives were also shadowing yet another mental patient, and began to question him in January of 1966. The new suspect was in Coby's ward but AWOL at the time of the murders. He claimed he was at his parents' home, yet his mother only recalled seeing him at home on the Sunday after the crime.

Police from Reading, Ohio, informed Coby detectives that they found the suspect publicly intoxicated on the morning of the murders. Yet that was at 1AM, while the Cobys were killed later that afternoon.

This 42-year-old man had been brandishing a weapon in various Cincinnati cafes during the previous week. So when cops recovered a .38-caliber colt revolver from his parents' home, the homicide squad was thrilled to have a promising suspect at last.

But this lead didn't pan out, just like all the others in this unfathomable murder riddle. Tests showed the gun had never been fired. And a vague alibi provided by his parents seemed to clear him for the murder day.

The suspect himself denied any guilt. During a 12-hour interrogation, he said, "I know no more about it than I've read in the newspapers." He was eventually released.

The Coby case was a glacier, inexorably pushing farther away as manpower was diverted to other crimes.

Tommy Coby is the only surviving child of the murdered couple. Dennis and Evelyn's other two children died in infancy. In a recent interview, he lamented the false hopes and enduring doubt left behind by the killer.

Now in his early 50s, Tom holds no illusions about cracking this faded case. But he wants people to know that his parents were not a statistic—and that they still deserve a slice of social justice.

Dennis Coby had developed a passion for cooking while serving in the army. Tom has fond memories of waking up to the smell of fresh baked bread, placed on the radiator for its final rise. He recalls long afternoons on father-and-son fishing trips.

Evelyn Flanigan was introduced to Dennis when her sister married his brother. A petite woman who weighed less than 100 pounds, Evelyn did not drive and was always waiting when Tommy came home from school—every day, except one.

The Cobys frequented the Arthur Murray Studios for a reason. According to Tom, they were "very good dancers who won their share of ribbons and trophies." Ballroom was their specialty. A photo he gave me showed them decked out in tuxedo and formal gown as they left for yet another competition.

Tom was the light of their lives, especially after the Cobys lost their next two children. And after being so cruelly orphaned, Tommy was doted on by his many cousins after going to live with Uncle Ray Temke, the man who found his parents dead in their garage.

When he turned 16 Tom began to wonder what had really happened. He could still recall the frenzied hours when "detectives were flying around the house and tearing drawers open" as he played silently in his room. It was nothing if not surreal for an eight-year-old.

When first contacted by this writer, he was reluctant to speak. Even after all this time, some relatives were worried that the killer might retaliate against the family. But during our interview he opened up. Tom Coby reached through the aching years and surrendered two details that had never been reported.

When I asked him if the garage was empty when he arrived home from school, Tom said that he didn't know. Approaching the steps from the west, he pointed out that he "never got that far." A quick look at the crime scene confirms that he couldn't see into the structure from the bottom of the steps.

Tom is adamant that he never said the car was gone: "The newspapers had it wrong." Notes from the case file are inconclusive, and witnesses claiming the garage was empty were not identified. Given Dennis Coby's work schedule, it would have been normal for the garage to be empty in the afternoon—the presence of the station wagon would have been odd.

If the couple were shot as Dennis left for work, that would clear up the "when and where" questions. So it's possible the car was there when Tommy got home, even though this scenario is at odds with the coroner's report on time of death.

It's just another example of the tortured path this case has crawled.

Tom saved the best tip for last—one that investigators had never revealed.

He vividly remembers a phone call to his grandmother's house a few days after the murders. She told detectives that "some woman claimed that her son had done it, and that he didn't mean to kill 'the Mrs.'—but that she got in the way." Then the woman hung up and never called back.

Over 44 years later, this sparse tale still glimmers.

2009

This was Tommy's view of the garage from the steps (top). The Coby station wagon would have stuck out the garage doorway (bottom)

SUMMATION:

This is the toughest summation of the entire book. Paradox reigns over this king of Queen City unsolved murders.

Like the detectives who worked the Coby case, this writer is wrestling with his theories. The further anyone delves into this crime, the less sense it makes.

So let's start with what we can eliminate, and then see what's left.

Number One suspect scenario: This was the roving maniac/mental patient who knew Dennis Coby. Investigators took a hard look at three such individuals, and never satisfactorily eliminated two of them.

Lacking a firm motive, a good cop always looks for either passion or gain.

If an inmate on Coby's ward felt mistreated by him, his mind could fixate on retribution. But the degree of planning and stalking required seems improbable for a mental patient, especially one who depended on his next pass to roam free.

Add to this the victim's apparent popularity with his charges, and the crazy interloper theory retreats to the back of the file.

Number Two suspect scenario: This was the opportunist who believed the Cobys were worth robbing, and then shot them in a panic. He could have been a fringe player at the dance studio.

Again, there would be prior planning/stalking. The logistics of the Coby automobile don't support this theory, unless the killer kidnapped them to make bank withdrawals. Yet there was no activity on the Coby accounts that day.

The Cobys were a working class couple with virtually no savings—it stretches credibility that they would be targeted for a big score robbery. But gain could still be the motive for murder.

Number Three suspect scenario: The Cobys surprised someone trying to steal their car and were abducted. At first glance this seems improbable, but upon further review this theory merits a closer look.

Emma Bertsch saw the Cobys descending toward the garage at around 2:15PM. Had she not turned back to her housework, she might have witnessed the confrontation and the abduction.

What was the killer doing with the victims for 2-1/2 hours? This question became the kingpin puzzler of the entire case. A novice car thief turned kidnapper would need time to sort things out. He made Coby drive somewhere, and then shot them at a remote location.

Why didn't he leave the car where he shot them? He may have wanted to draw attention away from the murder site, and drove his victims back to their garage to set up a false crime scene. It's hard to fathom how a young criminal had the composure to weigh these options—while dealing with the cold, hard fact that he'd just murdered two people.

One thing is certain: Whether intentional or not, he left enough red herrings to stalemate any inquiry. As detective Sandman had explained to the press: "The intangible elements have fallen in favor of the killer."

EPILOGUE:

This unsolved mystery, 45 years later, is the shattered legacy left to Tom Coby.

He understands that it will take the spoken word to bring his parents' faceless murderer to justice. Someone knows what happened on that long ago Thanksgiving Eve—it could be the shooter, or someone to whom he, in a moment of weakness, unburdened himself.

Tom hopes this renewed publicity and over four decades of thrusting conscience will finally provoke the gunman to cross over into atonement.

Perhaps that ancient key can still lead to the front door of a killer.

POSTSCRIPT: FEBRUARY 2010

"This may sound strange, but when I went out to my parent's grave site I took your book with me and read the whole chapter to them. I know it was well appreciated. Take care, Tom."

This email from Tom Coby dazed me. I picture him crouching over their headstones, reading my narrative in a faltering yet firm cadence, pausing to wipe away dormant tears.

And in my own misty eyes I now see closure.

Let no victim's ghost say we didn't try. This detective creed echoes along the ramparts of **Queen City Gothic**—and never more so than with the impenetrable murder of Dennis and Evelyn Coby.

Their only son has finally crossed over. The tears have cleared his vision, and the legacy of his father and mother has been forever burnished beyond their inexplicable deaths.

Tom Coby has buried his restless ghosts, never to be forgotten. By him or me . . .

I WITNESS:

The thief just turned 18 years old. His days of juvenile detention are behind him—he's on the hustle now and ready to pull a real caper. And carrying his first piece.

His partner wants him to "boost a jitney" for this next job. So on the chilly Wednesday before Thanksgiving, he's prowling Marshall Avenue, looking for the perfect car to steal.

He ducks out of the slanting rain and into the Coby garage. A station wagon is exactly what they're looking for, with plenty of room for their haul. But just as he opens the driver's door, a voice stops him cold.

"What are you doing here?" Dennis Coby's intonation carries the natural authority that he uses on his ward. And there's a hint of recognition. A wide-eyed woman stands, staring, with her mouth open.

The thief lives nearby, on one of the streets behind Marshall. He knows the couple by sight—the tall, stocky husband with the tiny wife. And he is certain that they can "make" him.

He orders them into their car at gunpoint. He takes the back seat, with Dennis driving and Evelyn shivering next to him. His .38-caliber Colt is leveled and at the ready. "I just need you to drive me someplace," he tries to reassure them.

His legs vibrate as he watches Coby shift into reverse and back into the street. He sits in glowering silence, wrestling his demons. He's in a real pickle now. Leave these two alive, and this is no small beef—kidnapping and robbery convictions will fetch some serious prison time. As the couple pleads to be released, the thief nods with icy calm.

He directs Coby to head toward nearby Burnet Woods. The park is desolate on this gray, drizzly day, and he needs time to weigh his options. Then he thinks, *What options?* There's only one, unless he wants to spend years, decades in a cramped cell.

He nudges the couple into the back. Once there, Evelyn starts to panic, and as he commands her to shut the hell up, Dennis makes a grab for the gun. But the young shooter gets the drop on him, unloading a fusillade into the quivering pair as Evelyn valiantly tries to shield her husband.

Shots resonate throughout the car; then the click of the empty revolver brings the young killer back to reality. The big man gave him no choice—and his hysterical wife just got in the way. There's no time for remorse, only steely resolve.

He waits another hour, listening to their ragged breathing. *God, they're taking so long!* When both finally expire, he has another decision to make. There is just enough time to drive the car back to the Coby garage. Returning with two dead bodies is a definite risk, but one he is willing to take.

Self-preservation is a powerful instinct, and this young man has infernal luck on his side.

He eases the car into the garage and takes one last backward glance at the couple. It is nearly 5:00 PM, and the oncoming holiday rush hour unnerves him. He needs to get moving. In a whirling panic he stumbles from the car and hits the sidewalk running.

As the killer sprints down Marshall Avenue, a woman coming home from work notices his haste. The Cobys will be discovered within minutes, and this enticing lead will be the last best hope of ever cracking the case.

But the young man continues running and disappears into obscurity.

Two nights later, he stands speechless as his mother calls Dennis Coby's mother to apologize. She barely has time to explain that it was an accident. He glares at her, and she hangs up the phone before spilling the beans.

Probably still alive today, the aging killer, who once tried through desperate means to prove himself a man, still bears the sheer affliction of guilt in his shuttered eyes.

2009

Except for a remodeled front porch, the Bricca house is unchanged since that horrifying September discovery in 1966.

A VISION OF DEADLY DESIRE

THE BRICCA FAMILY MURDER ROCKS THE WEST SIDE: 1966

"Put your shoes at the door, sleep, prepare for life. The last twist of the knife."

T.S. Eliot

PROLOGUE:

A murder investigation with an obvious suspect becomes a battle of wills, as detectives try to expedite justice through negotiation and coercion. With no proof other than motive, they must handle their target with care, gathering furtive corroboration while trying not to blow it on a legal technicality.

The slaughter of the Gerald Bricca Family on Cincinnati's West Side remains this city's most obsessive unsolved mystery. Rumor and innuendo flourished in 1966 and still resound today. Those with inside knowledge are reluctant to speak on the record, yet the crime has generated more gossip than any cold case in local history.

It's a terminal case with a fading pulse. After 43 years, police still haven't gathered enough evidence to charge the murderer, even though they are certain of his identity.

NARRATIVE:

Cincinnati's mood in September of 1966 was apprehensive. Against a national backdrop of strident Vietnam protests and churning race riots, the Queen City trembled in the thrall of the Cincinnati Strangler, a faceless black man who had slain four white women within the past eight months. Amid rising tension, many Negroes were being hauled in on vague charges of "suspicious behavior."

September 25 was a cool, rainy Sunday night on the cusp of autumn. On Greenway Avenue in Bridgetown, muted voices and tinkling wind chimes drifted though the drizzle, as hasty figures and wet vehicles darted about the neighborhood.

Cloaked by the haze of vanishing summer, a stranger stepped out of the fog and into West Side legend, when his lethal desire became a mortal storm for one Bridgetown family.

Sometime around 8:45PM during a lull in the rain, Mrs. Joan Janzen took her Chihuahua for a short walk. The young housewife was aware of the time, because she was anxious to watch the TV premiere of *The Bridge on the River Kwai* at 9 o'clock.

The temperature had dipped to 53 degrees, and a steady breeze rippled the mist through the trees lining Greenway as the rain started up again, looking like flurries of moths in the yellow street light. Joan pulled her jacket tighter and hurried along the sidewalk.

As she passed 3381 Greenway, she was startled by a man in the driveway. She was about to cry out when she recognized neighbor Jerry Bricca, standing near his garbage cans. They greeted each other, and Joan watched the young engineer trudge into his garage, dressed as if he'd just come home from work. She mused about the long hours Jerry put in—working the entire weekend was not unusual for him.

Joan Janzen would later insist: "I know it was Jerry. If it had been a stranger, everybody on the street would have heard me screaming."

She was the last person outside his house to see Jerry Bricca alive.

Inside the Bricca home the evening was winding down. Jerry and his wife Linda were in the family room watching television. He kicked off his shoes as Linda folded a stack of towels and waited to change over her laundry. Their two dogs were already bedded down for the night.

Linda's father called around 9:30PM and spoke to his daughter. She mentioned that Jerry was leaving for West Virginia early Monday on a business trip. During this conversation she expressed no anxiety or fear.

Shortly afterward Jerry put his young daughter Deborah to bed, as was his habit. He got so far as to remove one red stocking from her foot.

Then the turbulence of one rainy night ripped open the walls.

On Monday morning Jerry Bricca missed his flight to West Virginia. Several calls from his employer went unanswered.

Next door neighbor Richard Meyer noticed the Briccas' back patio floodlights were still on at 6AM. He left for work wondering—he had never seen that before. Late Monday Meyer noticed the family's trash cans were still on the street, their cars had not been moved, and newspapers were lying in the front yard.

By Tuesday neighbors had become alarmed. Linda Bricca was not playing in the backyard with her dogs, and her pet rabbits hadn't been fed. No one recalled seeing Jerry's beautiful wife since the weekend.

Around 10:00PM, Meyer consulted with Joan Janzen's husband Richard—he had called the Bricca residence repeatedly with no response. They decided to try the front door. Finding it ajar, Meyer leaned in and called Linda's name.

Instantly his senses were assaulted by the explicit odor of death. The war veteran later told reporters "I knew what it was as soon as I opened the front door. Nothing else smells like that."

At 10:40PM Hamilton County officers converged on the scene of an atrocity. In the master bedroom they found 28-year-old Jerry Bricca and his 23-year-old wife stabbed to death. Jerry was face down, his shirt drenched with blood. Linda was sprawled across her husband, negligee and robe pushed aside to reveal stab wounds around her breasts.

In the next room four-year-old Debbie lay crumpled against the wall if as she had been flung there. She had been stabbed in the back so violently that the blade sliced completely through her body.

Meyer and Janzen were asked to identify the victims. Meyer was devastated after seeing his neighbors lying in their own blood: "My God, I can hardly even remember what I saw; it's just like a fog now."

He recalled seeing Linda's rabbits out in the rain earlier that day: "I know she wouldn't let those rabbits sit out there, because she loved animals." Then Meyer broke into tears and sobbed, "My God, what they did to that baby!"

As reporters swarmed to the crime scene, a detective was seen vomiting on the front lawn. Police refused the press permission to view the interior of the home, but county fireman and neighbors flocked to the area shortly before midnight. Rumors persist to this day that unauthorized persons walked through the house and compromised the crime scene.

The only survivors of the massacre were the Briccas' two dogs. Thumper, a cocker spaniel, and Dusty, a medium-sized poodle, were found in the basement playroom, hungry but strangely subdued. Dusty was known to bark and bite when anyone came near Linda.

By dawn Wednesday officers had secured the scene.

It was just outside the jurisdiction of the Cincinnati police, and county investigators knew they would have their hands full with this grisly triple homicide.

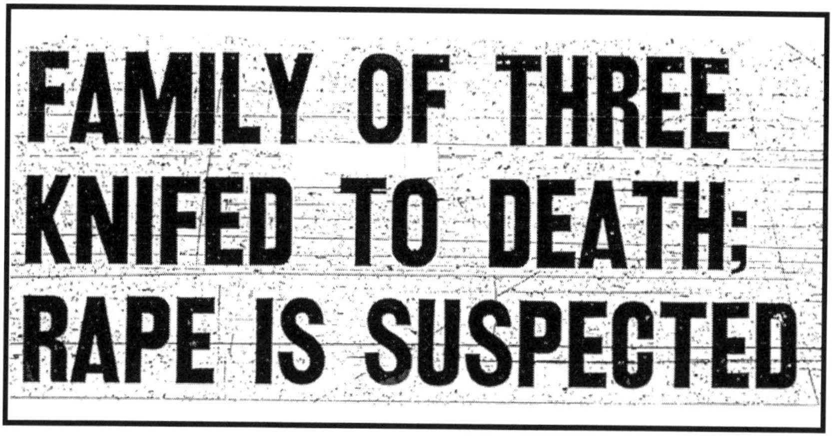
FAMILY OF THREE KNIFED TO DEATH; RAPE IS SUSPECTED

Coming during the height of the Cincinnati Strangler terror, the massacre of the young family was a stunning blow to the community.

It was like a shadowy horror fable—a suburban dream shattered by the specter of madness.

Late Wednesday autopsies were still ongoing. Detectives had sweated through an intense day long investigation, and emotions were frayed. The murder of the child had repulsed everyone.

After 24 hours, this is what they knew:

- The killer wielded the knife over twenty times in snuffing out the lives of the young family.
- The family had been stabbed repeatedly in their backs and chests, sometime between 10PM Sunday and 8:30AM Monday—the crime scene was already 36-48 hours old when the bodies were discovered.
- Both parents may have been bound with adhesive tape. A small piece clung to Jerry Bricca's face, and a sock had been stuffed in his mouth.
- Both adults sustained "penetrative head wounds" apparently not made by a knife, characterized as "unspecified mutilations."
- The murder weapon was between 5-1/2" to 7" long—the same size as a carving knife that was missing from the home.

- The front and rear doors of the residence were found closed but unlocked.
- Robbery may have been a "partial motive." There was no money in the house, and Jerry's empty billfold was found on the bed.
- Coroner Frank Cleveland confirmed that Linda Bricca had been raped.

"Family of Three Knifed to Death! Rape Is Suspected!" was the *Enquirer's* roaring headline, establishing the sexual assault of lovely Linda as the early motive.

Chief Investigator Lieutenant Herb Vogel had a different view about the "rape" angle, but for now he kept it to himself. "I am inclined to believe that robbery was only a secondary motive," was his first of many official statements to the press.

Vogel understood that the 48-hour gap between murder and discovery would hamstring the investigation. In any crime the first two days are critical—after that, leads drift. Now he questioned why the neighbors waited so long to investigate.

Late Wednesday night, a box of items including the victims' clothing, bed sheets, and some bloody towels was sent to the local FBI. Hair samples and latent fingerprints found in the house were also forwarded for analysis.

Linda's parents, who lived in the exclusive Chicago suburb of Barrington, had flown in Wednesday afternoon and were being interviewed at county headquarters. As their meeting ran past midnight, investigators were getting an earful about the marriage of Jerry Bricca and their beautiful daughter.

On Thursday morning Vogel's men began to prepare an interview schedule. Their plan was to talk to everyone who had contact with the family—an early implication that police believed the killer knew them.

A profile of the Briccas was compiled. At first glance they looked to be the ideal couple living in suburban Bridgetown. Jerry Bricca was a 28-year-old chemical engineer in charge

Known to their neighbors as "the kids," Gerry and Linda were a popular couple.

THE BRICCA MYSTERY

...AND NOBODY IS TALKING

"The most beautiful child you could imagine."

CINCINNATI, OHIO, APRIL 6, 1967

■ For two days the neat house on the quiet street in the suburb where the Briccas lived had been strangely quiet. So quiet that at the close of the second day, a worried neighbor went to the front door and opened it. He saw a foot lying on the floor at the top of the stairs, too still to calm his fears. Opening that door was the act that launched an investigation into the slaughter of the Bricca family, man, wife and child. This was on September 27, 1966. And in the seven month investigation that followed, the problem of getting at the truth has been a problem of opening the right door. In that time, the police have, by their own count, talked to more than 400 people. No one has been able to tell them anything that has brought them closer to a solution.

But there is one man whose story they would like to hear. They don't say that the solution to the Bricca massacre hinges on what this man

Pictures of the family as they appeared in *Front Page Detective's* 1967 Bricca case feature article. "Ánd Nobody is Talking" was the perfect title for this secretive investigation.

of planning at the Monsanto plant in nearby Addyston. He was memorialized by a company official as "friendly and conscientious" and "a rising star". They also confirmed that Jerry spent the entire weekend before his murder at the plant.

Originally from San Francisco, Jerry had taken Linda to his sister's wedding in the Bay Area just two weeks before the murders. He was short but a muscular 160 pounds, with close-cropped hair and a dark complexion. An excellent swimmer, he was described by neighbors as "always joking" and "nuts about kids."

Everyone commented on what a hard worker Jerry was—nights, weekends, and holidays, sometimes not getting home for more than a few hours' time. Investigators raised their eyebrows and scribbled in their notebooks.

Linda Bulaw Bricca was almost 24, a former airline stewardess described by all who knew her as stunningly beautiful. The former Chicagoan was a brunette with enormous dark eyes who often wore her hair in a French roll. After graduating at age 16 from Barrington High School, Linda lied about her age to get into United Airlines School. She met her husband while working a flight to Seattle, where Jerry was employed at the Monsanto branch.

Everyone mentioned that she was "crazy about animals," and her passion extended beyond their own dogs and rabbits. She fed the birds all winter long and worked part time at two veterinary clinics on nearby Glenway Avenue. She once told a neighbor that she briefly joined a circus as a child just to feed the animals.

Richard Meyer's wife said Linda was "easy to know" and "very tasteful and neat." Yet other neighbors seemed reluctant to go into any detail about her.

Everyone agreed that four-year-old Debbie was a well-behaved child who "talked like an adult." One of her frequent baby-sitters said the child would often ask to be called "Carol."

The family had moved from Seattle three years prior. Jerry was climbing the ladder at Monsanto, and his new Cincinnati

. . . AND NOBODY IS TALKING continued

Trash cans, papers on porch drew worried visit.

Patio lights had burned two days and nights.

Front and back photos of the murder house appeared in the *Front Page Detective* magazine feature.

position placed him on the fast track. Known as "the kids" because they were the youngest on the block, the Briccas were "well liked" and attended the many backyard barbecues and holiday parties on Greenway Avenue.

Home was a brick and wood tri-level house similar to many others on the street, with a playroom and garage on the first level, kitchen and dining room in the middle, and three bedrooms on the third level. The backyard had a patio, a rabbit hutch, and a swing set. Houses on either side were only 15 feet away.

The Briccas read like the textbook American family of the 1960s, and there was no outward sign of any misprints in this narrative. Yet investigators could not overlook the allure of the workaholic husband and the glamorous wife.

As county detectives began wading through a swarm of interviews, the Bricca case was seeping into the Queen City psyche. Already paralyzed by the Cincinnati Strangler, this latest outrage left the city petrified.

The Strangler was alleged to be a black man, so Vogel quickly quelled any racial tension brewing on the primarily white West Side. He assured everyone that "the Bricca slayer was believed white, certainly not of Negroid origin."

He listed the investigation's prevailing theories as "a matter of revenge, a sex crime, or the unforeseen outcome of a burglary." Vogel also officially contradicted the coroner's report on Linda Bricca's rape, saying that she only "had recent intercourse."

By Friday things quieted down on Greenway Avenue. The parade of the morbidly curious was now a trickle past the roped-off murder house at 3381. Kids on backyard swings, wagons strewn in driveways, and lawnmowers droning seemed to indicate that life was still vibrant.

But caution was now a cliché throughout Bridgetown—doors were bolted, large dogs were conspicuous, women and children hurried home before dark.

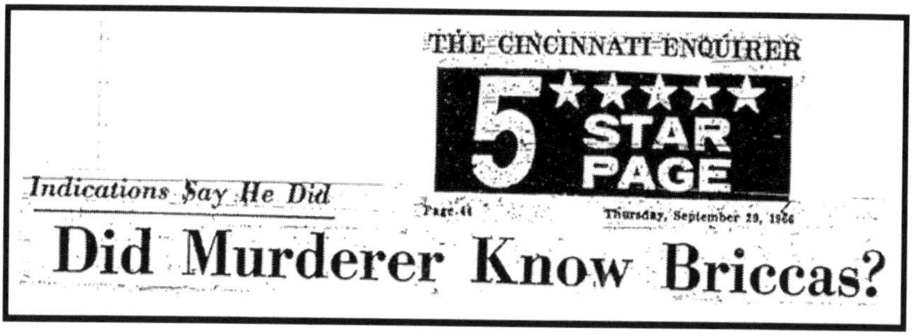
THE CINCINNATI ENQUIRER

5 ★★★★★ STAR PAGE

Page 41

Thursday, September 29, 1966

Indications Say He Did

Did Murderer Know Briccas?

The logistics of the crime scene indicated a confident killer who knew both the victims and the house.

Neighbor Richard Meyer had not recovered from his tour of the murder scene with police. Still considered a suspect due to proximity, his fear was a palpable warning for all West Side residents. "This happened only 15 feet away from us," he said. "It shakes us up. It could have been our house."

County officers were getting nowhere by canvassing the area. When Vogel was asked by a reporter if an outsider would go unnoticed on Greenway Avenue, he gave a wry smile and said it was likely. Another cop called it "the kind of street where everybody knows in five minutes if a man takes a strange woman into his house . . . but let something like this happen, and they haven't seen anything."

Yet Greenway residents were talking to reporters. The *Cincinnati Post* headline on Friday proclaimed that **"Neighbors Think Bricca Killer No Stranger."** The *Enquirer* asked, **"Did Murderer Know Briccas? Indications Say He Did."** Investigators combing these articles vowed to speed up their interview process.

Several factors pointed to the killer knowing the family:

- A carving knife was missing from a set. It may have been kept in a drawer found standing open—the knife's wooden scabbard had also disappeared.
- The house had been searched, but not ransacked—removal of incriminating evidence seemed to be the intention rather than robbery.

- The Briccas' two dogs, often aggressive toward strangers, were found locked in the basement and weren't heard barking Sunday night. Meyer said the dogs normally "had the run of the house."
- There were no sounds from the house and no signs of a struggle inside.
- Debbie was murdered because she knew the man who killed her parents.

The search for the missing knife was the top priority. A neighbor had described it as 6-1/2" long with the inscription "Rajba Bros. India", and he was certain the carving set was kept in the dining room cupboard.

Herb Vogel revealed that the Monday morning *Cincinnati Enquirer* was missing from the home, while the Monday afternoon, Tuesday morning, and Tuesday afternoon papers were found on the front porch where Richard Meyer had tossed them. Vogel theorized the killer may have wrapped the murder weapon in the paper and tossed it into a dumpster. He had already requested a search at the city dump.

Vogel pondered that missing paper, which would have been delivered between 4:30-5:00AM on Greenway Avenue. If the murderer used it to conceal bloody evidence, then he had remained in the house long after the killings. And since the trash was picked up on Monday morning, he could have dumped everything in the Briccas' can.

Detectives were interviewing anyone who had contact with the family. Over 400 persons were eventually questioned—no case in the Hamilton County jurisdiction was ever worked harder. From this overwhelming process a clear picture emerged.

Jerry Bricca worked long hours and was rarely home. Linda was "a stunning brunette" who worked part time as a veterinary assistant. Their daughter spent a great deal of time with baby-sitters.

Police learned "some very interesting things" about the Bricca family life from Linda's mother, information they would not divulge. Rumors of a love triangle floated around the West Side. Jerry had worked all weekend, arriving home in time to be killed Sunday night. If his wife wasn't raped, then who had "recent intercourse" with her?

On the Saturday following the murders, Vogel did say his investigators had some "promising leads." But he also tried to suppress the persistent rumor that an illicit romance was the motive behind the slayings. His official statement said that everything they had uncovered suggested that Jerry and Linda "were a devoted married couple".

Vogel was stalling. There's an old saying among cops: "A rumor is just a premature fact." Love's dark ride was looming over the case, and trying to annul that marriage was like trying to un-ring a bell.

On Sunday Herb Vogel called a press conference to review the investigation's progress. A horde of reporters heard him say that the surge of information had everyone working overtime. His men had received leads from as far away as Florida and Missouri, and each one was being checked out.

He complained about the slow pace of the FBI testing lab. Thirty items had been forwarded to the Washington Bureau the previous Wednesday, fragments and traces which could tell detectives how the killer worked. Vogel admitted these items were "the thinnest of clues," and that information about the crime was "meager."

What investigators were willing to make public shaped up like this:

- The Weapon: An "intense search" was on for the carving knife missing from the Bricca home. Coroner Cleveland said based on the wounds, "it could very well have been the knife" used in the killings.
- The Wounds: Linda Bricca was stabbed six times in the chest and side, twice on the head and twice in the neck. Jerry was knifed four times in the back, three in the neck,

and twice in the head. Debbie was stabbed four times in the back—each time the blade went through her body, as if the killer held her by the neck and hacked.

- The Motive: A gray area. Vogel repeated that it could have been a revenge killing, a sexual attack, or a robbery. While Coroner Cleveland insisted Linda Bricca had been raped, Vogel countered that "the coroner told me that she had recent intercourse before the killing."
- The Time: Between 9PM Sunday and 6:30AM Monday, but leaning closer to Sunday night. The victims' digestion indicated they had eaten not long before their deaths. Jerry was seen by two neighbors just before 9PM taking out the garbage, and there was no answer to a 6:30AM phone call Monday morning. Linda's parents were confused about whether they had called Saturday or Sunday night at 9:30PM. If it was Sunday, the killer could not have been in the house when Jerry arrived home.
- The Dogs: This bothered Vogel—the dogs locked away and strangely docile while the slaughter took place: "It is quite possible Mr. Bricca put the dogs in the playroom before opening the front door to let the killer in."
- The Evidence: Markings on their wrists suggested the couple's hands were tied with adhesive tape that was later removed. Some partial palm prints and fingerprints were found—Vogel didn't know if they were left by the killer, the victims, or investigators themselves.
- The Reconstruction: Vogel believed that Jerry and Linda were in the lower level playroom watching TV. His shoes were there, next to her folded laundry, and damp clothes were found in the washer and dryer. Investigators learned Jerry usually put Debbie to bed—when he took her up to the third level, Linda was left alone.

Vogel speculated that someone watching from the patio chose this moment to enter the playroom. Asked if this "someone" was an intruder or friend of the family, Vogel said it could have been either, or an "acquaintance." But he waffled: "I'm not saying either."

YOU DON'T FEEL SECURE ANY MORE

Shocked Bricca Neighbors Learn to Live With Fear

The cliché "it couldn't happen here" was shattered for the residents of the quiet street in Bridgetown.

The killer, intent on rape, seized the carving knife and forced Linda Bricca to the master bedroom. Alerted by the commotion, Jerry left Debbie's room and was stabbed immediately. Linda was then killed, perhaps while trying to aid her husband. The killer then turned his fury on the child to eliminate the last witness.

Yet Vogel admitted that the murder sequence was "still not clear. I don't know who was killed first. I don't know why there was no sign of a struggle." He reversed himself at one point, saying, "We now think the intruder came in the front door, but the back door is possible. Anything's possible in this thing!"

With that last vent of frustration, the lead investigator ended the news conference.

More than a week after the murders, the *Enquirer* ran a story headlined, **"Shocked Bricca Neighbors Learn to Live with Fear."**

Greenway Avenue housewives clustered on front steps and in driveways, whispering platitudes like "This is too close for comfort," and "How could it happen here?" And since everyone was certain the killer was no stranger, residents dealt with the added anxiety that a murderer might be walking among them.

Joan Janzen was even more direct. She lived across the street and was the last person outside the house see Jerry alive. Her husband had helped to identify the bodies, and he had not talked to the press since that night. "You just can't feel secure anymore, "she sighed. "Even when your husband is home, you still have doubt. Jerry was home when his family was killed, and he was young and strong."

She shivered in the first blush of autumn: "It gives you the creeps."

It didn't help that the *Enquirer* was currently running a serialization of *In Cold Blood*, Truman Capote's best seller about the slaughter of a Kansas family by two ex-convicts.

City Council members were speaking out on Bricca and the four rape strangulations. Phil Collins, chairman of the city's upcoming hearings on crime, admitted that, "If my wife is any indication of the public reaction to this thing, well, she's just petrified."

Collins stressed that cooperation between city and county police was essential to the investigation. The Bricca murders occurred only a few blocks from the city limits, yet County detectives were showing no inclination to involve Cincinnati cops.

Councilman John Held vowed that he would bring in "nationally known criminologists who will have an objective view of Cincinnati's troubles." He noted that the crime rate in Hamilton County had increased 300% in the past ten years.

Albers supermarket offered a $5000 reward for information leading to an arrest, bringing the total amount to $15,000—"a reward fund to flush out the Bricca fiend!" An Albers' vice president said his executives were "incensed" over the murder of the child, a sentiment that echoed throughout the community: "It was merciless. She could not have been a witness . . . it was utterly unnecessary even for a maniac."

Perhaps they could comprehend a double murder in the heat of passion. But the cold-blooded killing of a four-year-old was just too much.

On Sunday, funeral services for the family were held in Barrington, Illinois, the suburb of Chicago where Linda grew up. Violent death had reunited a young couple with a troubled marriage, clasped together in a premature eternity.

On Monday, October 3, Herb Vogel announced that he was expecting the FBI report within two days: "They are keeping me informed of things as they go along . . . the lab analysis will tell us a lot—if we're lucky." The results on the hair samples, fingerprints, and blood types were eagerly awaited.

Vogel believed the investigation was "closer to a solution than we were a week ago," and he was counting on the overdue FBI report to "narrow the field a little more." He added that certain fingerprints lifted from the crime scene could not be matched to either the victims or any investigators.

Once again, Vogel reminded everyone that he had "no racial determination" from the preliminary examination of the hair samples. Though he claimed early on that the killer was white, the possibility of a black assailant had not been ruled out by the press.

Vogel's team was waist deep in interviews and action items, even with all 13 detectives from the county squad working the case full time. They had dispatched bulldozers to the dump to find contents from Bricca garbage cans, and directed County engineers to scan the Greenway sewer line with a closed circuit television, both in a vain hunt for the missing knife.

Vogel tried to lower expectations: "We have no strong leads and no suspects."

According to the chief investigator, the recent Supreme Court Miranda ruling had "slowed the interview process. Two years ago we would have already brought people in here for questioning. Now we have to go out and gather backgrounds' that we could have gotten by direct questioning."

He stressed that those interviewed had come in "voluntarily in the spirit of cooperation . . . I wouldn't call them suspects, but we eventually get around to asking them where they were on the night of September 25th," Vogel said with a smile.

Vogel closed this press conference with another warning: "Criminals these days are thinking that even if they are caught, there is a slim chance they will be convicted."

By the tenth day of the investigation, over 250 interviews had been completed and typed. "We know a lot about the Bricca family," claimed Vogel, who wouldn't elaborate.

Buried in the interview file was one in particular that resonated with investigators.

On October 8, detectives questioned employees at the veterinary clinic where Linda Bricca began working two weeks before her murder. A 45-minute interview with one man raised concerns when he became evasive about his "relationship" with her.

Vogel himself conducted the session. The next afternoon, after considering some of the man's statements, the lieutenant visited his wife. She said her husband had been upset by the interview, and further questions should be directed to the attorney he had retained that very morning.

This was a significant break for Vogel, yet he didn't share it with the press. Several days later he denied rumors that the investigation was focusing on one man: "We have not yet zeroed in on any one person as a suspect."

He implied that his investigators were waiting until the full results of FBI testing were sent to Cincinnati. But the process was hardly languishing. Based on the excavation into the life of their new suspect, a theory was evolving.

Vogel now maintained that the killer had the home under surveillance before he entered. "There was a little ground work, a little advance observation. I don't think the home was just chosen at random." He added that burglary as a motive was "not a strong factor in my mind now." Then he speculated that Linda Bricca's "love of animals might have a bearing on the case."

Sounding upbeat, Vogel denied that the investigation was deadlocked: "We're rolling, we're not discouraged . . . we have been talking to friends and acquaintances of the family both in and out of town."

That group did not include a certain man who was hiding

behind his lawyer.

On October 11, the Cincinnati Strangler struck again.

Alice Hochhausler, wife of a prominent physician, was slain just steps away from her back door in the gaslight district of Clifton (Chapter 11). Like the Bricca murders two weeks before, this latest outrage occurred in a "nice" neighborhood where residents thought they were safe.

The juxtaposition of these two crimes shoved Cincinnati to the breaking point. A network of security guards, civil service employees, and delivery persons was established to put 5000 more eyes on the street. City Council moved Halloween trick-or-treating to the daytime.

That a case as incendiary as the Bricca bloodbath would occur during the reign of a serial killer struck most as a heinous coincidence. Yet the local press still tried to connect the murdered family and the black man being sought in the stranglings.

Meanwhile, the national crime tabloids were having a field day with the Queen City's plight. The October issue of *True Detective* ran a cover blurb announcing a **"Special Double-Length Feature! Exclusive Report on Cincinnati's Phantom Assault-Slayer."**

Their sidebar about the Bricca murders was rampant with errors: The number of stab wounds became 70 instead 20 and "Linda never left the house except to walk the dogs" are just two examples.

Here's a sample of the overwrought prose:

> **Dr. Cleveland revealed that Linda had been raped. A sock had been stuffed halfway down her husband's throat . . . To keep him from crying as he lay bleeding to death while his pretty wife was being violated? To choke down his screams as he witnessed the slashing and stabbing of his only child?**

This article stated with confidence that "few persons would believe that the phantom slayer **had not** moved to Bridgetown."

Vogel stepped in to defuse this notion. Now in possession of the long-awaited FBI report, he made it clear that his killer was a white man: "We have nothing to indicate the perpetrator of the Bricca homicide is of Negroid origin."

He offered more details at a press conference. Fingerprints lifted from the two murder bedrooms were not from the victims and were found "on items that would not be touched by the ordinary visitor," yet the FBI had searched its national fingerprint file of known criminals without a match. Vogel promised to send prints of probable suspects to the Bureau for comparison. "This doesn't mean those prints belong to the killer." He warned. "They might have belonged to a recent house guest."

His men were still puzzling over the ligatures. Linda had been bound with white adhesive tape, but her husband's hands seem to have been tied with rope. Both ligatures were missing from the scene. Vogel was impressed—this killer was cool enough to truss up both victims while controlling the child and the dogs.

He also revealed that a suspect "who bragged he had killed the Briccas" had been released after questioning. The young man had been "mouthing off to a friend, just trying to be a big shot." After checking his alibi, "We released him after it appeared he wasn't a suspect."

Vogel took no questions from the press, saying, "There is nothing further in the report that I can comment on." Pressed for an explanation, he remarked, "The Supreme Court is mighty funny these days," a reference to the recently enacted Miranda Rights.

In the weeks to come Vogel would field serious tips from other states. In Florida there was a similar triple homicide of a family by knife. A 22-year-old Monsanto employee in Nitro, West Virginia, was being held for stabbing a 12-year-old girl—Jerry Bricca's visit to that plant had been canceled by his own murder the night before.

A high profile national case provided a slender link to Linda Bricca. Valerie Percy, daughter of Illinois Senatorial candidate Charles Percy, was beaten to death in her suburban Chicago bedroom the week before the Bricca murders. The 21-year-old blonde had attended Barrington High School three years behind Linda.

Bricca Slayer Believed White

Lt. Herbert Vogel of Hamilton County Police today said the slayer of the Bricca family apparently is a white man.

"At this point in our investigation we have nothing to indicate that the perpetrator of the Bricca homicide is of Negroid origin," Lt. Vogel said.

The Chief Investigator took the proactive step of assuring the terrified city that the Bricca killer was not a black man.

Two former students from the same school mysteriously murdered within days of each other? It strained coincidence, but no connection could be established.

Vogel certainly didn't need wild leads or bogus braggarts. He had been stalking his prime suspect since early October.

By November the papers got wind of the gridlock—a leak by a frustrated detective finally drove Herb Vogel to go public. **"Family Slaying Probe Narrows to Single Suspect"** headlined a *Cincinnati Post* story that claimed "a noose of evidence is slowly beginning to tighten around the neck of one man."

Vogel refused to name the suspect, and evaded questions about building a case around one person. But the Post learned that the man had hired a prominent attorney to advise him. They reported that he refused to supply fingerprints and hadn't agreed to a follow-up interview since his initial questioning at his place of business.

Several people came forward who had seen the suspect with Linda Bricca walking on back roads or parked in lovers' lanes. The tinge of a romantic triangle weeks before was now staring detectives in the face. The rape angle had never gained traction—now Vogel's theory of "recent intercourse" was falling into place.

On November 15 Vogel finally admitted their investigation centered on one man. He confirmed the suspect had hired an attorney and would not cooperate. The chief investigator complained that lawyer Richard Morr imposed such "restrictive conditions" on any future interview that he could not accept them.

Police had talked to the man briefly in September while gathering Bricca background. Then the 45-minute interrogation on October 8th galvanized detectives looking for red flags. Showing consciousness of guilt, the suspect became agitated during the questioning and was distressed when Vogel contacted his wife.

His attorney challenged them to either arrest his client or leave him alone. Vogel didn't have enough evidence to charge the man, but now a motive was glistening.

On the same day, police took the overdue step of clearing Bricca neighbor Richard Meyer. He had identified the bodies for police and was profoundly affected, enduring crank calls at home and harassment at work. Vogel confirmed that Meyer "was not actually a bona fide suspect," yet this didn't explain why it took more than six weeks to exonerate the poor man.

Within weeks everyone quizzed about the case had been eliminated except the prime suspect. Vogel still refused to identify him, and complained they "were unable to question him because he is hiding behind his attorney." He added that "full cooperation by all citizens would make the homicide investigators' job a little easier."

Rumors that the suspect was a local veterinarian would not die. And in an opportune coincidence, an *Enquirer* article claiming police "wanted to question a certain man" casually mentioned that Linda Bricca worked several weeks for Dr.

Fred Leininger of the Glenway Animal Hospital before her murder.

The inclusion of the doctor in this specific article ramped up the chatter all along the West Side. Right or wrong, residents finally had a name.

On February 2 1967, the *Cincinnati Enquirer* ran an update on the Bricca case.

Herb Vogel would not admit the inquiry was stalled. "We still have an investigation going, although the number of detectives has been reduced from 10 to two," he explained. "We can't afford to use more men full time, because burglaries are knocking us cold."

Vogel also commented on "the man", saying he would not accept the lawyer's terms for another interview: "This is still an obstacle, until we find a way to circumvent it."

He was still at odds with the coroner over the rape issue. He repeated that there was evidence of recent sexual relations before the killing, and "nothing has been turned up to indicate definitely to me that it was rape." Vogel added that "recent intercourse" could mean 36 to 48 hours before Linda Bricca was slain.

The *Enquirer* posted another update as spring blustered in. Their headline of March 28, 1967, was incisive: **"Bricca Case Probe Stymied."** And the lead said it all: "Sheriff's deputies want to question a man in the Bricca murder case, but his attorney says, 'NO!' The deputies have offered to meet several conditions set by attorney Richard Morr, yet he says the police offer is 'only half' of what he wants for his client."

Herbert Vogel was at the end of his tether: "We feel as if we are being hindered even though we agree to most of the conditions laid down by Mr. Morr. We feel his client could supply us with information that may prove important to an ultimate solution to this triple homicide."

After interviewing everyone who had any contact with the family, Morr's client was the only person not eliminated as a suspect. Yet police had not spoken to him since October 8, 1966.

Vogel had agreed to the following interview conditions in February: He would provide in advance the seven questions he wanted to ask the man personally; the attorney would be present at all times; and Morr and his client would choose a time and place of "mutual convenience."

These were generous concessions by law enforcement. Yet Morr never responded, despite repeated phone calls to his office. When Detective Gerald Taylor finally caught up with Morr at the County Courthouse on March 21, the lawyer added another stipulation. He wanted the tape recording of the only interview with his client, but wouldn't commit to another session even if he received it.

According to Vogel, the seven questions requested by Morr were the same ones asked in the other 400 interviews:

- When did you last see Linda Bricca alive?
- Did you see Linda Bricca on Thursday, September 22, 1966?
- When did you last visit the Bricca residence?
- For what reason did you last visit the Bricca residence?
- Did Linda Bricca ever discuss with you any of her personal problems?
- Were you ever out with Linda Bricca socially?
- Where were you on Sunday night, September 26, 1966, between 9PM and midnight?

But the suspect declined to answer any questions about his relationship with Linda, and rejected all requests to submit samples of blood, hair, and fingerprints for crime scene comparison.

The Bricca case was now poised to pass into myth.

In July *Front Page Detective* ran a feature aptly titled **"The Bricca Mystery . . . And Nobody is Talking."** The national

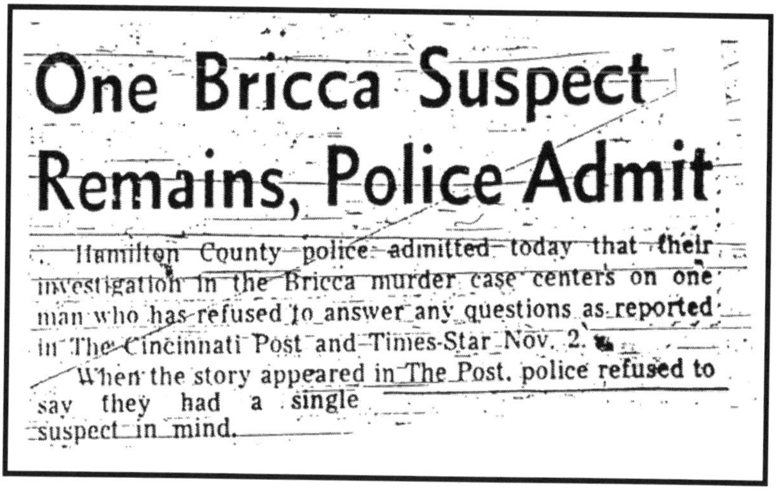

One Bricca Suspect Remains, Police Admit

Hamilton County police admitted today that their investigation in the Bricca murder case centers on one man who has refused to answer any questions as reported in The Cincinnati Post and Times-Star Nov. 2.

When the story appeared in The Post, police refused to say they had a single suspect in mind.

This February *Post* headline confirmed the rumored impasse with the prime suspect.

crime tabloid confronted the silent suspect in a manner that the local papers would not touch.

The writer quoted an unnamed Hamilton County detective complaining about "a door we haven't been able to open since it was slammed shut," and "a man whose attitude is puzzling and disturbing."

The article didn't diminish the frustration:

> **What is a police officer entitled to think when one man out of 400 refuses to cooperate? Four Hundred people saw it as their Responsibility to assist in every way to find the killer at large among them. One man has elected to use his constitutional privileges to flaunt the good will and best interests of an entire community.**
>
> **And the man who slaughtered three people without regard to their Constitutional rights to summer nights around the barbeque pit along Greenway Avenue—running the dogs, raking the leaves, or just growing up—will never be brought to justice.**
>
> **Is the Bricca atrocity ready to take its place as another statistic in the growing file of protected criminals?**

On September 26, 1967, exactly one year after the murders, law enforcement fired off a final salvo in the Bricca case. This time it was Hamilton County prosecutor Melvin Rueger's turn to vent.

The *Enquirer* headline was provocative: **"Prosecutor Believes He Knows Who Killed Bricca Family."** The article asked "How can a murderer kill a family of three and then vanish without a trace? Hamilton County officials don't think he has. They're convinced they know who the killer is . . . Then why don't they make an arrest?"

Prosecutor Rueger confronted the crime that had haunted Cincinnati's West Side for 12 months. "This is a classic case where recent Supreme Court rulings thwart law and justice," he explained. "Here is a case where a man kills three persons, there are no living witnesses, and he doesn't leave any clues behind."

An unidentified detective was even more blunt: "You would tear a guy apart if it was ethical, but you're prevented by law from doing some things."

Rueger explained that he lacked sufficient grand jury evidence, so the only chance investigators had was to talk to the suspect. "But we can't question the man, because the Supreme Court says that would be infringing on his Constitutional rights." Yet attorney Richard Morr was proving to be a larger obstruction than the nine Chief Justices.

County officials also leaked new details. Apparently Linda Bricca had become acquainted with the suspect in 1963, shortly after the family moved to Cincinnati. The couple was seen together numerous times on a secluded back road.

Jerry Bricca, after working through Saturday night at the Monsanto plant, attended 10AM Mass at St. Aloysius Church in Bridgetown on the last day of his life. The church was close to his house, yet he chose to return to work and didn't arrive home until late Sunday evening.

A YEAR GOES BY—STILL NO ARREST, ALTHOUGH . . .

Prosecutor Believes He Knows Who Killed Bricca Family

One year after the murders, this headline summed up the stalemate between investigators and "their man."

Some detectives now theorized that Jerry surprised the suspect by coming home at an unexpected time: "He heard Jerry carrying out the garbage cans and speaking to Mrs. Janzsen. I think the man in the house hit him as he walked in," one official said.

Others pointed out that Sunday night was not good timing for a tryst—something else was going on. They believed the married suspect confronted Bricca and killed him because he was afraid of the scandal. Linda was killed while possibly defending her husband. Then the deed that stuck in everyone's throat: "There was only one reason he would have to kill the little girl," one cop spat. "She knew him too well."

Rueger had the last word. "We always inform suspects of their rights before questioning them. But we could use psychology and sales talk to get them to confess. Now we have been deprived of those two tools by the Supreme Court, and men are walking around free who should be behind bars."

Predator and prey retreated into a lingering psychological stalemate, evocative of Dostoyevsky's classic novel *Crime and Punishment*, yet enduring much longer.

Cincinnati's West Side has embraced a folklore all its own.

People there have adopted the "womb to tomb" philosophy. They were born and raised there, married and started families there, grew old and died there. Census statistics bear this out—around 80% of current residents never left.

The West Side is a stronghold for conservative Republicans of German descent, and an enclave for Catholics. Ask someone where they live, and the answer will likely be a parish instead of a street.

It is an area long on tradition but short on tolerance. In 1966 98% of residents were white. Minorities were discouraged from living there, sometimes by questionable tactics.

The community has a long memory too. The Bricca murders would become an obsession for justice that eventually spread from Bridgetown to the whole West Side. Why this case didn't just fade away is a mystery—but then an obsession has no reason.

My colleague George Stimson, author of ***The Cincinnati Crime Book,*** told me about a talk he gave to the Bridgetown VFW in 1990. The topic was the Queen City's infamous murders, but it never got past the Bricca case. He fielded question after question about the unsolved triple homicide, the fascination of his audience still smoldering after 24 years.

In 1982, *Cincinnati Magazine* published an article about unsolved murders in the Queen City, and they featured the Bricca case. Captain Bernard Henke of the sheriff's department shared some insights into the original investigation during a lengthy interview. "They looked at everybody who ever had contact with that family," he said. "They looked at the mailman, the water meter reader, and the paper man. Anybody that ever was around that house—they even interviewed Mrs. Bricca's beautician."

He admitted the delay in finding the bodies hurt the investigation. Leads dry up after the first 48 hours. "You might be able to pin a witness's memory down to the last 24 hours, but not 48," he said. "What did you have for breakfast two days ago? How many people can remember details like that?"

Henke cut to the chase: "There are pictures in here of the scene, of the little girl . . . I have two daughters, and between three and six they are at their cutest stage. It's hard to imagine how anybody could do what they did to that little girl . . . In police work you get callous to a lot of things . . . but when a child gets killed . . . You don't even want to see these photos."

Henke insisted the case was still open. "At this point we'd need the spoken word. Somebody's conscience would have to get the better of them. It's happened before. They'll walk up to a policeman in another town and say, 'I can't stand it anymore; I killed a whole family back in 1966.'"

And there was this telltale quote at the end of the *Cincinnati Magazine* article:

> **Rumors and innuendo abounded. Police questioned a local businessman witnesses claimed to have seen with Mrs. Bricca while her husband was at work. But Captain Henke dismissed those ancient suspicions.**

Why would he do that? The focus on the prime suspect had been well documented. The sensitivity regarding him is perplexing—almost as if the man had connections in high places.

Because trying to spin the Bricca case into a real mystery was at odds with what everyone already knew.

The *Cincinnati Magazine* article was the last Bricca feature until this author profiled the case in *Snitch Magazine* ("Unsolved Bricca Case Haunts West Side," March 2, 2002). George Stimson's 1998 book also contained a chapter on the case.

The Bricca legend endures: on the internet, on the streets of Bridgetown, and in the minds of other murderers.

When Della Sutorius was growing up on the West Side, Cincinnati's future black widow killer became obsessed with the triple murder. In *Della's Web*, author Aphrodite Jones notes: "The Bricca case had become rather infamous in Western Hills . . . 16-year-old Della taunted her sister that she did it."

She didn't, but she did kill her husband in 1996. She's serving 20 years—perhaps she still fantasizes about murdering the Bricca family.

Some of the internet postings are the most poignant.

Date 5-25-2000: "I hope they find the person who did the crime—it's so awful, not to mention sick. Especially to kill the little girl, who was totally innocent?"

Date 1-27-2001: "Because it is a subject no one in my family wants to discuss, I've never known the details of the murders . . . Thank you for keeping the information available and offering the hope of finding some answers."—Bay area Bricca

Date 1-29-2001: "Gerald was my cousin, we all saw him a week before his death at a family wedding. It has been 33 years and the thought that this has never been solved is devastating. Also his parents died without ever knowing the truth."—A Bricca now in Texas.

I received correspondence from my *Snitch* article as well:

Date 2-20-2002: "I grew up on the West Side. There was always a controversy over who the veterinarian was since there are two vet hospitals on Glenway Avenue. Which vet hospital was it, Glenway Animal Hospital or Bridgetown Pet Hospital?"

Linda Bricca worked part time at both clinics. Both veterinarians came under suspicion, and one became the prime suspect.

Date 5-25-2002: "I worked at the car wash across the street from Glenway Animal Hospital, which was around the corner from the Bricca home . . . . Occasionally customers that stopped by the car wash would comment that the vet across the street was a murderer . . . I took a personal interest in the case because the vet across the street, Fred Leininger, was our family vet."

Fred Leininger was mentioned as Linda Bricca's final employer in an *Enquirer* article focusing on the unnamed suspect.

Date 5-27-2002 : "Most of the people in the Bridgetown area believe it was Fred who was the murderer. His practice seemed to do well, so I guess not enough people knew the story."

Date 5-28-2002: "The thing with Fred, he was my vet and I did see him on a regular basis. My overall impression of him is not of a killer. But everyone on the news who lives next to a killer says the same thing . . . I really didn't know him on a personal level."

This author has been casually researching the Bricca murders for over two decades. I find the reluctance of people to go on the record about the case fascinating. Forty two years later, the silence is deafening.

Here are some vignettes from my attempts to interview those connected with this most infamous crime.

After arranging a tour of the murder house in 1981 with the owners, I spent an hour recreating the crime for them. They told me that cars still stopped and stared at their house. When I left they thanked me, and then wrote down my license number and called the police. I received a call from an officer who berated me for "bothering those people" and questioned why I would "want to write about this terrible crime."

When the house was for sale in 1984, I arranged a tour with the listing agent. I don't know if he realized my true interest or not, but he never mentioned the notorious history of the home he was trying to sell me.

A phone interview with a former Bricca baby-sitter abruptly ended when the woman refused to discuss the case.

A phone conversation with a former Bricca investigator was frustrating because of his sudden amnesia. He claimed not to remember the details of any particular case—I reminded him that this was the BRICCA CASE! He also denied that the investigation had narrowed to a single suspect in 1966, which seems to be the County's official stance.

A lawyer I know had handled Linda Bricca's probate back in 1966. He told me her parents made a plea to him in 1990 to get the case reopened. He took this request to the Hamilton County sheriff's office and was harshly told to let it drop.

Neighbor Richard Meyer, who discovered the bodies, was at first reluctant to talk to me, but finally couldn't resist commenting on the 43 year old mystery that still lives next door to him. He believes the killings were "professional, somehow tied to the business interests of Linda's father, who was a "wealthy Chicago industrialist."

And Meyer shared this tidbit from the murder night: A Cincinnati police detective asked to use his phone after consulting with Hamilton County officers, who had jurisdiction over the crime. Meyer, still in shock from identifying the dead family, heard the detective complain to his superior about the lack of procedure being followed by county investigators.

Last year, after making a request for file access from Hamilton County Law Enforcement, I was amazed to receive a preliminary agreement. But when they decided to run it by their law director, I knew it was hopeless. As they confirmed their final rejection, I was told "90% of the file would have to be redacted because the information was too sensitive."

They were the only jurisdiction to turn down a file request during research for this book.

Why do so many refuse to talk about this case—while others thrive on a stealthy stream of gossip? I've heard every wild piece of conjecture out there. Here's a sampling of the word-of-mouth:

1. Jerry Bricca was castrated and his genitals were stuffed into his mouth: The coroner did mention unspecified "mutilations" to both adults, and Jerry allegedly had a pair of socks stuffed in his mouth. Recent information from a Bridgetown woman who knew the EMT responding to the scene seemed to confirm this rumor. Yet Richard Meyer discounts the castration theory, assuring me he saw no evidence of "any mutilations on Jerry or the baby," and confirming the "black socks" in Jerry's mouth.

2. Police had to let the killer go on a technicality: It's long rumored that investigators screwed up somehow, from contaminating the crime scene to violating the suspect's rights. The barrier of silence supports this contention.

3. The Bricca murders were connected to the Valerie Percy slaying the week before: The two women were allegedly part of a drug smuggling ring. Yet Linda was three years ahead of Valerie at Barrington High and graduated at age 16. It's doubtful that 13-year-old rich girl Valerie would have made a criminal connection with her. This is just a stubborn coincidence.

4. Linda and Debbie were both mutilated in a strange manner: This goes back to Rumor #1, and the evidence is inconclusive. Police implied there were mutilations, but refused to elaborate, citing the need for polygraph keys to weed out false confessions.

5. A psychic was brought in for consultation on the case: Questionable—Hamilton County investigators were old-school lawmen. Psychics working on police cases in the Midwest are more hype than reality.

6. Neighbors knew something was wrong, but deliberately delayed notifying police: The lack of activity at the Bricca home should have made any neighbor curious. Yet I think Meyer and Janzsen didn't come together on it until getting home from work Tuesday night, and at that point they acted expediently.

7. Undercover cops sat near the suspect when he went to bars, hoping to hear a drunken confession: This is too delicious to discard—one hopes they did just that. After the case went dark, two investigators made reference to "psychological games" and "sales talk" used as probing techniques. I feel certain the suspect was stalked for years after the crime.

8. The killer was so repulsed by his actions that he vomited in the house: There was no mention of vomit at the crime scene, and a suspect with a medical background would not be revolted by the sight of blood. But shortly after the discovery a cop was seen throwing up in the front yard.

9. Linda Bricca was a "knockout" and had numerous affairs: Everyone commented on her remarkable beauty. Combine that with the "former airline stewardess" label and Jerry's workaholic lifestyle, and we have the makings of a bored, wayward housewife. Whether she was really "hell on wheels" is just conjecture—and trashing the victim is an easy out. But we do know that one affair turned deadly.

10. The dogs were injected with something to keep them quiet: Almost everyone remembers the suddenly passive dogs. With the main suspect a veterinarian this becomes an intriguing possibility. The dogs weren't heard barking until Tuesday night—this could have been a tactic to delay discovery of the bodies.

11. Jerry had a violent temper and was beaten unmercifully: Neighbors all remarked on Jerry's good humor and even disposition. It's possible he attacked the killer to protect his family and started a chain reaction stabbing. If he was physically beaten, it was held back from the press.

12. The murderer stayed inside the house for hours after the crime, took a shower, and wiped everything clean: Probably true—it was late at night, and he had time to regain his composure and secure the scene. If Linda kept any hidden mementos of their affair, he found and removed them.

13. The killer checked himself into a sanitarium in California sometime after the murders: Fred Leininger remained at his veterinary clinic until 1995—he made no effort to run away. There is no indication that his practice ever suffered from the whispers about his past. If he had something to hide, he had the presence of mind to hire a good attorney to protect his rights.

14. Investigators used psychological pressure, forensic hypnosis, and innovative fingerprint techniques on the suspect: Goes back to Rumor #7 and has endless possibility: obtaining his empty beer glass from the waitress—bumping into him on the street and getting confrontational—making further attempts to question his wife. Anything to set his teeth on edge.

15. A local sports star was linked to the slayings: Supposedly a member of the Cincinnati Reds had incriminating evidence in his car trunk during a routine airport search. Yet the player most often mentioned wasn't with the club in 1966. This rumor is undoubtedly fiction.

16. The killer was big and strong, based on the wounds to Debbie Bricca: To hold a child in the air with one arm and stab with the other takes strength. One of my internet correspondents described Fred Leininger as "a decent sized man, around 6 feet tall and 220 pounds. He had big hands and fingers."

To engage in supposition and scandal is risky business—it can skew objectivity. But no recounting of the Bricca murders is complete without releasing the tumbling load of dirty laundry that sullies the case to this very day.

SUMMATION:

So what really happened the night of September 25, 1966, at 3381 Greenway Avenue in Bridgetown? What was the catalyst for murder?

Though he was never officially identified, Dr. Fred Leininger was the prime suspect. It was and still is common knowledge on the West Side. Two retired detectives have confirmed his status to this author.

Yet in this summation, we'll give him the presumption of innocence.

The killer was Linda Bricca's lover. I suspect Jerry caught wind of the affair—the smoke from another cigarette or the promise of his wife's perfume. He gave Linda an ultimatum to end it over the weekend while he worked.

What caused murder instead of withdrawal in a situation whose sole investment was emotional? Passion is not logical, and love/hate murders are often sparked by an extra element of irrationality, a motive so convoluted that it's difficult to determine where passion ends and insanity begins.

And when a rage killing subsides, other persons can be murdered out of an overwhelming fear.

EPILOGUE:

Over four decades later, the Bricca case survives on whispers. Questions abound. Why will no one go on the record about an unsolved triple homicide? What skeletons lurk deep within the files? And how could such a tenacious investigation uncover a killer without capturing him?

The suspect retired in 1995 and lived for many years in Florida before his death in 2004. All secrets were safe with him, because none were more deadly than his own.

If there is justice for the Briccas, the face in his mirror was that of an exiled stranger, waiting for a final judgment from beyond any earthly court: Is getting away with murder worse than getting caught?

POSTCRIPT:

Jack Heffron exhumed the case in an article for *Cincinnati Magazine's* April 2008 issue. Heffron writes a regular column called "West Side Story"—together with ex-cop John Boertline they tackled the Bricca legend head on.

Among their startling conclusions:

- The long buried autopsy report suggested that the killer was left-handed, based on the position of the wounds.
- The report makes no mention of Linda Bricca's rape.
- In January 2008 Hamilton County detectives still denied that the original investigation narrowed to a single suspect.
- A neighbor had noticed "that Linda seemed particularly nervous a month or so before the murder."
- Linda told the neighbor that she'd worked with two stewardesses who were attacked earlier that summer in their Seattle apartment. One died, and serial killer Ted Bundy was later considered a suspect.
- Linda also told next door neighbor Richard Meyer that her "friend" Valerie Percy, the Senate candidate's daughter, had been murdered—this was one week before her own death.
- Greenway Avenue residents have their own theories, and "none of them believe the killer was having an affair with Linda."

Heffron was able to dodge the rumors surrounding the case and provide an interesting revisionist spin. But he was left with a chain of unresolved coincidences—none of the other murders can be linked to the Bricca case.

POSTCRIPT: OCTOBER 2010

Since the publication of **Queen City Gothic** in October 2009, I have received more email about the Bricca case than the other 12 chapters combined!

And the Rumor Mill is still spinning:

❖ "The Unabomber" killed the Briccas.

There is a website dedicated to the proposition that Ted Kaczynski not only murdered the Briccas, but that he also killed Valerie Percy and all the Zodiac victims in California. And after proactively getting his hands bloody for ten years, he then decided to become a recluse who sent death packages through the mail.

❖ "Skipper Ryle" killed the Briccas.

Kiddy show host Glen Ryle was a close friend of chief suspect Fred Leininger, and his signature motorcycle was seen parked outside Leininger's veterinary clinic "every day of the two weeks leading up to the murders." Which coincides with the period Linda Bricca was working there. And that's why little Debby was killed—because even a 4 year old could identify Skipper Ryle.

❖ Linda Bricca was pregnant.

A Bricca relative told me pictures of her at a family wedding in San Francisco two weeks before the murders show her to be "noticeably pregnant". And the unspecified "mutilations" may have been the removal of her lover's baby.

❖ The Killer visited the gravesite.

A friend of Linda Bricca's parents visited the Barrington Hills cemetery with them in 1990, only to find that someone had outlined Linda's grave in Marlboro cigarette butts. She had been a closet smoker during her marriage to Jerry (who did not smoke). And surprisingly, Fred Leininger had purchased property in Barrington close to the cemetery. Perhaps the cigarettes had been a private joke between them, and now served as an expression of remorse from her lover turned killer.

❖ Fred Leininger did not die in Florida.

His obituary has him passing away in Sarasota February 2004. Yet he has an Ohio death certificate. So is this rumor just a premature fact?

Stories surrounding Fred Leininger's final exit have ebbed and flowed for years, with this writer mostly evading the sinister allegations. But this year, the hearsay became too deafening to ignore.

There is now credible evidence that the prime suspect and his wife traveled to Cincinnati, checked into a downtown hotel, tied plastic bags around their heads, and took an overdose of morphine. He died—she lapsed into a coma and expired in December 2004.

A suicide pact for the alleged Bricca killer and his faithful wife? Perhaps revenge IS best served cold, when the burden of guilt and the weight of conscience conspire to deliver some overdue justice.

He got away with murder—but he did not escape punishment . . .

I WITNESS:

Against a backdrop of incessant rain and steady drinking, this long, dreary Sunday is overwhelming him. Ice clinks in the bottom of his glass. A mockery. No one should ever try to get tipsy alone; it fills no voids. That requires company, someone else to listen and sympathize.

And the room is empty.

After making love one last time on Saturday, Linda delivered Jerry's edict: "End it now," her husband demanded, "or else I'll call his wife."

At first he shrugged and laughed it off. Who died and made Jerry Bricca king? But then he saw the look in Linda's eyes, a defeated compliance never there before.

She certainly chose a hell of a time to become the chaste, obedient wife. He stared at her in shaken disbelief, feeling utterly bereft.

"We both knew it had to end sometime," she reminded him gently. "Didn't we?" Then she flashed that irresistible United Airlines smile that everyone remarked upon. His heart raced. He grasped her hand. She pulled away. Stung, he rose to leave, then hurried home to stew, grateful only that he managed not to break down in front of her.

Now he broods his way through Sunday afternoon, feeling hollow and heavy as he remembers every single moment of their time together.

During their first lunch date, he had confessed his growing obsession. She nodded and ducked her head, feigning modesty. She'd felt his eye prints all over her at work; it was intoxicating. Jerry was hardly ever home, she admitted. Always working, always traveling. She sometimes felt like a widow. It was just a matter of time before she stopped trying so hard to please him, ceased fiddling with her hair, her clothes, her makeup. Then she giggled. Okay, maybe not.

Their eyes met in the shared joke. He reached across the table for her hand and gallantly kissed it, inhaling her scent, feeling the sweet, joyous pain of wanting her.

Now that pain is a raging desire for vengeance that twists and crumples him like a leaf in a flame. Her careless sendoff stokes the fire further. He is ready to turn Jerry's picture to the wall.

As night falls, he drives to Greenway Avenue and drunkenly cruises the neighborhood, parking three doors down from the tri-level. He watches as Jerry arrives home, eases into the garage and then drags the trash cans to the curb.

He waits, gets out of the car and approaches. He paces the exterior for several minutes, and peers through windows. Nothing. He walks back to the patio and squints into the dimly lit basement, where the couple sits together with their little girl, watching television. A pile of folded laundry is stacked nearby.

Oh, yeah, he remembers. Tonight is the premiere of *The Bridge On the River Kwai.* The three seem the very picture of happy domesticity. His stomach churns.

Suddenly Jerry leaps up, scoops Debbie into his arms, nuzzles her and heads toward the stairs. Time to put the child to bed. Perhaps he'll read her a story, maybe even retire for the night. A good chance for him to make his move.

He pushes open the patio door and glides into the room. Linda is folding more laundry and doesn't see him. She's wearing a frilly robe over her nightgown.

He must make her understand, before Jerry comes back. He must tell her that if they can only be together once more, if she can only know how much he truly loves her . . .

But Linda is startled, and cries out in alarm. She looks past him. He whirls. Jerry is standing on the top kitchen step, his face a thundercloud. He springs forward, threatening to call the man's wife, and the police if he doesn't go away immediately. Linda begs both of them to remain calm.

This is not going at all according to plan. He expected to confront Linda, first alone, then in Jerry's presence, get everything out in the open, convince both of them that he and she belong together, that no one should stand in their way.

But the two exchange meaningful glances, indicating that he's the one who will be leaving—for good. He gives a magnificent performance of docility, allowing them to escort him upstairs and toward the front door. But at the last moment he seizes the carving knife resting in the block on the dining room credenza and unsheathes it. Now *he* is in control.

He presses against her body with the knife to her throat. Her scent is a montage, propelling him back to their lazy afternoons of lovemaking, lying there adrift on her skin. He would give everything to have it once more.

Yet he feels Linda trembling in his arms. He snarls at Jerry to fetch the utility tape from the kitchen, and to close up the dogs in the playroom. Then he herds the couple up the steps to the third level.

Halfway there, he sees something that unnerves him—Linda, clearly shaken, places her small, timid hand inside Jerry's. His gives hers a reassuring squeeze.

So that's the way it is. The man who can't stay home with his wife and daughter for more than a few days at a time, who's too busy playing Mr. Corporate Big Shot; the woman who baits other men, who dresses like a fashion model and can't ever seem to get enough attention from passersby—now they're behaving like the bride and groom perched atop a wedding cake.

He pushes them toward the upstairs bedroom, where he commands Linda at knifepoint to bind Jerry's wrists before he tapes hers. They are surprisingly cooperative.

What now? He isn't sure. He'd only meant to scare them, convince Linda that she made a huge mistake by trifling with him. Then convince Jerry that he's the better man, have the pleasure of relating in orgiastic detail how his wife writhed and moaned whenever they made love. Perhaps he'd like to see it for himself—*Hey, Jer, care for a demonstration?*

Then he notices that Linda is crying. Pleading and remorseful now, she begs her husband to forgive her and tells him she's so very, very sorry.

Sorry?

Everything else seems to flow from that word and that moment. His fury flashes into an explosive seizure, demanding instant release. The knife, as if springing to life on its own, thrusts in frenzied motions. Jerry tries to defend himself—he is killed first. Linda attacks, attempting to pull him away from her husband. But it's too late. She too is stabbed repeatedly and then flung across his dead body.

The man stands, looking downward. Grief returns. He kneels and brushes Linda's damp hair off her lovely face, begins to weep and then realizes—he can still smell her perfume.

Abruptly, he hears a whimpering sound coming from the next bedroom.

Debbie.

Has she just now awakened? Or did she peek from her darkened doorway into the hall as the trio was ascending the stairs?

He cannot know. But in an instant grief becomes cold calculation.

He enters the child's room, where a tiny night light burns. He doesn't need to switch on the overhead; he can see her well enough. He slinks toward the bed, then places a large hand at the back of the girl's neck, lifts her into a vertical position and pierces her chest four times. It happens so fast that she makes only a small gasping sound, and then slides like a rag doll to the floor.

The killer resurfaces from his fugue state and waxes obsessive-compulsive. He sweeps through the crime scene and removes all traces of his existence. His letters are in Linda's bureau drawer, hidden beneath her blue silk nightgown, a location she revealed during a tender moment weeks earlier. The jewelry is inside a box under the bed. Everything disappears.

He wipes his fingerprints from each doorknob. He wraps the bloody knife in discarded newspaper. He showers and dresses. Then he slips out the back door into the early morning fog.

For the next four decades, his past will follow him like an ever-lengthening shadow. He may laugh again someday, but only to escape the terror of silence.

It's a Faustian bargain—but he is the one who lives in perpetual hell.

2009

Alice was almost home when the Cincinnati Strangler waylaid her in this driveway and dragged her into the garage.

TERROR IN THE GASLIGHT DISTRICT

ALICE HOCHHAUSLER FALLS VICTIM TO THE CINCINNATI STRANGLER: 1966

"Like one on that lonesome road
Doth walk in fear and dread,
Because he knows a frightful fiend
Doth close behind him tread."

Samuel Taylor Coleridge

PROLOGUE:

The rape-strangulation of Alice Hochhausler in Clifton's gaslight district is the Queen City's most seminal murder in recent memory. Struck down in her driveway just steps from her back door, Alice's death inflamed the citizenry and launched the largest law enforcement mobilization in Cincinnati history.

The wife of a prominent surgeon, she became the 5th victim of the "Cincinnati Strangler." Her slaying was the climactic outrage from a phantom who ravaged the innocence of the entire city.

If Alice Hochhausler could be taken, then none of us was truly safe.

NARRATIVE:

A conservative Midwestern city in the 1960s confronts a mysterious serial killer and its own escalating racial turmoil. No, not a cover blurb from the latest John Grisham novel—this is the unknown legend of the Cincinnati Strangler.

In 1966 the Queen City was the hunting ground for a brutal and elusive slayer who preyed on older women, murdering six and assaulting several others. They were killed in seedy flats, Victorian districts, and tree-lined parks. The assassin struck morning, noon, and night.

Like Boston several years earlier, Cincinnati was in the thrall of a ruthless strangler. This plot even had a twist. The victims were white, and when police announced the killer was a "Negro," fear and rage held the city in the cruel grip of racism.

In October of 1965 the national mood was apprehensive. A Gallup Poll cited Civil Rights problems as citizens' #1 worry, overtaking the Vietnam War. President Johnson called crime "a sore on the face of America," amid growing concerns that recent court decisions protecting the rights of the accused would virtually handcuff law enforcement.

Citizens of the Queen City were confident that such troubles "could never happen here." Yet they were on the verge of an unrivaled crime wave that would manacle police for over a year.

Around noon on October 12, 1965, 65-year-old Elizabeth Kreco was leaving her apartment in Walnut Hills when a short black man approached her, looking for the caretaker. She guided him to the basement, where he suddenly dragged her into a toilet room, raped her, and choked her until she passed out. She was found barely alive with a double-knotted piece of clothesline dangling from her neck.

Nine days later, two more women in Walnut Hills were assaulted. Both attackers were black males, but otherwise the descriptions differed.

Around 7PM on October 25, 39-year-old Margie Helton was leaving work in Walnut Hills when a young black man jumped into her car. "This is a robbery," he hissed. "Give me your money, and you won't get hurt." As she handed over $10, he tried to put a rope around her neck. She screamed, pounding the car horn as he broke off the attack and fled.

"Sex Crimes Prove Nightmarish Problem to Citizens," was the *Post* headline on October 27. Until now, Cincinnati had always depended on the kindness of strangers.

On December 2, 56-year-old Emogene Harrington eased her station wagon to the curb in front of the Clermont Apartments in East Walnut Hills. Mrs. Harrington, the wife of a University of Cincinnati scientist, was returning from grocery shopping. She locked her car and was seen searching for the janitor, who often helped carry the bags up to the 2nd floor.

At about 1:20 PM, the elderly custodian discovered her body in the restroom of the dimly lit basement. Emogene had been strangled with a section of plastic cord still hanging around her neck. Her clothing was ripped—she had been beaten and raped.

The cord was-double knotted at each end, just like the Elizabeth Kreco rape. Sergeant Russell Jackson was convinced the same man had committed this murder and the October onslaught.

Witnesses had seen a restless looking black man near the Clermont early that Thursday afternoon. A similar male was observed just before the crime in a neighboring building full of female tenants.

Dozens of sexual predators were questioned concerning their whereabouts that afternoon. But as winter beckoned, the killer's trail grew cold.

"New Fears Raised by Phantom!" exclaimed the *Enquirer* in January when a prowler tried to choke a woman in her Walnut Hills basement. Her husband chased off a tall Negro wearing a trench coat. The Strangler detail responded twice more to Walnut Hills that week, when two women encountered strange black men skulking around their basements.

On April 4, 1966, the phantom struck again.

Emogene Harrington was the strangler's first victim. Her station wagon is parked outside the Clermont Apartments after her murder.

At 10:40AM Frank Dant returned to his apartment on Rutledge Avenue in Price Hill. It was his custom to help count the Sunday church collection on Monday mornings, the only time of the week when 58-year-old Mrs. Lois Dant was home alone.

Frank walked in and stumbled over the battered body of his wife, strangled with one of her own stockings, her housecoat ripped open and her underwear torn off. She had been dead only a short time—Dant had just missed the killer.

Lois had been on the phone with her cousin just before her murder. The woman remembered their conversation being interrupted by the Dant's front doorbell. Lois put down the phone, then returned and said it was "just some man looking for the caretaker." A minute later she said, "There's the door again. Maybe it's the same man. I'll call you back." She expressed no anxiety as she said goodbye.

Sometime before 11:00, an upstairs neighbor overheard a man's voice downstairs: "I heard a startled cry or an excited yell. I can't describe it," she said later. "Then I heard a door slam. I looked down the stairs but saw nothing."

Police would question several suspects, some of them white. The FBI had confirmed the killer's blood type as O, but tests to determine race were inconclusive.

Lois Dant was killed inside her apartment on Monday morning—the only time of the week her husband was never home.

Some detectives hesitated to link this crime to the Harrington murder. Price Hill was a white community, and the man (or men) terrorizing Walnut Hills could not have loitered there by day with impunity. A black man at her door would have been a singular event for Mrs. Dant, and she would likely have mentioned the caller's race to her cousin.

Within weeks the investigation stalled.

Just before sunrise on June 10, a man walking his dog in Clifton's Burnet Woods discovered a woman's badly beaten body. Her clothing had been torn off, and a yellow necktie was knotted around her throat. A small terrier had been tied to a nearby tree. Tags verified the owner as Jeannette Messer of nearby Jefferson Avenue. The 56-year-old widow walked her dog in the park most mornings, telling concerned friends that it provided ample protection.

"Mad Strangler Catches Widow Strolling Alone," headlined the *Enquirer* interview of detective chief Jacob Schott. "He is definitely the same man who raped and strangled the two other women," claimed Schott. "The man is a maniac."

The killer had bludgeoned her, fracturing both cheekbones and several ribs. She was dragged off the trail, then raped and strangled. As more details were released, the *Enquirer* led with a story headlined, **"Fear Gripping Women While Strangler Roams."**

By late June, after police had worked over 1000 leads, Jake Schott finally put a face on the suspect—the *Enquirer* headline confirmed that a **"Negro Killed Three Women"**. His men had found Negroid hair on both Harrington and Messer. Though he admitted that none was found on Lois Dant, Schott reiterated that there was a serial killer loose.

The long, hot summer of dread had begun.

By July's end, Richard Speck and Charles Whitman had ushered in the era of modern mass murder. Speck, a mutant drifter, butchered eight student nurses in Chicago. Whitman, a brooding sniper, killed 13 from atop the University of Texas Tower.

On the rainy night of August 14, 1966, the Strangler struck again—or did he?

Pretty 31-year-old secretary Barbara Bowman was last seen leaving Clifton's Lark Café around 2AM. Witnesses at the bar described a short Negro cab driver around 30 years old who picked her up.

At the end of the ride to her Price Hill apartment everything went terribly wrong. She broke away from the cab, but the driver lurched the car over the curb and ran her down. Lying helpless in the pelting rain with her leg shattered, Barbara's last image was the taxi driver looming over her with a knife.

She was found minutes later, dying in the gutter at the corner of Ring and Grand, just down the street from her home. She'd been stabbed in the neck seven times with a paring knife found next to her.

The cab was abandoned nearby with a broken axle—police later confirmed it was stolen from the Yellow Taxi lot.

Strewn outside the vehicle were her purse, glasses, shoes, and the beads from a broken necklace. Barbara had ditched her high heels in a frantic effort to escape, only to be mowed

Mad Strangler Catches Widow Strolling Alone

Fear gripped Cincinnati anew Friday as the mad rapist-strangler claimed his third victim.

This time the killer struck at dawn in heavily wooded Burnet Woods.

His victim was Mrs. Jeannette M. Messer, 56, a widow who lived at 3249 Jefferson Ave.

THE CINCINNATI ENQUIRER

Tuesday, June 14, 1966, Page 23

5 ★★★★★ STAR PAGE

Fear-Gripping Women While Strangler Roams

Tension mounted when the third victim in six months was taken in a popular city park.

down by a killer whose methods the *Enquirer* called the "Most Bizarre in City History."

The bootleg driver had taken eight fares before picking up Miss Bowman, responding with call number 186 throughout the night on his radio. Yellow Cab furnished a tape where the suspect announcing himself as 186 was clearly heard.

Another lead came from a cabby who picked up a suspicious fare in lower Price Hill shortly after the murder. A drenched and breathless black man jumped into his back seat and demanded to go to the West End. He scooted over so the driver couldn't view him in the mirror, and leaped out just before arriving at his destination.

Negro Killed Three Women, Police Say

Trace evidence and witness statements convinced investigators that the lone killer was a black man.

Working with some Lark Café patrons, an FBI artist created two composites of the Bowman suspect, which were cross-checked against a list of Negro cab drivers in the ballpark of 5'8" and 160 pounds, 25-35 years old. Black men were quickly brought in for questioning and pulled into lineups for the Bowman witnesses.

Civil Rights groups became outraged over this "roundup mentality," but their protests were buried under the wave of anxiety sweeping the white neighborhoods.

As leads withered, detectives remained divided on whether to connect the Bowman slaying with the rape-strangulations. There had been ligature burns on her neck, but no sign of sexual assault—and she was much younger than the other victims.

In September, a Walnut Hills melee seized their attention. Virginia Hinners, age 40, was accosted in the office of the New Thought Unity Center by a young black man looking for work. He grabbed her abruptly and then threw her around the room, whispering, "Do you want what the others got?" When an elderly janitor intervened, the assailant knocked him unconscious, slugged Hinners, rifled her purse of $28, and strolled out into the night.

The Unity Center was across the street from the scene of the Emogene Harrington slaying, considered the first Strangler murder back in December 1965.

The slaughter of the Bricca family in Bridgetown (Chapter 10) is intertwined with the Strangler case. Jerry, Linda, and their

Barbara Bowman was found dying in the gutter, run over by the taxi and then stabbed 6 times by the driver.

daughter Debbie were slashed to death inside their home in late September. Mindful of the panic and unrest in the streets, Hamilton County detectives reported that their killer was "believed white, certainly not of Negroid origin."

As October arrived, the phantom was rousing again in Walnut Hills. First, 69-year-old Delle Ernst was knocked down and robbed by "a Negro youth" in the hallway of her apartment. Two nights later, a young black man attempted to garrote a 48-year-old woman in the elevator of her Park Avenue apartment building.

The Cincinnati Strangler was on the brink of a deadly rapture.

Alice Hochhausler was a vivacious, 51-year-old mother of nine who lived in Clifton's gaslight district. She had met her husband, Dr. Carl Hochhausler, while attending nursing school. Daughter Beth, their second oldest child at age 22, worked as a nurse at Good Samaritan, where her father was now the head of surgery.

Like most women, Mrs. Hochhausler was concerned about the violence gripping the city, so she had recently begun driving Beth home from her job at night. She would get ready for bed, slip a robe over her nightgown, and then drop Beth at her Ludlow Avenue apartment without ever leaving her car.

October 11, 1966, was a calm and cool Tuesday evening. Alice returned home from a PTA meeting at 10PM, changed into her night clothes as her husband dozed in front of the TV, and left the house just after 11PM.

Alice got into her 1964 Mercury station wagon and made the short drive to the hospital, picking up her daughter about 11:30PM. As they drove back from the hospital, the women became aware that a car was following them. When they parked at the corner of Ludlow and Cornell, across from Beth's apartment, this car pulled alongside the curb behind them and stopped.

"I wonder what he wants," Mrs. Hochhausler muttered, as both women checked the rear view mirror. "Do you suppose he's going to go around me?" The lone driver was a young black man in a brown and tan Chevy.

Beth thanked her mother and crossed the street to her building. As she turned to wave, she noticed the two-tone car had pulled around and was driving off. Her mother waved back.

The time was now 11:50PM. Alice turned up Cornell and pulled into her driveway minutes later, parking outside the brick and stone garage behind the house. The outdoor floodlights were not turned on. Inside her husband and seven of her children were asleep.

The Hochhauslers owned an aging German shepherd named Rex, whom some neighbors described as "fierce." The dog was tied in the yard during the day and kept in the garage or basement after dark.

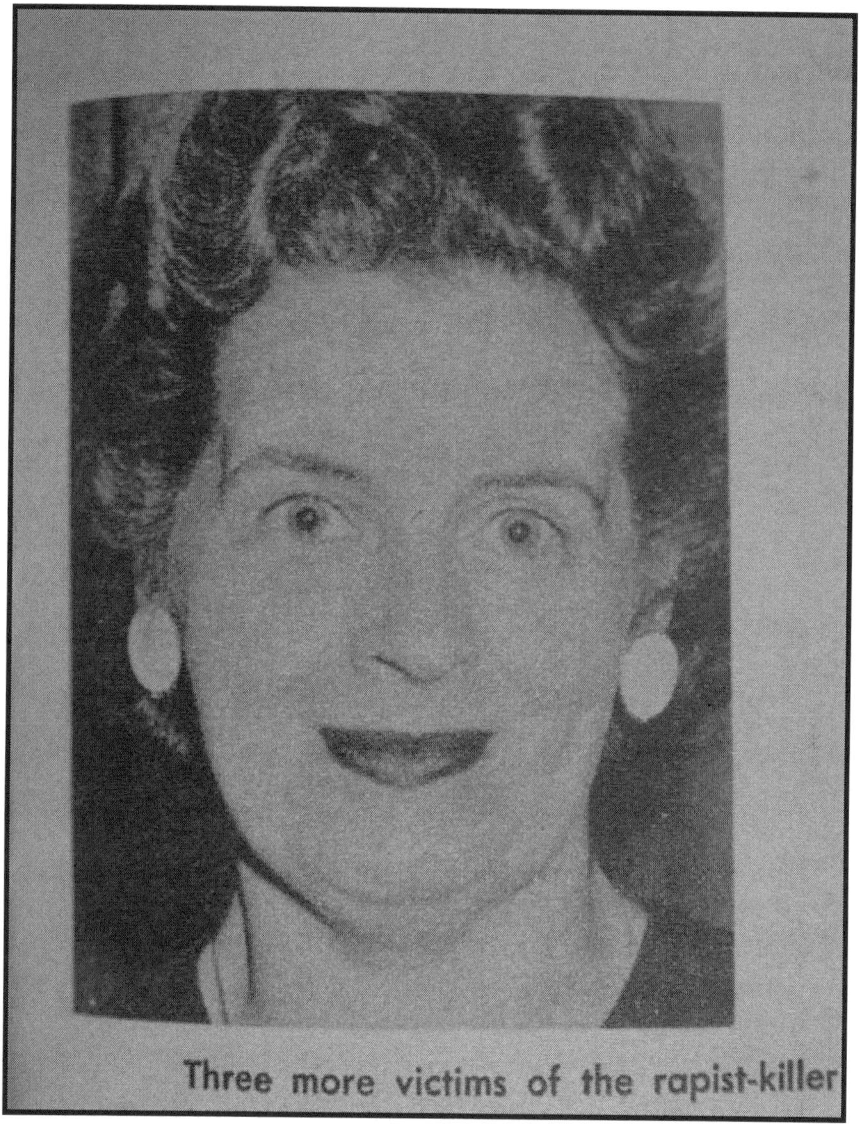
Three more victims of the rapist-killer

Mother of nine children, Alice was beloved by all who knew her.

As fate would have it, on this night Rex was in the basement.

Alice walked down a driveway flanked by deep bushes, toward the steps to her back door. Sounds from an outdoor party two doors down drifted across the green lawns and leafy streets. The last thing she heard was the furious barking of her neighbor's dog.

She must have become aware, in that final moment, of the man whose approach meant deadly peril.

Like a shark, the killer glided from the shadows and delivered a crushing blow to the back of her head, knocking her car keys and her dentures halfway down the driveway. He dragged the prostrate woman into the garage by her ankles, where he raped her and then strangled her with the belt from her bathrobe.

When her husband awoke next morning, he realized Alice had never come to bed. Mildly concerned, he assumed she was in the basement. After checking the laundry room, he looked out the window and saw her car parked near the garage.

He went outside—one of her shoes was lying in the driveway. Overcome by a wave of dread, Carl Hochhausler entered the garage, found his wife, checked her vital signs, and stumbled back inside to call the police. Then he called a priest to administer the last rites.

Hochhausler had reported it as a possible suicide, because a piece of rope was hanging from a rafter over his wife's body. But the first patrolman on the scene immediately summoned the homicide squad.

More than a dozen police cars soon arrived at the residence, an intense response that was in reverence to Clifton's historic gaslight district. As cops flooded the scene and stunned neighbors gathered, someone said, "My God, this is getting awfully close."

The Hochhausler home sat on the corner of Cornell Place and Evanswood Avenue. Detectives quickly theorized that the killer parked on Evanswood, then slipped through the thick bushes and ambushed Alice as she left her car.

Initial clues pointed at "The Strangler." Negro pubic hair was found in the victim's clothing, and a witness had observed a black man walking with "quick, jerky steps" on Ludlow Avenue at around 12:20AM.

The dense bushes around the Hochhausler driveway were just right for an ambush. (Below) The scene on murder morning.

While the rest of the household slept that night, daughters Rita and Judy were awake until 12:30AM. Their windows were closed, and neither girl heard their mother's car in the driveway, nor did they hear Rex—the dog usually barked if someone came into the yard. Both teenagers were chatting and not listening for anything, certainly not the sounds of their mother's murder 40 feet away.

Another daughter had arrived home from baby-sitting at around 11PM. She saw no one on the street and did not notice any strange cars parked nearby.

Other facts learned from the family:

- Picking up Beth was not a regular habit for Mrs. Hochhausler—she'd only done it on the past two Tuesday nights.
- She never turned on the backyard light when going out—police noted the yard was "very poorly lighted."
- No one in the family drank Colt 45 beer, yet an empty can had been found in the bushes along the driveway.
- The Hochhauslers had trouble with a flasher on their property in August and had reported this to police.
- The night before the murder their dog barked at around 2AM—the doctor got up to investigate but saw no one.

On Wednesday Cincinnati City Council moved to end the panic created by "a crazed rapist at large in the city." The entire police department was placed on emergency call. This unprecedented action added over 100 officers to the force on a contingency basis.

Detective Chief Jake Schott was blunt when telling his men how to investigate the Hochhausler murder: "Our orders are to stop any suspicious-looking person you see. If they don't give the right answers, bring them in. The department will back you 1000%. We need aggressive action. We can put 1000 men on the street, but without aggressive action we accomplish nothing."

They were not concerned about recent Supreme Court decisions protecting the rights of suspects. "The city manager has given me a mandate to stop this reign of terror," Schott continued, "and to question all persons who fall under suspicion. Nobody likes to be stopped on the street. We will do it as tactfully as possible, but we must have freedom to pursue this investigation."

In a 1997 interview with this writer, former Police Chief Stanley Schrotel recalled the escalating tension: "The news carried the stories in a very aggressive way—there were nosecrets. Anxiety was so keen that every member of the force was actively engaged to solve the case. People wanted an answer!"

5000-Man Posse Beefs Up Hunt For Sex Maniac

The *Cincinnati Enquirer* headline on October 14th said it all—the start of a massive manhunt for a rapist-killer known as the "Cincinnati Strangler".

The mobilization for a manhunt had begun.

The *Cincinnati Enquirer* headline of October 14, 1966, was a blockbuster. In huge type reserved for Pearl Harbor and the Kennedy assassination, the desperation of a city screamed from the front page: **"5000 Man Posse Beefs Up Hunt For Sex Maniac!"**

The "posse" was a network of retired cops, security guards, firemen, mail carriers, and meter readers, deployed "to extend the eyes and ears of the 900-man police force."

Their mission was to report all tan and cream 1959 model automobiles, which matched the car described by Beth Hochhausler. They were also given the latitude to report "anything of a suspicious nature."

The homicide squad had already assigned an unprecedented 23 detectives to the case full time. A phone hotline was set up, and the operators at "Station X" logged 800 calls the first day. The vintage two-tone Chevrolet was the most popular tip, as over 1000 cars were eventually checked without a match.

The car struck a chord with one detective—a check of the Jeanette Messer file turned up the same auto cruising Burnet

Woods just before her body was found. And the Lois Dant file mentioned a similar car seen near her building the day she was murdered.

Colonel Guy York, acting police chief after Stanley Schrotel's sudden retirement, characterized the Strangler as an emboldened predator who "glories in outsmarting the police. This last killing was almost an act of defiance." York knew what they were up against. "He must be pretty intelligent, because he gives his victims no time to scream and makes his getaway quickly and unobserved."

York was certain someone was harboring the Strangler, but wouldn't tell out of love or fear. He urged them to give up the killer: "Someone—a wife, a mother, a girlfriend—must have heard him talk about it. No one ever does anything without someone knowing about it."

Anxiety coursed through the city. The demand for large watchdogs became so great that they were imported from other cities. Locks and guns flew off the shelves, and self-defense classes were suddenly overbooked. The Kroger Company gave away 100,000 whistles to female customers, while deliverymen worked out passwords for their regular route stops.

An example of the hysteria triggered by the Hochhausler murder played out in City Hall. Council decided this would be the first daytime Halloween in recent memory.

York assured civic leaders that all the routine steps were being taken: grilling of sexual undesirables, sending evidence to the FBI, canvassing for witnesses. In fact, several people had reported suspicious activity in the gaslight district leading up to the murder.

On the night before the slaying, waitress Ruby Kennedy was accosted by a driver. She was leaving her job on Ludlow Avenue when a young black male cruised by and shouted, "Waiting for a taxicab, lady?" She retorted, "Hell, no, I don't want no cab!" She said the car was a two tone '59 Chevy.

Helene Muhsam, a Hochhausler neighbor on Evanswood, saw a "strange colored man" around 4:30PM on the day of the murder. While parking her car, she said she "felt somebody looking right through me," and turned around to observe a man watching her. He greeted her with a bow, which made her angry: "I knew this fellow didn't belong here." She watched him saunter down toward Ludlow Avenue, noting that he was short in stature and wearing a beret.

After dark, a man walking his dog at around 8:30PM heard something in the bushes bordering the Hochhausler driveway. Two hours later, a woman one street over claimed someone tried her kitchen door and shined a flashlight in the window. A man on Ludlow saw a cream over bronze '59 Chevy driven by a black male just before midnight—he later saw this man wandering around the gaslight district.

The fixation with a black suspect knew no bounds. There is a roster in the case file dated 10-21-66 with the heading "Colored Police Officers either resigned or separated from police division in last five years." Another list is titled "Male Negroes with records from Courter Tech High," a nearby vocational school.

While his men scrounged for local suspects, chief of detectives Jacob Schott was reaching out to other cities in his search for the Strangler. Schott was a tall, handsome man straight out of central casting, with Gary Cooper's looks but not his temperament.

He first contacted a Connecticut doctor about a former morgue attendant at Good Samaritan Hospital. Dr. Wolf had worked there in 1956 when James Fox was discharged for molesting dead bodies. Schott requested more details of Fox's offense.

He also queried Indianapolis police about Eddie Phelps, a known predator who'd left Cincinnati shortly after the murder. Described as a "male Negro, 26 years of age," he was laid off work on the day of the crime, and was not seen again after cashing his final check. Schott wanted the Indy cops to pick him up and find out how long he had been in Cincinnati.

And why did he suddenly leave?

Newspaper headlines fast-tracked the terror that was spellbinding the Queen City—it rivaled the feverish coverage spawned by the Cumminsville Railroad Killer in 1904 (Chapter 1). This vehemence was a tribute to Alice Hochhausler. The murder of the lovely wife and mother had provoked the wrath of the city, and the press ran with it:

- **"Grim Manhunt on For Mad Strangler."**
- **"Thousands Hunt Strangler."**
- **"City Police on Overtime as Strangler Strikes Again."**
- **"Psychiatric Aid Asked for in Hunt for the Strangler."**

The *Enquirer* also ran a three-day feature called **"Spotlight on Danger."**

The murder transformed quiet Cornell Place. Neighbors who days before had admired the beauty of autumn-tinged trees now gathered in tight little knots, talking about strange men and debating the ambiance of the gaslights. By now most residents considered the historic district to be poorly lit.

Patrolmen went door to door in Clifton and Walnut Hills, blanketing the other crime scene areas with leaflets that shouted "TELL THE POLICE!" They implored residents to give up "some bit of information that may lead police to the right man, and lift the fear that the series of crimes has aroused . . . here is the chance for someone to help all citizens frightened and fearful as long as this killer is free to strike again!"

Police hurled manpower at the case, with 14 extra cars prowling the streets, and all 12 vice officers transferred to the homicide unit. The 5000-man posse continued to interact with citizens while keeping their eyes on the street.

The volume of leads was daunting. Station X's hotline at police headquarters was logging 300 calls daily after receiving800 the first day. But Guy York was unwavering: "Even if we get 10,000 bad ones and one good one, it will be worth it."

At a press conference, Jake Schott announced that the blood type of Alice Hochhausler's killer matched the perpetrator of the other three murders. And he noted that the Hochhausler slaying occurred exactly one year from the October 12, 1965,

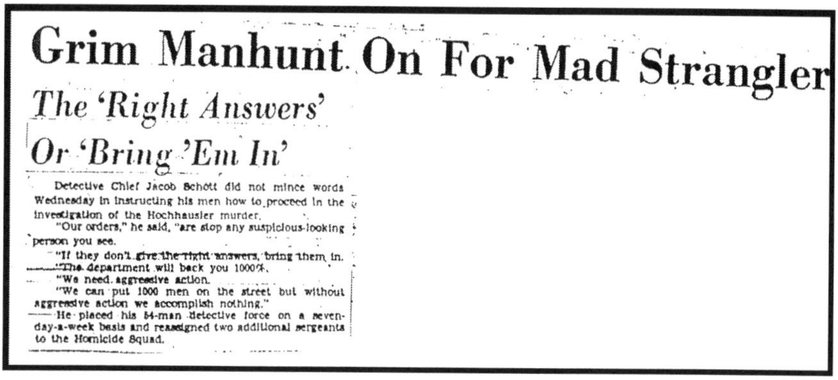

Grim Manhunt On For Mad Strangler

The 'Right Answers' Or 'Bring 'Em In'

Detective Chief Jacob Schott did not mince words Wednesday in instructing his men how to proceed in the investigation of the Hochhausler murder.

"Our orders," he said, "are stop any suspicious-looking person you see.

"If they don't give the right answers, bring them in. "The department will back you 1000%.

"We need aggressive action.

"We can put 1000 men on the street but without aggressive action we accomplish nothing."

He placed his 54-man detective force on a seven-day-a-week basis and reassigned two additional sergeants to the Homicide Squad.

The roundup mentality of the police was part of the immense mobilization, but nevertheless bothered local civil rights leaders.

assault and rape of Elizabeth Kreco in Walnut Hills—a grim anniversary of the Strangler's first attack.

There were other parallels to support his serial killer theory:

- All victims were over 50 years of age. Alice was the youngest at 51; Kreco the oldest at 65.
- All victims were beaten, strangled, and raped.
- All were choked with a ligature rather than the killer's hands: Kreco with a Venetian blind cord; Harringon with a plastic clothes line; Dant with a nylon stocking; Messer with a necktie; Hochhausler with the belt of her bathrobe.
- Robbery occurred in all cases but Hochhausler.
- They were daylight attacks in all cases but Hochhausler.
- All victims were dragged by the assailant—even Lois Dant had been dragged several feet inside her apartment.
- Four of the five attacks took place in the Walnut Hills/ Clifton area.

Schott called the Hochhausler slaying "a crime of chance . . . the killer just happened to be in the area of their home and saw his opportunity to strike. He prowls the city looking for the right opportunity—a woman alone at the right place and right time."

He maintained they had "no definite suspects at this time," adding that "several" had taken lie detector tests and been cleared. His investigators had actually questioned and released 15 men.

Schott closed his conference by praising the efforts of his detectives, and thanking the many retired cops who had volunteered their services. And he welcomed gas station owners and transit drivers, the latest groups to join the 5000-man network of "eyes on the street."

Alice Hochhausler was laid to rest on October 14. After the funeral, one friend spoke to reporters and summed it up for all the mourners: "We're going to miss those glowing eyes, that contagious smile. She was always cheerful, patient, and happy. She had that staunch faith, and she will always be here in spirit."

In an interview with this author in 1997, her daughter Beth talked about her mother on behalf of the family: "She was our champion and our nurturer. I don't know how you measure that kind of loss."

By the investigation's second week, desperation was creeping in.

Jake Schott admitted they were seeking psychiatric help to profile the Strangler. Schott believed that "the man is psychotic," and "may be engaging in a duel with police," implying that the Hochhausler murder was a personal taunt from the killer.

He sent an investigator to the Lima State Hospital for the Criminally Insane to pull records on all patients released one year prior to October 12, 1965 (the Kreco attack). And he arranged a conference at the mental ward of Cincinnati's General Hospital, where detectives met with leading psychiatrists and mental health experts.

Any insights gained into the mind of their perpetrator were not released.

Police were not reticent about one thing—their opinion that the killer was black. They felt the hair evidence and witness statements pointed to a Negro slayer.

The local NAACP took issue, and President Dr. Bruce Green was blunt: "There is tension in the Negro neighborhoods, because people are being stopped and questioned. We do not know whether the killer is white or Negro—we don't know who he is. Whoever he is, he is sick."

Green offered to act as an intermediary for any friend or relative of the killer who was afraid to approach the police, while reminding everyone that "there are as many Negroes interested in the apprehension of this slayer as there are white citizens."

Frank Weikel, a newspaper columnist whose beat was the city's underbelly, wrote an open letter to the killer, begging him to "seek the help you need" while offering his assistance. Weikel tried to get inside his head: "It is more than possible that you cannot forgive yourself for these senseless murders. Maybe your dreams are filled with the faces of your victims and your mind filled with their terrified voices pleading for mercy."

The Strangler never took up the offer.

On October 19 the City Council Crime Commission voted unanimously to hold Halloween trick-or-treating from 3-6PM. Under cover of darkness, the Strangler might assault a child, or wear a mask to invade another home.

That day, the Department of Safety issued a projection, calculating the time of the next strangulation if the suspect were not apprehended. Noting that none of the crimes occurred after the 15th day of any month, they forecast the next killing zone as between December 10th and the 15th.

They couldn't have been more wrong.

Less than two weeks after the Hochhausler murder the Strangler struck again.

A *Newsweek* except from October 22, 1966, captured the mood:

> **The chain latch gave easily in the decaying wood and the intruder was quickly inside the narrow old house on Cincinnati's seedy upper Vine Street. He found Miss Rose Winstel, an 81-year-old spinster, in her bedroom. If she screamed, no one heard; not till next evening did a nephew find her body, bludgeoned, raped, strangled with an electric cord . . . Five such killings in ten months had made the**

signature fearfully plain to Cincinnatians—and yet hard for police to read.

She had been dragged from bed with the covers still around her. Beaten more severely than the other victims, her body was wedged under the bed. Nearly blind, the last thing Rose heard was the horrifying sound of the wolf breaking down her door.

"Series of Sex Crimes Shatters Calm of Serene Cincinnati" was the *Enquirer's* front page headline on October 23. *Newsweek* noted that "frightened Cincinnati wondered not only who the Strangler was but where and when he might strike next."

This was the first national publicity for the Strangler case. Yet detectives were hesitant to link this murder to the others. It was too soon after the last one, the victim was much older, and the forced entry indicated prior knowledge that she was alone.

On December 2, one year after the Harringon slaying, Jake Schott admitted, "We don't have any good leads right now." The sketchy description of the slender black man had haunted police since the previous October, but they still hungered for one good tip.

Early on Friday December 9, in the heart of downtown Cincinnati, they got it.

Around 12:30AM, 22-year-old Sandra Chapas was followed by a Negro driving a two tone car and chased up the stairs of her apartment building. Neighbor Ethel Hall heard the commotion and peeked out her door. She spied a short, slightly built black man, "grabbing his crotch and panting like a dog."

Upon being spotted, he vaulted down the stairs, nearly knocking down Ethel's husband. As his car roared away, Lawrence Hall made note of the license number. Then his wife got off the phone with Sandra Chapas and said, "Call the police."

They couldn't locate the man – and it cost them. Despite cops swarming the downtown area, the Strangler was able to take another victim and slip through the next to safety.

Chapas had been menaced eight hours earlier and just one street over from the Brittany Apartments on Nine Street. Just after 8AM that Friday, a detective knocked on the door of the

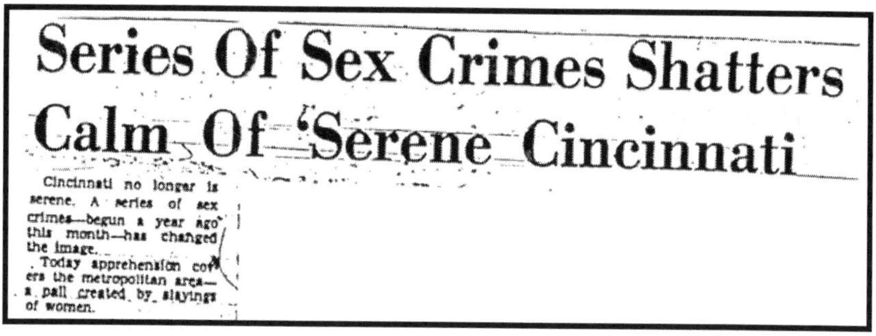

Series Of Sex Crimes Shatters Calm Of 'Serene' Cincinnati

Cincinnati no longer is serene. A series of sex crimes—begun a year ago this month—has changed the image.

Today apprehension covers the metropolitan area—a pall created by slayings of women.

An *Enquirer* story about the growing horror confirmed that all residents, both black and white, were living in fear.

Brittany's owners. "There's a dead lady in your elevator," he informed them. She lay crumpled on the floor of the cramped lift, a stocking taut around her neck.

Identified as 81-year-old Lula Kerrick, the shy, frail woman had just attended Mass nearby, leaving at 7:30 for the short walk home. The killer had followed her into the elevator—this time there was no rape.

At 9AM detectives converged on a West End factory. They had traced the license of the Chapas stalker, and his landlady said he left his room at about 7:40 to go to work. His timecard showed he clocked in at 8:07. One likely route would have taken him down Ninth Street past the scene of the Kerrick murder.

They hauled in for questioning one Posteal Laskey Jr., age 29. Paul Morgan was one of the arresting officers. In a 1997 interview with this author, Morgan expressed surprise at the demeanor of a suspect who may have just committed murder: "He was pretty calm—he didn't try to resist."

Laskey was one of the sex offenders quizzed earlier in the Strangler probe, and also a former Yellow Cab driver checked out in the Bowman stabbing. His rap sheet revealed that the part-time musician was no stranger to violence—there were four previous assault convictions, the first dating back to 1953.

The couple who witnessed the Chapas incident identified him as the intruder. This new charge violated his current probation for the October 1965 assault of a 16-year-old Clifton girl.

Laskey's troubles mushroomed. The Yellow Cab connection prompted police to bring the Bowman witnesses in for a lineup, and all six identified him as the cab driver. Virginia Hinners also recognized Laskey as her attacker from the previous September.

On December 15, the Hamilton County Grand Jury indicted Laskey for the murder of Barbara Bowman. He was held in the Cincinnati Workhouse without bond. **"Jailed Suspect In Spotlight Of 7-Murder Probe"** was the headline amid speculation that Laskey might be charged as the Strangler.

As rumors spread in the black community that an "all white" Grand Jury had indicted Laskey (there were four blacks on the panel), his attorneys tried to quash the indictment, claiming Laskey was "illegally and surreptitiously" taken from the Workhouse and "placed in a wire cage" for viewing.

With Black Nationalism rising across the country, leaflets began circulating in Cincinnati demanding a slice of racial justice: "Will we stand by as in the past and see one of our BLACK BROTHERS being sacrificed?"

The Bowman murder trial was set for March 27 before Judge Simon Leis Sr., who had a history with the defendant. While sentencing Posteal Laskey for an assault conviction in 1958, Judge Leis told him, "Men like you should be put out of society for life." A motion was filed to remove him for bias, but a District Court judge denied it.

Defense attorneys then filed for a change of venue, charging that Laskey couldn't get a fair trial in Cincinnati because of the "climate of fear." They cited detective magazines and local news reports linking him "with some unknown person called the Cincinnati Strangler." Judge Leis denied the motion.

The trial got underway at the Courthouse after an all white pro-death penalty jury was seated. Soon members of the city's Black Muslim sect began showing up to observe the proceedings.

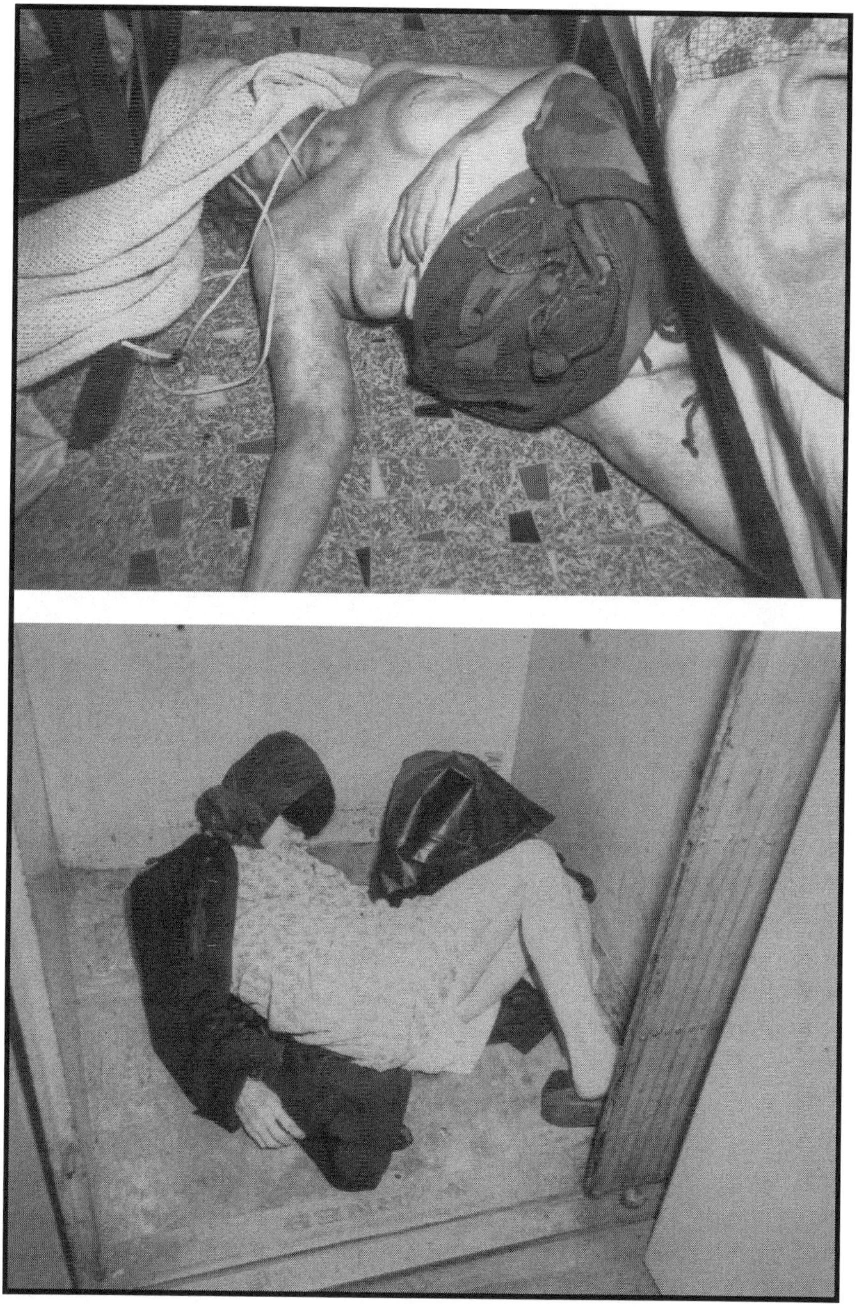

Rose Winstel's killer (top) broke down her door. Lulu Kerrick (bottom) was ambushed coming home from church.

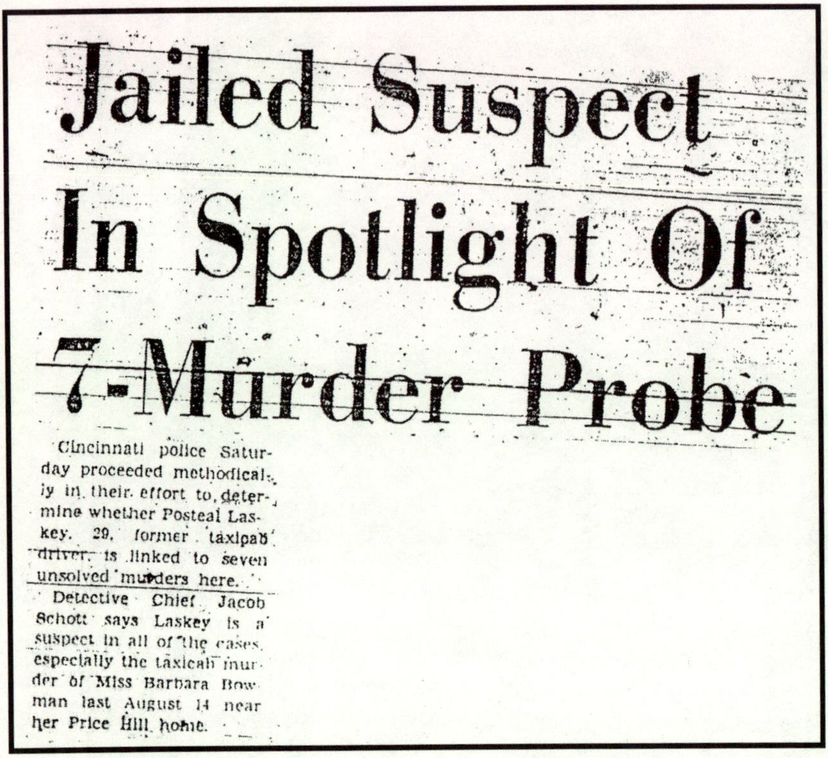

Jailed Suspect In Spotlight Of 7-Murder Probe

Cincinnati police Saturday proceeded methodically in their effort to determine whether Posteal Laskey, 29, former taxicab driver, is linked to seven unsolved murders here.

Detective Chief Jacob Schott says Laskey is a suspect in all of the cases, especially the taxicab murder of Miss Barbara Bowman last August 14 near her Price Hill home.

The evidence was strong against Laskey in the Bowman case, but strictly circumstantial in the six rape—strangulations.

With no physical evidence against Laskey, the prosecution relied heavily on eyewitness testimony. Three Lark Café customers identified him as the driver who'd picked up Bowman, but their descriptions of his clothing and facial hair differed. A dispatcher testified that call number 186 used by the killer was Laskey's number when he worked for Yellow Cab in 1962.

Over strong objections, Virginia Hinners described her harrowing assault the previous September in the Unity Center, identifying Laskey as the intruder who threatened her with "what the others got."

Two surprise witnesses surrendered some dramatic testimony. These women had driven by the cab parked at the murder scene and stopped to ask directions from a black man

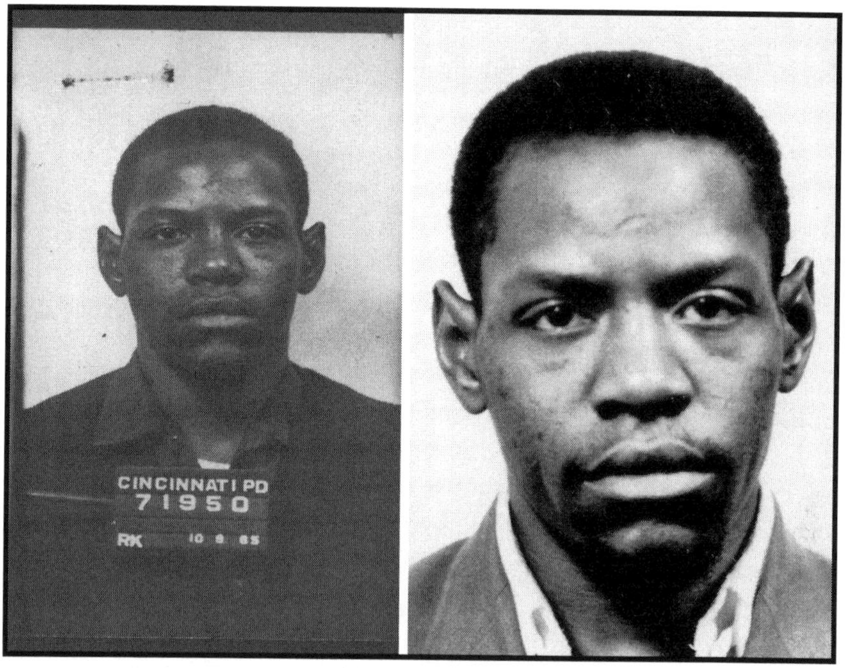

Posteal Laskey was arrested (left) in 1965 for assault, but was given probation despite his record. In custody shortly after the Kerrick murder (right) a year later, the change in his physical appearance is remarkable—possibly the emotional weight of seven killings?

sitting in the rear seat. Suddenly someone else rose up, and Mrs. Eileen Aultz exclaimed, “My God, that’s a white woman!”

Despite rain and darkness, she identified the man as Posteal Laskey.

Five defense witnesses, including his mother and brother, corroborated Laskey’s alibi for the Bowman slaying, swearing that “Junior” was home in bed that night. The defendant himself took the stand to proclaim his innocence—prosecutor Melvin Rueger spent an unbelievably short 17 minutes on cross-examination.

The jury deliberated for eight hours before finding him guilty of first degree murder on April 13th, with no recommendation for mercy. “I expected it,” was Laskey’s only comment. Prosecutors were vague on whether the conviction closed the six strangling cases, but no other charges were ever brought against Laskey.

Civil Rights groups assailed the verdict. The NAACP called it "circumstantial evidence of white witnesses versus Negro witnesses." CORE condemned "the wanton desire for blood which led to selection of an all-white jury," and "a trial held in an atmosphere where fear reigned and desire to kill a nigger held sway."

Two days later Black Power advocate Stokley Carmichael ratcheted up the racial tension with an inflammatory speech at the University of Cincinnati campus. And when Laskey was sentenced to death in May, his cousin Peter Frakes began walking downtown streets with a picket sign proclaiming, "Cincinnati Guilty—Laskey Innocent!"

On his June 11th visit to the Queen City, Dr. Martin Luther King, Jr. preached nonviolence before two Sunday church groups, encouraging them to "learn, baby, learn!" Mindful that seething hostility was boiling over, Dr. King warned that "hate and violence can destroy us all."

Later that day police arrested Frakes for blocking the sidewalk with his picketing. Incensed Negro leaders held a protest meeting the next night, but a roving band of black youths showed up and started throwing firebombs through windows. The arrival of 200 police further incited the crowd, and the insurrection exploded on Cincinnati.

The city was under siege for several days as bedlam flared through the black districts. Youths pillaged stores and destroyed cars—firemen were pelted with rocks while trying to extinguish countless fires. Only the deployment of 1000 Ohio National Guard eventually helped quell the riot.

The bottom line: 362 arrested, more than 70 people hospitalized, and over $3 million in property damage. Two government studies would later link Posteal Laskey's conviction and death sentence to the rioting.

Laskey confirms with attorneys Donald Roney and Burton Signer during a break in his murder trial.

The city simmered throughout the summer, nursing a giant hangover from the violence of June. When Dr. King was assassinated the following April, the second riot in ten months left two people dead, and forever splintered Cincinnati's image as the serene, majestic Queen City of the Midwest.

SUMMATION:

The Cincinnati Strangler case was back in the news with the death of Posteal Laskey in May, 2007. Spared the electric chair when capital punishment was declared unconstitutional in 1972, he was rejected for parole five times beginning in 1984.

Laskey forever proclaimed his innocence and took his secrets to the grave.

Recent coverage barely used "alleged" when naming him the Strangler. Yet he was never tried for any of those murders, and the evidence against him is scant. So was Laskey the killer?

Sergeant Russell Jackson told the *Enquirer* in 1970, "There's no doubt in my mind that Laskey was the Strangler. The day we arrested him was the day of the last one." Most proponents of his guilt allude to this—the killings ceased once he was captured.

There are two common serial killer myths: They can't stop, and they're invariably white. Yet many, like Jack the Ripper and the Zodiac, quit killing without being identified. And black serial killers have been around since the term was coined.

The Cincinnati Strangler might have been more than one man. Both the Winstel and Dant slayings had an element of planning that suggested the killer knew the victim.

There are other doubts. Laskey's blood type did not match the Strangler's, but in pre-DNA days the testing methods could be unreliable. He was in custody several times after the Bowman murder in August, yet no one identified him until his December arrest. And he was incriminated by conflicting eyewitness testimony—over half of all wrongly convicted persons are mistakenly identified.

Yet Posteal Laskey remains the prime Strangler suspect 43 years later, and the probable killer of Alice Hochhausler.

Both he and his car fit the descriptions of perpetrator and vehicle seen near some of the crime scenes.

His lengthy record exposed him as a cold-blooded predator who lulled his victims before attacking them. Laskey's rap sheet included four convictions where the women were bludgeoned and robbed, and many serial killers have evolved from hit and run assaults to murder.

Perhaps he grew tired of being identified and switched to murder. And perhaps Judge Simon Leis, Sr. was prophetic when he scolded Laskey while sentencing him in 1958 ("Men like you should be put out of society for life.").

Laskey began stalking the gaslight district the day before the Hochhausler murder, when witness Ruby Kennedy was accosted by a black man who wanted to give her a taxi ride. Helene Muhsam was unnerved by a black man walking near the Hochhausler home just seven hours before the murder. Her description fit Laskey right down to the beret—he was photographed wearing one after his December arrest.

And a man fitting Laskey's description was following Alice and her daughter just before the murder, driving a car that matched the Strangler's vehicle.

There is an infuriating postscript to this bleak tale.

Posteal Laskey was two months out of prison when he was arrested for a vicious attack on a 16-year-old Clifton girl in October 1965. At his arraignment, the judge noted his prior record but nevertheless gave Laskey probation for this latest offense. Police were stunned at this slap on the wrist, considering his history of violent assaults.

Three days after probation was granted, Elizabeth Kreco was attacked and raped in her Walnut Hills basement. Consider the grim irony: If Laskey had been rightfully imprisoned for his Clifton assault, the "Cincinnati Strangler" might never have existed—except in a novel.

From the London Correctional Facility, Posteal Laskey wrote me in 1997 that he would "like to have my side of the story told, if it is done in an evenhanded way."

But impartiality was a scarce commodity during the racially charged atmosphere of 1966. And more than four decades later, it is still too easy to recall the emotions that ripped apart the community.

For Beth Hochhausler it was more personal: "My mother was the light of our lives," she told this author in 1997. "It's been 30 years, and it still hurts."

EPILOGUE:

A good detective knows that the killer always leaves something at the scene and always takes something with him.

Posteal Laskey's conviction in the Barbara Bowman case did nothing to close the Strangler files, even though investigators were certain they had their killer. But there was never enough evidence to go to trial in any of the six rape-strangulations.

So Alice Hochhausler became the face of the Cincinnati Strangler investigation, and will always be the victim remembered by cops and citizens alike.

Her death was the stake though the heart of the Queen City's innocence, a cruel reminder that our fine houses and groomed lawns were no protection against a frightful fiend. The Cincinnati Strangler left an infamous landmark, and stole our legacy of immunity from random acts of madness.

I WITNESS:

By nightfall he is drinking heavily and prowling for a fresh victim. City lights blur through his alcoholic haze—his vision is cloudy, his head humming from the malt liquor.

The moon, a pale crescent, nestles between the clouds, hovering over the gaslight district. Laskey has been roaming these streets all day long, looking for an opportunity. The thought of boosting another rich, white woman from one of these stately Victorian homes has become a potent force.

People are talking about him now, calling him the Cincinnati Strangler. He smiles, smacking his lips in satisfaction and delight. What do you know; the big, bad wolf comes to the Queen City. He might soon be as renowned as Jack the Ripper. Laskey relishes every newspaper account of the police's dogged pursuit and their unending frustration.

That first murder was the ultimate impulsive act. He wasn't entirely certain of what he'd do if he got her alone. But then she escorted him right into the basement! How can anyone be so guileless, so unsuspecting?

Old ladies, protected and catered to all of their lives by first their fathers, then their husbands, then their sons, have no idea what a hardscrabble life is all about, let alone the danger which may lurk mere steps away. Whether they live in Clifton mansions or in cramped apartments, their residences are luxurious compared to his own. It just isn't fair.

Call this his attempt to even the score.

But there's something else at work, something he discovers only after killing the Messer woman last June: There is immense power in knowing how to terrorize people. And performing unspeakable acts on grandmothers sends a vile, horrifying message: No conscience, no remorse. None.

Now, in October, his passion is the beast that fouls its lair. The hunger shudders through his loins. It is once more the hour of the Strangler.

Laskey cruises up Evanswood, hoping to encounter the woman he startled that afternoon. He parks his car and hides in the Hochhausler bushes—a man walking by hears him moving. Unnerved, he gets back into his car and resumes the hunt.

As he turns the corner onto Cornell, he notices the activity at the Hochhausler house—females coming and going on errands and from baby-sitting jobs. His eyes linger on the darkened garage behind the house.

He knows patrols have been stepped up in Burnet Woods since he killed the Messer woman there. So he avoids the park and turns back into the gaslight district.

He parks again and tries a locked back door, even shining his flashlight in the window. Quickly retreating to his car, Laskey scolds himself for his drunken approach to an unknown house.

As he comes back up Evanswood just after 11PM, he sees Alice Hochhausler driving away. He follows her to the hospital, noting the empty streets. It is nearing midnight on a Tuesday, and the predator's prospects are diminishing by the minute.

He stays with Alice and watches Beth coming out to her car. Trailing them from the hospital, he follows too closely, alarming the women. As they stop at the corner of Ludlow and Cornell, Laskey pulls in behind them.

He sees both heads twisting to stare at him and realizes he is their topic of concerned discussion. So when Beth moves toward her apartment, he steers around and pretends to drive off. But once she is inside, he takes a quick U-turn and heads up Cornell.

With invisible swiftness he maneuvers into the bushes as Alice pulls into the driveway. The booze has heightened his senses—he has evolved into primitive awareness, oblivious to the furious barking of the dog across the street.

He knows this one is dicey. His approach must be perfect, not slapdash—there is a yard full of witnesses at a party two doors down.

Alice is a mere 30 feet from safety when he strikes, but it might as well be a mile. She is outside at this late hour only because of the Strangler, and she is no match for the macabre irony of her own murder.

2009

The murder house remains unchanged from when the Dumlers were butchered here in 1969.

PERSON OR PERSONS UNKNOWN

THE DUMLER TRIPLE MURDER IN MOUNT LOOKOUT: 1969

"Other sins only speak: Murder shrieks out."

John Webster

PROLOGUE:

Detectives will insist that every homicide is aggressively investigated, yet if the victims have social position it becomes a top priority for a long time. So when three members of the Dumler family were slaughtered inside their home on Cincinnati's upscale East Side, police ran down every hint, tangent, and nuance.

Following their primary rule, cops "looked close" for someone personally involved with the victims. And privately, they wondered why Dumler relatives were not more interested in their progress.

The killer remained in shadow, and the file jacket would become a moldering montage for every homicide cop who worked the case. Because like the Bricca family three years earlier, this triple murder was rife with rumor and innuendo.

NARRATIVE:

The turbulence of the 1960s was going out like a lamb.

The summer of 1969 saw the U.S. land the first man on the moon. In September, "peace and love" ruled at the youth movement's seminal event, a defiantly indulgent three day concert called Woodstock.

In the Queen City, Thursday October 23, 1969, was looking like a perfect Indian summer day. In the affluent neighborhood of Mount Lookout, sunshine was bathing the landscape with morning autumn gold. Birds were chirping in the dying vines, their songs wavering through the shiny suburban gloss. Tree-lined streets enclosed spacious homes and spruced lawns—driveways were strewn with toys and bicycles.

Mount Lookout was Cincinnati's incarnation of the American dream. But following the events of this lovely morning, it would become synonymous with shattered trust.

Just after 8AM, two young children toddled across the grass and knocked on their neighbor's door, complaining that they couldn't "wake up Mommy and Daddy." Mrs. Louis Lobert peered toward the brick and frame house at 1192 Beverly Hills Drive—a Halloween harbinger of jack o' lanterns sat on the porch, grinning back at her.

Her neighbors were the Dumler family, and the children were in obvious distress. Mrs. Lobert calmed them down, noticing that they had dressed themselves. After phoning the Dumlers and getting a busy signal, she sent the children back home, telling them to wait for the maid to arrive.

When Mrs. Lobert saw the Dumlers' housekeeper pull up at 8:30, she assumed everything would be fine. Yet within minutes the maid dashed out the front door and ran screaming across the yard, gasping to Mrs. Lobert, "Thank God the children weren't able to get into their parents' bedroom!"

The housekeeper was Mrs. Ruby Boehner, who was almost like a member of the family. She had found the back door ajar, and in a moment was upstairs pushing open the door to the master bedroom. What she saw staggered her like a blow between the eyes. Gasps tearing her throat, Ruby somehow managed to call the police—the patrolman who responded at 8:46 took one look in the bedroom and instantly requested backup. A squad of detectives was soon swarming over the house.

The Dumlers' bedroom was a killing zone. Martin Dumler was sprawled on the floor, shot twice in the head and stabbed twice in the chest. Patricia Dumler was lying on the bed, shot once in the head and stabbed three times in the chest. Her mother was on the floor beside Martin, shot once in the head.

Martin G. Dumler was the 29-year-old sales manager of the Chatfield and Woods Sack Company, a business founded by his grandfather and currently run by his father. He was wearing slacks and a t-shirt soaked through with his blood.

Patricia Dumler, age 27, had been Martin's college sweetheart and married him after they'd both graduated from the University of Cincinnati. Now she was slumped on the bed, dressed in a bloody blouse and skirt.

Patricia's mother, 50-year-old Mrs. Mary Wilson, had been staying with the Dumlers while her husband was in the hospital. Clad in a dinner dress, she had raised her hand to ward off the fatal shot—the bullet had gone through her palm and into her brain.

Ballistics would reveal the weapon as a .38-caliber revolver loaded with dumdum ammunition. "Wad cutters used by target shooters, with a nose and sharp edges," one cop explained to reporters. "They lose their effectiveness over distances of 25 yards, but when they're used up close, they spread when they hit the target. It's a vicious bullet to use on a human being."

Robbery was quickly ruled out—there was cash on Martin's dresser and both Patricia and Mary were wearing expensive jewelry. Neither woman had been sexually molested.

Noticing ligature marks on all three victims, detectives surmised that Dumler and his mother-in-law had been bound hand and foot, while only Patricia's hands had been tied. Electrical cords were missing from two lamps and the downstairs TV, and two steak knives dropped in the house had apparently been used to cut the cords.

Police Chief Jacob Schott was on the scene within an hour of the discovery. His grim assessment: "The victims were corralled in the master bedroom while dressed in their casual clothes. This is a nasty murder."

Against a backdrop of escalating national violence, Schott couldn't contain his anger as he surveyed the bloodbath: "Since we have practically eliminated the death penalty, it seems people will kill you for a nickel . . . We've had one senseless killing after another. We'll have to get back to the day where the punishment fits the crime."

It was the second multiple homicide in Cincinnati that fall. On September 24, four women had been shot to death during a bank holdup on the west side of town.

As word of this new outrage spread, a river of cars nosed their way through Beverly Hills Drive. The smiling pumpkins on the Dumlers' front porch added a macabre touch to a grisly mystery.

Investigators began by getting up close and personal. The lives of the three victims were put under a microscope, along with everyone who knew them.

Martin Dumler seemed to have a desirable existence. He came from a socially prominent, old-money Cincinnati family. His grandfather was a painter and composer of some renown who'd established Chatfield and Woods Company during the Great Depression. Martin was in line to succeed his father as president.

He had been a handsome young college student, but at age 29 was a hefty, round-faced man who looked older than his years. Several friends would later describe "Marty" as the "playboy" type while in college. His parents were Martin H. and Jane Dumler, who drove back from a North Carolina vacation upon getting the bad news. His sister was Mrs. Louise Kepley, whose husband Keith was also Martin's lawyer.

THE CINCINNATI ENQUIRER

7TH YEAR NO. 198- FINAL EDITION FRIDAY MORNING, OCTOBER 24, 1969 PRICE 10 CEN

‘Pointless’ Slaying Of 3 Baffles Police

Police speculated that Sanders and Carpenter slayings might be linked to wanton murders of Mr. and Mrs. Martin Dumler (above) and Mrs. Dumler's mother, Mrs. Mary Wilson

The murder of Patricia and Martin Dumler in upscale Mt. Lookout was a front page fixture up until Halloween of 1969.

Patricia Dumler was described as an attractive and buxom blonde. She modeled part time for Lillian’s Dress Shop, and was an active bowler and tennis player. According to one neighbor, she had recently resolved to quit smoking.

The couple was survived by their two children, five-year-old Martin III and four-year-old Janie, who had somehow slept through a night of unspeakable horror.

Mary Wilson lived in suburban Wyoming. Her husband Fred had been hospitalized while recovering from a heart attack and

Mary was staying with her daughter's family until his release. They were planning to visit Fred Wednesday night when the hospital called to say he was too ill and that their visit should be postponed.

Martin Dumler had arrived home at about 8:00PM. With the hospital visit cancelled, he changed his clothes and began to putter around the house. A teenage neighbor was already there to baby-sit, and she went home at 8:10PM. As the last person to see the victims alive, the young girl was not identified by police. She told investigators the trio seemed in good spirits, and she didn't observe anything suspicious or alarming.

It was a clear and brisk Wednesday evening. The sun had vanished shortly after 7PM, but some teenage boys from the neighborhood continued to play football in the Dumlers' lengthy back yard. As young Jim Farrell took a pass near the picture window, he saw Martin walk past it. His sleeves were rolled up, and to Jim it looked as if he were in the middle of some project. He saw no sign of distress on Martin's face.

After the bodies were discovered, the boys recalled their evening game behind the Dumler house, just before the murders went down. They realized there could have been additional victims. The baby-sitter would have stayed until after the intended hospital visit, or the boys themselves might have rested on the porch steps for a moment to chat.

It was a chilling insight.

"How could it happen here?" sounds like a cliché when something dreadful occurs in a "nice" neighborhood. But if three people are butchered in their home on your block it takes on new import. You pray it wasn't random, secretly yearning for something in the victim's life to turn up and make sense of it all.

"It could have been our house," said Kathy Farrell, a Dumler babysitter whose brother Jim had played in their backyard that night. "God, those poor children."

Her mother watched police and reporters milling around the Dumler home. "You just don't think it can happen on your street," she said. "I am going to get a dog."

Other neighbors stared out their windows, pale and anxious as they searched for an explanation. One noted that Mr. Dumler traveled a great deal, but insisted that "Marty and Pat were very stable. There was nothing wrong with that couple."

As residents eulogized they were also being pressed for information. Anything they had seen on Wednesday was of paramount importance to police, who had 40 men working the case.

Of the hundreds of impending tips, the first two involved a stranger. A neighbor had seen Patty Dumler talking to a man in a car in front of the Dumler home Wednesday afternoon. And a student reported seeing a man sitting in a car in "the semicircle," which was a wide loop where the road turned near the Dumler house. She saw him at about 8:10PM, just ten minutes after Martin arrived home.

Several factors separated the Dumler case from ordinary Cincinnati homicides, and investigator Paul Morgan was well aware of them. In this town, murder usually involved one killer and one victim in a rough locality. Yet this was a triple homicide in a suburban enclave, and he couldn't rule out a second killer.

Morgan wondered how the Dumler children had slept through the massacre in the adjoining bedroom. Did the killer use a silencer on his gun? And the missing appliance cords were something he had never seen before.

Speaking to reporters, Morgan confirmed that "Nothing else was taken. There wasn't a robbery or sign of forced entry." He admitted that this case was their top priority—the Dumlers' social status ensured a vigorous pursuit—and he believed that complex cases were easier to solve. "Planned murders always leave too many loose ends," Morgan explained. "The killer always misses something, or leaves something while they're trying to cover their tracks."

Then he threw in a veiled comment: "The Dumlers were shot by someone who knew what they were doing . . . there are indications the killer stayed at the scene for some time after the murders."

In other words—the victims knew their murderer.

The deluge of leads was a logistical nightmare. They all had to be checked.

A man named Raymond Cole walked into a Norwood bar the night of the murders and claimed to have killed three people. He asked to see a priest, but got a detective instead. Cole's story didn't check out, and was filed away with other drunk and delusional tales.

A married Dumler neighbor was questioned, but his girlfriend provided an alibi for the murder night. He still needed an explanation, however, to pacify his irate wife.

They quizzed Martin Dumler's caddy at his country club. It seemed Marty had lost the Presidents' Cup Golf Tournament the previous summer and accused the winner of cheating. This hint of competitive animosity went nowhere.

There were reports from Patricia Dumler's friends in her Wednesday bowling league that strange men were flirting with her at the alley. This led one detective to write the question in the case file: "Was Pat having an affair?" It deserved consideration—she was an attractive, voluptuous young woman whose husband was a traveling workaholic. The rumor wafted through the case file, yet was never pinned down.

Another suspect's name jumped out with some resonance. Charles Milles Maddox, originally born in Cincinnati but now a resident of California, was also known as Charlie Manson. He had recently been arrested in Los Angeles for the murders of actress Sharon Tate and six others in August. It wasn't that much of a stretch—the Manson family was already suspected in a Kentucky killing of a former group member.

But Helter Skelter had not arrived in the Queen City.

A paint-spattered man roaming the neighborhood Wednesday afternoon was being sought. Since the Dumler house had been painted two weeks before, police went through Martin's checkbook to determine who had done the work. There was no obvious connection, but investigators still wanted to quiz this man.

The Dumler children were being gently questioned. Five-year-old Martin and four-year-old Janie could not yet grasp what had happened to their parents, yet their proximity to the crime made them valuable witnesses. They confirmed watching "The Patty Duke Show" and "Batman" before being put to bed at 9:00PM, and they were certain that their grandmother was the only other person in the house.

Some detectives wondered why the killer hadn't eliminated all the witnesses. Paul Morgan speculated that the children were spared because the killer was close to the family, and knew he hadn't been seen by them.

Two days after the murders, police admitted they had not identified a suspect. They had scoured the house and backyard on Thursday morning, so now they retraced their steps on Saturday. The "first 48 hours" were gone, and they had nothing.

The two knives found lying in the house tested negative for blood or fingerprints. Tests confirmed they were used to cut the cords—three with the smooth knife found in the hallway, the others with the serrated knife found in the master bathroom.

The killer had improvised to muffle the shots. There were entry and exit holes on two pillows, one on the bed near Pat's body, the other on the floor between Martin and Mrs. Wilson.

Chief Schott's first press conference showed he was under pressure to make an arrest. First he reaffirmed the obvious by reminding them that he had ruled out murder-suicide. Then he claimed an extra shot had been fired, and that the fifth bullet was missing. Initial reports had accounted for three bullets in the victims and one in the floor. Schott guessed the other bullet was inside the mattress, and confirmed that it was sent out for testing.

Responding to shouted questions, Schott refused to confirm or deny any signs of struggle in the bedroom or elsewhere, saying only that the Dumlers "put up a passive resistance to the killer—or killers." And he disagreed with the coroner about the stab wounds. Schott's men were certain they were post-mortem, which supported their theory that the killer had remained in the house for a long time.

Or killers. Some investigators would not concede that one man could murder three adults. The thing with the cords would have taken time, and perhaps a second person to hogtie the victims.

Schott ended the conference by pointing out that his men were trolling the sewers for the weapon, chasing down reports of prowlers, and talking to everyone. Their schedule of interviews now stretched into the hundreds.

Everything was in motion—except the solution.

By the weekend detectives had recreated the last days of Martin and Patricia Dumler. They were certain the couple had been targeted—mother-in-law Mary Wilson was just a "wrong place at the wrong time" victim.

On the final day of his life, Martin had a normal workday, including lunch at his club. He left work sometime after 7PM and made two stops on the way home—first at a bakery in Hyde Park and then at a service station on Erie Avenue. Arriving home just before 8PM. he placed the baked goods on the kitchen table.

On her last day, Patricia was busy with the errands of a typical suburban housewife. She dropped some neighbor children off at school, went to her Wednesday morning bowling league, and did some afternoon shopping. She was also seen talking to someone in a parked car after she arrived home.

It was an ordinary day for both husband and wife. They were seemingly unaware of any sign that their lives were now measured in hours.

3 Victims Untied After Slayings

Mt. Lookout Killings Still Baffle Police

Whoever shot and stabbed to death Mr. and Mrs. Martin G. Dumler II, and her mother, Mrs. Mary Wilson, bound them hand and foot and then untied them after the slayings. This is the theory police are working on now.

There are no suspects. But police were told by some neighbors of the Dumlers' that a man, in his 30s, wearing paint-spattered clothing, was seen walking in the neighborhood between 2 and 4 p.m. Wednesday.

PATRICIA ANN DUMLER

MARTIN G. DUMLER II

This *Post* article featured a younger photo of Martin, and speculated about the missing appliance cords.

Chief Schott said he would welcome any information citizens might have, "no matter how scanty." He guaranteed that informants would remain anonymous, but declined to offer rewards. By the end of the weekend, police were swimming in lurid gossip, creepy calls, and wacky letters.

Today, the Dumler file jacket is a cumbersome dossier of fading documents and remote leads. It takes up four boxes in the Cincinnati police cold case squad room—this author was granted permission to examine the aged contents.

There is a box of 3 x 5 index cards catalogued with over 500 individual tips from Cincinnati residents. Here are some of the intriguing tales that were never released to the press:

- A man called to say his wife and three other men killed the Dumlers. Detective Meiszer arranged a meeting in a bar, but the caller didn't show.
- A Dr. Armstrong was treating Pat Dumler for a "nervous condition," probably relating to the "numerous crank calls" she had recently received.
- A waitress at the Cincinnati Country Club thought "Marty had a dominating attitude" toward Pat. A bartender said that Dumler often became "belligerent" when drinking.
- A business associate claimed Marty had talked with him about "ousting his father as president" of the company because he drank to excess and made some bad business deals. Dumler had said his father was also "upset with Keith"—that would be brother-in-law and company lawyer Keith Kepley.
- Speaking of Martin's job—there was a rumor that he'd fired four male employees for having "illicit sex with a female coworker." The company would later deny this.
- The owner of the dress shop where Martin's wife modeled said that Pat was harassed by an overly attentive male customer a month before the murders. She also denied the rumor that two other models were fired in order to provide Pat with her job.
- A family friend noted that Marty often charged items to his grandmother's account. He believed that Marty's parents

were stingy, but that his grandmother spoiled him with money and gifts.

- A Dr. Lippert, who had treated brother-in-law Keith Kepley, heard that Pat Dumler was "messing around" on Martin.

Several anonymous letters voiced good ideas about the direction of the investigation. One urged the focus be shifted to Martin Dumler's employees, who might gain professionally or financially from his death. Another suggested checking the baby-sitter's friends—after all, she was the one who was supposed to be there while the Dumlers were at the hospital.

But for every earnest letter there were several weird ones, kept in a file labeled "Eccentric Letters."

- Local psychic Mildred Barton received a vision of the killer: He was 5'-8" with dark hair and glasses, and his name was Dave Berry.
- A woman wrote that her Ouija board had determined the motive for the crime—it was an escalating feud between Pat Dumler and her "gardener."
- Someone revived an old forensic myth, calling for the victims' eyes to be photographed! They thought the killer's image would still be there, since he was the last thing they saw.

This ludicrous idea had first surfaced during the Jack the Ripper investigation in 1888, with negative results. Yet some people still believed that a murder victim's eyes could develop into the ultimate camera.

Most of these leads faded after the initial run through. But about 10% were chosen for additional follow-up.

According to family friend Yvonne Buss, Pat Dumler had been "blackballed" for unknown reasons from membership in the Junior Women's League of Cincinnati. Yvonne also bowled with her on that fateful Wednesday. She said Pat expressed concern about her children if "something would happen" to her and confided that Martin "gambled heavily" on golf and poker.

Buss was earmarked for a second interview. Her statement about Pat's demeanor hours before her murder was astonishing.

During the next session they inquired about her ex-husband, a compulsive gambler who often golfed with Marty Dumler. She said he suffered from "mental problems" and had recently been fired from his job.

A Dumler neighbor had reported that a .38-caliber colt revolver was stolen from his car a few days before the murders. After reading the ballistics evidence in the paper, he contacted police and told them that the missing weapon was loaded with four wad cutter bullets, just like the target ammunition used on the victims.

It was probable that the killer lifted this gun, a weapon that could never be traced to him. And only someone familiar with the neighborhood would know the gun was in that car.

A neighbor of Martin's father and mother saw him talking to another man in the parents' driveway (they were out of town) the day before the murders. The stranger was a tall man in his 40s, and the witness described their interaction as both "agreeable" and "agitated." After a 30-minute conversation, Martin and the other man got into separate cars and drove away.

Why would Martin arrange a meeting at his parents' house while they were away? Did he need something from his father's files?

An almost forgotten tip dovetailed nicely with this one. A man playing golf with Martin the weekend prior to the murders had witnessed something unusual. The club ranger had driven all the way out to the back nine to summon Marty to the clubhouse—there was an urgent call from his father.

Did the key to this case turn somewhere in Martin Dumler's "extramural activities?"

During that weekend after the slayings, the first real suspect dropped back into the case. Edward Forster, a Dumler neighbor, was the married man whose girlfriend had provided an alibi that seemed to clear him.Now he was picked up again because of his "evasive and suspicious behavior." Arrested at Lunken Airport

Official file photographs show the "circle" in front of the house, and the back entry where the killer probably entered.

Saturday night while trying to charter a plane to a southern city, Forster was with a 16-year-old boy "with whom he had changed clothes so that police could not identify him," according to Sergeant Russ Jackson.

His spurned wife told detectives that he hadn't been home since the murders. When Forster finally called her, she told him police and the FBI were looking for him, yet "he didn't want to be bothered talking."

A local dry cleaner had identified him as the suspicious man who changed clothes at his store on the night after the murders. He said Forster was agitated, and after donning a different outfit he took the other clothing with him. The dry cleaner noticed that the clothes were stained.

Since losing his job the previous spring, Forster had become known throughout the neighborhood for his erratic behavior. Police considered him a "mental case."

But they could not consider him the killer. Forster was released Sunday afternoon, his alibi for the murders still unshakable. "We found a female he was definitely with that evening, "confirmed Russ Jackson. "No question about that. So we are releasing him and the 16-year-old boy."

Forster was "ashen faced" when let go—his adulterous and elusive conduct had thrust him into the glare of publicity. Yet like all "persons of interest" questioned in the Dumler case, he walked away unscathed. By the end of the weekend police had interviewed 100 people at headquarters and another 300-plus were questioned door-to-door. The case jacket is still bulging with the harvest from this epic endeavor.

On Sunday, the housekeeper who discovered the bodies finally spoke on the record. Still stunned by her gruesome discovery, Ruby Boehner was under a doctor's care. The 57-year-old domestic had known Mary Wilson all of her life. "I knew the family through five generations. I took care of Pat when she was a baby," she explained, her voice breaking. But she was thankful about the children: "I was glad I was the one to keep the children from seeing all of that. Can you imagine them being there all night?"

Detectives couldn't imagine it. They were bewildered that Martin Jr. and Janie heard nothing of the mayhem in the next bedroom.

On Monday morning all three victims were laid to rest, beginning with a private service for Mrs. Wilson. The murdered couple was buried after a Requiem High Mass with no visitation. Several members of the funeral party wore shoulder holsters.

Certain that the killer was close to the family and in attendance, undercover detectives kept everyone under scrutiny.

As Schott prepared to review evidence with the coroner that afternoon, he gave this curt appraisal to the press: "No significant developments and no new suspects—the investigation will continue."

Yet one week after the murders they were still deadlocked. The police mantra of "no new leads" was wearing thin, especially when they refused to discuss specifics.

Captain Carl Lind, head of the crime bureau, defended the sudden information blackout: "We're naturally hesitant to reveal too much, not because we don't feel the public should know, but to protect them . . . Speculation becomes rumor, and rumor tends to be accepted as fact. It is misleading and can slow down our investigation . . . Some things are known only to us, and to the people that did it."

Reporters jumped on his use of "people" instead of "person," and Lind agreed: "There could very well be more than one person who committed the crime."

They had questioned everyone who had a connection with the Dumlers, including "tradesman, plumbers, repairmen, and painters," according to Russ Jackson. "We have no suspects. We've talked to some people two or three times, and we may want to talk to some of them again. It's the only way we can develop new information."

Jackson was convinced the killer was known to the family—someone whose arrival at the house would not arouse suspicion. But he admitted that the answers to their questions were elusive.

- How did the slayer gain entrance so readily? Even though the back door was found ajar, there was no sign of forced entry. Did Martin let the killers in?
- Why were the victims stabbed after being shot? If the killer had limited ammunition, perhaps he hadn't counted on Mrs. Wilson being there. After searching the house, he came back to stab Martin and Pat to make sure they were dead.
- Why did he/they untie the victims after killing them? And what happened to the ligatures? The cords were a bizarre

twist, but they also pointed to a second killer. A solitary assassin would have to cut six cords with two different knives while holding three persons at gunpoint.

- What was the motive for killing the three victims? Investigators had ruled out the two women. They were certain the incentive for this triple homicide was buried somewhere in the intricate life of Martin Dumler, either through his business dealings or his gambling habit.

The Mount Lookout neighborhood remained jittery as the investigation stalled. “Night is the worst,” sniffed a Dumler neighbor. “I let on that I’m not affected by the whole thing, but I keep hearing strange noises.” A mother of three lamented, “It’s almost impossible to get a baby-sitter.”

Another Beverly Hills Drive housewife found a deeper meaning. “We have been jolted out of our little world, grown up, matured in a way,” she sighed. “The night of the killings none of us would have noticed anything out of the ordinary . . . it just never occurred to us that something might happen here.”

Crime was in the nationwide spotlight as well. The National Violence Commission declared that fear of violent crime “is gnawing at the vitals of urban America,” and predicted high income families would some day be living in “fortified cells”. “Fear of crime,” they stated, “is destroying some of the basic human freedoms which any society is supposed to safeguard—freedom of movement, freedom from harm, and freedom from fear itself.” They also noted that one third of American homeowners kept a gun to protect against intruders.

On October 31, Mount Lookout celebrated Halloween as a policeman posted on the Dumler porch turned away trick-or-treating children. Inside, two armed men waited and listened, part of the team of cops stationed around the clock to protect the crime scene from theft and vandalism. So as not to contaminate evidence, the officers were restricted to the kitchen and living room. If they smoked, they brought their own ashtrays—any debris they created was removed after their shift.

E CINCINNATI ENQUIRER

L EDITION SUNDAY MORNING, OCTOBER 26, 1969 PRICE 30 CENTS

Neighbor Man Quizzed In Mt. Lookout Murders

URDAY, OCTOBER 25, 1969 WEATHER: Cloudy, mild. (For Details See Page 7.) Phone: 721-1111

Police Question 275 In Triple Slaying

Earlier headlines were optimistic, but as the investigation wore on the number of interviews was daunting for the detectives

They also found themselves directing traffic during the first week. "Things got so bad that we put up temporary 'no stopping at any time' signs to keep people from parking and gawking," one noted. In addition to checking for prowlers, they answered the telephone and recorded the time and purpose of each call. A few were official, but most were wrong numbers or hang-ups.

In the second week of the investigation two new leads provided fleeting hope.

A triple murder in St. Louis on Halloween night caught the attention of Dumler detectives. A woman, her daughter, and the daughter's husband were found stabbed to death in their home—both women had been raped. St. Louis police eventually arrested their plumber for the crime.

Also on Halloween night, a man walked into a Detroit police station and claimed he "killed three people in Cincinnati." Identified as Donald Franklin Fry, the former Detroit resident never mentioned the Dumler case. After questioning his relatives,

Cincinnati investigators could not place Fry in Mount Lookout at the time of the slayings, and assigned his confession to the back of the file.

With the release of Donald Fry, the investigation went into a coma. As 1969 closed the decade, it became apparent that the killer or killers were beyond apprehension.

The Dumler case flickered for the next four decades. Yet unlike the Bricca murders (Chapter 10), there was no gush of rumor staining the East Side.

One neighbor summed it up in a 1977 *Enquirer* article recalling the crime. “No one mentions the murders,” he said. “No one wants to talk about it. It’s a complete mystery; that’s what’s so scary.”

A detective quoted in the article claimed the case was still open, even though police were no longer actively working it. “The circumstances are so unusual,” he said. “We must have interviewed at least 500 people. We spent all those hours on it, and it was never solved.” At that time, over 90% of all cases were closed each year.

In the 1980s and ‘90s the wealth of tips dwindled down to a couple per year. A Crime Stoppers segment on a local news station in 2002 revived the case for several days. Police received 15 calls with “new” information. Most were discounted right away, but two leads were encouraging.

A former employee urged police to look at the man who did the auditing for Dumler’s company. He was certain “this man and Marty were up to something.” Another caller stated her friend was married to a man who claimed to have “cut electrical cords in the Dumler house.” This man also told his wife that he had killed someone.

In an interview with this writer in 1997, retired investigator Paul Morgan shed some light on this lifeless case. “We just never got any good solid leads, or good solid suspects, which in itself is unusual,” Morgan lamented. “Normally with so much digging, there’s something. But not in this case.”

Morgan was candid about his frustration with the Dumler relatives. He found it strange that no one from the family ever checked the progress of the investigation. Other than official interviews, none of them spoke on the record or to the press.

He remembers calling Martin's mother on that morning in 1969 to break the terrible news of the murders. When he first identified himself as a police detective, he was shocked by her response: "What's Marty done now?"

But when I asked Paul Morgan, "Whom do you like the best of all the suspects?" he declined to name one.

SUMMATION:

The Dumler's killer was someone known to the family, someone comfortable enough to remain in the house despite the sleeping children. A cool customer to say the least.

An interesting name is buried in the bloated case file—Martin's brother-in-law Gregory Keith Kepley.

A former marine who'd served in Vietnam, Kepley was Martin's company attorney in 1969, and a routine background check had turned over some dirt. He was investigated by the CID on suspicion of smuggling a weapon from Vietnam into the states. During this time he was examined by a doctor for a mental problem, although Kepley later claimed he was treated only for a physical ailment.

Keith Kepley has his own folder in the swollen Dumler case jacket, replete with tantalizing remarks. One detective wondered whether Kepley had a drinking problem. Several others observed how he always looked away during the interviews: "He would not meet your eyes" was one notation. These veteran investigators had detected a hint of menace in Martin Dumler's brother-in-law.

Kepley had a good alibi that was backed up by his wife. He'd called Marty that night to set up a squash game, and left a message with Pat—rendered irrelevant by the next few hours of madness.

The detective's "feel" for Kepley as a suspect was not supported by any physical evidence. He fit the theory of a killer close to the victims, but he could not be placed in the Dumler home on the murder night. There will never be any proof that the crime was committed by Keith Kepley.

Or by anyone else, for that matter.

EPILOGUE:

Dumler investigators never got any eye-catching leads, even though the brutal, baffling nature of the crime spawned its share of suspects. But the killer never came into focus—remaining forever a soft blur.

The Dumlers were slaughtered in their cozy neighborhood, in the bedroom of their charming home, by person or persons unknown. So unless there's a quarrel between criminals or the killer's conscience is ready to snitch, the 1969 slaying that devastated a revered Cincinnati family will forever remain a mystery.

POSTSCRIPT: AUGUST 2011

I recently discovered an *Enquirer* interview with Homicide Squad Chief Russell Jackson from 1971. The unsolved slaying of the Dumler family was still bothering him.

And he provided a new twist to the logistics of the killings.

"Marty may have struggled a little bit but not much", claimed Jackson. "He was stabbed a couple of times in the chest at an upward angle, then shot in the head. I think Marty was stabbed while standing up. This is unusual. He fell on his chest on the rug."

His lead investigator had always maintained that both Martin and his wife were stabbed post mortem.

Jackson confirmed that the cautious killer remained on the scene for some time, without taking anything of value. "Marty was turned over after death and the wires removed from his arms and legs. You could tell this was done after he bled out because most of the wire marks were clear—like the white band in a suntan where you wear your watch. They did the same thing with Mrs. Wilson."

After indicating that Pat Dumler's hands had been bound with adhesive tape instead of electrical cords, Jackson spoke about the macabre twist that still puzzled him. "About an hour after the three victims were dead, they (the killers) turned Pat over on her back and stabbed her in the heart", Jackson revealed. "There was absolutely no blood in the wound in Pat's heart, showing she was stabbed there quite some time after death."

Multiple killers, adhesive tape, stabbing before and after the shootings? Time had veered Jackson's theory farther away from the conventional wisdom held in 1969.

But the veteran detective was certain of one thing. "It was someone they (the Dumlers) knew. If it was an intruder, somebody who was going to hurt your wife . . . I think you would put up quite a fight."

Russell Jackson retired shortly after giving this interview.

I WITNESS:

Martin Dumler is out of his league—and in over his head.

Through some shady business pact, he hooks up with a man he thinks he can trust. But things are progressing badly, and his partner is becoming abrasive and threatening.

Yet Martin is oblivious to his cohort's insinuations. He's not as slick or as charming—or even as smart—as he thinks he is. And he fails to recognize the inexorable tightening of the web around his life.

The man is finished with Martin. Dumler is putting him in an untenable position, and Marty's big mouth is backing him further into a corner. Their unethical covenant, ensnared in a thicket of lies, is on the verge of exposure.

He will not be dragged down by the likes of Marty Dumler. It's time to cut loose this excess baggage.

Desiring a weapon that can't be traced, he steals the .38-caliber revolver with four wad cutter rounds from a neighbor's car. He knows the gun will be there.

He promises himself he'll talk to Dumler first—but Marty better have the right answers. On Tuesday afternoon they meet in his father's driveway and are seen bickering by a neighbor. Dumler leaves, thinking all is resolved. His partner drives away to finalize his murder plan.

After dark on Wednesday night he slides his car into the semicircle of posh Beverly Hills Drive. As he moves toward the objective, his footsteps ring hollow on the lonely street.

Inside the Dumler home, the family is winding down.

Both kids are in bed; the adults are in the living room enjoying drinks. With their hospital visit canceled at the last minute, it is becoming a relaxing evening for Martin, Pat, and her mother.

Suddenly they hear an insistent rapping on the back door. Martin goes to answer it, growling, "Who could that be at this hour?" But perhaps he already knows the answer.

The killer stands there for a moment, his silhouette framed in the doorway. Then he steps into the kitchen—and into the Dumlers' escalating nightmare.

He is thrumming like a live wire. He brushes past Martin and into the living room, entering voice first. Pat recognizes him from other visits, but his appearance this time alarms her.

As Martin follows him into the room, an argument erupts. Marty shushes him, asking his wife and Mrs. Wilson to give them some privacy. The two women scurry upstairs to the master bedroom. Pat gets out her sewing kit and sits on the bed. Her mother begins asking questions, her voice mingling curiosity with concern.

Downstairs, the conversation's tone gives Martin an odd sense of dread. His partner is staring at him in a creepy, unflinching way. Eager to end this confrontation, Marty, ever the glib salesman, draws on his gift of gab.

But the killer isn't buying. He smiles at the irony. Marty doesn't realize he has already negotiated for his life—yet didn't close the deal.

The gun is out now. The killer's eyes glaze with high-voltage determination as he passes sentence on his ex-partner: "I can't trust a man who's never lost anything."

Marty looks stunned, like a man fallen prey to an incredibly transparent scheme. He hears his own strident breathing and feels his bowels weaken.

Pointing the weapon, the killer directs him to sever the appliance cords. Not understanding the purpose, Martin complies. As he works on the first lamp, the swaying light casts shifting shadows on the walls.

Upstairs in the hallway, three more cords are cut. The killer tells Marty where to drop the knives. Then he herds his former partner toward the hushed voices murmuring in the master bedroom.

Once inside, the killer moves with deadly efficiency—he has mentally rehearsed this sequence over and over. He commands a protesting Martin to lay his mother-in-law on the bed and bind her hands and feet. Then he orders Pat to bind Martin. He pushes the husband to the floor and nudges Pat back to the bed, where he ties only her hands. She cooperates, not knowing what else to do, praying that the man won't think about the two small children lying sound asleep in the next room.

As Marty continues to complain, the killer hisses, "Let me tell you something!" He fires from the hip, but the bullet only grazes Martin's cheek. Pat stifles a scream. Marty howls and tries to roll away. This time the killer takes careful aim and puts a second one in his forehead. Pat covers her eyes with her bound hands, sobbing.

Mary Wilson rolls off the bed and tries to flee, but the man flings her to the floor and holds a pillow over her face. The shot barrels through her hand and plows right into her head. The old lady—well, that's a shame, but he couldn't foresee that she would be here tonight. He must deal with it, take total care of business.

Pat is squirming and moaning on the bed. As the killer looms, she turns her face away and blubbers in protesting horror. He sends his last bullet crashing through a pillow and into the back of her head.

The killer then spends an hour scouring the house to remove any trace of his alliance with Martin Dumler. Its touch and go with the children upstairs, but if they stay asleep, the risk of hanging around to finish the job is minimal.

Finally, he stands in the master bedroom doorway and surveys his work. Something, almost nothing, draws his attention to Marty. He pulls out his own knife and stabs him twice in the chest. He stabs Pat twice in the heart.

Then he walks outside into the brisk autumn night, his footsteps still ringing hollow as the moon peeks from between the rooftops.

He is never captured.

2009

Except for the missing phone kiosk, the north entrance of Spring Grove Cemetery is unchanged since Paul Mueller was killed there.

MURDER IN THREE ACTS

THE KILLINGS OF SALLY GLUECK BROWN, EUGENE PEARSON, AND PAUL MUELLER: 1971

"I must become a borrower of the night, for a dark hour or twain."

William Shakespeare

PROLOGUE:

The lethal force at work on that October evening was peerless, spawning an empty trail of blood and tears.

It was an unprecedented chapter in Cincinnati's unsolved history—three unrelated victims in three different locations murdered within the same hour. By morning city police were confronted with a trio of baffling, motiveless crimes. No connection between the killings was ever made, and the famine of clues doomed the investigations from the start.

If there was evil lurking in the shadows, it was a perfect evil, impervious to the black and white of small human choices. Now just a few strokes from midnight, the wicked play about to begin would depend on shades of gray.

NARRATIVE:

A national crime wave and a Nixon-era obsession with law and order made 1971 a banner year for cop movies—*The French Connection* won the Oscar, and Clint Eastwood defined the anti-hero as a vigilante detective in *Dirty Harry.* On television the irascible and bigoted Archie Bunker was fast becoming a satirical icon.

In September, the four day Attica prison riot ended with a bloody climax, as 28 inmates and 9 guards were killed by police officers trying to suppress the uprising.

And in Cincinnati, homicides were piling up at a record pace—79 by year's end. The sheer numbers were shocking enough. But it was the triple killing in one night that left the entire city thunderstruck.

As the sun set on October 3, the sky faded into a throng of stars against a full moon that was remote yet watchful. A lukewarm day was now an evening crisp around the edges.

It was Sunday. The Lord's Day was about to become the devil's night.

Across the city three people were winding down their days. One was coming home from a dinner banquet. Another was leaving a college party on foot. The third was talking on a pay phone. So secure is our future, so unknowable is our fate, that none of them could possibly fathom that their lives were now numbered in minutes, and that their names would engage their fellow citizens for weeks to come.

Mrs. Sally Glueck Brown, age 59 and recently widowed, had attended a tabernacle dinner at Hebrew Union College, where she had worked for the past eight years. Friends saw her leave at around 9:15, and just before 10PM she arrived home.

She pulled into the lot behind the Woodside Apartments, a secluded complex enclosed by trees on Galbraith Road in Hartwell, just west of Drake Memorial Hospital. She put her blue Oldsmobile sedan into reverse and prepared to back into her parking spot in carport #9.

Suddenly a single gunshot punctured the darkness. Several residents heard it and dashed out of their apartments—they found Sally Brown slumped behind the wheel, dying from a bullet through her left eye. She was gone by the time the ambulance arrived.

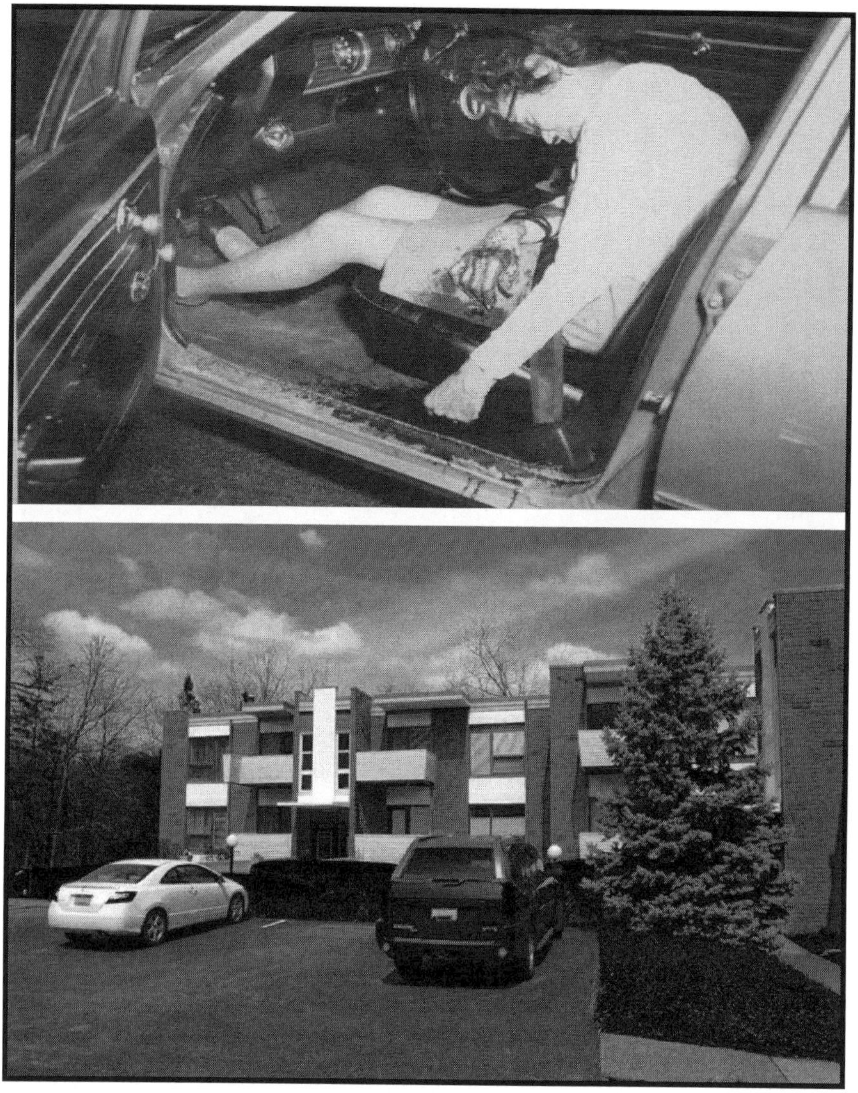

2009

Sally Brown was found slumped in her car and shot through the eye. In a recent picture of the murder scene (below), the white car at left is parked where the victim's car was that night—the shot probably came from a balcony.

As uniformed officers searched the dense woods surrounding the buildings, investigators surveyed the murder scene. Her driver's side window was down, with the engine running and lights still on. She had been shot though the open window, yet there were no powder burns, indicating the shooter was at a distance. Next to her on the seat was her untouched purse.

Gathering detectives were left with a conundrum: For no apparent reason, a socially active woman was killed within sight of her front door, in a neighborhood not known for crime, shot down by a phantom assassin—or sniper.

As Sally Brown died in the Woodside parking lot, across town in Clifton a campus party was breaking up. A University of Cincinnati professor had hosted a get-together for about 50 of his students, many of whom were starting to leave around 10PM.

Eugene Pearson, a 23-year-old graduate student, left the party after telling friends he was walking home. He lived on Victory Parkway, more than two miles away, but he was used to the pedestrian life. With his long hair and beard, Pearson looked the part of a pacifist loner. Politically active, he had protested the Vietnam War in Washington D.C. and organized a free clinic in the Walnut Hills area.

At 10:30PM, a mile and a half on his way, Pearson was abruptly caught up in a violent confrontation. Someone accosted him, and before he could comprehend his own murder, he was viciously hacked to death by a heavy bladed weapon.

Pearson had no chance to resist—he was nearly decapitated.

He was found by some teenagers just before 11PM, sprawled on the sidewalk of Wehrman Avenue, a vacant road with few houses that was ideal for an ambush. He'd been slain where he was found, facing his killer as the first deadly blow found its mark. Pearson fell face down and bled out in a wide pool, yet his rimless glasses had not been dislodged. One detective speculated that the weapon was a machete.

Eugene Pearson was butchered in his own blood on the freeway overpass of deserted Wehrman Avenue.

The victim's knapsack lay nearby, with his volumes of Russian literature spilling out across the pavement. There was money in his billfold but no driver's license—he was eventually identified by his passport. His clothing was not disarrayed, and he had suffered no injuries other than the terrible gashes in his neck.

Pearson had foreshadowed his own death several weeks before. He told a friend that he "wouldn't resist if someone came at me with a knife. If my life means that much to them they can have it."

Cincinnati detectives were now working two crime scenes five miles apart. They were stretched thin, with ten members of the 16-man homicide squad on the job, scrounging for meager clues and canvassing for scarce witnesses.

But the wicked entity prowling the darkness was not finished yet.

Paul Robert Mueller was having a busy night. The 33-year-old father of four, recently separated from his wife, was living with his parents near the back entrance to Spring Grove Cemetery.

Spring Grove is the oldest burial ground in the Queen City, and the beauty and serenity of the grounds are stunning. Ornate mausoleums and elaborate crypts embellish the peaceful gardens and lakes, while stone carvings and mosaic sculpture languish in the shady glades of this Cincinnati landmark.

The north side of the cemetery hugs Gray Road, and the north entrance had a distinguishing feature—a public telephone box to the left of the driveway. A driver could pull up and make a call without getting out of his car. Residents of Gray Road were used to seeing heavy traffic at this phone kiosk, especially at night.

The nature of these calls was open to speculation, but police suspected that drug activity was likely.

Witnesses later said they had seen Mueller's car parked by the phone several times earlier that night. Sometime after 11PM he pulled up to the box again and made a call.

Someone walked up to his car and pumped two shots into his head at point blank range, killing him instantly. Whether he was lured there by his murderer or fell prey to a random shooting, the former golf pro had been ambushed.

Residents of Gray Road would report hearing gunshots at various times that night. Mrs. Katherine Brunswick heard one shot at 11:40 and two at 1AM. Mrs. Joan Osterbrock claimed to hear three shots at 1:45AM, but admitted she "may have looked at the clock wrong." Bob Funke placed the shots at 1AM.

Paul Mueller lay dead in his car until morning. In a tragic irony, his father was employed at the cemetery and discovered his son's body at 8:10AM when he arrived for work. A fresh group of detectives awoke and responded to yet another crime scene.

The shooter got the drop on Paul Mueller while he was talking to his married girlfriend at the cemetery's north gate.

Powder burns indicated the shooter was standing next to the open driver's window. The victim's billfold containing $45 was intact next to the body, and the phone receiver was in Mueller's lap—a tangle of lost connections.

The kiosk was in an open area next to the road. Other than the cemetery gateposts, there was little cover to hide the killer's approach.

Perhaps this was a personal interaction that turned deadly.

A Sunday evening in October had transpired into a distinctively sinister night.

By 8AM Monday the harried homicide squad was processing three crime scenes that appeared random and motiveless—cases that are often unbreakable. Weary detectives rotated in and out, shaking their heads. Murders like these were rare and usually occurred one at a time.

All three victims had been killed either going home or arriving there. All still had money on their persons. No weapons were found, and there were no suspects.

Investigators began digging into the lives of the deceased. By Monday afternoon, Sergeant Russell Jackson had his men "working around the clock" on the slayings, primarily interviewing friends and family members. Jackson would not confirm the caliber of the guns, and had "no comment" about a connection between the Brown and Mueller shootings, crimes that occurred less than three miles apart.

Within the week they had two more killings to deal with.

Mrs. Katie Walther, age 90, died on October 9 from injuries sustained during a savage beating in her apartment on September 12. She had never regained consciousness, and detectives inherited a cold case with no witnesses or suspects.

That same night a city fireman was slain in Avondale, the third Cincinnatian killed in a parked car that week. Edward J. Reisinger, age 28, was found in the front seat of his auto in Woodward Park, clad only in his underwear and shot once in the back of the head. His clothing was on the front seat and his fireman's uniform was in the back. The engine was off and the

CINNATI ENQUIRER

TUESDAY MORNING, OCTOBER 5, 1971

SINGLE COPY 15c
Home Delivered 6 Days 75c

Three Baffling Killings Confronting City Police

Eugene S. Pearson
"wouldn't resist"

Mrs. Sally Glueck Brown
murder victim

Eugene Pearson and Sally Brown wound up on the front page for the wrong reason.

windows were closed—his wallet, Timex wristwatch, and gold wedding band were missing.

Tracing his movements, cops learned his last shift was Thursday morning, after which he'd left for his part-time job at Swallen's department store on Red Bank Road. He worked there until 5PM and then returned home. Coworkers said it was normal for him to put his uniform on the back seat.

Not normal was a young husband and father leaving his home Thursday night and winding up almost naked in a rough part of town with a bullet in his brain. What was the nature of the Edward Reisinger's fatal assignation in the park? The place was a known haven for prostitution, and detectives eventually made several arrests to close the case—apparently the fireman was killed during a private transaction gone awry.

Mrs. Walther's killer was never apprehended. Her hopeless case jacket was condemned to the back of the file.

The Reisinger and Walther murders prolonged the homicide squad's sleepless week, as they continued to quiz anyone who knew the trio of victims from the Sunday night bloodbath.

Examining the life of Sally Glueck Brown confirmed what detectives had already guessed—no one had an obvious motive to kill her.

Besides her involvement with Hebrew Union College, which had been founded by her brother Dr. Nelson Glueck, Brown had been past president of the Jewish Women's Organization, president of the Wise Temple Sisterhood and the Cincinnati Chapter of Hadassah. Her friends described her as a young 59-year-old, with an enthusiasm for life and new experiences.

Her friend Esther Shapiro told police that Sally had recently confided in her. She had been distraught and talked about dying, but wouldn't say why she was so upset. Esther also revealed that there was friction between Sally and another woman at Hebrew Union.

Another early tip still has resonance today. A co-worker pointed out that Sally Brown was "very active in raising bonds for Israel." He suggested that "any Arabs in Cincinnati who object to this" just might resort to killing her.

A terrorist murder in 1971? Detectives discounted it, but put the tip in the active file.

Brown's carport backed onto thick woods perched on a steep hill behind the complex. If the killer was lurking in the thicket, his approach and exit would be effortless. Yet after surveying residents, investigators found no evidence of a shooter in the parking area. Fred Miller's dogs did not react to any movement behind the building just before the shot, and no one saw a person fleeing or a car speeding away immediately afterwards.

Miller did see someone standing near the murder car less than a minute after the shot. He hurried outside to discover it was neighbor Phil Lumpkin. They looked at Mrs. Brown and called the police, who would find Lumpkin a puzzling witness. He drove a blue Pontiac—Sally Brown drove a blue Oldsmobile—and he usually parked two spots away from where she was shot. He had dark hair and wore glasses, just like the victim.

Now Lumpkin wondered aloud if someone was after him and "shot her by mistake." Police later determined that he was in his apartment entertaining the wife of a business associate at the time of the murder. Even though the scene was sealed off, Lumpkin managed to whisk her away in his car.

Detectives looked hard at Lumpkin's personal life—there is a 30-page interview with his female companion in the case file. He was described as a numismatist, a collector of historic money, and he had a house full of cash that he was buying and selling for profit. According to the file, he "had the joint bugged with all kinds of electric devices."

Lumpkin was an oddball. But his married girlfriend was his alibi, and he could not be connected to the murder.

Another lead was also rooted in adultery. A week before the murder, a male Woodside Apartments resident had informed a Mrs. Reynolds that her husband was having an affair with his wife. After being confronted, Mr. Reynolds had threatened the resident, who arrived home just after the shooting and whose car was "very similar" to Sally Brown's.

Yet investigators were already moving in a different direction from the mistaken identity scenario. During my research, this writer pulled an offense report from the case jacket that hinted at a new theory, one that never reached the newspapers in 1971:

> **We have experienced approximately 18 robberies which have occurred within the past three months where the victims were accosted in the driveway or garage . . . The suspects are operating in the better apartment building areas. It is our opinion that the victims are picked up while driving on one of the main arteries near their residence and then followed home by the suspects . . . Shots have been fired in two of these cases.**

A young black man wearing a stocking mask was picked up on the fly by a maroon auto after several of the robberies. This strong arm blitz began July 1, 1971, and continued through October 11, a week after the Brown killing. Several arrests were eventually made, but there were no links to the murder.

Seven days into the investigation police came upon a suspicious coincidence. They learned that a long time resident of the Woodside Apartments was in the habit of firing guns out of his window when he was intoxicated. Police believed one of his guns matched the caliber of the murder weapon, but they could not locate it.

This man denied any connection to the shooting of Sally Brown. Detectives couldn't come up with the physical evidence to charge him, even though they were convinced he had accidentally shot Brown. One cop commented dryly, "Nowadays we are limited as to how far we can go—everybody has certain civil rights."

When the suspect died years later, his widow allegedly told a friend that her husband had fired a gun out the window the night Mrs. Brown was killed. Yet when confronted by detectives hot to revive the case, she denied making the statement.

The investigation into the near beheading of Eugene Pearson wasn't going much better. Like the Brown slaying, Pearson's murder appeared to be a random act.

Interviews revealed that although many people knew him, he was an enigma to most. The graduate student was described as "a young man who had everything to live for"—yet no one understood what he was living for.

His legal guardian William Fisher summed him up: "He was no monkey-around guy. He was serious. I don't understand things like this." The Fishers had adopted Eugene after his parents were killed in a 1962 auto accident. "He was working and going to school. He was so busy he didn't have time to come and say hello to us."

Russ Jackson told the press that Pearson associated with "a lot of different people" at the University of Cincinnati. He called

Eugene "a remote individual" who "kept to himself quite a bit", and whose own brother didn't know much about him. Jackson noted that Pearson had several girlfriends, including one who claimed they had been briefly engaged the previous spring. She said they were "still friends" and had talked about living together, which was news to those who knew Pearson.

The inquiry also uncovered UC students who took an active dislike to the arrogant Pearson and who had "beaten him up several times." Some of these young men had weapons in their dorm rooms. Police tested a machete, a sword, and a long bladed knife for blood with negative results.

Other personal details soon emerged. Pearson worked at Frisch's restaurant in Clifton, and he was known to "associate with Negroes" there. He was a socialist proponent of the doctrine of Marx who "smoked marijuana but not to excess." A bartender at the 226 bar (a known homosexual hangout) recalled seeing Pearson there several times three months prior to his murder. Yet regardless of his sexual orientation, investigators discounted his love life as a factor in his death.

Everyone agreed that Pearson was a pacifist who wouldn't have resisted an attack. His strident antiwar stance had alienated some people—detectives probed whether his militant activism might have angered some opponents to the point of violence.

While canvassing near the Wehrman Avenue crime scene, a motive for Pearson's murder was staring cops in the face. They realized that the surrounding neighborhood was mostly black residents. Was there a racial overtone to the killing?

Russ Jackson had received an inquiry from a district attorney in Oakland, California, because aspects of Pearson's murder were similar to ten recent attacks with a machete in the San Francisco area. Like Pearson, all the victims were young white men with long hair, and eyewitness accounts identified the perpetrators as black. Jackson believed the weapon that killed Pearson was a machete or a meat cleaver.

Jackson also consulted with Louisville detectives over two similar cases in August. One man died and another was severely hacked by black attackers—again the victims were young white males with long hair.

Investigators could not link the cases to Pearson, but privately they liked the racial angle. Tensions had subsided somewhat since the riots of the late 1960s, but in 1971 Cincinnati remained the most segregated city north of the Mason Dixon line.

Eugene Pearson's vicious slaying could have resulted from a dare or an initiation—black males taking an opportunity to "off whitey" on their turf. And the young graduate student was the ideal victim, a gentle peacekeeper who would have forfeited his life without protest.

An offense report pulled from the Pearson file dovetailed perfectly with this theory. Three men of the Black Muslim faith were arrested the day after the murder for a nearby assault—they had attacked a white man in his driveway an hour prior to and five blocks away from the Pearson homicide.

Their mug shots revealed a coldness of expression that said they needed no reason to hate whites. And Eugene Pearson's effeminate appearance could have stoked their rage, since some Black Muslims believed that long-haired white males were homosexuals who would attempt to lure a black man.

These three men were investigated extensively but could not be linked to the crime. Cops squeezed their informants in Walnut Hills, but hit a dry well. Nobody knew anything—or they chose not to give up a killer to "The Man."

The murder of Eugene Pearson was destined to be unavenged. Just as the victim would have wanted it.

As Paul Mueller lay shot to death in his car on Monday morning, detectives who had worked the other two crime scenes began to arrive. It was soon apparent that while those slayings seemed wanton and unprovoked, the shooting at the north gate of Spring Grove Cemetery had a different texture. Investigators were quickly convinced that this killer had a motive.

Initial checks into Mueller's background delivered conflicting opinions about the father of four. A former All-City football player at Hughes High School, Mueller had attended Miami University

These black Muslims were later arrested for attacking a white male four blocks away from and one hour earlier than the Pearson slaying

for two years and later worked as a golf pro at Wyoming and Western Hills Golf Clubs. Recently separated from his wife, the Procter & Gamble welder appeared to be living large as a bachelor.

Russell Jackson, so effusive in discussing the Brown and Pearson cases, clammed up on this one. Other than confirming the marital separation, Jackson offered a terse, "I can't tell you anything for publication" to the press.

During the separation, Paul Mueller lived with his parents on Beechwood Avenue, less than a quarter mile from the crime scene. Residents along Gray Road confirmed that Mueller used the phone kiosk several times that night—his father's house had a phone, yet for some reason he was compelled to use an outdoor line.

Russell Jackson continued to stonewall. Though inquiries into the victim's stints as a golf pro had uncovered some questionable behavior, Jackson would not comment on any scandalous activity by Paul Mueller. Yet their focus remained Mueller's private life, and centered on two possible motives: drug activity or a love triangle.

The fact that Mueller wasn't robbed seemed to rule out a simple holdup or drug deal turned violent. Detectives theorized the killer had waited behind the gate, knowing that Mueller would stop to use the phone again. A note from the case file reads: "Paul was a man of habits; he used the same route or did the same thing." Once talking, the victim's distraction enabled his assassin to get up close.

A review of the case file today reveals a number of men who had reason to kill Paul Mueller. The following are just some of suspects who had previously crossed paths with the dead man:

- Mueller was rumored to be the "go between in a bad grass deal," and was suspected of selling the pot after helping to steal it. An informant told police that "Moose (Mueller) got out of the deal," but thought "they might knock him off."
- Mueller "had trouble recently with an ex-con" named Habisch, who told others at the "Brass Boot" bar (a favorite Mueller hangout) that he "would get Paul." On the night of the murder, Habisch entered the bar around 11:30PM, but "quickly left when he saw Mueller there," according to witnesses.
- Another bar called the Sugar Bear Lounge had a club called "Black Legion," a group of white racists who may have killed Mueller as an initiation—he allegedly owed $1000 to their leader. This group "stayed high on dope all the time," and was suspected of "killing a woman at the bar in July."
- Mueller had been charged with assaulting David Mandery the previous May. Paul was having an affair with Mandery's wife, and had "beat David up pretty good" after intentionally crashing his car into Mandery's vehicle.

Investigators also withheld from the press that they had an ear witness to the murder: Paula Mandery. Yes—David's

Rites tomorrow for Mrs. Brown;
Search for her killer continues

Slaying Victim 'Gentle,' Wouldn't Resist Force

By MARGARET JOSTEN
Enquirer Reporter

The victim of a throat-slashing in Walnut Hills emerged Tuesday as a pacifist and loner who may have predicted his own death around Christmas, 1969.

Eugene S. Pearson, 23, 2640 Victory Pky., hacked to death Sunday night, was quoted by a longtime acquaintance as saying, "If someone came at me with a knife I wouldn't resist. If my life means that much to them they can have it.

Murder of welder lacking in motive

Robbery does not appear to be a motive in the slaying of Paul R. Mueller, who was found about 8:20 a.m. yesterday at 4800 Gray road near the north entrance of Spring Grove Cemetery.

While Brown was eulogized and Pearson praised, the personal life of Paul Mueller was blacked out in the press.

wife was on the phone with Paul Mueller when he was shot to death!

In a lengthy police interview, Paula described what she had heard over the line: "I didn't know if it was a knocking on the door or a banging with a stick—it sounded like a piece of steel to me at first. But later on it just dawned on me that it could've been gunshots." She confirmed that Paul had expressed no fear prior to the shots, nor did he indicate that "he was in any kind of trouble." Mrs. Mandery heard no other voices or any cars driving away—just the dead silence of her lover's final moment.

She placed the shooting at "around 12:30AM", and exonerated her husband, who was driving a truck back from West Virginia and didn't get home until 2AM. Whether he knew about his wife's relationship with Mueller or not, David Mandery volunteered for a polygraph and passed it on October 19.

The Mueller file was awash with "persons of interest"—as if a line had been forming to knock off the man called "Moose," a man known for his "violent temper." Yet none of these individuals could ever be connected to the murder.

In 1993, new technology provided one last gasp for the Mueller case. The Automated Fingerprint Identification System (AFIS) got a hit when a latent from the Mueller file was entered against the data base. A man named Earl Burton was a match for the forgotten fingerprint taken from the phone booth in 1971. Burton admitted to working at a green house on Gray Road in the early '70s, but denied knowing Paul Mueller or anything about his death. He agreed to a polygraph test, but was advised by his doctor not to take it because of his heart condition. Detectives could not eliminate him, but privately felt he was telling the truth.

Recently, a longtime resident of Gray Road discussed the Mueller murder with me. He knew the victim, and saw Mueller use the phone often in the weeks before his death. He remembered seeing Mueller's car there at 7AM that morning but thought nothing of it—the body wasn't discovered until 8:10.

Weeks later, investigators hinted that they had a good suspect. During our interview, the Gray Road resident claimed, "The police knew who did it, but couldn't make a case."

Former homicide detective Tom Oberschmidt, a classmate of Mueller's at Hughes, had run into the victim the week before the shooting. In an interview with this writer, he described Mueller as a "good-looking guy, a ladies' man who was well liked, but not a bully." At "about 6'-1" and 230 pounds," he was a "good athlete" who could handle himself. Oberschmidt assured me that "You didn't screw around with Paul Mueller!"

Mueller's killer would forever roam the city a free man, but he did effect one positive change. A month after his murder, the phone kiosk was removed permanently.

Sergeant Russell Jackson gave the *Cincinnati Enquirer* a rather testy interview in late February 1972. He used the trio of unsolved killings to plead his case that his detectives were unsung and underpaid.

"The biggest difference between today and when I took over the squad ten years ago is the increase in pressure on me and my men, "Jackson complained. "A few years ago you only got one baffling murder, the kind that tied up manpower, about every six months. Today they come so fast and furious that you can never catch up. Now this is real pressure."

So how do you solve a pointless killing where the clues are imaginary and the witnesses are extinct? "The answer is still the dogged homicide detective who gets out and beats the bushes, interviews people, and utilizes informants," explained Jackson. "You have to be a good investigator and a good interrogator."

But he grumbled about the recent lack of cooperation from the public, something he didn't encounter when he first joined the force in 1943. "Potential witnesses just back away from us," he said. "They just don't want to get involved unless the victim was a friend or relative of theirs."

Jackson aimed at the Brown/Pearson/Mueller murder parlay to drive home his point about staffing: "I don't think we have the personnel to cope with the crime increase, and I don't know if we ever will. The homicide squad has grown from six men when I took over to 16 men today, but it's still not nearly enough manpower."

"This should be done and done soon," he continued, "because of exactly what happened to us in October, 1971." And he conceded that while the three cases were given top priority, some "loose ends and dangling leads" didn't get the "proper attention" from his investigators.

It was a startling admission from an old school cop like Russ Jackson.

He closed the interview by confiding how these open cases haunted the detectives working them. "When your workday is over you just don't leave an unsolved case at the office. You take it home with you in your mind. You worry that you're not doing things right, or that something isn't being done that should be."

Jackson's comments revealed how the toil of thundering hours had carved the three murders into his psyche.

SUMMATION:

The ominous events of October 3, 1971, swiftly faded from memory. The case jackets took a meandering trip to the dead file, waiting for a new pair of eyes to harvest clues that others had missed.

The shooting of Sally Glueck Brown appeared to be a careless accident—as if she had been struck by lightning. The crime scene dictated the logistics of the shooting. Detectives were certain the killer had shot her from a distance, as the trajectory favored a sniper firing from a perch above the parking lot.

Brown investigators had uncovered the drunken resident who sometimes discharged weapons from his window. This coincidence offered the best resolution: a woman mistakenly shot by an intoxicated neighbor, who concealed it with the help of his wife. She incriminated her husband after his death, and then denied making statements her best friend swore she had. Giving up a dead spouse was not on her agenda, and the truth of this case would reside with her.

The brutal attack on Eugene Pearson also presented a coincidence to taunt detectives. He was found in the "VFW" section of Walnut Hills—"very few whites." Nothing suggested his murder was a racial hate crime, but similar attacks had occurred in other cities in the fall of 1971.

This was more than being in the wrong place at the wrong time. It was an inadvertent opportunity—Pearson was slaughtered because of what he was while being where he was.

The excavation into the life of Paul Mueller undoubtedly tripped over his killer. The two men knew each other, and there was lingering animosity. The killer was aware of what Tom Oberschmidt later told me—that "Mueller was a rough son of a gun." He brought the gun along as an equalizer, and picked a time and place when Mueller would be sitting in his car. He knew he had to get the drop on the strapping welder.

It can be easy to blame the victim in crimes like this one. Hearsay from the case file suggests Mueller was a dangerous man living on the edge—the reticence of police to publicly address the reputation of the young husband and father speaks volumes.

EPILOGUE:

It was the bloodiest, most frustrating period in Cincinnati homicide squad history.

On October 3rd 1971, The killings transpired at a livid pace and piled up into the existing backlog of 79 homicides that year—at the time a Queen City record. Detectives and street cops hammered away at all three crimes, an unrelenting offensive of shoe leather and lip service. They worked double shifts and caught naps on the fly.

But persistence never had a chance of paying off. Sally Brown, Eugene Pearson, and Paul Mueller were cut down in their prime by assassins protected by fate and providence.

Their souls were snared by destiny, falling victim to a sinister moon. When that night was finally given back to the living, all three lives had ended in deaths that were overwhelming and unanswerable.

POSTSCRIPT: OCTOBER 2010

Earlier this year I was contacted by Sherry Mueller Morse, the oldest daughter of victim Paul Mueller.

I dedicated this book to the victims, hoping to give each one a piece of social justice. But until I spent time with Sherry, I never truly experienced the devastation an unsolved murder visits upon the loved ones left behind.

Sherry was in 6th grade when Paul was killed, yet beyond the hints and whispers that her father was "doing bad things," her family never spoke about the crime. And since press coverage at the time was scant, she grew up without a trace of truth about her father's murder.

Sherry reminded me that her grandfather had found her father's body when he arrived for work at the north gate of Spring Grove cemetery. Then she dropped an irony bomb on me—that fateful October Sunday was her 11th birthday, and her father had taken her on an autumn picnic in that beautiful graveyard, just ten hours before and 100 feet away from where he was killed.

Paul Mueller was no saint, but he was a man's man, well liked and loyal to his friends. And he was a father of four, a dad who shared an unbreakable bond with his daughter Sherry.

We met at Spring Grove, where Paul was ambushed and gunned down in the prime of his life, and where he now rests. During those few hours I saw it all: her grief, her loss, her pain, her strength, and her resilience in the face of indescribable heartbreak.

But most of all, I felt her hunger for the truth, and we are now joined in that search.

Sherry revealed her thoughts about her father, Paul Robert Mueller, in an email to me. What she wrote rendered me wordless.

To a killer from a survivor:

It does not matter who you are or why you did this. It is over and done. Those days so long ago are in my memory forever. I can see them like time is standing still.

If you are still out there, I only have this to say to you. My life was never the same after that day . . . I give you that.

He will never see me play my favorite sport.

He will never teach me how to drive a car.

He will never attend a Father/Daughter Dance or see my Prom Dress.

He will never see me graduate from High School or College.

He will never meet the man I married or dance with me at my wedding.

He will never be a guest in my home.

He will never see the beautiful Grandchildren I was able to give him.

He will never be able to comfort me through my divorce.

He will never meet the true love of my life.

Will he ever know how much I loved him? How much I needed him in my life? He was my Dad not just a man. He was not perfect . . . no one is. You took his life, he deserved to live.

You took a life and for that I pity you. Pity because you have no soul. He knows . . . he knows that I hold him in my heart always; you can never take that away from us. You can never take away that despite all the ugly pain over the years . . . I am survivor despite the odds.

You took his life, but he lives in me despite you . . .

I WITNESS:

He is feeling the usual liberating effects of Jack Daniels, but his problems aren't shrinking; in fact, they're growing larger, magnified by the bottom of his shot glass. The bottle is nearly empty. His only kindred spirit now is his upcoming hangover—and the revolver cradled in his drunken lap.

Spooking his neighbors by firing guns into the darkness has become a perverse kind of hobby. Sometimes he overhears them talking the following morning in the parking lot, their voices hushed and frightened. *Did you hear those shots? This used to be such a nice area. What is happening to our city?*

He peers through the parted drapes and guffaws.

Tonight the view from his balcony takes on a hazy clarity. The October moon seems so huge, so close. His vision zooms, and then doubles—the evening shadows tremble and lurch in the moonlight.

Just after 10PM he sees the blue Pontiac pull into the lot. The driver has dark hair and is wearing glasses. Phil Lumpkin! That weasel coin collector from downstairs!

The man drains his glass and focuses on the car. How he'd love to throw a giant scare into that little punk. Rigging his apartment with all that security stuff—how does he afford it, anyway? He'd like to give Lumpkin something to be really afraid of.

I'll just shoot out one of his tires, the man chuckles to himself. That guy will never tell, much less call the cops. He's too paranoid.

If not for the sound and the recoil, he would never believe he actually discharges the gun. And unlike most errant gunshots, this one finds its mark—right through the eye of Sally Glueck Brown.

As the drunken killer stares in horror, he spots Phil Lumpkin rushing up to the car and opening the door. The shock propels him out of his fog, and he is instantly scared sober.

Oh Christ, he murmurs. *Who did I just shoot?*

The three young black men believe in the tenets of the Nation of Islam—these blue-eyed crackers are really just "grafted snakes," an inferior race conjured up centuries ago in a laboratory by some mad scientist.

The only remedy for the proliferation of these white devils is hate. And willful extermination. Racism has lit the fire which now burns as brightly as the moon overhead.

Earlier that night they attacked one in his own driveway. But this devil fought back, with a vigor that belied his long hair and small physique. The knife proved useless up close, and the devil yelled at the top of his lungs. They had no choice but to flee.

Now they have a machete, the preferred weapon in San Francisco. As they prowl deserted Wehrman Avenue their resolve is strong. Their failed attempt has shamed them. Their appetite for blood is whetted. Tonight they kill a white devil.

They spy Eugene Pearson heading toward them on foot. He is exactly what they're looking for. His thin build, long hair, and skin color are an abomination. And he is a defenseless weakling who carries a book bag and wears rimless glasses. This one will not have the will to resist.

"You took a wrong turn, devil," one of them sneers. "This is our turf." The hippie grad student says nothing and with an obliging shrug, reaches for his wallet—he's been robbed before.

"We don't need no money from no snake," they taunt him. One man orders Pearson to kneel down and begins unzipping his pants, yet Eugene just stands there. His passivity enrages them, setting off enough madness to devour a life. They crave victory—if not through a courageous display, then slaughter will suffice.

One swift stroke of the machete nearly severs Pearson's head. He falls face-forward on the pavement and several other wanton blows rain down against his neck. As his blood washes over the sidewalk, they hoot and jeer at his quivering form, pointing at the rimless glasses still perched foolishly upon his nose.

Habisch has been sitting in the Brass Boot, fidgeting impatiently for about an hour when Paul Mueller finally shows up. God, how he hates that son of a bitch! He's always got some dodge working, always running his mouth.

He is afraid of Mueller—the guy has a wicked temper and can back it up. He knocked Habisch down several weeks ago during a brief fracas at the Boot, threatening to kick his ass in front of everyone there. Afterward Habisch boasted to several drunken patrons that he would eventually "get" Paul Mueller.

But first he needs a plan.

Habisch leaves the Boot and drives away, checking for his gun in the glove compartment. He's an ex-con who shouldn't be carrying, but he's running with a rough crowd.

He knows where Mueller will wind up—using the phone on Gray Road to call Paula. Perfect. The scheme is clear now; it just grabs him. He can settle his score with "Moose" and simultaneously do a favor for the Black Legion, who put a bounty on Mueller after he burned them on that pot deal.

Habisch parks alongside a nearby greenhouse and takes his position behind the cemetery gate. The full moon bathes the north entry in subtle light. His approach must be swift, precise. Sure enough, shortly after midnight Mueller pulls up and grabs the phone. The killer waits until the burly welder is ensconced in his call—he hears Mueller begging Paula to meet him somewhere. Despite his impassioned pleas, she apparently refuses.

When Paul finally backs down and says he is going home to bed, Habisch makes his move. He steps around the gate, strides to the car, and fires two shots into the guy's head from a foot away. The phone flops onto his lap, drenched with his blood, and Mueller slumps in his seat. The killer hears Paula's disembodied voice demanding, "Paul? Paul, are you OK?"

The big man never saw it coming—the notion of death stalking him from inside the marble orchard where his father worked was unthinkable. Habisch bolts for his car, his heart pounding. He drives away, knowing they can never pin this one on him.

He has the last laugh on Paul Mueller. And the moon's shimmering face smiles down upon him.

FINAL EXIT:

THE LEGACY OF A LANDMARK

"I know death hath ten thousand several doors for men to take their exits."

John Webster

Let no victim's ghost say we did not try.

Yet history is written by the survivors, those who gather in the cloak of dusk to drink bottoms up to their memory.

And for those who pass empty bedrooms, suffer lonely holidays, and push away unbearable images—murder has left a landmark of grief and a legacy of loss.

An unsolved murder blurs the line between light and dark, madness and reason, sin and redemption. It is the ultimate gray area. The answers remain elusive, tangled in the killer's phantom footsteps.

In these chapters we have encountered innocent victims, faceless killers, ardent detectives, and frightened citizens. We have been forced to confront the persistence of evil without the reassurance of punishment.

What remains is the fascination. The mystery.

And forever having one more question to ask.

This book is dedicated to the victims. May their restless ghosts find peace . . .

REFERENCE AND BIBLIOGRAPHY

Books

Baird, Adrion: *My Long Journey Home.* Tennessee: Pathway Press 2002.

Buss, David M: *The Murderer Next Door—Why the Mind is Designed to Kill.* New York: Penguin, 2005

Glennon, Lorraine, editor: *The 20th Century—An Illustrated History of Our Lives and Times.* New York: JG Press, 1999

Halttunen, Karen: *Murder Most Foul—The Killer and the American Gothic Imagination.* Cambridge, Mass.: Harvard University Press, 1998

Hopkins, William Foster: *Murder is My Business.* Cleveland, Ohio: The World Publishing Company, 1970

Lester, Dr. David: *Questions and Answers About Murder.* Philadelphia, Pa.: The Charles Press, 1991

Mestemaker, Albert: *Courtroom Gladiator.* Cincinnati: Brandenburg Publications; 1998

Newton, Michael. *Hunting Humans.* Port Townsend, Washington: Loompanics Unlimited, 1990.

Rhodes, Richard: *Why They Kill—The Discoveries of a Maverick Criminologist.* New York: Alfred A. Knopf, 1999

Stimson, George: *The Cincinnati Crime Book.* Cincinnati, Ohio: The Peasenhall Press, 1998

Strean, Dr. Herbert & Freeman, Lucy: *Our Wish to Kill—The Murder in All Our Hearts.* New York: St. Martin's Press, 1991

Newspapers

The Cincinnati Enquirer

The Cincinnati Post

The Cincinnati Times Star

The Kentucky Post

The Kentucky Times Star

Periodicals

City Beat Magazine:

Newsweek Magazine:

Cincinnati Magazine

Snitch Magazine

True Detective Magazine

Front Page Detective Magazine

Inside Detective Magazine

Official Detective Stories Magazine

Unsolved Mysteries Magazine

Miscellaneous

Cincinnati Police Homicide Division Case File Jackets

Greenhills Police Patricia Rebholz Case File Jacket

CHAPTER SOURCES:

CHAPTER 1: Embrace the Beast—Cumminsville Railroad Killer 1904-1910.

- *Cincinnati Enquirer*
- *Cincinnati Post*
- *Cincinnati Times Star*
- *Cincinnati Commercial Tribune*
- Halttunen, Karen: *Murder Most Foul—The Killer and the American Gothic Imagination.* Cambridge, Mass.: Harvard University Press, 1998
- Newton, Michael. *Hunting Humans.* Port Townsend, Washington: Loompanics Unlimited, 1990.

CHAPTER 2: Into the Wind—Three Missing Girls 1915-1922.

- *Cincinnati Enquirer*
- *Cincinnati Post*
- *Cincinnati Times Star*

CHAPTER 3: The Bride In the Casket—Frances Brady Shooting 1936.

- *Cincinnati Enquirer*
- *Cincinnati Post*
- *Kentucky Times Star*
- *Kentucky Post*
- *Kentucky Enquirer*
- "Who Killed the Bride on the Threshold?" *True Detective Magazine.* December, 1936.

CHAPTER 4: To Be or Not To Be—Willard Armstrong Murder/Suicide 1939.

- *Cincinnati Enquirer*
- *Cincinnati Post*
- *Cincinnati Times Star*

CHAPTER 5: Caught in a Whirlwind Tailspin—Sophia Baird Hotel Stabbing 1943.

- *Cincinnati Enquirer*
- *Cincinnati Post*
- *Cincinnati Enquirer*
- *Cincinnati Enquirer* special. *Visions of Sophia.* 6-17-84 thru 6-21-84.
- Baird, Adrion. *My Long Journey Home.* Tennessee: Pathway Press 2002.
- Interview with Adrion Baird: 5-13-2008
- Cincinnati Police Homicide Squad Case File: Sophia Baird

CHAPTER 6: The Man Who Knew Too Much—Oda Apple Assassination 1953.

- *Cincinnati Enquirer*
- *Cincinnati Post*
- *Cincinnati Times Star*
- Cincinnati Police Homicide Squad Case File: Oda Apple

CHAPTER 7: The Matron and the Meter Man—Audrey Pugh and Robert Lyons 1956.

- *Cincinnati Enquirer*
- *Cincinnati Post*
- *Cincinnati Times Star*
- Hopkins, William Foster. *Murder is My Business.* New York: World Publishing Company: 1970.
- Stimson, George. *The Cincinnati Crime Book.* Cincinnati: Peasenhall; 1998.
- "The Society Beauty and the Woman Hater." *True Detective Magazine.* September, 1956.
- "No Time for Alibis." *Official Detective Stories.* October, 1956.
- Interview with Stanley Schrotel: 6-5-1997
- Cincinnati Police Homicide Squad Case File: Audrey Pugh

CHAPTER 8: The Whistling Shadow—Patty Rebholz Bludgeoning 1963.

- *Cincinnati Enquirer*
- *Cincinnati Post Times Star*
- *Cincinnati Post*
- "Her Last Wish." *City Beat Magazine.* January 10, 2002.
- "An Innocent Man." *Cincinnati Magazine.* April, 2002.
- "Cold Cases: Talk of the Town." *CBS News.com.* July 10, 2004.
- "Martha Moxley and Patty Rebholz." *48 Hours Mystery.* July 11, 2004
- Interview with Tom Doyle: 2-21-2008
- Greenhills Police Department Case File: Patricia Rebholz

CHAPTER 9: Less Than Meets the Eye—Cobys Shot to Death 1964.

- *Cincinnati Enquirer*
- *Cincinnati Post Times Star*
- Interview with Tom Coby: 5-20-2008

- Cincinnati Police Homicide Squad Case File: Dennis and Evelyn Coby

CHAPTER 10: A Vision of Deadly Desire—Bricca Family Murders 1966.

- *Cincinnati Enquirer*
- *Cincinnati Post Times Star*
- *Cincinnati Post*
- Stimson, George. *The Cincinnati Crime Book.* Cincinnati: Peasenhall; 1998.
- "Exclusive Report on Cincinnati's Phantom Slayer." *True Detective Magazine.* October, 1966.
- "The Bricca Mystery . . . And No One is Talking." *Front Page Detective.* July, 1967.
- "Getting Away with Murder." *Cincinnati Magazine.* January, 1982.
- "The Still Unsolved Murder of a Cincinnati Family." *Unsolved Mysteries Magazine.* May, 2000
- "Unsolved Bricca Case Haunts the West Side." *Snitch Magazine.* March, 2002
- "Death on a Quiet Street." *Cincinnati Magazine.* April, 2008

CHAPTER 11: Terror in the Gaslight District—Alice Hochhausler and The Strangler 1966.

- *Cincinnati Enquirer*
- *Cincinnati Post Times Star*
- Mestemaker, Albert: *Courtroom Gladiator.* Cincinnati: Brandenburg Publications; 1998
- Newton, Michael. *Hunting Humans.* Washington: Loompanics Unlimited, 1990.
- Stimson, George. *The Cincinnati Crime Book.* Cincinnati: Peasenhall; 1998.
- "Cincinnati: The Strangler." *Newsweek Magazine.* October 31, 1966.

- "If this is Barbara's Slayer—Will the Stranglings End?" *Inside Detective Magazine.* March, 1967.
- "Cincinnati's Phantom Rapist." *True Detective Magazine.* April 1967.
- "The Legacy of the Cincinnati Strangler." *Cincinnati Magazine.* August,1997.
- Interview with Paul Morgan: 3-8-1997
- Interview with Stanley Schrotel: 6-5-1997.
- Phone interview with Beth Hochhausler Placke: 6-7-1997
- Cincinnati Police Homicide Squad Case File: Alice Hochhausler
- Cincinnati Police Homicide Squad Case File: Barbara Bowman

CHAPTER 12: Person or Persons Unknown—Dumler Triple Homicide 1969.

- *Cincinnati Enquirer*
- *Cincinnati Post Times Star*
- *Cincinnati Post*
- "Coed Killer At Large In Ohio." *Official Detective Stories.* July, 1970.
- Interview with Paul Morgan: 3-8-1997.
- Cincinnati Police Homicide Squad Case File: Dumler Family

CHAPTER 13: Murder in Three Acts—Killings of Brown, Pearson, Mueller 1971.

- *Cincinnati Enquirer*
- *Cincinnati Post Times Star*
- *Cincinnati Post*
- "Getting Away with Murder." *Cincinnati Magazine.* January, 1982.
- Interview with Tom Oberschmidt: 8-2-2008
- Cincinnati Police Homicide Squad Case File: Sally Glueck Brown
- Cincinnati Police Homicide Squad Case File: Paul Mueller

- Cincinnati Police Homicide Squad Case File: Eugene Pearson

PHOTO AND NEWSPAPER CREDITS

Cover:	Author's Collection
Dedication:	Author's Collection
Introduction:	Author's Collection
Chapter 1:	Page 6, Author's Collection Page 9, *Cincinnati Enquirer*, May 7, 1904 Page 13, Author Page 17, Author Page 20, *Cincinnati Post*, January 3, 1910 Page 24, *Post*, January 4, 1910 Page 25, *Enquirer*, January 3, 1910 Page 27, *Enquirer*, January 4, 1910 Page 29, *Post*, October 28, 1910 Page 33, *Enquirer*, October 26, 1910
Chapter 2:	Page 42, Author Page 46, *Cincinnati Enquirer*, June 19, 1915 Page 53, Author Page 55, *Enquirer*, November 16, 1919 Page 57, *Cincinnati Post*, August 3, 1948 Page 59, *Enquirer*, August 25, 1921 Page 62, *Cincinnati Times Star*, September 23, 1957 Page 63, *Enquirer*, August 22, 1948

Chapter 3:

Page 70, Author
Page 74, *Kentucky Post*, October 2, 1936
Page 75, *Post*, October 2, 1936
Page 77, Author
Page 81, *Kentucky Times-Star*, October 2, 1936
Page 83, *Post*, October 7, 1936
Page 86, *Post*, October 7, 1936
Page 91, *Times-Star*, October 20, 1937
Page 93, *Kentucky Enquirer*, August 18, 1937

Chapter 4:

Page 102, Author
Page 106, *Cincinnati Post*, February 6, 1939
Page 110, *Cincinnati Enquirer*, February 9, 1939
Page 116, Enquirer, April 15, 1939

Chapter 5:

Page 120, Adrion Baird Collection
Page 124, Adrion Baird
Page 129, *Cincinnati Post*, April 23, 1943
Page 131, *Cincinnati Enquirer*, April 26, 1943
Page 138, *Enquirer*, May 4, 1956
Page 145, *Enquirer*, June 17, 1984

Chapter 6:

Page 150, Author
Page 155, Apple Case File
Page 157, Apple Case File
Page 159, *Cincinnati Post*, August 26, 1953
Page 162, *Cincinnati Enquirer*, August 12, 1953

Page 164, *Enquirer*, August 9, 1959
Page 165, Author

Chapter 7:

Page 170, Author
Page 174, *Cincinnati Enquirer*, April 12, 1956
Page 175, *Official Detective Stories Magazine*, October 1956
Page 176, *Official Detective*
Page 178, Pugh Case File
Page 179, *Enquirer*, April 16, 1956
Page 181, Pugh Case File
Page 184, *Enquirer*, May 27, 1956
Page 185, *Official Detective*
Page 189, *Official Detective*
Page 198, *Enquirer*, November 15, 1956

Chapter 8:

Page 206, Author
Page 209, Rebholz Case File
Page 212, Rebholz Case File
Page 217, *Cincinnati Enquirer*, August 12, 1963
Page 218, Rebholz Case File
Page 221, Rebholz Case File
Page 223, Rebholz Case File
Page 225, *Enquirer*, August 13, 1963
Page 234, *Enquirer*, December, 20, 2000
Page 238, *Enquirer*, November 23, 2001
Page 240, *Enquirer*, November 30, 2001
Page 248, *Enquirer*, December 7, 2001

Chapter 9:

Page 252, Author
Page 256, *Cincinnati Enquirer*, November 28, 1964
Page 260, *Enquirer*, November 28, 1964

Page 261, Tom Coby collection
Page 263, *Enquirer*, November 30, 1964
Page 264, *Enquirer*, December 4, 1964
Page 271, Author

Chapter 10:

Page 278, Author
Page 282, *Cincinnati Enquirer*, September 28, 1966
Page 285, *Front Page Detective*, June 1967
Page 287, *Front Page Detective*
Page 289, *Enquirer*, September 29, 1966
Page 294, Cincinnati Post-Times Star, October 4, 1966
Page 299, *Post Times Star*, October 29, 1966
Page 302, Post Times Star, November 15, 1966
Page 304, Post Times Star, September 22, 1967

Chapter 11:

Page 322, Author
Page 326, Author
Page 327, Author
Page 329, *Cincinnati Enquirer*, June 11, 1966
Page 330, *Enquirer*, June 15, 1966
Page 331, Author
Page 334, Hochhausler Case File
Page 335, *True Detective Magazine*, April 1967
Page 338, *Enquirer*, October 14, 1966
Page 342, *Enquirer*, October 13, 1966
Page 344, *Enquirer*, October 15, 1966
Page 347, Winstel/Kerrick Case Files

	Page 348, Author Page 349, *Enquirer*, December 11, 1966 Page 351, *Inside Detective Magazine*, March 1967
Chapter 12:	Page 358, Author Page 362, *Cincinnati Enquirer*, October 24, 1969 Page 369, *Cincinnati Post*, October 24, 1969 Page 373, Dumler Case File Page 379, *Enquirer,* October 26, 1966
Chapter 13:	Page 386, Author Page 389, Brown Case File/Author Collection Page 391, Pearson Case File Page 393, Mueller Case File Page 395, Cincinnati Enquirer, October 3, 1971 Page 400, Cincinnati Post, October 3, 1971 Page 402, Pearson Case File
Epilogue:	Page 414, Author

CHAPTER APPENDIX AND CITATIONS:

Chapter 1: EMBRACE THE BEAST

Denied It: Witnesses Say They Did Not See Mueller Suspect In Saloon
Post 11/03/1904 11:2
Breaks Down Over The Tragedy: Frank Eastman, Murdered Girl's Lover, Accompanied Detectives On Investigation—Crutches With Spots Resembling Blood
Post 10/03/1904 1:1 pic
Murdered Young Phone Girl: Human Fiend Frightfully Attacked Miss Alma Steinigeweg, of Winton Place
Post 11/03/1904 1:4
Did One Man Murder The Three Girl Victims? Murder Of Miss Steinigeweg Recalls The Tragedies Of McDonald And Mueller
Post 11/03/1904 11:5
Girl Telephone Operator Victim Like Louisa Mueller, Who Was Slain!
Cincinnati Times Star 11/03/1904 1:1 pic
Fog Concealed Assassin, Whose Victim Was Found In A Vacant Lot, With Head Crushed By Frightful Blows
Cincinnati Enquirer 11/04/1904 12:1 pic

Victim Was Uneasy Just A Month Ago: Indications That She Feared Some Man Just About The First, When Exchange Girls Were Formerly Paid
Post 11/04/1904 14:3 pic
Tracing Suspect: Police Have Chain Of Circumstantial Evidence And Description
Post 11/04/1904 1:1 pic
Continued: Cases Of Wilson and Salmon, Charged With Mueller Murder
Post 11/04/1904 5:1
Where Pretty Alma Steingeweg Lost Her Life
Cincinnati Enquirer 11/04/1904 4:4 pic
Positive Proof Of Foul Crime Now Leaves No Doubt Whatever That Alma Steinway Was Murdered: Dead Victim Had Also Suffered Outrage From The Brute Who Took Her Life
Cincinnati Enquirer 11/05/1904 9:1 pic
Now Suspected That Two Men Were Implicated In The Murder Of Alma Steinigeweg
Post 11/05/1904 1:1
Slayer Of Alma Steinway Has Not Been Found: Clew After Clew Run To Earth By Police And Employees Of Traction Company Without Success
Commercial Tribune 11/05/1904 1:2+
John Kilgour Emphatic In Denouncing the Crime: Says He Would Have No Hesitation In Shooting Down A Man Who Would Harm One Of His Girls
Post 11/05/1904 11:3
Stoutly Built Man With Slouch Hat Being Hunted As The Brutal Murderer Of Alma Steinway: Many Witnesses Saw Such A Person In The Vicinity On Wednesday Night
Cincinnati Enquirer 11/06/1904 9:1

Slain Girl Buried; No Clew To Murderer: Thousands Crowd About Little Church Where The Funeral Services Are Held—More Clews Run Down Without Success
Commercial Tribune 11/06/1904 6:1

Suspect Now Sought; Find A Trail Of Blood: Important Developments May Lead To Solving Murder Mystery
Post 11/07/1904 1:1

Detectives Question Dead Girl's Admirer: Benjamin Renner Unable To Give Any Information Which May Lead To The Identity Of The Murderer Of Alma Steinway
Commercial Tribune 11/07/1904 5:4

Reward Offered For Slayer: City Council Authorizes Payment Of $2,500 For Capture Of The Fiend Who Slew Miss Lloyd
Cincinnati Enquirer 01/04/1910 9:3+

Chopped Her Head Almost Off After Failing to Ravish The Dying Woman: Fiendish Crime Committed In Fairmount
Cincinnati Enquirer 01/02/1910 Sec.2 1:1 pic

Police Say Anna Lloyd Was The Victim Of Hired Assassin; Hunt For Eye-Witnesses: Police Hear That Engineer On C. H. & D. Train Saw Two Men Struggling With Woman In Ravine
Post 01/04/1910 1:7

Dying Mother Had Premonition Of Daughter's Death—Hearts Quail
Post 01/03/1910 2:2

Murder Of Anna Lloyd, Fourth Woman Victim, Still A Mystery: Three Men Are Held In Case And Are Being Questioned Closely by Police Officials—Developments Are Expected
Post 01/03/1910 1:7+ pic

Two Arrests In Connection With Lloyd Murder: Henry Cook, A Butcher, And James Fields, Negro Laborer, Held At Police Headquarters On Suspicion
Commercial Tribune 01/03/1910 1:7+ pic

Miss Neely, Post Writer, Visits Scene Of Crime And Tells Of Shuddering As Passing Through Isolated Spot
Post 01/05/1910 1:1

How Engineer Saw Death Struggle In Dark Raving; Map Of The Murder Zone
Post 01/05/1910 1:2 pic
Crime Recalls Three Similar Cases In 1904; All Still Unsolved
Post 01/03/1910 3:1
5th Murder Is Mystery: Prisoner Begs Chance to Hunt Slayer Of Wife
Post 10/26/1910 1:1+ pic
Mutilated Body Of Young Wife Is Found In Her Home In Cumminsville, With Throat Cut And Head Horribly Chopped: Husband, A Boarder And Negro Are Under Arrest
Cincinnati Enquirer 10/26/1910 8:4
Thinks Same Man Killed Daughter: Mother Of Mueller Visited The Hackney Home
Cincinnati Times Star 10/26/1910 3:4+
Hackney Hunts Murderer; All Men Arrested in Mystery Freed
Post 10/28/1910 1:6 pic
Police Make New Arrest In Cumminsville Murder: Negro Is Questioned By Police Concerning Murder
Cincinnati Times Star 10/27/1910 1:3+ pic
Hackney Case Shrouded In Deeper Cloud: Police Baffled By Murder Mystery—Husband And Boarder Are Freed From Custody
Commercial Tribune 10/28/1910 1:3+
Speculation At Police Headquarters As To The Cumminsville Murder Mysteries
Cincinnati Enquirer 11/26/1912 8:3
Murders And Manhunts—No.2: The Mad Killer Of Cumminsville
Post 05/03/1956 28:1 Pic
The Cumminsville Murder Zone
Cincinnati Times Star 04/05/1958 Sup5:1 Pic

Mad Killer's Shadow Fell Over City During Six Long Years Of Terror
Cincinnati Enquirer 06/09/1963 40:3

Chapter 2: INTO THE WIND

Clews to Child's Slayer-Bloody Clothes Found in Vacant House
Cincinnati Enquirer 06/19/1915 1:2
Slight Clue in Lost Child Case Given to Police
Cincinnati Enquirer 11/15/1919 1:5
Grief Stricken Mother Keeps Constant Vigil
Cincinnati Time Star 11/16/1919 1:2
Stranger Trailed Young Girl For Two Weeks Before She Disappeared, Says Father
Cincinnati Post Times Star 8/22/1921 1:6
Photos of 200 Girls in Room of Suspect Held in Mystery
Cincinnati Enquirer 8/30/1921 1:2
Hornberger Boy Also Missing: Gone From Home Three Days, But Seen Nearby
Post 09/26/1922 1:3
Gump Hornberger Mysteries Rotten Boards Give Police First Clew In 29 Year Search
Post 08/21/1948 1:7
Search For Bodies Fails Old Cistern Holds Only Water Police Had Hoped To Solve Mysteries
Post 08/23/1948 1:8
Old Timers Recall Lost Girl Mysteries Draining Of Old Cistern Starts Flood Of Memories
Post 08/23/1948 17:4
Emptied Cistern Fails To Solve Mysteries
Cincinnati Times Star 08/23/1948 8:4
Death Of Father Recalls Mystery Of Emily Gump Rudolph Gump 72, 852 Poplar Street
Post 07/02/1954 2:4

Kidnapped Girls Never Found Death Recalls 30 Year Old Mystery 9 Year Old . . . Disappeared
Cincinnati Times Star 07/02/1954 :
Rubble May Hold Key To Mysteries
Cincinnati Times Star 9/23/1957

Chapter 3: THE BRIDE IN THE CASKET

Bride-To-Be Slain in Covington
Kentucky Post 10/02/1936 1:6
Bride-To-Be's Murder Baffles Police
Kentucky Times Star 10/02/1936 1:3
Mystery Deepens In Murder of Covington Bride-To-Be
Cincinnati Enquirer 10/02/1936 1:4
A Cowardly Crime
Kentucky Times Star 20/03/1936 5:5
Murder That Blocked Wedding Plans Keeps Authorities Baffled
Kentucky Times Star 10/03/1936 1:2
Druggist First To Reach Brady Home After Shot Startles Him And His Wife
Kentucky Times Star 10/03/1936 1:3
Brady Slaying Still Mystery
Kentucky Post 10/05/1936 1:5
Jealousy Denied In Murder Quiz; No Other Girl, O'Donnell Says
Kentucky Post 10/07/1936 1:4
Powder Burn Complicates Investigation
Kentucky Post 10/07/1936 1:5
Man and Woman Fled Murder Scene
Kentucky Times Star 10/07/1936 1:4
Is Brady Killing To Be Listed As Perfect Crime
Kentucky Post 10/08/36 1:4
Detectives At Blind Wall In Murder Probe
Kentucky Post 10-08/1936

Business Men Band To Track Slayer
Kentucky Times Star 10/10/1936 1:3
Van Venison May be Called to Testify In Murder Inquiry
Kentucky Times Star 10/20/1937 1:1
Suspect Is Charged With Brady Murder
Cincinnati Enquirer 12/01/1937 1:7
Verdict Acquits Bradshaw Of Part In Brady Murder; Venison Story Is Refuted
Cincinnati Enquirer 3/18/1938 1:3
1936 Murder Never Solved
Cincinnati Times Star 10/28/1947 21:6
Murders And Manhunts-No.4: Bride-To-Be's Slaying Unsolved In 20 Years
Post 05/07/1956 12:1

Chapter 4: TO BE OR NOT TO BE

Norwood Man Clubbed Asphyxiated
Cincinnati Enquirer 02/06/1939 1:1
Hunt Visitor To Man Slain In Moth Bag
Post 02/06/1939 1:1
Chief Coroner Argue Point In Mothbag Case
Post 02/07/1939 1:5
Federal Agent Is Called In Prosecutors Force Also Aids In Norwood Murder Inquiry
Cincinnati Enquirer 02/09/1939 1:2
Mothbag Death Recalls Killing Of Kirschner
Post 02/09/1939 3:1
Rich 2 Aides Take Plane To Quiz Mrs
Post 02/13/1939 1:8
Clues To Habits Worthless Murder Investigators Say
Cincinnati Enquirer 02/15/1939 1:6
Moth Bag Case Probe Is Reopened
Post 02/28/1939 1:8

Coroners Verdict Returned In Mothbag Death Case Mystery Is Still Unsolved
Cincinnati Enquirer 04/05/1939 1:6
Moth Bag Case Not Closed Yet
Post 04/06/1939 22:5
Murder And Manhunts No.6: You Be The Judge Murder Or Suicide? Young Executive Found Trusse
Post 05/09/1956 20:1

Chapter 5: CAUGHT IN A WHIRLWIND TAILSPIN

Pretty Blonde Stabbed To Death In Hotel
Cincinnati Enquirer 04/26/1943 1:8
Easter Slayer Leaves Trail Of Fingerprints In Wild Flight
Post 04/26/1943 1:8
Report Second Attack By Murder Suspect Mt Auburn Woman Victim Of Assault In Home
Cincinnati Times Star 04/26/1943 1:2
Middletown Man Offers Clue In Search For Girls Slayer Saw Negroes Around Hotel
Cincinnati Enquirer 04/27/1943 1:2
Slayer May Have Carved Initial On Victims Hand
Post 04/27/1943 1:3
Suspect In Waitress Slaying Is Seized
Cincinnati Times Star 04/27/1943 1:1
Waitress Slaying Is Still Mystery
Cincinnati Times Star 04/29/1943 1:1
Hat Clue In Hotel Slaying Leads To Arrest
Cincinnati Times Star 05/04/1943 23:4
West Virginia Man Held As Hotel Murder Suspect
Cincinnati Enquirer 05/05/1943 11:6
Store Owner Indentifies Hat Found In Alley After Killing
Cincinnati Enquirer 05/08/1943 1:2
New Suspect Quizzed In Easter Slaying
Post 07/09/1943 1:2

New Suspect Quizzed In Easter Slaying
Cincinnati Times Star 07/09/1943 1:1
Rumor Of Confession False Negro Suspect Sought In Hotel Murder Found At Clinic But Admits
Cincinnati Enquirer 07/10/1943 8:6
Baird Case Suspect Is Held Again
Post 07/12/1943 2:5
Musician Held As Suspect In Hotel Murder
Cincinnati Times Star 07/12/1943 3:5
Man 33 Is Identified In Murder Of Girl 19 At Hotel Police Say
Cincinnati Enquirer 07/13/1943 1:2
Witness Identifies Suspect In Slaying
Post 07/13/1943 1:4
Slaying Of Waitress Denied By Suspect As Officers Seek Witness Who Saw Fleeing Killer
Cincinnati Enquirer 07/14/1943 10:3
Slaying Suspect Held On Weapon Charge
Post 07/14/1943 1:7
Bond $10,000 For Negro Accused Of Carrying Concealed Weapon
Cincinnati Enquirer 07/15/1943 10:5
Girls Slaying Still Mystery Year Produces Few Clues In Easter 1943 Tragedy
Post 03/31/1945 2:4
1943 Hotel Slaying Among City's Unsolved Crimes
Cincinnati Times Star 09/22/1953 9:1
Murders And Manhunts-No. 3-Killer Struck In 1943 But Escaped Justice
Post 05/04/1956 34:1
Murder Mystery Lives On For Brother
Post 07/24/1981 1b:1
Chapter 1 Visions Of Sophia
Cincinnati Enquirer 06/17/1984 A1:1
Chapter 2 Life In The Big City
Cincinnati Enquirer 06/18/1984 A1:1

Chapter 3 A Trail Of Blood
Cincinnati Enquirer 06/19/1984 A1:1
Chapter 4 Nothing But Ashes
Cincinnati Enquirer 06/20/1984 A1:1
Chapter 5 Tying The Threads Together
Cincinnati Enquirer 06/21/1984 A1:1

Chapter 6: THE MAN WHO KNEW TOO MUCH

Father Shot From Rear As He Walks With Boy Close To His Home 3123 Hackberry St
Cincinnati Enquirer 08/10/1953 1:3
Mystery Of Hackberry St Boy 3 Holds Secret To Baffling Bullet That Dilled His Dad
Post 08/10/1953 1:5
East Walnut Hills Area Combed For Clues In Mysterious Slaying
Cincinnati Times Star 08/10/1953 1:4
Police Lack Clue And Motive In Fatal Shooting Of
Cincinnati Enquirer 08/11/1953 1:5
2 New Theories Developed In Fatal Shooting New Witness Found
Post 08/11/1953 1:1
Slain Man Had Premonition Of Danger Enquirer Learns
Cincinnati Enquirer 08/12/1953 14:7
Car Abandoned Near Scene Of Slaying In Walnut Hills
Cincinnati Enquirer 08/13/1953 1:2
Auto Clew Is Useless In Mystery Claying
Post 08/14/1953 5:2
Auto Clew Is Useless In Mystery Claying
Cincinnati Enquirer 08/15/1953 3:2
Neighbors Plan Slaying Reward
Post 08/17/1953 6:2
Neighbors Plan Slaying Reward
Cincinnati Times Star 08/18/1953 1:4

Hackberry Slaying Witness Arrested On A Charge Not Related To The Slaying Mrs Della Carmos
Post 08/19/1953 1:6
Hackberry Slaying Witness Arrested On A Charge Not Related To The Slaying Mrs Della Carmos
Cincinnati Enquirer 08/20/1953 22:3
Mystery Deepens As Slaying Is Studied Here's The Story Step by Step In Weird Unsolved Hackberry Murder
Post 08/26/1953 4:1
Reward Fund Being Solicited
Cincinnati Times Star 08/27/1953 4:4
. . . Shooting Ruled Homicide
Cincinnati Enquirer 09/04/1953 14:7
Mysterious slaying of Oda Apple most baffling of unsolved murders
Post 01/05/1954 24:1 pic
Reward Money To Be Returned
Cincinnati Times Star 03/29/1955 5:1
Murders And Manhunts No.5: Motiveless Slaying Still Awaits Break
Post 05/08/1956 31:1 Pic
Boy, 3, Holds Only Clue In Death In His "Firecrackers Got Daddy": Stray Bullet Kills
Cincinnati Enquirer 05/21/1956 13:1
Apple Murder Confession Proves Hoax
Post 10/29/1956 4:1
Pugh Murderer Is Not Alone; Near Perfect Crimes Recalled
Cincinnati Enquirer 05/20/1956 56:1
Oda Apples Death Is Mystery 6 Years After Found Shot
Cincinnati Enquirer 08/09/1959 5b:4

Chapter 7: THE MATRON AND THE METER MAN

Hyde Park Matron Murdered
Cincinnati Enquirer 04/12/1956 1:6

Stained Carpet May Unlock Mystery Of Slaying
Post 04/12/1956 1:1
Police Question Salesman About Slaying Of Socialite
Cincinnati Times Star 04/12/1956 1:8
Shocking Crime
Cincinnati Enquirer 04/13/1956 4:2
New Evidence Boosts Prowler Murder View
Post 04/13/1956 1:5
New Suspect Is Quizzed In Pugh Slaying
Cincinnati Enquirer 04/14/1956 1:7
Former Mental Patient Taken To Hospital Pending Tests For Police In Pugh Murder
Cincinnati Enquirer 04/14/1956 6:1
Alibi Clears Man Quizzed About Mysterious Slaying
Cincinnati Times Star 04/14/1956 1:1
Police Ask Publics Help In Pugh Case
Post 04/16/1956 1:1
Meter Reader Held Quizzed In Slaying
Cincinnati Enquirer 04/17/1956 1:4
Quiz Ex Convict In Murder
Cincinnati Times Star 04/18/1956 3:7
Autopsy Indicates Right Hander As Pugh Slayer
Cincinnati Enquirer 04/19/1956 1:1
New Slaying Suspect Checked
Cincinnati Times Star 04/19/1956 1:1
Don't Go Near The Door
Cincinnati Enquirer 04/24/1956 16:4
Police Begin Screening Of C800 Studebakers In Search For Mystery Car In Pugh Case
Cincinnati Enquirer 04/25/1956 10:2
Curtain Descends On Wait By Police For Pugh Suspect
Cincinnati Enquirer 04/29/1956 1:1
A Perfect Crime Hamilton's View In Pugh Murder
Cincinnati Enquirer 05/03/1956 1:5
Month On Pugh Case Police Have Nothing
Post 05/11/1956 1:2

New Pugh Murder Suspect Held
Cincinnati Enquirer 05/19/1956 1:7
Pugh Murderer Is Not Alone; Near Perfect Crimes Recalled
Cincinnati Enquirer 05/20/1956 56:1
Weird Characters On The Loose
Cincinnati Times Star 05/23/1956 10:1
Break In The Pugh Case
Cincinnati Times Star 05/26/1956 6:1
Meter Reader Admits He Killed Audrey Pugh Seized Paring Knife During Argument
Post 05/26/1956 1:1
Stabbed Mrs Pugh In Fight For Knife Meter Reader Says
Cincinnati Times Star 05/26/1956 1:7
Two Women Point Finger Of Guilt At Robert Lyons
Cincinnati Times Star 05/26/1956 1:7
Fbi Lab Report Is Clincher In Pugh Murder Case
Cincinnati Enquirer 05/27/1956 22:1
Pugh Murder Case Is Solved On Meter Mans Confession Nearly Perfect Crime
Cincinnati Enquirer 05/27/1956 1:6
Case Closed
Cincinnati Enquirer 05/28/1956 4:1
Whole Story Sought In Murder Entire Truth Lacking In Lyons Confession Of Mrs Pugh Slaying
Cincinnati Enquirer 05/28/1956 1:6
Had To Handle Robert Lyons With Kid Gloves
Cincinnati Enquirer 05/28/1956 45:1
Old Argument Of Mrs Pugh Lyons Revealed Husband Tells How He Changed Window After Dispute
Post 05/28/1956 1:6
Surprise Found General Along His Meter Route That Lyons Was Killer
Cincinnati Enquirer 05/29/1956 13:2
Meter Reader Hires Hopkins As His Lawyer
Post 05/29/1956 1:2

William Hopkins Retained As . . . 's Attorney In Mrs Pugh Death Case
Cincinnati Enquirer 05/30/1956 46:1
The Four Big Lies How Police Trapped Audrey's Killer
Post 05/30/1956 1:1
Echo Of Pugh Case Woman Recalls Violent Brush With Lyons
Cincinnati Times Star 06/04/1956 1:1
Meter Man Changes Story Says He Didn't Kill Mrs Pugh
Post 06/05/1956 1:7
Meter Reader Indicted For First Degree Murder
Post 06/15/1956 1:6
Lyons Calmly Denies Guilt Fails To Ask Bond When Arraigned
Post 06/18/1956 1:5
Surprises Promised In Trial Of Lyons For Pugh Murder
Cincinnati Times Star 09/26/1956 1:7
Judge Bans Tv During . . . Trial
Cincinnati Times Star 09/27/1956 3:3
100 Seat Limit Set For . . . Trial
Cincinnati Times Star 10/31/1956 3:3
Lyons Trial Jury May See Police Movie
Post 11/02/1956 1:3
Testimony Is Due To Begin Monday In . . . Trial
Cincinnati Times Star 11/03/1956 3:3
Lyons And Jury Visit Scene Of Slaying
Post 11/05/1956 1:1
Opening Curtain Rises In Murder Trial Of . . . Jury Hears First Plea
Cincinnati Enquirer 11/06/1956 18:1
Confession Movie Is Key To Lyons Case Prosecution
Cincinnati Times Star 11/06/1956 3:6
Courtroom Hit Lyons Case Played Before Standing Room Only House
Cincinnati Times Star 11/07/1956 1:2

Accounts For Time Pugh Testifies In Lyons Trial
Cincinnati Times Star 11/08/1956 1:6

Lyons Meter Book Erased Expert Says G Man Tells Of Tests
Post 11/09/1956 1:7

Boss Calls Lyons Ideal Meter Reader
Cincinnati Times Star 11/09/1956 1:1

Lyons Lawyer Seeks To Set Up Alibi
Post 11/10/1956 1:6

Lyons To Face Several Witnesses Prosecution Expects To Wind Up Case Late Wednesday
Post 11/12/1956 4:8

Lyons Defense Rips Into Blood Evidence
Post 11/13/1956 1:7

Poker Bluff Used On Lyons Police Say
Cincinnati Times Star 11/14/1956 1:3

Confession Allowed As Evidence At . . . Trial
Cincinnati Enquirer 11/15/1956 1:2

Murder Jurors Witness Picture Of Lyons Re Enacting Crime
Cincinnati Enquirer 11/16/1956 1:1

Lyons Is Placed On Another Street At Time Of Slaying
Cincinnati Enquirer 11/17/1956 1:5

Admitted Crime To Beat Chair On Prosecutors Tip
Cincinnati Enquirer 11/20/1956 1:6

Lyons Holds Fast In Denial Of Slaying Defense Rests
Post 11/20/1956 1:6

Roney Denies Threat Of Chair To Lyons
Cincinnati Enquirer 11/21/1956 1:6

Lyons Termed Trickster In Fight For Life As State Demands Death
Cincinnati Enquirer 11/22/1956 1:2

Lyons Is Acquitted Jury Finds Verdict After Seven Hrs
Cincinnati Enquirer 11/24/1956 1:6

The Meter Reader Is Freed
Post 11/24/1956 4:1

Glad You're Back Old Friends Tell
Post 11/24/1956 12:1
Missing Death Weapon Lyons Key To Freedom
Cincinnati Times Star 11/24/1956 3:3
Free Air For A Free Man In A Free Land
Cincinnati Enquirer 11/25/1956 1:1
The Lyons Verdict
Cincinnati Enquirer 11/26/1956 4:1
City Job Waits Lyons
Post 11/26/1956 1:7
Chief Calls Inquiry Into Lyons Trial Seeks Police Error
Cincinnati Enquirer 12/10/1956 1:3
Police Action Called Sound In Lyons Case
Post 12/12/1956 22:1
Police Work Lauded In Lyons Case
Cincinnati Times Star 02/18/1957 22:4
$10,000 Found Near Body Of 1950s Murder Figure
Cincinnati Enquirer 05/20/1977 A1:2
Memories Still Fresh
Cincinnati Enquirer 05/20/1977 C2:2
Police Won't Probe Meter Readers Death
Post 05/20/1977 11:3
Coroner Rules Natural Causes In Lyons Death
Post 06/01/1977 19:6
Slices Of Cincinnati (Pugh Murder)
Post 08/07/1990 5a:3

Chapter 8: THE WHISTLING SHADOW

High School Cheerleader 15 Found Slain In Greenhills Killer May Have Been Seen By Boy
Cincinnati Post Times Star 08/09/1963 1:6
Mystery Deepens In Girls Slaying
Cincinnati Enquirer 08/10/1963 1:7

Lab Tests Reveal Heavy Blows On Head Killed Cheerleader
Cincinnati Post Times Star 08/10/1963 1:7
Maniac Ruled Out As Girl Killer
Cincinnati Enquirer 08/12/1963 1:7
2 Names Given Police In Probe Of Girl Slaying
Cincinnati Post Times Star 08/12/1963 1:7
Slain Girls Beau Given Tests To Determine Type Of Blood
Cincinnati Enquirer 08/13/1963 1:7
Patricia Not Followed Walked From Dance Alone Witnesses Say
Cincinnati Post Times Star 08/13/1963 1:7
A Once Quiet Street Where Murder Stalked
Cincinnati Post Times Star 08/14/1963 8:1
Third Lie Detector Test To Be Given To Friend In Patricia Rebholzs Murder
Cincinnati Enquirer 08/14/1963 1:7
Blood Stains On Boys Pants Of Same Type As Patricias
Cincinnati Post Times Star 08/14/1963 1:7
Wehrung Youth Is Quizzed Again
Cincinnati Enquirer 08/21/1963 1:5
Wehrung Parents Make Son Ward Of Juvenile Authorities
Cincinnati Enquirer 09/02/1963 1:7
Judge Explains Code In Wehrung Becoming Ward
Cincinnati Enquirer 09/02/1963 7c:1
Juvenile Court Takes Custody Of Michael
Cincinnati Post Times Star 09/02/1963 1:7
Wehrung Background Is Studied By Court
Cincinnati Post Times Star 09/04/1963 1:6
For Normal Life-Wehrung Sent Away To School
Cincinnati Post Times Star 09/16/1963 1:1
Rebholz Slaying Witness Found In New Probe
Cincinnati Post Times Star 06/02/1965 1:5
Greenhills Murder Report Awaited
Cincinnati Enquirer 06/03/1965 1:3

Agencies Mum About New Rebholz Murder Probe
Cincinnati Enquirer 06/17/1965 1:6
Prosecuter Gets Report On . . . Slaying
Cincinnati Post Times Star 06/17/1965 1:2
No New Charge In Rebholz Case
Cincinnati Post Times Star 06/23/1965 1:4
. . . Released As Juvenile Court Ward
Cincinnati Enquirer 07/28/1965 1:6
Michaels Back In Class
Cincinnati Enquirer 02/01/1966 7:1
Unsolved Murders (Patricia Rebholz 08/08/63)
Post 11/12/1991 11a:4
Murder, He Wrote (Play Based On 1963 Unsolved Rebholz Murder)
Cincinnati Enquirer 02/05/1996 C1:2 Pics
Trying Again For Patty: Thirty-Six Years Have Passed Since The Killing Of A Popular Cheerleader
Cincinnati Enquirer 11/17/1999 A1:2+ Pic
‘63 Murder Case Talk Of Greenhills
Post 11/19/1999 1a:1+ Pic
Unsolved 1963 Slaying Of Cheerleader Reopened
Post 11/17/1999 1a:2+ Pic
Law Officials Close In: Evidence In 1963 Murder Unsealed By Prosecutors
Cincinnati Enquirer 01/06/2000 B1:2+ Pic
Reporter Revisits ‘63 Case
Cincinnati Enquirer 01/22/2000 B2:6
Help Sought In Old Slaying: ‘someone Knows Something’ Of Killing
Post 01/06/2000 4a:1 Pic
Indictment Sought In 37-Year-Old Murder: Prosecutor Wanting To Skip Juvenile Court
Post 03/17/2000 18a:1 Pic
37 Years After Cheerleader’s Death, Boyfriend Charged: Patty Rebholz Was Bludgeoned After
Cincinnati Enquirer 05/03/2000 A1:2+ Pic

Man Pleads Not Guilty In Killing 37 Years Ago
Cincinnati Enquirer 05/04/2000 D2:1
'48 Hours' Covers Greenhills Murder
Cincinnati Enquirer 05/11/2000 E4:4
Court Urged To Treat Suspect As 15: Slaying From 1963 Still Juvenile Case, Wehrung Lawyers
Cincinnati Enquirer 05/20/2000 D7:1 Pic
Accused, 53, Seeks Juvenile Trial
Post 05/19/2000 21a:1
Judge Befriended Teen Suspect: 1963 Slaying Case Reopened
Post 05/04/2000 1a:2+ Pic
Adult Trial Sought In Slaying: Decades-Old Case Raises Age Issue
Cincinnati Enquirer 06/03/2000 B2:3 Pic
Prosecutor Argues Right To Try Man In '63 Killing
Post 06/03/2000 8a:1
Judge's Testimony Key In '63 Slaying
Post 06/07/2000 1a:1+
'Adult Juvenile' Poses Dilemma: Court To Weigh Designation For Teen Suspect, Now 52
Cincinnati Enquirer 06/08/2000 A1:2+
Wehrung Will Be Tried As An Adult
Post 06/13/2000 1a:1+
Accused As A Teen-Ager, Suspect To Be Tried As Adult: Wehrung Faces Life In 1963 Patty Reb
Cincinnati Enquirer 06/14/2000 A1:2
Trial For Suspect, 52, Awaits Apellate Ruling: Wehrung Wants Case In Juvenile Court
Cincinnati Enquirer 07/18/2000 B2:3
Lawyers For Suspect, 52, Argue He's Still A Juvenile In 1963 Slaying: Appeals Court Judges
Cincinnati Enquirer 09/14/2000 C13:1
Wehrung Trial Stays In Adult Court
Cincinnati Enquirer 10/14/2000 B1:2+

Wehrung To Face Adult Murder Charge
Post 10/14/2000 9a:1
Ill Health May Lead Witness In '63 Murder To Testify Now
Post 10/17/2000 11a:3 Pic
1963 Killing In High Court: At Issue: Adult Or Juvenile Prosecution For Accused Man
Cincinnati Enquirer 10/25/2000 B5:4
Ex-Reporter Could Testify In '63 Slaying
Cincinnati Enquirer 11/01/2000 B3:6 Hom
Rebholz Case May Bar Public: Attorneys Want Reporter Questioning Private
Cincinnati Enquirer 11/11/2000 B2:3
Wehrung Trial Deposition To Be Closed: Ex-Reporter To Be Queried
Post 11/21/2000 10a:2
Deposition May Be Open To Public: Ex-Reporter To Talk About Slaying Case
Post 11/28/2000 11a:3 Pic
Wehrung Admitted Hitting Girl: 'Another Self' Killed Teen
Post 11/29/2000 18a:3
Ex-Reporter: Why He Stayed Mum
Post 11/29/2000 18a:3
Tv Reporter Recalls Chilling Interview: Suspect In '63 Told Him He'd Hit Patty
Cincinnati Enquirer 11/29/2000 A1:2+
Judge Denies File Access In '63 Slaying
Cincinnati Enquirer 12/19/2000 B2:3
Report Sheds Light On 1963 Slaying: 'Other Self' Could Have Killed Patty Rebholz, Suspect
Cincinnati Enquirer 12/20/2000 A1:2+
Sanctions Sought For Prosecutors: Wehrung's Lawyers Angry Over Release Of 'Prejudicial' Re
Cincinnati Enquirer 12/21/2000 C2:3
Dismissal Sought In Rebholz Slaying
Post 01/19/2001 13a:1 Pic

Prosecutors: Friend's Testimony Provides Motive In '63 Slaying
Post 02/17/2001 8a:2
Friend Testifies About Breakup: Prosecutors Say Girl Killed In 1963 Over Split
Cincinnati Enquirer 02/17/2001 B1:5 Pic
Judge Deals Blow To Wehrung
Post 03/06/2001 5a:2
Murder Trial To Proceed: Ruling Defends 38-Year Delay
Cincinnati Enquirer 03/07/2001 B2:3
Wehrung: Try Me In Juvenile Court
Post 05/15/2001 5a:2
Ohio Court Weighs Jurisdiction In '63 Beating Death Of Teen Girl
Cincinnati Enquirer 05/16/2001 B2:3
Try Wehrung As An Adult, Court Rules
Post 07/19/2001 12a:4
Flashbacks To '63 Slaying
Post 08/04/2001 1a:1+
Wehrung To Be Tried As An Adult
Cincinnati Enquirer 07/19/2001 B1:2
Suspect On Trial-38 Years Later: Proceedings Begin Monday In Slaying Of Greenhills Teen
Cincinnati Enquirer 11/23/2001 B1:1+ Pic
Jurors Walk Greenhills Site Where Girl Was Killed In 1963
Cincinnati Enquirer 11/27/2001 B2:3
Breakup Of Teen Romance Recounted: Friend Testifies About Aptty's Intentions
Cincinnati Enquirer 11/28/2001 A1:2+
Trial Begins In Teen's '63 Death
Post 11/26/2001 6a:2+
'63 Slaying Case Writing Final Chapter
Post 11/27/2001 1a:1
Brother: Wehrung In Search
Post 11/27/2001 6a:1

Coronor: Patty Didn't Fight: No Medical Evidence She Defended Herself
Cincinnati Enquirer 11/29/2001 B1:2+
Testimony Places Couple In Field
Post 11/28/2001 17a:2+ Pic
Jurors To Hear Wehrung 'confess'
Post 11/29/2001 1a:5
Coroner: Victim Was Strangled, Then Beaten
Post 11/29/2001 15a:1
Wehrung Changed Story He Told Cops
Post 11/30/2001 16a:6
Witness:'I Had A Chilling Feeling'
Post 11/30/2001 17a:1
Tape Played Of '63 Interrogation Of Wehrung: Blood Was His, He Told Police
Cincinnati Enquirer 11/30/2001 B1:2+
Trial Is Talk Of Village: 38-Year-Old Murder Case Changed Town
Cincinnati Enquirer 12/02/2001 B3:2
Witness Recounts Wehrung Talk: Retired TV Reporter Testifies
Cincinnati Enquirer 12/01/2001 B1:1
Other Boy Seen Trailing Patty: Witness Describes Dark Pants, Glasses
Cincinnati Enquirer 12/04/2001 B1:2+
Would-Be Boyfriend Testifies: He Asked Rebholz To Drop Wehrung
Post 12/04/2001 1a:4+ Pic
Wehrung Defence Wraps Up: Witness Casts Doubt On Breakup Theory
Cincinnati Enquirer 12/05/2001 B1:2+
Jury Deliberating '63 Murder Case: Defense Indicated 3 Other Suspects
Post 12/05/2001 16a:2+ Pic

A Cop's 1963 Notes The Jury Never Saw: Wehrung Described As Cruel Boyfriend
Post 12/06/2001 1a:3+
Defense: Ignore 'mike's White Lie': Jurors Deliberate '63 Murder Case
Post 12/06/2001 20a:2+
Wehrung Not Guilty In 1963 Slaying: Who Killed Patty Rebholz Still A Mystery
Cincinnati Enquirer 12/07/2001 A1:2+ Pic
Untangling Rebholz Case Formidable Task For Jury
Post 12/07/2001 1a:4:+
At First, Jurors Voted To Convict Wehrung
Post 12/08/2001 1a:3+
Trial A Landmark For Attorney: Wehrung's Defense Had First Criminal Case
Cincinnati Enquirer 12/09/2001 B1:2+
Wehrung Talks-On National TV
Post 02/06/2002 A1:1+
Wehrung Interview Airs On 'Inside Edition'
Cincinnati Enquirer 02/06/2002 B2:1
An Innocent Man
Cincinnati Magazine 04/01/2002 68+
Wehrung Record Expunged
Post 05/22/2002 17a:1
Cincinnati Enquirer 11/11/2000 B2:3
An Innocent Man
Cincinnati Magazine 04/01/2002 68+ Pic
Wehrung Asks That His Record Be Expunged
Cincinnati Enquirer 04/23/2002 B5:1
Judge Agrees To Seal Record Of Wehrung: Murder Charge Expunged
Cincinnati Enquirer 05/23/2002 B3:6

Chapter 9: LESS THAN MEETS THE EYE

Mystery In Camp Washington, Bullet-Riddled Bodies Of . . . And His Wife Found In Their Parked
Cincinnati Enquirer 11/26/1964 1:4
Police Say Murder In Camp Washington-Motive Mystery In Double Killing
Cincinnati Enquirer 11/27/1964 1:5
Slain Couple Appeared Normal, Neighbors Say
Cincinnati Post Times Star 11/27/1964 1:6
What Was Motive-Seek Murder Clues
Cincinnati Enquirer 11/28/1964 1:1
Killer, Lurking In Coby Garage, Fired 6 Shots, Police Believe-Autopsy Shows Couple Lived
Cincinnati Post Times Star 11/28/1964 1:5
Neighbors Fear Killer Of Couple May Lurk Nearby
Cincinnati Enquirer 11/30/1964 1:1
Police Attend Coby's Funeral
Cincinnati Post Times Star 11/30/1964 1:3
Couple Believed Slain Earlier Than Time Neighbor Saw Them
Cincinnati Enquirer 12/02/1964 39:1
Former VA Patient Cleared Of Any Part In . . . Slayings
Cincinnati Post Times Star 12/03/1964 1:1
Police On Wrong Track-Cobys Not Slain By Psycho Former Patient Says
Cincinnati Enquirer 12/04/1964 37:1
Sniper Slug, Coby Bullets Compared
Cincinnati Enquirer 12/05/1964 3:4
Police Seek Owner Of Key Found With Slain Cobys In Auto
Cincinnati Post Times Star 12/12/1964 1:1
Quizzed In Coby Killings
Cincinnati Enquirer 12/14/1964 46:8
Coby Slayer's Gun Identified By Fbi
Cincinnati Enquirer 12/18/1964 1:6

Polograph Test Made On Police-Clues Sought In . . . Case
Cincinnati Enquirer 01/15/1965 1:1
After 90 Days-Unsolved Mystery-Fleeing Youth Still Sought In Coby Double Murder
Cincinnati Enquirer 02/04/1965 28:1
Firemen Reject Lie Tests In Coby Slaying
Cincinnati Post Times Star 02/12/1965 34:4

Chapter 10: A VISION OF DEADLY DESIRE

Family Of 3 Knifed To Death Bridgetown Ohio
Cincinnati Enquirer 09/28/1966 1:4
Neighbors Think Bricca Killer No Stranger
Cincinnati Enquirer 09/29/1966 1:1
Fbi Lab To Check 30 Items Found At Scene Of Triple Slaying
Cincinnati Post Times Star 09/29/1966 1:5
Slain Familys Neighbors Recall The Little Things
Cincinnati Post Times Star 09/30/1966 38:4
Reconstruction Of A Murder Murder Solution Worth $7000
Cincinnati Enquirer 10/01/1966 1:3
No Solid Lead Yet In Bricca Probe Coroners Report Will Help Solve Several Questions
Cincinnati Post Times Star 10/01/1966 1:6
Reward Upped In Bricca Case Total $12,000
Cincinnati Enquirer 10/03/1966 1:8
Shocked Bricca Neighbors Learn To Live With Fear
Cincinnati Post Times Star 10/05/1966 42:4
Bricca Employer Gives $5000 For Murder Hunt
Cincinnati Enquirer 10/12/1966 1:1
Bricca Slayer Scouted Home Then Struck Vogel Says
Cincinnati Post Times Star 10/12/1966 4:3
Strange Fingerprints Found By Fbi On Bricca Property
Cincinnati Enquirer 10/16/1966 1:6

Police Mum On Report In . . . Murder Case
Cincinnati Enquirer 10/20/1966 1:5
Bricca Slayer Believed White
Cincinnati Post Times Star 10/21/1966 1:3
Bricca Case Confession Retracted
Cincinnati Post Times Star 10/24/1966 1:3
Prober Mum On Bricca Report
Cincinnati Enquirer 11/02/1966 10:4
Florida Seeks Bricca Details
Cincinnati Enquirer 11/05/1966 4:3
Briccas Neighbor Cleared By Police
Cincinnati Enquirer 11/15/1966 1:5
One Bricca Suspect Remains Police Admit
Cincinnati Post Times Star 11/15/1966 1:7
Bricca Murder Probers Seek Link With Girls Slaying In WV
Cincinnati Post Times Star 11/22/1966 6:5
Obituaries
Cincinnati Enquirer 09/28/1966 1:4
Bricca Case Still Open Investigator Insists
Cincinnati Enquirer 02/02/1967 41:1
Triple Homicide Bricca Case Probe Stymied
Cincinnati Enquirer 03/28/1967 1:7
A Year Goes By Still No Arrest Although . . . Prosecutor Believes He Knows Who Killed Bricca
Cincinnati Post Times Star 09/22/1967 1:3
Update . . . Triple Murder
Cincinnati Enquirer 05/06/1977 D1:1
Unsolved Murders (Bricca Family 09-27-1966)
Post 12/24/1991 5a:4
Death on a quiet street
Cincinnati Magazine 04/01/2008 116:1+ pic

Chapter 11: TERROR IN THE GASLIGHT DISTRICT

Scientist's Wife Found Slain—Victim of Strangler
Cincinnati Enquirer 12/03/1965 1:3
Strangler Struck in Dim and Dusty Basement
Cincinnati Enquirer 12/03/1965 7:2
Housewife Raped, Slain in Price Hill—Killer Strikes Again
Cincinnati Enquirer 04/05/1966 1:1
Strangulation Shocks Victim's Neighborhood
Cincinnati Post 04/05/1966 1:5
Third Woman Raped, Slain, Body Found In Burnet Woods
Cincinnati Post 06/10/1966 1:4
Mad Strangler Catches Widow Strolling Alone
Cincinnati Enquirer 06/11/1966 1:2
The Strangler . . . Who, What, Why?
Cincinnati Enquirer 06/11/1966 9:2
Fear Gripping Women While Strangler Roams
Cincinnati Enquirer 06/14/1966 23:3
Negro Killed Three Women, Police Say
Cincinnati Enquirer 06/15/1966 13:3
City Police On Overtime As Strangler Strikes Again
Cincinnati Enquirer 10/13/1966 1:3
Grim Manhunt On For Mad Strangler
Cincinnati Enquirer 10/13/1966 1:5
Someone Knows Strangler—York Asks Help
Cincinnati Post 10/13/1966 1:4
Citizens Cooperate With Police In Mobilizing Against Killer
Cincinnati Post 10/13/1966 12:2
5000 Man Posse Beefs Up Hunt For Sex Maniac
Cincinnati Enquirer 10/14/1966 1:1
Similarities Startling—All Point To One Man
Cincinnati Enquirer 10/14/1966 10:1
Thousands Hunt Strangler
Cincinnati Post 10/14/1966 1:2

Psychiatric Aid Asked In Hunt For Strangler
Cincinnati Enquirer 10/15/1966 1:6
Another Woman Strangled—Rape Verified
Cincinnati Enquirer 10/22/1966 1:6
Police Think 5th Slaying Planned
Cincinnati Post 10/22/1966 1:3
Strangler Strikes Again! Body Found In Elevator
Cincinnati Post 12/09/1966 1:1
Strangler's Victims—6 or 7?
Cincinnati Enquirer 12/10/1966 28:3
Jailed Suspect In Spotlight Of Seven Murder Probe
Cincinnati Enquirer 12/11/1966 1:1
Suspect Quizzed In Strangling Also In Taxi Slaying Questioned In Death Of Miss Lula Kerrick
Cincinnati Enquirer 12/10/1966 1:5
Faces New Charge Mrs Virginia Hinners Secretary At New Thought Unity Center Identifies
Cincinnati Post Times Star 12/12/1966 1:7
Bowman Case Murder Charge Looms Today
Cincinnati Enquirer 12/13/1966 1:1
Laskey Claims He Has Alibi With Girl At Same Time Of Alleged Assault Faces Bowman Slaying
Cincinnati Post Times Star 12/14/1966 1:7
Jury Indicts Laskey In Bowman Slaying
Cincinnati Post Times Star 12/16/1966 1:8
I Need Help . . . Asked At Avondale Branch Office Of The Hamilton County Legal Aid Society
Cincinnati Enquirer 12/21/1966 7:1
Attempt To Set Aside Murder Indictment Fails
Cincinnati Enquirer 12/23/1966 4:3
Laskey Enters Not Guilty Plea To Murder Robbery Indictments
Cincinnati Post Times Star 12/23/1966 1:6
Judge Leis studies Laskey appeal, attorney lists major arguments
Cincinnati Post Times Star 04/21/1967 34:3

Defense fund set for Laskey
Cincinnati Post Times Star 04/21/1967 34:5
Brief Filed Seeking Laskey Case Evidence
Cincinnati Post Times Star 01/04/1967 12:1
Laskey Death Sentence Upheld In Ruling By Appeals Court
Cincinnati Post Times Star 02/13/1968 1:1
Laskey Case Started Reign Of Fear In City
Cincinnati Enquirer 03/03/1968 11a:1
Posteal . . . Is Granted Stay Of Execution
Cincinnati Post Times Star 03/26/1970 45:6
Terror In New York Brings To Mind Fearful Days Of Cincinnati Strangler
Cincinnati Enquirer 08/12/1977 A13:1
Leis Fights Parole For Man Jailed As 'Strangler' In '67
Post 01/04/1980 9:4
Parole Denied For Alleged City Strangler
Post 01/10/1980 12:1
Prospect Of Laskey Parole Enrages Mother Of Victim
Cincinnati Enquirer 04/09/1982 A1:5
Laskey's Conviction Touched Off A Tinderbox Of Racial Tensions
Cincinnati Enquirer 04/09/1982 C1:4
Laskey Denied Parole
Post 05/05/1982 1a:1
Living With The Cincinnati Strangler-Panic Was City's Reaction To Strangler
Cincinnati Enquirer 10/06/1985 E1:2
Strangler Conviction Sparked Riot
Post 05/05/1986 2b:1
Officials Protest Killers' Parole Requests
Cincinnati Enquirer 03/11/1988 4d:1
Serial Killers In Local History
Cincinnati Enquirer 03/24/1991 B3:1

Strangler Up For Parole (30 Years After City Was Terrorized)
Post 01/24/1997 1a:4 Pic +
A Reign Of Terror (Cincinnati Strangler)
Post 02/08/1997 1a:2+ Pic
Strangler To Remain Locked Up; Parole Board Rejects Laskey's Try At Freedom
Post 02/10/1997 1a:1+
The Legacy Of The Cincinnati Strangler
Cincinnati Magazine 08/01/1997 31+ Pic
Cases Of The Century: The 10 Top Cases Of Cincinnati's Legal Legacy
Cincinnati Magazine 08/01/2001 Sup
Strangler Denied Parole: Posteal Laskey Remains In Prison
Post 03/05/2002 8a:2
Strangler Is Denied Parol: He Must Serve 10 More Years
Cincinnati Enquirer 02/14/2007 B2:1
'Strangler' Goes To Grave; '60s Saga Concludes
Cincinnati Enquirer 06/13/2007 B1:2+ Pic

Chapter 12: PERSON OR PERSONS UNKNOWN

Three Slain In Mt Lookout . . . And Wife Her Mother
Cincinnati Post Times Star 10/23/1969 1:8
Pointless Slaying Of 3 Baffles Police
Cincinnati Enquirer 10/24/1969 1:1
Paint-Spattered Man Dumler Case Target
Cincinnati Post 10/24/1969 1:5
Sitter Could Have Been Dumler Slaying Victim
Cincinnati Post 10/24/1969 12:2
Police Sifting Clues Hunt For Stranger In Triple Murder
Cincinnati Enquirer 10/25/1969 1:1
Neighbor Man Quizzed in Mt. Lookout Murders
Cincinnati Enquirer 10/26/1969 1:5

Dumler Case a Mystery, Police Say
Cincinnati Post 10/27/1969 1:2
Police Retrace Steps for Dumler Clues
Cincinnati Post 10/29/1969 5:4
Slaying Probe Centers on Man in Detroit
Cincinnati Enquirer 11/01/1969 20:4
Wills Of Slain Couple Filed In Probate Court
Cincinnati Enquirer 11/06/1969 45:1

Chapter 13: MURDER IN THREE ACTS

Dr. Glueck's Sister Among Three Slain: Body Found In Car
Cincinnati Post Times Star 10/04/1971 1:1 Pic
Bullet Victim Found In Auto
Cincinnati Post Times Star 10/04/1971 1:5 Pic
Three Baffling Killings Confronting City Police
Cincinnati Enquirer 10/05/1971 1:1
Slaying Victim 'Gentle," Wouldn't Resist Force
Cincinnati Enquirer 10/05/1971 1:5 Pic
Rights Tomorrow For Mrs. Brown
Cincinnati Post 10/05/1971 10:2
Murder Of Welder Lacking In Motive
Cincinnati Post Times Star 10/05/1971 33:1
No Clues Found in Three Slayings
Cincinnati Post 10/05/1971
Robbery Still Not Ruled Out In Slayings
Cincinnati Post 10/07/1971 1: 3
Reward Set In Slayings—Clues, Motives Lacking
Cincinnati Enquirer 10/07/1971 27:2
Lack Of Evidence Common In City's Mysterious Slayings
Cincinnati Enquirer 01/28/1979 B1:2
Homicide Squad Faces Crime Hike, Apathy
Cincinnati Enquirer 02/23/1972 1:5

ACKNOWLEDGMENTS:

There are three people who were integral to the creation of *Queen City Gothic.*

My Editor, Coleen Armstrong, who prodded, cajoled, kicked, coaxed, inspired, and amazed me through the entire process, renovating my words into prose while convincing me that I was good enough.

My Photo Designer (and good friend), John Farnham, whose obsessive precision collided with my retentive vision to create the headline and picture layouts. And he heckled me into sticking with this project.

My artist wife, Sheryl, who doubles as my Reader. She bridged the demographic between true crime and mystery genres, and she conceived the "I Witness" segments. Plus she pointed out when something didn't make sense.

My sincere thanks to Amanda Koumoutsos and Cortney Fleck at Author House.

I would like to thank all law enforcement personnel who cooperated in the research for this book. Cincinnati Police Division cold case officers Gary Conner, Mike Miller, and Sal Tufano were invaluable, as was detective Tim Gormley, whose dogged pursuit of missing files eventually paid off. Retired homicide cops like Paul Morgan, Tom Oberschmidt, and Frank Sefton were able to fill in the blanks.

My deep gratitude to Greenhills Police Chief Tom Doyle, whose passion for unresolved justice matches my own.

To my friends and minions who endured my macabre obsessions and morbid lunch conversations, your support and encouragement were tenacious: Eric Ford, Steve Berninger, Veronica Wilkins, Robert "Juggy" Sturdevant, Maria Dowling, Cheryl Ware, Don and Kim Nickol, Marilyn Sims, Diane Pfister Epstein, Tina Parker, Patsy Stephenson, and my tennis mates Leon Starks and Larry Handley.

To Kim Ryan—my marketing ace and Haiku protégé—who convinced me that "the dream that keeps coming back is your destiny."

To my colleague George Stimson, who planted the seed for this book during our many conversations, and with his own excellent anthology *The Cincinnati Crime Book*.

To Tom Coby, who opened up a painful chapter of his life.

To Adrion Baird, whose inspirational life showed me that someone could overcome the tragic loss of their sister.

And lastly to my other family members: Beth King and Blythe Pietila, AKA "the famous Nettleton twins", and Roxanne Burnette, all three of whom became my surrogate sisters after Trina died.

To my nephew Sean, who finally got it right by marrying Andrea.

To my brother Tim, for bestowing me with the sarcastic sobriquet "true crime writer"—and spurring me to prove you wrong.

To Cassie—there are no words to express how proud I am of you.

And finally to my dear and departed mother Margaret: Your love will outlive life's sorrow. And your beauty lingers like a poem I shall never write…or abandon. Thank you for being unforgettable…

J. T. Townsend is a freelance writer and lifelong resident of Cincinnati. He is the former true crime historian for *Snitch Magazine*, and his work has appeared in the *Cincinnati Enquirer, Cincinnati Magazine, Word Magazine,* and *Clews.* In addition, he appeared in the 2008 British Documentary *Conversations With a Serial Killer.* He has also appeared on WCPO News with Catherine Nero and Jenell Walton, as well as 700 WLW Radio with Mike McConnell and Bill Cunningham. Visit his website at www.jttownsend.com

Made in the USA
Monee, IL
11 February 2024

53332400R00280